The Murders at Wildgoose Lodge

FROM SOME REVIEWS:

'Terence Dooley recreates what happened on the night and the aftermath in an intriguing story of a local incident that had national implications'

Ireland's Own.

'The burning of Wildgoose Lodge is an episode that has assumed mythic proportions. This is the first fully researched and comprehensive analysis of the burning of Wildgoose Lodge and the events that subsequently unfolded [...] Dooley tells all this with a steady hand and a good feel for the period. While concentrating on the events in that part of county Louth, he does not lose sight of the bigger picture and illustrates how the authorities all the way up to the Irish Secretary, Robert Peel, were involved in the prosecution of the suspects. He discusses in detail all the various theories about who was involved and why the Lynch-Rooney family was attacked and is certain enough to come to his own conclusions. All in all this is a fascinating book that not only throws new light on an infamous outrage but on Irish society in this period'

Tony Canavan, *Books Ireland.*

Book-of-the-Year choice (2007), Paul Bew, *Irish Times.*

'It is to Terence Dooley's credit that he has placed the murders in the context of local agrarian crime and has completed an immense amount of research in order to do so [...] Dooley's excellent book, meticulously documented and argued, deepens our perception of the background and should send readers back to Carleton with renewed interest and understanding'

Maurice Harmon, *Ríocht na Midhe.*

D1609871

The Murders at Wildgoose Lodge

Agrarian Crime and Punishment
in Pre-Famine Ireland

TERENCE DOOLEY

FOUR COURTS PRESS

Set in 11 on 13 point AGaramond for
FOUR COURTS PRESS LTD
7 Malpas Street, Dublin 8, Ireland
e-mail: info@fourcourtspress.ie
http://www.fourcourtspress.ie
and in North America by
FOUR COURTS PRESS
c/o ISBS, 920 N.E. 58th Avenue, Suite 300, Portland, OR 97213.

First printed 2007
First paperback edition 2008

ISBN 978-1-84682-112-7

A catalogue record for this title
is available from the British Library.

Printed in England
by Athenaeum Press, Gateshead, Tyne & Wear.

Contents

Illustrations

*This book is dedicated to the memory of
Pat Dooley (6 April 1917 – 23 November 2007),
my father, mentor and dearest friend.*

Preface and acknowledgments

… I inclined
To lose my faith in Ballyrush and Gortin
Till Homer's Ghost came whispering to my mind.
He said: I made the Iliad from such
A local row. Gods make their own importance.

Patrick Kavanagh, 'Epic'.

While a youth growing up in Monaghan in the parish of Killanny, along the same Inniskeen road on which Patrick Kavanagh was reared, the stories of the murders at Wildgoose Lodge were as current then in local lore as they had been in Kavanagh's time. Around the age of twelve, my father showed me the spot at Corcreaghy crossroads where he thought a notorious Ribbonman named Patrick Devan had been hanged and gibbeted. Stories of a man being hanged and his body left to rot for months suspended from the branches of a tree (as he thought happened) probably rocked my youthful sensibilities and they certainly aroused my curiosity so that from then on I was captivated by who that man was (revealingly my father knew little about him) and why he was hanged. Over the years my father told me other bits and pieces of the story, most of which he had heard from his grandfather, John Dooley (1842–1926), when as a young boy he helped him thin turnips and weed potatoes among the hills of Dunelty and Ballingarry. John Dooley had lived through the Great Famine. He had many stories to tell but amongst his favourite was 'the burning of Wildgoose Lodge'. However, the version that he undoubtedly believed was true, because it had been handed down to him by his mother, was more or less a reworking of William Carleton's version of events published over a decade before John Dooley was born.

Down through the years some of my father's contemporaries added to my knowledge. Two in particular – George 'Judd' Garland and John 'Sapper' Thornton – are remembered with fondness. To a young inquisitive mind, details of the incident remained sketchy and elusive: Devan was the only name that came up time and again and he was invariably represented as the victim of injustice. But details of his crime did not seem compatible with this representation: he had led a mob of men to burn to death a family (whose names were forgotten or at least not mentioned); during the outrage a mother passed her infant out through the window of the burning house and begged for mercy only to see her child piked by Devan and thrust back into the flames with the shout: 'the nits must burn with the louse'.

Then at the age of fifteen, as a student in the Patrician High School, Carrickmacross, my history teacher, Tom Flanagan, introduced me to a published version of events for the first time – an 1897 pamphlet by John Mathews. I read it aloud for the class. We all came from the areas mentioned therein: Killanny, Reaghstown, Carrickmacross, Inniskeen, Corcreaghy, Stonetown, Drumcondra and Meath Hill. My fascination with the atrocity was intensified, and for that I am very grateful to Tom, so that when some years later I embarked on an academic career in History I began to conceive of the idea of investigating the historical evidence relating to the incident. Over a period of almost twenty years, a number of projects have taken priority but at every given opportunity I have found myself drawn back to Wildgoose Lodge. In the process of identifying and consulting sources, I have accumulated a large number of debts to the staffs of the following repositories, museums and libraries: British Library, London; British Museum, London; Department of Folklore, University College Dublin; John Paul II Library, NUI Maynooth; Louth County Library, Dundalk; Louth County Museum, Dundalk; Manuscripts, Archives and Rare Books Library, Emory University, Atlanta, Georgia; Monaghan County Museum, Monaghan; National Archives of Ireland; National Library of Ireland; Public Record Office Northern Ireland; Royal Irish Academy; Russell Library, Maynooth.

Many individuals have helped by providing leads, advice, answering numerous queries, reading individual chapters or offering support in a variety of other ways. A very sincere and warm thanks are, therefore, due to the following: Dr Aoife Bhreathnach, Shawn Nicols Boyle, John Bradley, Lorraine Buchanan, Padraig Clerkin (who has since sadly passed away), Patrick Cosgrove, Anne Donoghue, Sean Farrelly, Eddie Filgate, Paddy Friel, Dr Louise Fuller, Dr Neal Garnham, Kevin Gartlan, Professor Ray Gillespie, Dr Brian Griffin, Brendan Hall, Donal Hall, Dr Brian Hanley, Catherine Heslin, Professor Jackie Hill, Niamh Howlin, Collette Jordan, Dr Jennifer Kelly, Brian Keoghegan, Des Konopka, Simon Kress, Dr David Lederer, Professor Colm Lennon, Kevin Lynch, Gerard Lyne, Brendan McCaul, Dr Sinead McEnaney, Dr Philip McEvansonea, Seamus MacGabhann, Dr Dympna McLoughlin, Michael McMahon, Dr Eddie McParland, Dr Anthony Malcomson, Dr Chris Morash, Dr Filipe Ribeiro de Meneses, Mary Murray, Isabell Murphy, Dr Naomi Nelson, Máire Ní Chearbhaill, Padráig Ó Conchubhair, Gregory O'Connor, Dr Thomas O'Connor, Niall Ó Muirgheasa, Pat O'Neill, Harold O'Sullivan, Professor Gary

Owens, Diane and Johnny Pollock, Dr Jacinta Prunty, Lord Roden, Noel Ross, Dr Ian Speller, Dr W.E. Vaughan, Walter Walsh, Willie White, Dr C.J. Woods and Penny Woods. Jim Keenan drew the maps contained herein with his usual expertise. Tom Larney gave me my most informative tour of the site of Wildgoose Lodge and the surrounding areas. I am indebted to my godfather, Johnny Murtagh, for introducing him to me.

Professor R.V. Comerford generously took the time to read an early draft of this book and improved it greatly with many sharp insights. I was fortunate that Dr Jennifer Kelly came to the History Department at NUI Maynooth before I finished this work. She, too, generously gave of her time, answered numerous queries and offered much appreciated erudite advice. I am also extremely grateful to Dr Richard McMahon who read a number of chapters and shared with me his expertise on nineteenth-century crime and punishment. It goes without saying that I alone am responsible for all errors and misconceptions that remain.

It has been a delight once again to work with Four Courts Press; my thanks to Michael Adams, Martin Fanning and Anthony Tierney.

As ever, I am extremely grateful to all my colleagues in the History Department at NUI Maynooth for their fellowship and friendship.

I reserve the final and most important word of thanks to my ever-supportive family. My father taught me more than he will ever realise and my mother inspired me through the love of folklore which she shared with her late brother, Dr Seán Ó hEochaidh, *ar dheis Dé go mara a anam*. My brothers and sisters and their families, as well as the Dolan family, have waited a long time for this book. I hope they enjoy reading it as much as I enjoyed writing it. *Táim fíor bhuíoch dibh go léir do gach rud a dhéanann sibh dom.*

Annette, as ever, has been a rock of support. Conor and Áine share my love of Killanny and have travelled the by-roads of north Louth and south Monaghan with me retracing the steps of those who converged on Wildgoose Lodge on the night of 29–30 October 1816. Conor's inquisitiveness and perceptiveness has helped me more than he can yet understand. Aine's sparkling smile simply brightens up every day. Without them none of what I do would be worthwhile.

Writing this book has presented a great number of challenges not least of which has been the decision as to where one should begin. To this author it seemed logical to begin with William Carleton's fictional version of events and then to present the historical evidence. In so doing it also became imperative to examine Carleton's motivation for writing the story, which was found to be extremely illuminating in its own right. Soon social memory and the murders at Wildgoose Lodge developed into a more substantial chapter than had been anticipated. I decided to begin with it because so much of what is believed to have happened at Wildgoose Lodge is based on Carleton's version of events. Some readers may, however, choose to go straight to the historical evidence therefore beginning with chapter two which establishes the context in which the murders took place as a necessary prelude to the remainder of the story. But the reader should not forget to return to chapter one to see, for example, how historical events can be reinterpreted to suit changing political agendas.

Finally, the sources are littered with variants in the spelling of personal and place-names. I have adopted the general rule of changing names and place-names to follow modern conventions (except where names appear in quotations in which case the given orthography is used within the quotation). Thus Devan is used instead of Devane, Devaun, Devine; McQuillan is used instead of Cullen, Cuillin McCuilinn; Killanny instead of Killaney; Corcreaghy instead of Corcria, Corcreagh and so on.

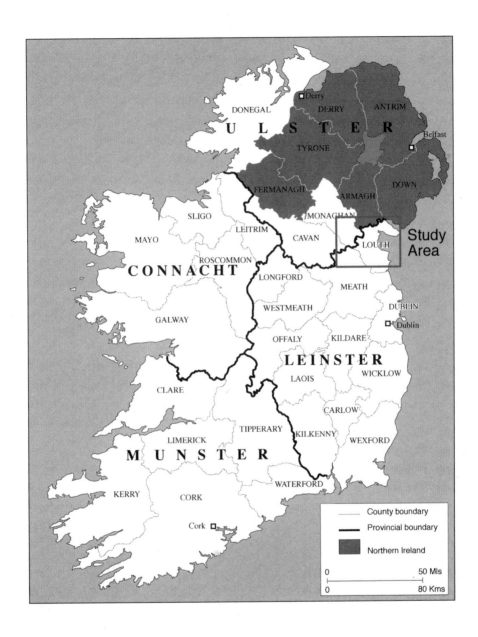

1 Map of Ireland showing the borderlands area under study.

PART ONE

CHAPTER ONE

Social memory and the burning of Wildgoose Lodge

The terrible event which resulted in the destruction, under circumstances of fiendish ferocity, of an entire household, consisting of a family
of eight, has exercised an influence not only on the mind of the morbid
but on the mind of the moralist for many years.

'Introduction' to John Mathews, *The burning of Wildgoose Lodge*
(1882), p. 1

Introduction

On 3 November 1816, a letter appeared in the *Freeman's Journal,* written by an
unnamed correspondent from Ardee in Co. Louth, who wanted to bring to the
attention of the public: 'the most monstrous and horrid occurrences that ever
disgraced human nature in Ireland – nay, as satanic a deed as ever was conceived
by the imagination of a Shakespeare or an Otway!'[1] The chilling report which
followed described briefly the circumstances surrounding the murder by burning of eight people in their home at nearby Reaghstown by a mob of 100 or so
men who at the time were styled Ribbonmen (Ribandmen) suggesting their
membership of a secret oath-bound society. The victims who had died on the
morning of 30 October were later identified as Edward Lynch, an elderly
Catholic farmer and linen weaver; his bachelor son, Michael; his married daughter, Bridget; her husband Thomas Rooney; their five-month-old son, Peter, and
three young servants: Ann Cassidy, Bridget Richards and James Rispin.[2]
Homicide was not an infrequent occurrence in nineteenth-century Ireland but
in the annals of modern Irish history, there are few multiple murders as grue-
some as that of Edward Lynch and his cohabitants.[3] According to the chief secretary of Ireland at the time, Sir Robert Peel, it equalled 'in atrocity' (though

1 *Freeman's Journal* [hereafter *FJ*], 3 Nov. 1816. 2 *Correspondent,* 2 Nov. 1816; *Belfast Newsletter,*
25 July 1817; Proclamation issued by the lord lieutenant and council of Ireland, 18 Nov. 1816
(Dundalk Library, WGL papers). 3 In 1882, for example, five members of the Joyce family were
brutally murdered at Maamtrasna in Co. Galway; see Jarlath Waldron, *Maamtrasna: the murders
and the mystery* (Dublin, 1992).

not in scale) the 1798 massacre at Scullabogue in Co. Wexford when 126 men, women and children, predominantly Protestant, were burned to death in a barn by rebels.[4]

The house in which Lynch and the others perished was known locally as Wildgoose Lodge. It was located about four miles from the town of Ardee, less than ten miles from Dundalk (both in Co. Louth) and another four miles from Carrickmacross in Co. Monaghan. Until the night of 29–30 October 1816 it had stood for generations on the brow of a hill, a respectable stone built, thatched house overlooking an expanse of marsh and bogland. The 'wild, mournful, desolate' Ardee bog with its 'wide tussocky tracks … great thorny lumps of furze, tangled nets of brambles, giant hillocks of rush, tufts of coarse, dead grass, acres of heather … [and] little black peat stacks' was the defining topographical division between the lodge and the more fertile lands of north Louth/south Monaghan so much so that neighbours usually described themselves as 'living across the bog' from the lodge.[5]

The Filgates of Lisrenny who had settled in Louth under the Cromwellian plantation of the seventeenth century had originally built the lodge as a shooting retreat.[6] By 1816 it was owned by Townley Patten Filgate, a brother of the then owner of Lisrenny, William Filgate Sr, and its function had changed to that of farmhouse. The lodge and its surrounding lands were leased to Edward Lynch whose father and grandfather had been retainers to the Filgates, probably as herds, although the elderly William Filgate Jr (1781–1875) in his 1867 account described 'Terence Lynch' – an indication of a fading memory – as the last in a line of 'huntsmen' to his father.[7]

The lodge was situated on a small rising piece of land, which, in the winter season, when the River Glyde burst its banks, became almost an island with only one narrow pass providing access to it from the south side of the high road near Reaghstown chapel.[8] The floodplain, which subsequently besieged the hill, attracted gaggles of wild geese, thereby giving the house its name of Wildgoose Lodge (which may have been a sobriquet as, according to Filgate's 1867 account, it was also known as Carthill House).

The area has long since been drained and wild geese no longer congregate on the lowlands during the winter. But on top of the hill, now only a few hun-

---

4 Robert Peel to John Foster, 31 Oct. 1816 (PRO, Peel papers, ADD 40291); for a comprehensive account of this episode, see Tom Dunne, *Rebellions: memoir, memory and 1798* (Dublin, 2004), pp 247–66. 5 John Mathews, *The burning of Wildgoose Lodge* (Dundalk, 1882), p. 3; see also evidence presented by neighbours in the later trials as described in chapters six and seven. 6 *Burke's landed gentry of Ireland* (London, 1958 ed.), pp 273–4. 7 Transcript of 'The story of the Wildgoose Lodge' as told by William Filgate to his daughter H.P.E. Filgate, 11 Mar. 1867 (Dundalk Library, Wild Goose Lodge [hereafter WGL] papers). 8 *Kilkenny Moderator*, 12 Mar. 1818.

dred yards from the main Dublin–Derry road (N2), the outline of the site of Wildgoose Lodge is still hauntingly visible. Decaying trees and twisted brambles cover what is left of the few stones that have survived but like the site of many ancient forts in Ireland, superstitiously guarded by the local communities, it has been nature rather than human intervention that has taken its toll. The site was never rebuilt upon. In fact, it is unlikely to have been touched by those who have farmed the surrounding fields since 1816. It has remained taboo, a place not to be meddled with because tradition has associated the site with great tragedy. While eight people were burned to death on the morning of 30 October 1816, almost double that number again were later executed within its walls or on nearby Reaghstown Hill for their part in the crime. In total twenty-nine people, victims and convicted suspects, for the most part from the surrounding area, died as a consequence of their association with events at Wildgoose Lodge in 1816.

The names of those who were murdered never resonated in the locality with the same power as the name of the house in which they died. The incident was usually referred to as 'the burning of Wildgoose Lodge' and hardly ever as 'the murder of the Lynches' and so it was the name of the house which became synonymous with the atrocity and not the name of the occupying family. Why this should be is open to interpretation. Some might argue that it was because the crime was so heinous that local people erased the names of the victims from their minds in order to be able to contemplate it and, therefore, Wildgoose Lodge became the label by which it was remembered. It is more likely, however, that the synonymy became a more or less permanent fixture after the most famous account of the incident, written by the Irish novelist and short story writer, William Carleton (1794–1869), was published under the title 'Wildgoose Lodge' in 1833. Widely regarded as Carleton's most gripping and compelling contribution to the short story genre, it brought the event to an international audience.[9] Just as significantly Carleton's fictional account became adjudged as authentic; it was quoted from by succeeding generations of writers and historians as authoritative; and it largely came to determine the description of events that continues to survive in the local lore to the present day. Because Carleton has remained so central to the perception of what happened at Wildgoose Lodge on the night of 29–30 October 1816, the section that follows simply recounts his version of events.

9 For critiques of this story as a literary work, see, for example, Barbara Hayley, 'Introduction' in William Carleton, *Traits and stories of the Irish peasantry*, vol. i (Gerrards Cross, 1990 [first ed., 1844]), p. 11; Barbara Hayley, *Carleton's traits and stories and the 19th century Anglo-Irish tradition* (Gerrards Cross, 1983), p. 73.

William Carleton's 'Wildgoose Lodge'

In 'Wildgoose Lodge', a young man identified only as Jim receives an anonymous summons to attend a 'special' meeting of the agrarian secret society to
which he belongs.[10] This is to be a select meeting rather than a general one; one
gets the impression it is to deal with extraordinary business of a serious and
nefarious nature. While Jim is initially flattered to be called as one of the chosen
few to attend 'on the next night at the solemn hour of midnight' his flattery
soon turns to trepidation. He is struck by a feeling of foreboding, sensing
'approaching evil' hang upon him and some innate force warning him of a 'fearful evil' that might shortly confront him.[11] He is unable to share his fears with
his father and brothers who are not members of the organisation. The turmoil
in his mind and the overall sense of impending disaster are then echoed in the
growing storm outside as the day turns 'gloomy and tempestuous almost beyond
any other' he can remember. During the evening dark clouds roll over the hills,
a sleet-like rain falls in slanting drifts and an unusually high wind sweeps through
the countryside in relentless gusts. As night approaches, the storm gathers
momentum, the rushing clouds almost obliterate the moon and the stars manage
to peep through only occasionally.[12]

Then, towards midnight, Jim readies himself to leave home to attend the
meeting; by now the storm has abated. He had contemplated staying at home
but changed his mind when he considered the implications of not turning up;
to be branded a traitor by the secret society would leave life much more intol-
erable than a soaking on a wet night. He travels the quarter mile from his home
to the meeting-place, the parish chapel, a long slated house that had not yet
been fully completed, situated in a solitary part of the neighbourhood:

> The scene which presented itself here was in keeping not only with the
> external appearance of the house, but with the darkness, the storm, and
> the hour, which was now a little after midnight. About forty persons
> were sitting in dead silence upon the circular steps of the altar. They
> did not seem to move; and as I entered and advanced, the echo of my
> footsteps rang through the building with a lonely distinctness which
> added to the solemnity and mystery of the circumstances about me.
> The windows were secured with shutters on the inside, and on the altar
> a candle was lighted, which burned dimly amid the surrounding dark-
> ness, and lengthened the shadow of the altar itself, and those of six or

10 William Carleton, *Traits and stories of the Irish peasantry*, vol. ii (Gerrards Cross, 1990 ed. [first
edition, 1844]), p. 349. 11 Ibid., pp 349–50. 12 Ibid., p. 349.

2 William Carleton (1794–1869).

seven persons who stood on its upper steps, until they mingled in the
obscurity which shrouded the lower end of the chapel. The faces of the
men who sat on the altar steps were not distinctly visible, yet their more
prominent and characteristic features were in sufficient relief, and I
observed, that some of the most malignant and reckless spirits in the
parish were assembled. In the eyes of those who stood at the altar, and
whom I knew to be invested with authority over the others, I could per-
ceive gleams of some latent and ferocious purpose, kindled, as I soon
observed, into a fiercer expression of vengeance, by the additional excitement of ardent spirits, with which they had stimulated themselves to a
point of determination that mocked at the apprehension of all future
responsibility, either in this world or the next.[13]

   The reception he receives is different to any he has experienced in the past;
it is not so boisterous or good-humoured. From the majority comes an occasional nod of the head, a suppressed '*Ghud dhemur tha thu?*' (How are you?),[14]
but from those who are 'evidently the projectors of the enterprise' comes 'a con-

13 Ibid., p. 351. 14 Ibid.

vulsive grasp of the hand, accompanied by a fierce and desperate look, that seemed to search my eye and countenance, to try if I were a person likely to shrink from whatever they had resolved to execute'.[15] Jim is reminded of his oath to the secret society and each man purposefully gives him 'the secret grip of ribbondism'. He is frightened by their cold determined stares that seem to tell him: 'We are bound upon a project of vengeance, and if you do not join us, remember that we can revenge.'[16] Then the leader, known as 'the Captain', reads out the names of those who were absent: 'in order that the real cause of their absence might be ascertained, declaring that they would be dealt with accordingly'.[17]

At this point the reader's attention is firmly concentrated upon the leader. His name is Paddy and he is the local schoolmaster who teaches his daily school in the same chapel where they now meet, and on Sundays he acts as clerk to the priest ('an excellent and amiable old man, who knew little of his illegal connexions and atrocious conduct').[18] Paddy is a man of slight build, probably no more than thirty. He is unremarkable in both dress and physical appearance, but he certainly commands the respect of his men. When he calls on them to prepare to fulfil their oaths, there is an enthusiastic response: 'By all that's sacred an' holy, we're willing,' exclaim his men in some form of unison.[19] 'You're our Captain, an' has yer orders from higher quarthers; of coorse, whatever ye command upon us we're bound to obey you in,' says another.[20] Most of those present have been cajoled by drink, which is freely passed around in a deliberate ploy by the Captain to further his undisclosed plans. He pours a glass of whiskey from a jar and offers it to Jim who is disgusted by the profanity of the act of drinking in the chapel and so peremptorily refuses to imbibe. Jim is in the minority. Most of those present drink two to three glasses, while a few who did not do so inside the chapel are encouraged to do so outside where: 'the sacrilege of the act was supposed to be evaded'.[21]

At 1 a.m. the Captain addresses the gathering. Six of those who have been summoned have still not arrived; they are castigated as potential 'thraitors' who will have to be dealt with at a later time.[22] The Captain locks the doors and makes his way up to the altar. It is from this point onwards that the narrator continuously refers to the satanic evilness he perceives in the Captain's countenance and actions. Time and again his 'satanic expression', 'hellish expression', 'malignant sneer' and his 'distinct malignity' are referred to. There is continuous emphasis on his obsessive drive for revenge. Placing the bible on the altar, the Captain swears to 'perform the action which we have met this night to accomplish, be that what it may'.[23] Then:

15 Ibid. 16 Ibid. 17 Ibid., p. 353. 18 Ibid., p. 352. 19 Ibid., p. 354. 20 Ibid., p. 354. 21 Ibid., p. 352. 22 Ibid., p. 353. 23 Ibid., p. 254.

the persons whose vengeance had been deepening more and more during the night, rushed to the altar in a body, where each, in a voice trembling with passionate eagerness, repeated the oath, and as every word was pronounced, the same echoes heightened the wildness of the horrible ceremony, by their long and unearthly tones. The countenances of these human tigers were livid with suppressed rage; their knit brows, compressed lips, and kindled eyes, fell upon the dim light of the taper, with an expression calculated to sicken any heart not absolutely diabolical.[24]

Seven men suddenly appear from a corner of the chapel. They are brothers and cousins of men who have been convicted some time before: 'for breaking into the house of an honest poor man in the neighbourhood, from whom, after having treated him with barbarous violence, they took away such firearms as he kept for his own protection'.[25] It now becomes increasingly evident that this is to be a mission of revenge. These men embody all the hateful characteristics of their leader: 'demons might have been proud of such horrible visages as they exhibited; for they worked under all the power of hatred, revenge, and joy; and these passions blended into one terrible scowl, enough almost to blast any human eye that would venture to look upon it'.[26] The Captain has deliberately kept these men out of sight, for he did not want the majority to presume their mission until he had sworn them to participation. As some begin to configure what lies ahead, there is a general exhilaration at what is anticipated:

> The scene which now took place was beyond all powers of description; peals of wild, fiend-like yells rang through the chapel, as the party which stood on the altar and that which had crouched in the darkness met; wringing of hands, leaping in triumph, striking of sticks and firearms against the ground and the altar itself, dancing and cracking of fingers, marked the triumph of some hellish determination.[27]

But there are another few who do not want to take a blindfold oath; they ask the Captain what is planned. He turns to his audience and tells them that 'the oath of secrecy must be taken' or woe be to him that will refuse: 'he won't know the day nor the hour, nor the minute, when he'll be made a spatch-cock of'. Then he turns back to the altar and taking up the bible swears: 'In the presence of God, and before His holy altar, that whatever might take place that night he would keep secret, from man or mortal, except the priest, and that neither bribery, nor imprisonment, nor death, would wring it from his heart.'[28]

24 Ibid., p. 355. 25 Ibid. 26 Ibid., p. 358. 27 Ibid., p. 355.

The gang then loads whatever firearms they possess. Bayonets and short pikes are made ready. A half-burned turf is placed in a pot, the men vacate the chapel, the Captain locks its doors and all begin on their journey of vengeance. It is now after 2 a.m., the rain has abated but it remains dark and windy. By the time they reach their destination the number of men has swollen to 130, having been joined en route by gangs converging from several other directions.[29] The result of the day's rains become apparent:

> At length, we arrived within fifty perches of the house, walking in a compact body, and with as little noise as possible; but it seemed as if the very elements had conspired to frustrate our design, for on advancing within the shade of the farm-hedge, two or three persons found themselves up to the middle in water, and on stooping to ascertain more accurately the state of the place, we could see nothing but one immense sheet of it – spread like a lake over the meadows which surrounded the spot we wished to reach.[30]

At this point the Captain brings his followers to another 'causeway', which was something like a wooden bridge erected for purposes of circumventing floods such as this. There is a breach in it too, so he orders twelve of his men to form a human bridge to allow the others climb across their backs onto the dry knoll where the house is situated.

The 130 or so men are composed of two separate parties: the first, with whom the Captain regularly confers, comprises a small band of around fifteen men, including those who appeared out of the shadows in the chapel. They are the ones who have been 'so vindictive all the night', the ones who are privy to the Captain's 'nefarious purpose'.[31] The Captain summonses five of these. They approach the house with the lighted coal which has been rekindled by 'two or three persons from a remote part of the county' who: 'entered a cabin on the wayside, and, under pretence of lighting their own and their comrades' pipes, procured a coal of fire, for so they called a lighted turf'.[32]

Within less than fifteen minutes one half of the house is on fire, fanned by the driving wind. Some of the larger group rush over to the Captain and his gang and remonstrate with them not to kill all who are inside. The former were having none of it: 'hell itself could hardly present anything more satanic than their countenances, now worked up into a paroxysm of infernal triumph at their own revenge'.[33] Those who try to intercede on behalf of the unfortunates in the house find themselves facing down the barrels of at least fifteen guns and pis-

28 Ibid., p. 356. 29 Ibid., p. 357. 30 Ibid. 31 Ibid., p. 358. 32 Ibid., p. 357. 33 Ibid., p. 358.

tols. The Captain warns those who would resist him that they will be killed just as surely as the family in the house. 'No mercy', he tells them is to be the password for the night. It is at this stage that the narrator becomes most explicit in his depiction of the Captain as a demonic creature:

> The Captain's look had lost all its calmness, every feature started out into distinct malignity, the curve in his brow was deep, and ran up to the root of the hair, dividing his face into two segments, that did not seem to have been designed for each other. His lips were half open, and the corners of his mouth a little brought back on each side, like those of a man expressing intense hatred and triumph over an enemy who is in the death-struggle under his grasp.[34]

Those who had set the fire cannot hide their glee.[35] The vast majority look on with horror, but none leave the scene for they fear that if they are not killed on the spot, they will surely meet an early death: 'from a quarter from which they had no means of defence'.[36] The Captain threatens them:

> Another word … and you're a corpse where you stand, or the first man who will dare to spake for them; no, no, it wasn't to spare them we came here. 'No mercy' is the password for the night, an' by the sacred oath, I swore beyant in the chapel, any one among yez that will attempt to show it, will find none at my hand. Surround the house, boys, I tell ye, I hear them stirring. 'No quarther – no mercy' is the order of the night.[37]

With that a ring of men encircle the house. It is now approximately 2.30 a.m. and the wind continues to fan the flames. Suddenly, a window shatters and a woman, her hair ablaze, sticks her head out. She cries out for mercy. The Captain replies to her anguished cries that there is to be no mercy. Two of his men rush at the woman, one stabbing her with a pike and another with a bayonet. She dies with the word 'mercy' divided in her mouth. As her head collapses on the window ledge her attackers plunge her body back into the flames. A cry of horror rises from all except the Captain's hardened cohort. Enraged by the lack of commitment of some of his followers, the Captain readies his bayonet and rushes at them but stopping short of plunging it into one man's body, he hisses into his ear for all to hear:

'It's no use now, you know; if one's to hang, all will hang; so our safest

34 Ibid. 35 Ibid. 36 Ibid., p. 359. 37 Ibid.

way, you persave, is to lave none of them to tell the story. Ye may go now, if you wish; but it won't save a hair of your heads. You cowardly set! I knew if I had told yez the sport, that none of you, except my own boys, would come, so I jist played a thrick upon you; but remimber what you are sworn to, and stand to the oath ye tuck.'[38]

Shouts and shrieks from inside the house rise above the crackling of the flames and the rush of the storm. The wind once again gathers momentum blowing the raging flames across the deeply thatched roof and the timbered eaves.[39] Those inside the house seeking escape rush to the breaking windows and doors. But time and again they are met with the cry of 'No mercy' and are driven back at the point of bayonet and pike. Their haunting screams hang in the air before being carried off with the wind. A man appears upon the side-wall of the house, nearly naked, his clothes scorched from his body. His appearance signals the climax of the horror experienced by the victims:

> Every muscle, now in motion by the powerful agitation of his suffer-
> ings, stood out upon his limbs and neck, giving him an appearance of
> desperate strength, to which by this time he must have been wrought
> up; the perspiration poured from his frame, and the veins and arteries
> of his neck were inflated to a surprising thickness. Every moment he
> looked down into the flames which were rising to where he stood; and
> as he looked, the indescribable horror which flitted over his features
> might have worked upon the devil himself to relent. His words were
> few: 'My child', said he, 'is still safe, she is an infant, a young crathur
> that never harmed you, nor anyone – she is still safe. Your mothers,
> your wives, have young innocent childhre like it. Oh, spare her, think
> for a moment that it's one of your own: spare it, as you hope to meet a
> just God, or if you don't in your mercy shoot me first – put an end to
> me, before I see her burned!'[40]

The Captain approaches him coolly and deliberately: 'You'll prosecute no one now, you bloody informer,' says he: 'you'll convict no more boys for takin' an ould gun an' pistol from you, or for givin' you a neighbourly knock or two into the bargain.' The motivation behind the raid has now been revealed: the victim had informed on men who had previously raided his house for arms. It is Ribbon revenge that has brought the Captain and his men to the Wildgoose Lodge. [41]

No sooner has the Captain's words been spoken than a screaming woman,

38 Ibid. **39** Ibid., p. 361. **40** Ibid., p. 360. **41** Ibid., pp 360–1.

herself almost scorched to death, appears at one of the windows with an infant in her arms. A raider runs to rescue the child but before he can do so the Captain bayonets the child and throws it back into the scorching flames. He then turns to the would-be rescuer, bayonets him and has his body flung into the flames. Turning to the child's father, the man sitting on the gable wall, the Captain mockingly tells him what he has just done. Then with the assistance of his gang, he hoists himself up on the wall and with his bayonet shoves the father into the burning house. His is the last 'wild and terrific cry' to be heard.[42] The narrator is not sure how many have actually perished, but he calculates it is between eight and eleven persons, including the infant child.

Those who along with the Captain had been intent on revenge rejoice in the completion of their mission. The faces of those who remain on the fringes are 'blanched to the whiteness of death: some of them fainted, and others were in such agitation that they were compelled to lean on their comrades'. The narrator concludes: 'they became actually powerless with horror: yet to such a scene were they brought by the pernicious influence of Ribbonism'.[43] The Captain's men search through the ashes to make sure that nobody has survived; he wants no more informers. 'Boys,' says he, 'we had better be sartin that all's safe; who knows but there might be some of the serpents crouchin' under a hape o'rub-bish, to come out an' gibbet us tomorrow or next day: we had better wait a while, anyhow, if it was only to see the blaze.'[44] And he leaves those present with a final warning that should anyone dare break the oath they had taken that night their lives would be short-lived.

The story ends with the narrator addressing his readers and informing them that a few months after the atrocity he saw the bodies of the Captain, whom he now names for the first time as Patrick Devan,[45] as well as many of those who were 'actively concerned in the perpetration of this deed of horror', wither in gibbets from which they hung for their crimes and he thanks God for his own escape.

Carleton's motive for writing 'Wildgoose Lodge'

William Carleton was born in Prillisk in Co. Tyrone on 20 February 1794.[46] The youngest of fourteen children of a small Catholic tenant farmer, he was reared in a 'humble house' (though probably not nearly as humble as he

42 Ibid., p. 361. 43 Ibid. 44 Ibid. 45 In contemporary accounts variously spelled Devann, Devaun, Devane, Devan. Because Devan was the one most commonly used by contemporaries and allegedly by Patrick Devan himself (see reference to his letters in chapters four and five), it is the spelling that will be adhered to throughout the rest of this text. 46 William Carleton, *The*

recalled) by parents who according to his claims were quite gifted – his father in the art of storytelling, his mother as a singer endowed with 'the sweetest and most exquisite of human voices'. Carleton benefited from the strong influence of an intelligent and articulate father (who could express himself just as competently in English as in his native Irish) and from intermittent education both in local hedge schools and classical schools.[47] He was very much brought up in a culture in which storytelling was an immensely important part of the social fabric.[48] He was also reared in a highly charged political atmosphere spawned by socio-political and religious resentments and bred by the competing political mindsets and cultural outlooks that had vied for supremacy in the eighteenth century.[49]

An articulate, intelligent young man, Carleton decided that manual work was not for him. Instead, he later wrote: 'I was unconsciously but rapidly preparing myself for a position in Irish literature.'[50] Inspired by Alain-René LeSage's (1668–1747) picaresque hero Gil Blas – who rose from servant to landed proprietor and nobleman – Carleton left Tyrone in the autumn of 1817, 'stimulated by this romantic love of adventure',[51] and made his way south to the parish of Killanny which straddled the counties of Louth and Monaghan. There he stayed for a few weeks with the Roman Catholic curate, Fr Edward McArdle, who he had known during his youth in Tyrone.[52] With no books to read and very little to pass his time, Carleton got into the habit of going for a lengthy walk each day. On one of these excursions he came to Corcreaghy crossroads, on the borders of Monaghan and Louth, where a group of soldiers were standing guard beneath: 'something like a tar sack dangling from a high beam of wood … long ropes of slime shining in the light, and dangling from the bottom'.[53] The sergeant on duty explained to him that this was the gibbet from which hung the decaying body of a notorious Ribbonman named Patrick Devan. It was then that Carleton heard for the first time 'the inhuman and hellish tragedy of Wildgoose Lodge'. Curious for more information, he listened that night as Fr McArdle related his version of events. He later wrote: 'The effect upon me was the most painful I ever felt from any narrative. It clung to me until I went to bed that night – it clung to me through my sleep with such vivid horror that

autobiography (Belfast, 1996 ed., [1st ed., 1896]); idem, 'Introduction' in Carleton, Traits and stories of the Irish peasantry (London, 1834); D.J. O'Donoghue, The life of William Carleton, 2 vols (Dublin, 1896); R. Wolff, William Carleton (1980); Benedict Kiely, Poor scholar: a study of the works and days of William Carleton (Dublin, 1948).   47 Carleton, Autobiography, pp 15–18.   48 Ibid., pp 18, 34.   49 Ibid., p. 37.   50 Carleton, 'Introduction', p. xv.   51 Ibid., p. xvii.   52 Fr McArdle became parish priest in 1820 and died c.1826; Raymond Murray, The burning of Wildgoose Lodge: Ribbonism in Louth, murder and the gallows (Monaghan, 2005), p. 5.   53 Carleton, Autobiography, p. 114.

sleep was anything but a relief to me.'[54]

After his stay with Fr McArdle, Carleton moved to Lowtown, less than two miles from Corcreaghy, where he was employed as a tutor to the children of Piers Murphy, a large Catholic farmer whom he described as 'the most over-bearing and most brutally tempered man I ever met – in fact, a low-minded, ignorant ruffian'.[55] Working with servants and labourers on the farm, Carleton must have been exposed to unrelenting stories of the burning of Wildgoose Lodge.[56] Moreover, he gathered with others at night in a public house at Corcreaghy crossroads kept by Peter Byrne and his three brothers, which was located a stone's throw from where he had come across Devan's gibbet. Once again it would have been difficult to avoid conversation on the atrocity partic-ularly as many local people had at that stage been arrested in connection with the murders and were awaiting trial in Dundalk jail. Thus there is a certain legit-imacy to Carleton's claim that: 'While I resided in the county of Louth, so near the scene of the outrage, I had the opportunity of learning, as every man had, that the incidents connected with it were as well known to the public as if that public had been present at them.'[57]

It is not clear when exactly Carleton left Killanny; he was unsure himself for he later wrote in his autobiography: 'I think the season was Lent ... I saw nothing on the tables but fish.'[58] But he certainly left with a store of lore about the burning of Wildgoose Lodge. He was still imbued by 'a spirit of romance'; his destination was Dublin where he believed his literary ambitions would be realised.[59] Very little is known of his earliest years in the capital. His autobiog-raphy tells us only that he held a number of teaching posts and that he was befriended by a family named Fox who introduced him to his future wife, Jane Anderson, a relative of theirs. What is more certain is that he made little or no progress in the literary sphere which led to a great deal of personal frustration; he later wrote that while some of his contemporaries such as Maria Edgeworth blossomed in London, others like himself 'laboured at home under all the dark privations of a literary famine'.[60]

By now Carleton was in his early thirties and had converted to Protestantism. For long after he was 'always at pains to give the impression that his embrace of the Anglican faith was the result of disinterested intellectual

54 Ibid., pp 114–15. 55 Ibid., p. 121. 56 According to the autobiography, Murphy 'had a great many cottages upon his property, in which those who worked on his immense farm resided'; ibid., p. 125. 57 Ibid., p. 116. 58 Carleton, *Autobiography*, p. 136. 59 Ibid., p. 151; idem, 'Introduction', p. xvii. 60 Carleton, 'Introduction', p. v; Brian Donnelly, 'William Carleton: novelist of the people' in Charles Dillon and H.A. Jefferies (eds), *Tyrone: history and society* (Dublin, 2000), pp 567–86.

scrutiny amongst the contending claims of the various Protestant churches, having already rejected the Catholic Church's claim to exclusive salvation'.[61] But, as Brian Donnelly argues, his conversion may have been much more pragmatic for it would have been extremely difficult for a young, aspiring Catholic writer to achieve the degree of patronage necessary to match Carleton's ambitions. Thus, in November 1826, when Carleton wrote to Sir Robert Peel, then British home secretary, 'offering to prove the involvement of O'Connell's Catholic Association and the Catholic priesthood in agrarian crimes',[62] he had a very clear agenda in mind. Playing to Peel's staunchly anti-Catholic emancipationist views Carleton was attempting to secure influential benefactors to allow him to widen his social network that, in turn, would progress his literary ambitions. Peel had been chief secretary of Ireland at the time of the burning of Wildgoose Lodge and as this work will show was central to most of what happened in the aftermath of the crime. In his letter Carleton's denunciation of the Catholic clergy was venomous: 'but the priests are those that I principally fear, not more from the habitual dissimulation of their character than from my knowledge of the unforgiving fire which burns within them black, malignant, and designing, systematically treacherous and false, and inherently inimical to Protestants'.[63] Significantly, he also suggested the seditious habits of Roman Catholic schoolteachers:

> If it can be proved that within a certain local extent (say of a few parishes) that the RC schoolmasters of the lower classes are with few exceptions the individuals who propagate with the greatest industry such seditious principles and who usually administer the unlawful oaths what a guide would not the certainty of this fact be to ministers.[64]

Carleton's letter was effectively a presagement of 'Wildgoose Lodge'. A short time later the Revd Caesar Otway befriended Carleton (the role of Peel in their meeting is not inferred). Otway was an evangelical proselytiser, a committed leader of the 'New Reformation' and a 'well-known anti-papal controversialist'.[65] Otway encouraged Carleton to write stories for his paper the *Christian Examiner* that would 'highlight the superstitious nature of much Catholic ritual as well as the corrupt practices of an ignorant clergy living off gullible congre-

61 Ibid., p. 575; Carleton, *Autobiography*, pp 180–1. **62** John Kelly, 'Carleton, William (1794–1869)' in *Oxford dictionary of national biography* (Oxford, 2004) [http://www.oxforddnb.com/view/article/4679, accessed 6 Sept. 2006]. **63** William Carleton to Sir Robert Peel, 3 Nov. 1826 (British Library, Peel papers, vol. ccx, fols 29–32, Add. MS 40390). **64** Ibid. **65** W.B. Yeats, *Representative Irish tales* (Gerrards Cross, 1979 ed.), p. 118.

gations'.[66] Carleton's first printed piece, 'A pilgrimage to Patrick's purgatory', which spotlighted the dangers of Roman Catholicism, appeared in the *Christian Examiner and Church of Ireland Gazette* in April 1828. It was around this time that the atrocity of Wildgoose Lodge must have proclaimed itself to Carleton as the perfect vehicle to consolidate his ingratiation with a literate Protestant ascendancy audience. Here was a heinous crime carried out by a Catholic secret society with the clandestine support of the clergy that needed little imaginative embellishment to serve his particular agenda. He had carried the lore around with him for twelve years or so; all he needed was to refresh his memory by researching the reports that had appeared in the newspapers between the perpetration of the crime in 1816 and the end of the trials in 1818. He wrote:

> Afterwards, when the trials took place, and the government prosecutions had closed, and when there was no apprehension of legal proceedings against any others than those who had been convicted, several whom Devaun had summoned without disclosing to them the frightful object in view, actually admitted that they had been present, and had no hesitation in giving full details of the deeds which were done. To this fact, added to another which I will mention, I owe the accuracy with which I have detailed the proceedings. These were, however known through the public papers which reported the trial. A copy of these papers I got afterwards from the Rev. Dr Stuart, rector of Lough Swilly.[67]

In January 1830, Carleton published 'Confessions of a reformed Ribbonman' in the *Dublin Literary Gazette*. The editor was happy to do so, as it was, he argued, 'a true record' from an authentic source and he pointed out that had it been 'a pure fiction, it would not have gained a place' in his paper.[68] From the end of that month and through most of February 'Confessions' was also serialised in the *Newry Telegraph*, a newspaper that was widely circulated in Louth and Monaghan. The editor added his own note to the final instalment: 'The main facts and circumstances set forth in the foregoing narrative are by no means fictitious. The readers of the *Telegraph,* who bear in memory the burning of Wildgoose Lodge and the utter destruction of its inmates (in 1816), will at once recognise the fidelity of the picture.'[69] Even at this stage, fourteen years after the event, it is clear that the crime was labelled 'the burning of Wildgoose Lodge'. It is also clear that from its first publication Carleton's story was being widely heralded as factual and authentic. That he used the narrative technique of telling

---

66 Donnelly, 'Novelist of the people', p. 576.   67 Carleton, *Autobiography*, p. 116.   68 Quoted in Hayley, *Carleton's traits and stories*, p. 123.   69 *Newry Telegraph*, 5 Feb. 1830.

the story in the first person, disguising it as an eyewitness account, undoubtedly had a misleading effect on a generally less sophisticated literary audience
than exists in the present day. Even for some of the more literate, such as Fr
Bernard Loughran, parish priest of Killeavy in Co. Armagh, the narrative technique blurred the distinction between fact and fiction. After it appeared in the
Newry Telegraph a very irate Fr Loughran, who had been curate in Ardee from
1812 to 1821, wrote to the editor decrying the author for having been hood-
winked: 'The wonder is that a person of such intellect should be seduced or
duped by so vulgar, so insignificant, or so illiterate a character as the inhuman
Devan.' Loughran claimed: 'the particulars of this horrid transaction are still
fresh in my memory – I then resided in the immediate vicinity of Wildgoose
Lodge, and could not be an inattentive observer of the tragical scenes I had to
witness'.[70] His letter focused on one very significant change made by Carleton
in the pursuit of his agenda: his representation of the owner of the burned house
as a Protestant. In 'Confessions' the narrator recalled: 'Our conjectures were
correct, for on leaving the chapel we directed our steps to the house in which
this man (the only Protestant in the parish) resided.' Fr Loughran vigorously
countered this representation:

> It is strange, indeed, that while this barefaced calumniator labours, with
> a perversion of truth and facts that bespeaks the dark workings of a
> malignant heart, to represent the appalling occurrence of Wildgoose
> Lodge, as a conspiracy against the lives of Protestants, should refer his
> readers to the files of the *Newry Telegraph,* for a confirmation of his
> statement. This ill-judged manoeuvre proves the truth of a well-known
> proverb, that 'liars should have a good memory'. It is unfortunate for
> this public defamer that the very contrary is recorded in the columns
> of the *Telegraph.* Should he take the trouble examining, he will learn
> from it that Lynch, whom he pompously designates with the epithet,
> *Mr,* was a *Roman Catholic* in a very humble sphere of life, that every
> individual that perished with him was a Catholic, that, as far as could
> be ascertained, all the conspirators were Catholics …[71]

Three years later, the story became the earliest of Carleton's to appear in
the first edition of his *Traits and stories of the Irish peasantry* (1833). By then two
major changes had been made. Firstly, the Edward Lynch character was no
longer represented as a Protestant; the relevant sentence was changed to: 'Our
conjectures were correct; for on leaving the chapel we directed our steps to the

70 Fr B.J. Loughran to editor, 13 Feb. 1830 in *Newry Telegraph*, 19 Feb. 1830.   71 Ibid.

house in which this devoted man resided.'[72] (The impact of the rest of the story was no less diluted by the fact that this was a barbaric crime committed by Catholics on Catholics.) Secondly, the title of the story was changed to 'Wildgoose Lodge'. Why this decision was taken is again open to interpretation. Fr Loughran's criticism had certainly suggested there were credibility issues concerning the concept of a 'reformed Ribbonman':

> Perhaps the 'reformed Ribbonman', if he ever belonged to that miscreant's standard [Patrick Devan], which I believe few of your readers will believe, has, since his secession from him and his banditti, applied himself to the cultivation of those [literary] talents. If so, it is to be lamented that his moral improvement has not kept pace with his astonishing march of intellect.

Carleton's literary mind may even have recognised that a dark irony attached itself to the name of the house, the mystique that the name exuded hinted at the wild goose chase undertaken by the authorities after the incident to capture the perpetrators. However, it was probably more a case that after 1816, as noted above, the atrocity was more popularly labelled according to the action ('the burning of Wildgoose Lodge') rather than the outcome (the murder of eight people). When Carleton followed suit he ensured that this would remain the case up to the present day.

In 'Wildgoose Lodge' Carleton borrowed from the editors of the *Dublin Literary Gazette* and the *Newry Telegraph* by adding his own footnote to what appeared in *Traits and stories:*

> This tale of terror is, unfortunately, too true. The scene of hellish murder detailed in it lies at Wildgoose Lodge, in the county of Louth, within about four miles of Carrickmacross [Co. Monaghan], and nine of Dundalk [Co. Louth]. No such multitudinous murder has occurred, under similar circumstances, except the burning of the Sheas, in the county of Tipperary. The name of the family burned in Wildgoose Lodge was Lynch. One of them had, shortly before this fatal night, prosecuted and convicted some of the neighbouring Ribbonmen, who visited him with severe marks of their displeasure, in consequence of his having refused to enrol himself as a member of their body. The language of the story is partly fictitious; but the facts are pretty closely such as were developed during the trial of the murderers. Both parties were

72 Carleton, 'Wildgoose Lodge', p. 256.

> Roman Catholics, and either twenty-five or twenty-eight of those who
> took an active part in the burning, were hanged and gibbeted in differ-
> ent parts of the county of Louth. Devan, the ringleader, hung for some
> months in chains, within a hundred yards of his own house, and about
> half a mile from Wildgoose Lodge. His mother could neither go into
> nor out of her cabin, without seeing his body swinging from the gibbet.
> Her usual exclamation on looking at him was 'God be good to the sowl
> of my poor marthyr!' The peasantry, too, frequently exclaimed, on seeing
> him, 'Poor Paddy!' A gloomy fact that speaks volumes.[73]

The footnote was an unashamed effort by Carleton to convince his readership
of the authenticity of his account. It might simply be viewed as part of a narrative technique that had become popular as a result of 'a resistance on the part
of readers to the very idea of invented or imagined worlds [which] led novelists like Defoe, Richardson and Fielding to disguise their works as autobiogra-
phies, memoirs, real-life adventures or eye-witness accounts'.[74] The footnote
was certainly a lazy and poor attempt at providing facts: it would not have taken
much research of the type supposedly carried out by him in the newspapers to
find that eighteen men were executed after the burning; having lived in Killanny
and seen Devan's gibbet at Corcreaghy he would have known the latter was a
good deal further than half a mile from Wildgoose Lodge and that Devan's
mother was dead by the time her son was hanged, but then describing her cries
of 'my poor marthyr' and the sympathetic exclamations of the peasantry could
be interpreted as another attempt by Carleton to highlight the potential menace
of lower class Catholic secret societies. In total, the footnote was no less fictional that the rest of the story.

    Carleton's claims of authenticity for literary effect contributed to the myth
that subsequently emerged that his was a historically accurate, factual account
so much so that he was later unfairly judged as a historian. For example, D.J.
Casey, a former professor of English at New York State University, contended:

> In summary, Carleton, as a Louth historian, is a dismal failure, for he
> deliberately distorts events, transmogrifies personalities, and misrepre-
> sents points of view. His pages are littered with inaccuracies and con-
> tradictions, and his demonstrated inability to interpret the event or
> respond to it objectively should immediately rule out historical credi-

---

73 Carleton, *Traits and stories 2*, p. 362; see also, Carleton, *Autobiography*, p. 118.   74 Tom Dunne,
'Fiction as "the best history of nations": Lady Morgan's Irish novels' in Tom Dunne (ed.), *The
writer as witness: literature as historical evidence* (Cork, 1987), p. 134.

bility.[75]

When Carleton set out to write 'Confessions of a reformed Ribbonman/ Wildgoose Lodge', he did not do so as a historian; he did so as a frustrated writer with ambitions who had a particular purpose in mind and that was to win absolute approval from the *Dublin Literary Gazette*'s predominantly upper class and Protestant readership.[76] (This was not lost on later nationalist commentators; Darrell Figgis, 1882–1925, a nationalist separatist, later criticised Carleton for having deserted the cause of his people to become a sycophant of the Protestant ascendancy 'who viewed his race askance, and who wished to find palliatives for their prejudice'.)[77] When he wrote again to Robert Peel in 1842 looking for an annual pension he concluded: 'For this I can appeal to my writing whose spirit is conservative and Protestant and I have reason to know that they have effected a more generous and liberal tone of thinking in religious matters among a large class of the leading Roman Catholics of Ireland.'[78] As will become clear later in this work, Carleton's version of events not only appealed to Peel but also to the Protestant and Catholic merchant and middle classes of Dundalk and the Protestant and Catholic gentry and large farmers in the surrounding area of north Louth because it focused on the atrocity and followed a line that took no account of mitigating biographical circumstances. Carleton represented the motivation behind the burning in terms of 'the pernicious influence of Ribbonism' and 'the following up of private and personal feuds and enmities amongst themselves [Ribbonmen]',[79] but without reference to the social, political, economic, demographic and cultural milieux in which the crime was incubated.

Carleton's story conformed to the agenda of the likes of the proselytising Caesar Otway who was intent on reforming the moral conduct of the lower orders (which is very much echoed in the title 'Confessions of a reformed Ribbonman'). His version suggested some covert form of alliance, however loose, between 'treacherous and false' Roman Catholic priests, Roman Catholic schoolmasters and local secret societies. In the version which appeared in the *Gazette* Carleton portrayed the burning in terms of an orchestrated sectarian raid – as noted he emphasised that the victim was the *only* Protestant in the

75 Casey, 'Carleton in Louth', p. 104.   **76** Margaret Chesnutt, *Studies in the short stories of William Carleton* (Gottenburg, 1976), p. 129.   **77** Hayley, 'Introduction' in Carleton, *Traits and stories, vol. 1*, p. 10; Darrell Figgis, 'Introduction' in William Carleton, *Stories of Irish life* (Dublin, n.d.), p. xii.   **78** William Carleton to Robert Peel, 21 Oct. 1842 (British Library, Peel papers, vol. cccxxvii, fols. 171–2, Add. MS 40517).   **79** Carleton, 'Wildgoose Lodge', p. 361; idem, *Stories of Irish life*, p. 115.

parish. In that and later versions he presented his audience with the type of stereotypical characters that would prey on their foreboding, as would the central action of the plot. His characters were 'the most malignant and reckless spirits in the parish'; profane enough to drink liberally in a place of worship; bound together by hideous oaths; with no regard for the laws or authority of the state; no respect for private property or life; and led by a satanic leader. And as Raymond Murray concludes: 'Great evil is accentuated in the sacrilegious activities of the beastly conspirators. The rituals of Ribbonmen replace the Catholic Mass rite.'[80]

Thus, the real importance of 'Confessions of a Ribbonman' or 'Wildgoose Lodge' to a historian lies in what they tell of Carleton's understanding of the attitudes and perceptions of his targeted audience towards the lower orders and in particular towards Catholic agrarian secret societies. His representation of Devan was almost a carbon copy of the way in which the judiciary and Crown prosecutors depicted him during his trial in 1817. Judge McClelland portrayed Devan as a 'monster' and his associates as 'nefarious ruffians'.[81] Judge Fletcher's charge to the juries at the later Wildgoose Lodge trials at the spring assizes of March 1818 was to be strongly echoed in Carleton's introduction to his *Traits and stories*. Fletcher said: 'It appears that the monster, Devan (who now on a gibbet pays the forfeit of his crimes), was clerk to the parish priest; he was, it seems, the parish schoolmaster too. It was to this wretch that the forming of the morals and the minds of the rising generation was committed.'[82] In his introduction to *Traits and stories* Carleton later wrote that the education of children 'was left altogether to hedge schoolmasters, a class of men who, with few exceptions, bestowed such an education upon the people as is sufficient almost, in the absence of all other causes, to account for much of the agrarian violence and erroneous principles which regulate their movements and feelings on that and similar subjects'.[83] It was reminiscent of his portrayal of such men to Robert Peel a number of years before.

Moreover, in the late 1820s, early 1830s Carleton very much played on the mindset of a Protestant ascendancy whose sensibilities had been severely shaken by the 1798 rebellion and to a lesser extent by the millenarianism of the 1820s when, in order to embellish his description of what happened at Wildgoose

80 Murray, *The burning of Wildgoose Lodge*, p. 7.   81 *Dublin Evening Post*, 14 Mar. 1818; *Drogheda Journal*, 18 Mar. 1818; *Correspondent*, 19 Mar. 1818.   82 *Correct abstract of the charge of Mr Justice Fletcher on the conviction of the persons charged with the burning of Wildgoose Lodge*, 1818 (Royal Irish Academy, 3B53–56/492).   83 This was a generalisation not exclusive to Carleton: L.M. Cullen has pointed out that in the early nineteenth century 'there was a growing belief that education was in the hands of persons who were morally dissolute and politically subversive'; Carleton, 'General introduction' in *Traits and stories 1*, p. xix–xx; Cullen, *Modern Ireland*, p. 237.

3 'By all that's sacred and holy we're willin': taken from William Carleton's *Traits and stories*, vol. ii (1865 ed.). Note the physical features of the 'miscreants' gathered around Patrick Devan.

Lodge, he drew inspiration from Richard Musgrave's *Memoirs of the different rebellions* (1801), a work which depicted the 1798 rebellion: 'as a priest-led conspiracy, continuing the pattern of consistent Catholic treachery earlier seen in the rising of 1641 and the reign of James II [which] strongly influenced conservative Protestant thinking'.[84] For example, Carleton's brutal descriptions of the helpless plight of the mother and child, the helpless man being piked and thrown back into the flames and the general terror of the night (all of which were largely imitated in later accounts) seem to have been strongly influenced by Musgrave's account of the Scullabogue massacre in 1798 when, as referred to earlier, 126 men, women and children, predominantly Protestants, were burned to death by rebel forces in a barn in Co. Wexford. Musgrave quoted Richard Sylvester, an eye-witness at Scullabogue, who: 'saw a child who got under the door, and was likely to escape, but much hurt and bruised; when a rebel perceiving it, darted his pike through it, and threw it into the flames'.[85] Likewise, the plight of the child's mother in 'Wildgoose Lodge' is echoed in another eye-witness account from Scullabogue:

> The roof was on fire, and the loyalists were trying to force open the door to effect their escape, but were prevented by the rebels, of whom the prisoner was one, and he made several stabs of his pike at those who endeavoured to get out, particularly a woman, and on striking her he bent his pike.[86]

On the other hand, it is erroneous for literary critics to have dismissed the idea that Carleton's account had no historical basis. Barbara Hayley, in her introduction to the 1990 facsimile edition of *Traits and stories,* described the story as a 'purely fictional account' (although she noted the irony that because it seems 'grippingly true ... it is frequently quoted as a factual source on this atrocity').[87] Barry Sloan regarded the meeting in the church as 'unnecessarily melodramatic' and 'a detail that belongs merely to the genre of Gothic horror tales'.[88] In a similar vein D.J. Casey who regarded the tale as 'more fiction than fact, more fantasy than history' wrote:

In Carleton's 'Wildgoose Lodge' there are all the elements of Gothicism

---

84 Neal Garnham, 'Musgrave, Sir Richard (c.1757–1818)' in S.J. Connolly (ed.), *The Oxford companion to Irish history* (Oxford, 1998), p. 373. **85** Richard Musgrave, *Memoirs of the different rebellions in Ireland from the arrival of the English* (2 vols, Dublin, 1802 ed.), vol. i, p. 528. **86** Quoted in Tom Dunne, *Rebellions: memoirs, memory and 1798* (Dublin, 2004), p. 252. **87** Hayley, 'Introduction' in Carleton, *Traits and stories of the Irish peasantry*, vol. i, p. 11. **88** Barry Sloan, *The pioneers of Anglo-Irish fiction, 1800–1850* (Gerrards Cross, 1986), pp 165–6.

– save perhaps the derelict castle. The tempest rages, lightning slices the heavens, and floods inundate the landscape. The chapel is transformed into a shadowy den of iniquity as 'the Captain', the clerk of the chapel, reigns over the midnight ceremony. There is even the nocturnal procession of maniacal disciples to the isolated lodge where the slaughter of innocents is to occur. There is dread, terror, and suspense. The Captain, not now Paddy Devaun, but a diabolical metamorphosis of him, ruthlessly orders death and destruction in the inferno that roars before him.[89]

Carleton was not at all being 'unnecessarily melodramatic' or Gothic when he situated the planning of the burning in a chapel; that is how it was. But literary licence was taken with much of the rest of the story and so there has been a gradual melting of fact with fiction down through the generations. Carleton's story can arguably be best described as fiction with a basis in fact. It is the objective of the main body of this work to set out the available evidence and to investigate the myths that have grown as a result of Carleton's account.

Earlier published accounts

Carleton was not the first to use the incident at Wildgoose Lodge for a purpose or to suit a particular agenda. In 1823 the first identified published reference to the atrocity (other than newspapers) appeared when John Graham (1776–1844) devoted nine stanzas to it in his epic poem, *Sir Harcourt's vision: an historical poem* (Dublin, 1823), which are reproduced in appendix I of this work. Graham was from a very different background – social, religious and cultural – to Carleton. His agenda for drawing on Wildgoose Lodge was less motivated by the prospect of personal gain but the incident served a somewhat similar purpose, to warn a Protestant audience of the dangers of Catholic Emancipation. A Fermanagh-born historian, whose ancestral family had moved from Cumberland to Ireland in the early seventeenth century, Graham was an ardent admirer of those who had defended Londonderry in 1688 and wrote a history of the siege of that city and the defence of Enniskillen in 1688 and 1689. He was 'a zealous and even fanatical participant in Protestant commemorations of the Williamite period'.[90]

The poem was an address to Sir Harcourt Lees (1776–1852), a prolific pam-

89 D.J. Casey, 'Wildgoose Lodge: the evidence and the lore' in *Journal of the County Louth Archaeological and Historical Society*, 18:1 (1973), pp 220–1. **90** Norman Moore, 'Graham, John',

4 Sir Harcourt Lees (1776–1852), rector of Killanny
(courtesy of National Portrait Gallery, London).

phleteer who had gained a reputation of being a notorious anti-emancipationist, acquiring for his efforts the sobriquet of 'No-popery Lees'.[91] He was the
eldest son of Sir John Lees (1739–1811) who in the 1790s was secretary to the
Irish Post Office and largely instrumental in using the mail as a means of gathering secret information 'of all those in any way suspected of planning treason-
able acts or even of harbouring "disloyal" thoughts' that helped break the United
Irish movement.[92] By the time of the burning of Wildgoose Lodge in 1816 Sir
Harcourt had been the Church of Ireland rector of the parish of Killanny for
ten years. He lived for part of the year in Drummoney glebe near Essexford

rev. Colm Lennon, http://www.oxforddnb.com/view/article/11212 (accessed 3 Feb. 2005). **91** See
Harcourt Lees, *A cursory view of the present state of Ireland* (Dublin, 1821); idem, *The crisis: or
patriotism explained and popery exposed in four letters addressed to that upright and eloquent barrister Daniel O'Connell esq.* (Dublin, 1821); idem, *The rehearsal: king and constitution and pope and
Catholic emancipation; recommended to the attention of the most stupid of the Protestant advocates
for unrestricted civil liberty* (Dublin, 1821). In a footnote to Carleton's *Autobiography*, Carleton
describes Lees as 'one of the most notable opponents of "popery" in Ireland during the early years
of the century'; Carleton, *Autobiography*, p. 121. **92** Thomas Bartlett, *Revolutionary Dublin,
1795–1801: the letters of Francis Higgins to Dublin Castle* (Dublin, 2004), p. 14.

(and for the other part in Blackrock, Co. Dublin), just over a mile from Corcreaghy crossroads where Carleton saw Devan's gibbet.[93]

In his works Lees repetitively warned of Catholic inspired conspiracies to murder Protestants and advocated the strongest repression of those who supported Catholic secret societies. He denounced 'those image-worshippers' who 'pay divine adoration to a mixture of flour and water made up by the hands of an illiterate and possibly profligate priest'.[94] Lees proposed to rescue the lower orders 'from the influence of ignorance and priest-craft' and 'the middling classes from the example and dictation of factious demagogues who really pant after, not so much emancipation, as the revolution which they firmly believe it would soon occasion'.[95] For Lees, the events of 1798 had served to harden his belief that a future 'popish rebellion' was inevitable.

In 1821 in a series of letters to Daniel O'Connell (which when published as a single volume went through at least seven editions), Lees defied the leader of the emancipation movement to 'shew me an instance since the commencement of your Church, where papists, enjoying power, did not persecute Protestants, murder them, burn them, torture them, imprison them'.[96] Two years later, Graham helped consolidate this perception in *Sir Harcourt's vision*. The relevant verses suggest that after the murders at Wildgoose Lodge Protestants of all classes could legitimately fear for their lives (even though the murders had not been sectarian). The publication coincided with the rapid spread of millenarian excitement in the early 1820s fuelled by the prophecies of Signor Pastorini's[97] *General history of the Christian Church* (1777) that had foretold the violent extermination of Protestants. The cult of Pastorini flourished particularly but not exclusively in the south of Ireland where it became caught up with the agrarian Rockite movement and subsequently in some areas: 'Protestants lived in dread because of the credence given by Catholic peasants to Pastorini's hopeful vision'.[98] A chief characteristic of the writings that appeared in response to Pastorini was the notion that the Catholic clergy conspired against the defeat

93 Killanny is divided between counties Monaghan and Louth and is not in Co. Down as is claimed in the revised version of Lees' biographical sketch in H.C.G. Matthew and Brian Harrison (eds), *Oxford dictionary of national biography vol. 33* (Oxford, 2004), p. 149. **94** Lees, *The crisis*, p. 46. **95** Idem, *The antidote: or 'Nouvelle a la main' recommended to the serious attention of the Right Hon. W. C. Plunkett* (Dublin, 1819), pp 69–70; see also idem, *The mystery: being a short but decisive counter-reply to the few friendly hints of the Rev Charles B. Stennett at present an officiating popish priest in the religious college of Maynooth* (Dublin, 1820). **96** Lees, *The crisis*, p. 21. **97** Pseudonym of Charles Walmesley (1722–97), an English Catholic bishop. **98** James S. Donnelly Jr, 'Pastorini and Captain Rock: millenarianism and sectarianism in the Rockite movement of 1821–4' in Samuel Clark and James S. Donnelly Jr., *Irish peasants: violence and political unrest, 1780–1914* (Madison, Wisconsin, 1983), pp 111–14.

of secret agrarian organisations by refusing to denounce their subversive activities. According to *Sir Harcourt's vision*:

> No meeting of bishops or clergy was call'd,
> At Reaghstown or Stonehouse to say,
> That deeds of such horror their pastors appall'd,
> Who these felons would drag into day.

Graham perceived the real titular leaders of the Catholic lower classes to be 'the Ribbonmen' and his stanzas, in the very best Pastorini-like tradition, portended dreadful things to come for Protestants:

> The other [oath] of Ribbonmen – dreadful to say,
> On a very short notice to rise,
> Their innocent Protestant neighbours to slay,
> And the sixth great commandment to despise.

Lees' proselytising activities and his teachings – which would have been widely known as his pamphlets were bestsellers in their day – were probably well articulated to his Catholic neighbours, of whom Patrick Devan, the local hedge schoolmaster, was one. From the late eighteenth century an increasing number of people began to read newspapers, or more precisely have them read to them. The thirst for the dissemination of ideas was evident in the south Armagh area that bordered on north Louth and south Monaghan from the early 1790s when it was reported that

> the change in the natives here is truly astonishing. Formerly a newspaper would have been a phenomenon amongst them. At present, they may vie with the northerns in their thirst after politics. He who can read has generally a large audience about the door of his cabin.[99]

In 1823, the editor of *The Times* went as far as to suggest that Lees' writings were recruitment propaganda for Ribbonmen.[1] Meanwhile in Killanny Lees found himself the target of aggressors. In 1820, he claimed that he captured an 'accredited Ribbon agent' in his house at Essexford who was endeavouring to seduce his servants from their allegiance and attempting to persuade them to

99 Quoted in Jim Smyth, *The men of no property: Irish radicals and popular politics in the late eighteenth century* (Basingstoke, Hampshire, 1992), p. 5. **1** *The Times*, 11 Jan. 1823.

assassinate their master. A few nights later, the barking of one of his pointer dogs alerted him to a fire in his home. He was later informed 'on the oaths of disinterested and credible witnesses that a foul and bloody conspiracy' had been formed to murder him.[2] The conspirators – Edward Slaven, Thomas Muckeins and Patrick Marron – were all tried for attempted murder at Monaghan assizes in July that year. John Milton, a soldier, swore that when he went into a public house in Carrickmacross he found the three accused talking there in Irish. When they began to talk in English he overheard Muckeins say: 'Sir Harcourt Lees was a d——d bad man, and sent a bad character of the Roman Catholics to Dublin, and said if he had him here he should not see morning.'[3] In his auto-biography, Carleton relates an anecdote of how his Catholic employer, Piers Murphy, was determined one night to shoot one of Lees' dogs that had strayed on to his lands.[4] The impression given by Carleton is that it was the owner rather than the dog that Murphy despised. While it is difficult to quantify, it is possible that Lees' presence in the parish of Killanny added an extra dimension to the Catholic question and became just another ingredient in a dangerous cocktail that led to social disorder.

Published accounts from Carleton to the land war

After Carleton, the next published account of the murders appeared in *Chambers' Edinburgh Journal* on 30 September 1837.[5] It was published anony-mously. However, the author can be identified from an almost verbatim piece that appeared in James Anton's memoirs, *Retrospect of a military life* published nine years later in 1846. The Scottish-born Anton was a soldier in the 42nd Foot Regiment who came to Ireland in May 1817, about seven months after the burn-ing and around the time that suspects, including Devan, were arrested. By June of the following year he was stationed in Dundalk, just a month before the majority of the Wildgoose Lodge trials were held there. His is a memoir pub-lished (though not necessarily written) twenty years after the event. Memoirs can be historically inaccurate to varying degrees due perhaps to gradual failure of memory (Anton, for example, mistakenly claimed that thirteen were mur-dered and only eleven executed)[6] or simply for embellishment. Anton's accounts of the Wildgoose Lodge incident show clear evidence that he borrowed heav-ily from Carleton. There are crucial points of agreement: the meeting to plan

---

2 Lees, *The crisis*, pp 9–10. **3** *The Times*, 2 Aug. 1820; see below for additional evidence concern-ing William Filgate given at this trial. **4** Carleton, *Autobiography*, pp 121–3. **5** http://www.jbhall.freeservers.com/1816_wildgoose_lodge.htm, 23 Oct. 2004. **6** Ibid.

the atrocity was held in a chapel; the leader was Patrick Devan, the clerk of the chapel; he forcibly reminded all present of the oath they had taken; he placed a piece of burning turf in a pot and led the way to the lodge.[7] Devan and followers are still the monsters of Carleton's account, who have duped their naïve followers. As they left the chapel:

> To the credit of human nature, it must be stated, that few of this numerous party had the slightest idea of what was intended by the originators of the movement. As the men went along, they were inquiring among themselves, in whispers, what was to be done; even those who had heard Devan's threats did not believe that they would be enforced, or that any further injury would be done than had been inflicted before.[8]

Like Carleton, Anton embroidered his account by drawing information from works describing other atrocities. The story of the distraught mother trying to save her child is once again the focus of the atrocity; in *Chambers' Edinburgh Journal* Anton wrongly identifies her as Lynch's wife instead of his daughter:

> The wife of Lynch, while her own body was already enveloped in flames, had endeavoured to preserve the infant at her breast, and she appeared at the windows, content to die herself, but holding out her child for mercy and protection. Frantically she threw it from her. And how was it received? On the point of pikes, and instantly tossed back into the burning ruins, into which at the same time sunk its hapless mother.[9]

Thus it echoed strongly of Carleton who, in turn, had drawn inspiration from Musgrave. In the account later published in Anton's *Retrospect*, this episode is more graphically described:

> The monsters stood ready with their pikes to thrust back those who should dare to escape, either from the door or window and when the burning mother held out her scorched child for protection it was thrust back on her bosom as she fell amidst the blazing fire. Not a tear of pity fell for the guiltless sufferers, no soothing sound mingled with their wailings but loud rose from the surrounding band the savage shouts of exultation as they beheld the struggling victims falling in the flames.[10]

There were nine years between Anton's two accounts. During that time,

7 Ibid.   8 Ibid.   9 Ibid.   10 Ibid.

5 George Cruickshank's drawing of the Scullabogue massacre, taken from
W.H. Maxwell's *History of the Irish rebellion in 1798* (1844).

George Cruikshank's expressive drawing of the massacre at Scullabogue in 1798
appeared in W.H. Maxwell's *History of the Irish rebellion in 1798* (1844). One of
the focal points of this illustration is a savage-looking pike man holding an
impaled child up to the burning thatch. There is murder and mayhem all
around. The armed raiders are determined to fire the charnel house so that none
will escape; victims trying to escape are crushed behind a door, some about to
be shot, stabbed or piked. Thus, atrocities separated in time by eighteen years
and geographically by the length of a province had become entwined in popular Protestant culture.

It is also significant that Anton's 1846 memoirs came in the aftermath of
the expose of Ribbonism which had taken place over the previous six years or
so when many of the most prominent leaders were arrested and tried, their trials
attracting widespread media attention. Over the previous two decades or so
Ribbonism had evolved beyond local secret societies into a more formal organisation in most of Ulster, north Leinster and north Connaught that exhibited

strong traits of Catholic sectarianism in response to Protestant Orangeism and embodied some concept of an independent and egalitarian Ireland to be achieved through armed insurrection. Lynch, Anton wrote, 'though a moderate man' joined a local secret oath-bound organisation believing that 'such a combination, on the part of those who held the same opinions with himself, was necessary to counteract similar demonstrations on the opposite or Protestant side'.[11] What Anton was describing here was the Ribbon organisation as was understood and exposed in the 1840s; it was not of the type of the local agrarian society that had carried out the murders at Wildgoose Lodge. The anti-Ribbonism rhetoric of the 1840s clearly influenced Anton's retelling of the Wildgoose atrocity. Anton specifically condemns the lack of effort made by the Catholic clergy of Louth to prevent their congregations from organising illegally just as in the 1840 trial of noted Ribbon leader, Richard Jones, the defence proclaimed:

> It must be obvious to all the world that a secret and criminal association like this, in which so many thousands of the lower order of Irish papists are implicated, could not, by any moral possibility, exist at all without the full knowledge of the Romish priests, or that it could continue to exist, without their warm approbation and encouragement.[12]

Anton's description of events fits in well with the idea of a reformed Ribbonman falling foul of his former comrades. He claimed that local Ribbonmen met for a time at Wildgoose Lodge – its remoteness gave it an obvious advantage – but that as the society increased in numbers and Lynch began to increase in prosperity, he began to fear that he would pay the price of coming under suspicion as one of its leaders. He, therefore, put an end to the meetings at his house, which subsequently: 'led the ringleaders to stimulate their sworn accomplices to inflict every annoyance on him which they could think of to accomplish his ruin and eject him from the place'.[13] Anton played up the suggestion that Lynch had violated his oath that 'no member should bring another before the bar of justice'.[14] By turning informer, he had separated himself irrevocably from his previous associates and soon: 'the whole strength of the fraternity was called together on purpose to witness the punishment about to be inflicted upon him for his apostacy'.[15] In a like manner, when Kennedy, the informer in the Jones' trial agreed to give evidence it was reported that 'such is the lawless condition of society throughout Ireland' that 'the only effective secu-

11 http://www.jbhall.freeservers.com/1816_wildgoose_lodge.htm, 23 Oct. 2004. 12 *Leitrim and Roscommon Gazette,* 4 July 1840; my thanks to Dr Jennifer Kelly for bringing this source to my attention. 13 Ibid. 14 Ibid. 15 Ibid.

rity against being himself murdered, has been subsisted, with his whole family in prison'.[16]

There is no surviving historical evidence to suggest that Edward Lynch was a Ribbonman nor was there ever any suggestion of the same made in the trials. Anton's contribution added another dimension to the mythology growing around the incident. However, in the context of the historical evidence presented later in this work Anton did make two interesting observations: firstly, that secret organisations 'were for controlling what the different parties considered local oppressions rather than government authority' and secondly that in a judicial system that was open to corruption individual magistrates were capable of falsely implicating suspects in order to secure convictions.[17]

The next published account appeared in 1857 in William Brett's *Reminiscences of Louth*. Brett was the proprietor of the first newspaper printed in Dundalk in 1829, the *Louth Free Press*. According to Pádraig Ua Dubhthaigh, Brett's enthusiasm for the cause of Catholic Emancipation aroused the suspicion of the local landed class; he became embroiled in a number of libel suits and within a year was forced out of business.[18] By the time he came to write his recollections, he had learned a publishing lesson that an alternative history to the now more or less established one of the murders at Wildgoose Lodge would not be popular with the readership he was targeting. Thus it remained a 'demonical crime', an 'infernal plot' and a 'dark and barbarous atrocity' carried out at the instigation of Devan whose 'heart must have been steeled by the archfiend'.[19] Brett concluded that Carleton had kept the story alive when it would have been much better if 'the recollection of this barbarous outrage, so revolting to the feelings of humanity could be buried in oblivion forever'.[20] His sentiments reflected the views of a local community that were to survive long into the future.

Seven years later, another account appeared in D'Alton and O'Flanagan's *The history of Dundalk* (1864). John D'Alton (1792–1867) had been born into a Westmeath landed family. He was educated at Trinity College and was called to the Irish Bar in 1813. J.R. O'Flanagan was a fellow barrister who agreed to help him complete his study of Dundalk.[21] They too were looking to a certain set for patronage – the book was dedicated to over 160 local benefactors whose subscriptions had made its publication possible, the majority of whom were members of the county gentry families or the urban middle classes. Their main

---

16 *Roscommon and Leitrim Gazette*, 4 July 1840. 17 http://www.jbhall.freeservers.com/1816_wild-goose_lodge.htm, 23 Oct. 2004; see also James Anton, *Retrospect of a military life* (Edinburgh, 1841), pp 163, 303. 18 Pádraig Ua Dubhthaigh, *The book of Dundalk* (Dundalk, 1946), p. 104. 19 William Brett, *Reminiscences of Louth* (Dundalk, 1913), p. 7. 20 Ibid. 21 'Obituary of John D'Alton, 1792–1857' in *Tempest's Annual, 1936*, pp 13–14.

benefactors included Lord Roden and Chichester Fortescue whose fathers played prominent roles in the arrest and trials of the Wildgoose suspects; Malcolm Brown and James McAlister who sat on the juries; Alexander and James Shekleton (sons of Alexander, iron manufacturer, who sat on the Devan jury and was manufacturer of the gibbet in which the latter was hanged), as well as family relations of other jurors including Robert Moritz, Henry Hale, Robert Dickie and John Baillie.[22]

D'Alton and O'Flanagan devoted a complete chapter to the crime, which they erroneously dated to 30 October 1817 instead of 1816.[23] In a footnote, the authors pointed their readers to 'a graphic account' to be found in Carleton's *Stories of the Irish peasantry*, and they clearly relied heavily upon it themselves, not least in the description of the foulness of the night, the goings on in the chapel and the burning. There is a slight deviation from Anton's account – Dalton and O'Flanagan contended that it was Lynch's son refused to join the Ribbonmen thereby becoming 'a mark for the displeasure of this lawless and wicked confederacy'.[24] The motivation for the burning is therefore again depicted in terms of Ribbon revenge and the crime was portrayed in the most barbaric terms:

> No mercy! was the order and no mercy was shown. A fearful sight appeared at one of the windows – a woman's head, with the fire burning like the glory around. She shrieked for mercy; she received the thrust of a pike, and was flung back into the flames. The whole dwelling soon showed one lurid blaze, and the shrieks of its perishing inmates rose fearfully above the cracking of the rafters. Doors were wrenched open, and windows shattered to atoms, in the efforts of the inmates to escape; but the fiends who guarded every egress, had their lesson, and *no mercy* was extended to man, woman or child – even an infant was doomed to perish. The owner of the house – Lynch – made a pathetic appeal on behalf of his daughter. She was yet unhurt, and he begged, in moving terms, for her life; or, if that was not granted, that he might be shot, rather than see her perish by fire. 'You'll prosecute no one now, you bloody informer,' was the inhuman response.[25]

This was clearly a reworking of Carleton's account which brought the horror of the crime to a new generation of Louth people and further enhanced its barbarism by exaggerating the number murdered to 'about a dozen' while simul-

22 John D'Alton and J.R. O'Flanagan, *The history of Dundalk and its environs; from the earliest historic period to the present time with memoirs of its eminent men* (Dundalk, 1864), pp vii–viii. 23 Ibid., pp 219–23. 24 Ibid., p. 220. 25 Ibid., pp 221–2.

taneously understating the number executed at thirteen. The authors also dubiously concluded that the suspects were 'ably defended by the well-known eminent criminal lawyer, the late Leonard MacNally'.[26]

The dating of Brett's and D'Alton and O'Flanagan's works is important. The borderlands – south Monaghan, east Cavan, north Louth, south Armagh and north Meath – had passed through another vicious period of Ribbon atrocities in the late 1840s, early 1850s, so much so that atrocities there in the years 1849–52 were given special consideration in government enquiries.[27] Along that notorious Ribbon belt, R.L. Mauleverer, agent on a number of south Armagh estates, was murdered near Crossmaglen in May 1850; Lord Templetown's agent, Thomas Bateson, was murdered near Castleblayney in December 1851; attempts were made on the life of W.S. Trench after he took over management of the Bath estate in south Monaghan in 1849.[28] By the early 1860s, Fenianism was attempting to replace Ribbonism in south Ulster and north Leinster during another period of economic crisis, rising evictions and growing agrarian tensions. Thus Brett, D'Alton and O'Flanagan were able to use the murders at Wildgoose Lodge as a warning against the growing threat of secret oath bound societies with possible revolutionary intent.

After the land war

Between 1864 and the next published account in 1882, Irish social life and politics went through significant change taking in the Fenian rebellion of 1867, the disestablishment of the church in 1869, the growth of the Home Rule movement from 1870, the rise of the Land League, the merging of the land and national questions under Charles Stewart Parnell during the Land War of 1879–82, and the beginning of the end of landlord influence. In this context, the burning of Wildgoose Lodge became subject to a major reinterpretation

---

26 Ibid.; for more on MacNally's participation see chapters four and six. 27 *A return of the number of murders, waylayings, assaults, threatening notices, incendiary fires or other crimes of an agrarian character, reported by the constabulary within the counties of Louth, Armagh and Monaghan, since the 1st of January 1849; distinguishing by name the persons murdered and waylaid; also, stating the numbers arrested for each offence; whether informations have been sworn in the case, and the result of any trial of the same*, HC 1852, xlvii; for the prevalence of crime in these areas, see also *Report from the select committee on outrages (Ireland); together with the proceedings of the committee, minutes of evidence, appendix and index*, HC 1852 (438), xiv. 28 M.B. McMahon, 'The murder of Thomas Bateson, 4 December 1851' (unpublished MA in Local History thesis, NUIM, 2003), pp 6–7; for a contemporary version of events, see W.S. Trench, *Realities of Irish life* (Boston, 1880), pp 188ff.

DUNDALK & NEWRY EXAMINER

AND

Louth Advertiser,

ESTABLISHED 1830.

One of the oldest Provincial Papers in the North of
Ireland.

ITS politics have always been independent of all political
parties, but its principles are embodied in the words " Irish
Nationality."

Its circulation extends, in addition to Louth, to the
Counties of Meath, Armagh, Cavan, Monaghan, and Down,
while it is widely read in England, Scotland, and America,
by expatriated Irishmen.

JOHN MATHEWS,

Proprietor,

CLANBRASSIL STREET,

DUNDALK.

JOB PRINTING

IS also carried on at the Office of THE EXAMINER, and all
orders neatly and expeditiously executed.

THE STATIONERY AND BOOKSELLING DEPARTMENT

Will be found to be supplied with all the newest samples of
Stationery and the latest publications of the works of the
best authors.

Second-hand Books bought and sold.

EXAMINER Office, Dundalk.

6 Advertisement taken from the *Dundalk
Examiner*, edited by John Mathews,
illustrating its political agenda.

7 John Mathews, proprietor and editor of
the *Dundalk Examiner*.

from the early 1880s because reworking the story had the potential to suit the
political agendas of the time. The narrative that evolved did not entirely sub-
sume the 'facts' as previously presented but it did much to change the foci of
blame and sympathy.

In August 1881, John Mathews purchased the copyright, plant and printing
material of the *Newry Examiner and Louth Advertiser* and continued in the role
of editor.[29] He relocated the newspaper office to Clanbrassil Street in Dundalk
and changed the name to the *Dundalk Examiner and Louth Advertiser*. Mathews
was: 'an ardent student of Irish history and literature and an industrious collector of ancient local events' and importantly a staunch nationalist.[30] His son and
successor as editor, Patrick, was a close personal friend of Timothy Healy and
he championed the latter's cause in the North Louth constituency after the
Parnellite split in the early 1890s.[31]

In the very first edition which Mathews edited on 27 August 1881, he began
to run a series in the *Dundalk Examiner* on the trials of the Wildgoose Lodge
suspects. In the main he reproduced reports that had appeared in newspapers
in 1817–18 but he also wrote a narrative and interpretation of the events leading up to and after the murders. The series appeared on the same pages as
accounts of evictions in Louth during the Land War, subjective accounts of the
activities of so-called 'emergency men' (outsiders, predominantly Protestants,
taken into an area by landlords to defend their properties and to carry out their
work); reports on the proclamation of Co. Louth in October 1881 under the
Protection of Property Act ('This recourse to draconian legislation cannot produce any other result than a widespread and ill-concealed disaffection among
the people'); and reports of the arrest of Charles Stewart Parnell in October
1881.[32] The series later formed the basis of a pamphlet published posthumously
in 1897, the content and rhetoric of which very much reflected the seismic shift
that had taken place in Irish politics in the post-Famine period.

In light of the changes in Irish nationalist politics since the beginning of
the Land War, Mathews' account can be seen not only as a deliberate attempt
to revise Carleton's version of events (which he claimed was both 'stunted and
inaccurate' even though he went on to draw from it himself, at least, as he put
it, 'the portions that may be coincident with the facts'),[33] but also as an opportunity for a nationalist such as him to draw parallels between the extension of
the Insurrection Act to Louth in 1817–18 and the proclamation of the county
in 1881 in order to highlight to his readership the unacceptability of the latter.

29 *Dundalk Examiner*, 27 Aug. 1881. **30** 'Biographical notes' in *Tempest's Annual, 1959*, p. 130.
31 Ua Dhubhthaigh, *Dundalk*, p. 104. **32** *Dundalk Examiner*, 8, 15 Oct. 1881. **33** Mathews, *The
burning of Wildgoose Lodge*, p. 1.

Mathews' account was nurtured during a decade that has become associated with the decline of deference towards landlords (if such can genuinely be quantitatively measured). Nationalist writing turned to blaming the evils of society on a corrupt landlord system. Locally, Denis Carolan Rushe, later secretary of Monaghan County Council, in his *Historical sketches of Monaghan* (1895), wrote of the pre-Famine secret societies:

> They soon began to use their secret conclaves as a means of protecting themselves against the insupportable tyranny of the local landlord or the proctor. And as in such cases, they could only make themselves felt by retaliating for injustice done, and as the heads of these societies were wholly irresponsible, this retaliation took shape in the perpetration of the most appalling acts of revenge.[34]

Thus Rushe portrayed the irresponsibility of Ribbon leaders and the appalling acts of revenge that they perpetrated as by-products of the tyranny of the landlord and the tithe proctor. Similarly, while Mathews referred to the 'fiendish ferocity' of the crime, he looked for underlying causes within the landlord system. His stated objective was to break the trend whereby 'so-called moralists' had used the Wildgoose Lodge incident as proof of the perceived natural inclination towards disturbance inherent in lower-class Roman Catholics,[35] as, for example, expressed by Sir Robert Peel when he blamed the disturbances of 1816–17 on 'that natural predilection for outrage and a lawless life which I believe nothing can control'.[36] The most significant aspect of Mathews' account is that the Lynches are no longer represented as the victims and the perpetrators are no longer satanic creatures:

> These writers have written rather from an embibed prejudice, than from a personal or communicated knowledge of the facts; and from such our late Irish novelist, Mr Carleton is not exempt. The burning of Wildgoose Lodge originated in one of those love jealousies which invariably prevail in rural districts, when the village maiden selects a husband from a host of admirers. As has already been stated, the whole damage done to Rooney's house [meaning Lynch's on the night of the April raid], only amounted to 7s. 6d., which was with an apology promptly tendered on the following day. This was indignantly refused, and 'the

34 D.C. Rushe, *Historical sketches of Monaghan from the earliest records to the Fenian movement* (Dublin, 1895), p. 82. 35 Mathews, *The burning of Wildgoose Lodge*, p. 1. 36 Quoted in Galen Broeker, *Rural disorder and police reform in Ireland, 1812–36* (London, 1970), p. 2.

mild and beneficient law', as Judge Fletcher called it, was appealed to
and the 'mild and beneficient law' hanged the three men, and buried
them like dogs in the jail yard, with nine barrels of lime. Then came
the determined spirit of retributive vengeance on the part of the people.
The awful measure of revenge which they took, none possessing the
slightest tinge of humanity, can excuse or palliate. But let us see what
steps the authorities took to dispense an even-handed justice and vindicate the majesty of the law. Thieves, murderers and outlaws, of every
description, were procured; men who had as little respect for the Gospels
by which they were swearing, as they would have for *Bony's Oraculum*
or a deck of cards. These were the characters whose testimony was
unscrupulously received and acted upon, in utter defiance of law or justice. Where was then that spirit of British law, which makes liberty com-
mensurate with and inseparable from British soil.[37]

Mathews painted the real villains in this piece as the approvers: 'thieves, murderers and outlaws'. Matched with the retributive policy of the administration, he
concluded that 'such was the thirsting desire of the authorities for retributive
vengeance, that the evidence of these desperate characters was unscrupulously
accepted'.[38] In conclusion he told his readership that they 'could calmly review the
whole and see if the barbarity of the laws did not far exceed that of the prisoners
– even of those who were actually guilty and of these there were but four'.[39]

Devan was no longer the archetypal villain. Mathews presented a case for
his conduct in a more sympathetic light, suggesting that the crime grew out of
the unjust circumstances of the time. Devan was portrayed as a man eminently
endowed with 'a determined and unconquerable disposition' who when arrested
was 'determined to meet his fate like a man', who defended himself stoically
during his trial, 'destroying the evidence of the informers', and who died refusing to name his accomplices.[40] Mathews tells us that when he reached the place
of execution he was spoken to by Lord Roden and his agent Major John Straton:
'Now, Devan, there's not five minutes' distance between you and your Creator,
give us the names of the men who were at the burning of Wildgoose Lodge,
and we'll send you to any part of the world you wish with a fortune that will
make you independent the rest of your life, where you will have time to repent
for your sins'. Devan ignored them and 'turned to the hangman and manfully
told him to go on with his work':

After he had been hanging the entire day, he was taken down and put

37 Mathews, *The burning of Wildgoose Lodge*, p. 14. 38 Ibid., p. 11. 39 *Dundalk Examiner*, 26
Nov. 1881. 40 Mathews, *The burning of Wildgoose Lodge*, pp 15–16.

in a gibbet just as he had stood when living, and here remained for
twelve months, swaying to and fro, the loud creaking of the gibbet min-
gling with the moaning of the night wind. The gibbet was so placed
that whenever the slightest breeze turned it in the swivel from which it
hung, the ghastly shadow of Devan would dance fantastically on the
floor of his mother's cottage. At length decomposition set in, and
Devan's legs dropped off. A pitch cap was then made for him and a bag
well tarred into which it was put and left hanging for a couple of years
more.[41]

Thus after the publication of Mathews' pamphlet on the eve of the 1798
centenary celebrations, Patrick Devan had begun his journey into nationalist
lore as something of a local folk hero, becoming just another foot soldier in the
army of violent resistance.

Other short and mainly inaccurate accounts of the burning of Wildgoose
Lodge followed in G.H. Bassett's *Louth county guide and directory* (1886) and
Pádraig Ua Dubhthaigh's *The book of Dundalk* (1946).[42] The only information
of note in Bassett is that by 1886 the lodge was the property of John Wildman,
that it once: 'stood on a slight elevation, and a small portion of one of its gables
is still in existence. It is a lonely spot partly sheltered by two or three trees'.[43]
Benedict Kiely published his biography of Carleton entitled *Poor scholar* in 1947.
But Kiely took Carleton's works too literally. He wrote, for example, that in
Killanny, Carleton walked into 'a terrible townland of death, where decaying
bodies swung on roadside gallows, poisoning the wind and the sun and the pure
air, making the whole earth not only a wicked place, but the abode of hideous
and unintelligible evil'.[44] The only gibbet that Carleton could have witnessed
was that of Devan; the others had not even been tried before he left Killanny
for Dublin.[45] Moreover, Kiely accepted that there were twenty-four bodies gibbeted and that two men had been transported for the original raid on Lynch's
home.[46] But he perceived a certain ambiguity in Devan's life, partially vindicat-
ing him as a victim of his surroundings:

> where men were bitterly discontented about rents and tithes, where
> men really knew slavery and oppression and the black neighbourhood
> of perpetually threatening hunger, where men hated each other because

---

41 Ibid., p. 10. 42 G.H. Bassett, *Louth County guide and directory* (Dublin, 1886), p. 237; Ua
Dubhthaigh, *Dundalk*, p. 37. 43 Bassett, *Louth County guide*, p. 237. 44 Benedict Kiely, *Poor
scholar* (Dublin, 1972 ed. [first ed., 1947]), p. 38. 45 T.G.F. Paterson, 'The burning of Wildgoose
Lodge' in *County Louth Archaeological Journal*, 12:2 (1950), p. 168. 46 Kiely, *Poor scholar*, p. 39.

of differing creeds … From one point of view Paddy Devaun was a
martyr. From another point of view he was a murderer. The truth was
somewhere between the two points of view.[47]

The next major account appeared in the *Journal of the County Louth
Archaeological and Historical Society* in 1950. It was written by T.G.F. Paterson
(1888–1971), a former curator of Armagh County Museum, and in his opening
paragraph he made his own important contribution to the telling of the story
by pointing out that

> In the neighbourhood of Reaghstown the tragic affair is still spoken of
> with horror, and local tradition affirms that certain people who were
> innocent of active participation in the burning of Wildgoose Lodge suf-
> fered the same penalty as those who were undoubtedly guilty of
> murder.[48]

The focus was not on the victims of the burning but on the victims of injustice, the innocent who had hanged because they had been unfairly implicated
in the crime. In the style of Carleton, Paterson recorded in a footnote:

> Devan's mother, however seems to have had no doubt as to her son's
> complicity in the crime and at the execution begged him not to betray
> his associates or save himself by the blood of other men. Later, when
> his lifeless body was hung in front of her dwelling, she is said to have
> been comforted by the fact that he had not purchased liberty in such a
> fashion.[49]

The content was similar but the tone was a good deal different. By the time
of Paterson's account, the association of a dying rebel/patriot/martyr with a
grieving mother had become very much a popular representation in Irish ballads such as, for example, 'Kevin Barry', a song commemorating the execution
of a young student in Mountjoy jail on 1 November 1920,[50] or the narrative
ballad, 'The valley of Knockanure', commemorating the deaths of Padraic
Dalton, Padraic Walsh and Diarmuid Lyons who were shot by Black and Tans

47 Ibid., p. 47. 48 Paterson, 'The burning of Wildgoose Lodge', p. 159. 49 Ibid., p. 179. 50
'Kevin Barry, do not leave us/On the Scaffold you must die!'/Cried his broken-hearted mother/As
she bade her son good-bye/ Kevin turned to her in silence/Saying, 'Mother, do not weep/For it's
all for dear old Ireland/And it's all for freedom's sake.'; http://www.bbc.co.uk/history/war/east-
errising/songs, (23 Feb. 2005).

during the War of Independence.[51]

In the early 1970s, D.J. Casey, a professor of English at the State University of New York, published another account in consecutive issues of the *Journal of the County Louth Archaeological and Historical Society* aptly entitled 'Wildgoose Lodge: the evidence and the lore'.[52] Casey saw the need to examine the actions of Devan by reference to the society in which he was reared. He pointed to the fact that Devan grew up in a climate of political, economic and agrarian turmoil. He recognised that one needs to go beyond being surprised at the fact that it was a murder of Catholics by Catholics and to consider it in light of 'Lynch's and Rooney's relationship to the Catholic community and to those members of the Catholic community who were bent on their destruction'.[53] Increasingly, questions were being asked about the wider motivation behind the crime. Casey's was the first informed critique of previously published accounts that also drew substantially from primary sources such as newspapers and the Foster papers on deposit in the Public Record Office of Northern Ireland. He also drew on an oral account from Annie Lynch taken by folklorist, M.J. Murphy, on deposit in the Folklore Department of UCD.[54] However, Casey, like Paterson, does not seem to have been aware of the wealth of material now available in the National Archives (then the State Paper Office) in the State of the Country Papers, which illuminated so much for this author. Nor did he draw on a myriad of other sources that are invaluable in reconstructing events surrounding the trials such as the Gregory papers, the Peel papers and a variety of estate papers, many of which have only become available since the publication of his work.

Raymond Murray (Reamonn Ó Muirí) later reproduced a selection of the National Archives material in a later article in the *Journal of the County Louth Archaeological and Historical Society* but he offered only a minimal narrative. Since then Monsignor Murray has published *The burning of Wildgoose Lodge: Ribbonism in Louth – murder and the gallows* (2005). Its importance lies in the fact that he has transcribed a great deal of the primary sources which were generated by the outrage in police reports and newspapers. While his book suggests the agrarian background to the crime, the use of the term 'Ribbonism' in the title is misleading when applied to that system as understood by historians

---

51 I met with Dalton's mother and she to me did say/May God be with my darling son who died in the glen today/If I could kiss his cold clay lips my aching heart 'twould cure/And I'd gladly lay him down to sleep in the valley of Knockanure; ibid. 52 Casey, 'Wildgoose Lodge: the evidence and the lore', pp 140–61; 211–31. 53 Ibid., pp 142–3. 54 The full transcript of this interview was not made available to this author; instead he has relied upon the transcript in Casey's work.

in the present day. The crime, as we shall see, was not carried out by the illegal formal organisation that was Ribbonism but rather by a local agrarian society with very little formal structure that was comprised of men some of whom were little more than banditti.

The lore

As T.G.F. Paterson pointed out, the atrocity at Wildgoose Lodge was still spoken of 'with horror' in the neighbourhood of Reaghstown in the 1950s. Decades later it was still difficult to find anybody who would talk openly of the incident. The burning of Wildgoose Lodge was not something to be remembered locally with pride. There were too many raw nerve ends. The victims were not policemen or soldiers, landlords, bailiffs or agents, the usual inspirers of balladeers, songsters and local bards and thus the incident could never be commemorated in 'the vengeful and triumphalist tone' that exemplified contemporary ballads celebrating, for example, a perceived victory by the tenantry over a landlord or the police.[55]

But the story of the burning of the lodge, or more specifically the threat to authority that it could conjure, continued to be used in a covert way. In 1823, seven years after the event, a tenant farmer, Philip Shirley, told his landlord William Filgate that 'the country accused his family of it [giving information leading to convictions] & the congregation of Reaghstown w[oul]d not clear them of it'.[56] From this early stage it is clear that if a local transgressed social boundaries his neighbours saw a means of retribution in associating him or his family with informing on the Wildgoose Lodge suspects. Similarly, on 29 July 1831, a threatening notice was posted on Baron Hussey's gate near Slane:

> This is a caution to the Baron not to continue any longer in his English practice of pounding cattle and charging trespass to the great annoyance of his poor tenantry but the Baron is not entirely to blame, but the set of villains he keeps about him – the first is Cooper Carney who was banished from Louth, who was a stag and got many an innocent man hung at Wildgoose Lodge …[57]

This type of associative stigmatisation continued for generations. In his

---

55 Owens, 'The Carrickshock incident, 1831', p. 41. 56 Philip Shirley to William Filgate, 20 January 1813 (Dundalk Library, WGL papers). 57 Quoted in S.R. Gibbons, *Captain Rock, night errant: the threatening letters of pre-Famine Ireland, 1801–1845* (Dublin, 2004), p. 221.

preface to the MacGibbon and Kee edition of Carleton's autobiography published in 1968, Patrick Kavanagh wrote that:

> The name of Wildgoose Lodge was whispered in my native parish of Inniskeen right up to my own time. It was believed that a large contingent of Ribbonmen took part in the destruction and I remember one October evening, when I was gathering potatoes as a boy for a neighbour, asking the man to tell me something about the business. He told me to ask my father. Another neighbour always swore by the name of one of those same Ribbonmen. When threatening to boot someone, he used to say, 'I'll raise you as high as the Van (Paddy Devaun) was hung.'[58]

Kavanagh's words are instructive: reference to the lodge was always 'whispered'. Few, including the neighbouring farmer, were willing to speak of the crime at Wildgoose Lodge even though it happened over a century and a half before. Devan's name lived on in local lore as the one who was 'hung'. Of all the versions that this author recalls hearing, the teller could always remember the name of Devan, but very often forgot (or perhaps never knew) the name of the family who perished.

Almost two centuries of inter-penetration between the written and oral traditions have undoubtedly shaped and reshaped each other. The facts have become distorted, and this is particularly true of the oral history of the incident. There have been, and continue to be, so many versions of the Wildgoose story in circulation in the oral tradition that it is impossible to relate them all here. We can, however, look at a number of examples to emphasise a point. In March 1904, James Gartland related what he had heard from his parents:

> Old Lynch, the morning after the cutting of the webs and spilling cream[59] – it was a Wednesday morning – went straight to Ardee and swore an information against Devan, McCullogh and others. My mother was teeming a pot of potatoes outside her father's house at Mullenstown when Lynch was passing on his way to Ardee. When her father spoke to Lynch in Irish, after some remarks Lynch told my grandfather, Patrick Cluskey, what happened the night before and where he was going to swear an information on the three young men referred to.

---

58 Patrick Kavanagh in 'Introduction' to Carleton, *Autobiography* (London, 1968 ed.), p. 10. **59** Reference to the raid carried out on Wildgoose Lodge in April 1816 which will be described in chapter two.

My grandfather put his walking stick before Lynch and asked him, in the name of God, to go back home, saying if he swore on those three boys that they would be taken under the Whiteboy Act and tried and hanged without judge or jury. Lynch replied: 'That is what I want.' Accordingly, he swore on them that morning. They were taken that same day and hanged in a day or two after and strapped to a gibbet opposite their parents' doors until their bones withered and fell asunder. Now, to avenge the death of those three men, Devan, the school-master,[60] plotted the destruction of Lynch's and Rooney's families together with four servants.[61]

As we shall see in chapter three, there was an earlier raid on Wildgoose Lodge in April 1816 that Lynch reported to William Filgate and which later resulted in the execution of three young men. But none of the latter was named Devan or McCullough. These were implicated in the second raid.

Cluskey's advice to his neighbour was given through the medium of the Irish language. Gartland may have emphasised this because the Gaelic revival was relatively strong in his area, Farney, in 1904. Or was it historically accurate that the Gaelic language was still very much a living language in the area in 1816? Carleton used a number of Gaelic phrases in 'Wildgoose Lodge' and having lived in the area possibly saw an authentic reason for doing so. English had made rapid progress particularly in areas most affected by commercialisation and modernisation such as Dundalk where in 1816, the Church of Ireland rector, the Revd Elias Thackeray wrote that 'it is gratifying to a person attached to British policy, to have it in his power to say, that the English language is gaining ground fast; and that it is very generally spoken and taught'.[62] Thackeray's comment, of course, suggests that English was not yet universally spoken (although obviously there was a growing desire to acquire the language). In his statistical account of the parish of Faughart (on the outskirts of Dundalk) in 1816, the Revd Gervais Tinley reported that 'most of them [the poorer classes] can speak English tolerably well; but their common language with each other is Irish'.[63] Moreover, in 1811, it was deemed important that Fr McCann, the parish priest of Louth, had: 'got an assistant who understands Irish'. This was

60 According to Gartland, Patrick Devan was a cousin of the Devan he mentioned above. 61 James Gartland to Fr Skelly, 16 Mar. 1904; quoted in Casey, 'Wildgoose Lodge: the evidence and the lore', p. 161. 62 Revd Elias Thackeray, 'Statistical survey of Ballymascanlon parish, 1816', consulted on www.jbhall.freeservers.com/clonmore_1815.htm. 63 Revd Gervais Tinley, 'Statistical account of the parish of Faughart' (from W. Mason Shaw (ed.), Parochial survey of Ireland, 1816), reproduced in Tempest's Annual, 1942, p. 2.

the aforementioned Fr Bernard Loughran (*c.*1790–1845) who had just finished his studies at Maynooth.[64] Statistical evidence corroborates these statements. Garret FitzGerald in his analysis of the approximate minimum level of Irish-speakers in the different baronies of Ireland 1771–1871 has shown that in 1771–81 an average of just over 68 per cent of young people in the seven baronies of most relevance to this study must have been Irish-speaking with the average falling to just over 53 per cent by 1801–11.

Table 1: Estimated minimum level (%) of Irish-speaking by baronies among successive decennial cohorts, born 1771–1821

Barony	1771–81	1781–91	1791–1801	1801–11	1811–21
Ardee (Co. Louth)	63	65	55	40	28
Dundalk Lower (Co. Louth)	67	66	59	54	43
Dundalk Upper (Co. Louth)	66	64	58	48	38
Louth (Co. Louth)	72	66	63	56	38
Morgallion (Co. Meath)	71	65	60	53	32
Fews Upper (Co. Armagh)	59	57	53	49	48
Farney (Co. Monaghan)	79	79	76	74	73

Source: Garret FitzGerald, 'Estimates of Irish-speaking', pp 131, 134.

Gartland's account also suggests that Mathews' nationalist interpretation had become the antidote to Carleton's version. For Gartland the Whiteboy Act was a retributive tool of government resented by the lower classes. There is great sympathy for the young men who would be 'tried and hanged without judge or jury'. The three who were eventually hanged were not gibbeted but the oral tradition clung on to the heinous nature of gibbeting opposite their parents' door until the victims' bones: 'withered and fell asunder'.

Gartland provided Patrick Devan with a personal motivation for his involvement in the second raid, his cousin had been executed as a result of the first one. There has often been a tendency in the local lore to ascribe the motivations for the attack to such localised and personal motives. William Filgate Jr, for example, in his 1867 account talked of 'a very good looking' second daughter of Lynch's that a Ribbonman named Tierney (notably the surname of one of those executed for the first raid) wanted to marry. When she refused to have anything to do with

64 Most Revd Richard Reilly, Archbishop of Armagh to Dr Conwell, vicar general, 31 Aug. 1811 (Ó Fiaich Memorial Library, folder 3).

him: 'He determined to carry her off by force & with a gang of his fellow Ribbonmen broke into Wildgoose Lodge, but Lynch and Rooney beat them off with pitchforks, wounding one of them'. Attempted abductions of this type were not uncommon in Ireland but this information is nowhere else referred to in any of the contemporary documentary evidence. Stories of Devan's unrequited/spurned love for Lynch's daughter also abound in the locality.[65] Some of these accounts go so far as to claim that the infant burned in the fire was Devan's illegitimate child and not Rooney's.[66] Given the close proximity of the lodge to where Devan lived (at least as the crow flies) it is possible that Lynch's daughter was well known to him but whether there was ever romantic involvement is an aspect of this story that will probably never be revealed. If Filgate preferred to consider the motivation for the first raid in terms of local love matches gone wrong it may have been because it detracted from the wider socio-economic circumstances in which the crime was incubated,[67] and the role of estate management policy on the Filgate estates that led local agitators to want to murder him and his father.[68]

In 1964–5, folklorist, M.J. Murphy recorded an account from Annie Lynch, a native of Louth although no relation of Edward Lynch.[69] According to her account, Lynch and his family were not the victims but the villains because they resorted to the authority of an alien government for protection from 'their own people'. Rooney was only a servant boy with Lynch. Devan was the only son of a widow; again, this held the emotive appeal of an aged mother left alone to fend for herself in a cruel world. He escaped to England where he was found working on the sewers. Once again, a failed love match between an unnamed suitor and Lynch's daughter comes to the fore:

> The fight started and they went to choke each other, and the crocks of cream that were sitting on a table in the kitchen, they had wooden lids just sitting on them – they spilled and broke the crocks outside and started to fling the lids at them when the girl wouldn't take this fellow … Well the eggs were chipping under the turkey and they took them out and the turkey, and walked on her and the eggs in the street, they were that mad at the girl for refusing them. That was the very beginning of it – the blackguards. I heard it all told in Louth.[70]

According to Annie Lynch, the original 'stag' (approver) was James

65 Paterson, 'The burning of Wildgoose Lodge', p. 178. 66 See also Annie Lynch's account below. 67 See chapter two. 68 See chapter three. 69 The relevant extracts from the interview were reproduced by Casey in 'Wildgoose Lodge: the evidence and the lore', ii, pp 213–15. 70 Quoted in Casey, 'Wildgoose Lodge: the evidence and the lore', p. 213.

McDermott, a servant boy at Stonetown chapel: 'He died after in a workhouse in America: he was still alive and the two legs rotting off him above the knee.' There is no reference to a James McDermott (or even to a name remotely like his) in any of the historical documents but Lynch's description of the horrendous end that McDermott suffered speaks volumes for the odium in which informers were held. Indeed, in Lynch's account all the approvers met an untimely death (as at least three of them did in reality): a man called Kavanagh was shot and left lying on the road for days 'for no one would go near him or bury him'; one was tied to a horse's tail which was 'galloped around the field till there wasn't a piece of him left together'; a whole family died in the asylum, just another inexplicable personal tragedy associated with the bad luck of having informed.[71] Those paid and or pardoned for providing the information leading to the arrests of the Wildgoose suspects are recorded in contemporary documents generated by the authorities, but none of these names are matched by Lynch.

Essentially what we get in Lynch's account is the overlap of historical fact and lore shaped perhaps by nothing more than begrudgery intended to tarnish a neighbour's name and further echoing the odium in which informers had traditionally been held in Ireland:

> There was people in Reaghstown and they were the breed of the stag Carey, but they changed their name to Carrey. Carey, they said, was the ring-leader of the stags there at the time. One man was the name of the Miller Reenan, he lived at the chapel … he stagged too. I was in Tommy McKeever's pub in my time too, and his sister Molly married The Miller, and McKeever never spoke to her after from that day till the day he died: what took her to marry that stag?[72]

Such odium was more widely discernible in the nationalist literature and songs of the nineteenth century; as G.D. Zimmerman concluded: 'informers, along with all those who accepted to give evidence at trials, were consigned to hell by the rhymers of broadsides, and cursing was traditionally resorted to against them.'[73] Those guilty or even suspected, along with their descendants, were in danger of becoming outcasts in local communities. In his folklore study of Ballymenone in south Fermanagh, Henry Glassie pointed out how: 'Old cases hardened into permanent "spite", silence, a scar on communal tissue, but hate remained a local matter, contained in the neighbourhood.'[74] Over a cen-

71 See ibid., p. 216. 72 Ibid. 73 G.D. Zimmerman, *Songs of Irish rebellion: Irish political street ballads and rebel songs, 1780–1900* (Dublin, 2002 ed.), p. 27.

tury after the Wildgoose Lodge murders the Inniskeen poet-novelist, Patrick
Kavanagh, declared that 'hating one's next-door neighbour' was as essential a
part of a small farmer's religion as knowing the beauty and pain of Monaghan's
drumlin landscape.[75] Annie Lynch's account, with its emphasis on informers,
goes some way to verifying this.

The burning of Wildgoose Lodge was an atrocity carried out within a local
community by neighbours on neighbours. The fallout from it in the locality
can be more easily imagined than described. When in July 1822 Samuel McNally
and three others wanted to intimidate Lawrence McMahon from
Carrickmacross, who was working as a coachmaker in Drogheda, they accused
him of informing on three men who were hanged at Wildgoose Lodge.
McMahon 'remonstrated with McNally on the danger of raising such a [false]
report concerning him'. McNally and three others were later indicted for 'an
unlawful combination to regulate the trade of coachmaking' but McMahon
was dismissed from his job, his employer obviously aware of some form of threat
to his business in employing one (wrongly) associated with informing.[76]

During later periods of political excitement, the atrocity could always be
called upon to scandalise some one. Thus, in 1852, following a bitter election
for Dundalk Borough, a poster was circulated in the area publicising the names
of 'the Orange Catholics ... [who] ... acted as traitors to Repeal and Old Ireland,
and did all in their power to sell the Borough of Dundalk to Lord Roden and
his Orange faction'. Amongst those named and shamed as 'the greatest traitors
among the Orange Catholics' was 'Wildgoose Lodge Dowdall', probably Patrick
Dowdall, proprietor of the pro-establishment *Newry Examiner* before John
Mathews.[77]

Similar to Gartland's account above, Annie Lynch heard of a servant girl
who had been warned several times to leave the lodge before the burning, but
did not heed the danger signs. Devan's behaviour is rather humorously excused
on the fact that he came from Tully (which is a neighbouring townland of
Corcreaghy): 'a sort of wild, isolated spot; and the people in it were all tol-therry
[drool] and quare. They'd never polish their boots going to mass, and they'd
put the clothes arse-ways on themselves.'[78] In the main, Lynch's account offers
evidence of the Chinese whispers syndrome that can affect the oral tradition.
The further one moves chronologically from the event, the less historically accurate it becomes and versions begin to take on the characteristics of folk tales in

74 Henry Glassie, *Passing the time: folklore and history of an Ulster community* (Dublin, 1982), p.
282.   **75** Patrick Kavanagh, *Tarry Flynn* (London, 1948), p. 176.   **76** *FJ*, 30 July 1822.   **77** Noel
Ross, 'Two nineteenth-century election posters' in *Journal of the County Louth Archaeological Society*,
16:4 (1968), pp 224, 227.   **78** Casey, 'Wildgoose Lodge: the evidence and the lore', ii, p. 214.

which the forces of good and evil are ranged against each other.

The burning of Wildgoose Lodge in modern drama

In February 1968, a play entitled *Wild Goose Lodge* written by Jack McQuoid and Michael Duffy was produced by Sam Hanna Bell for Radio 4 Northern Ireland. The play is based on an intelligent mixture of newspaper accounts and local lore. It opens in 1816, at a time when 'the potato crop began to fail in certain districts, and because of this discontent grew among the people'.[79] Edward Lynch is introduced as a prosperous, industrious farmer who facilitated meetings of a secret agrarian society in his home but whose son had refused to join the same. His wife is still alive and there is an infant in the house. His wife has reservations about having meetings in their house, which are attended by their son-in-law, Thomas Rooney, but Lynch tells her: 'There's crop failures, famine almost in some places, people are being treated cruelly by the powers that be. I don't like to turn them out.' Devan is regarded as 'the big boss of that crowd'. But Mrs Lynch also makes it clear that she mistrusts Devan, who she believes holds a grudge against her family since Thomas Rooney married into the Lynches. Lynch approaches Devan to ask him to stop holding meetings at the lodge. Devan reacts badly and this gives rise to the first attack on the lodge, which sets in train the series of events that leads to the trial and execution of three men Shanley, Conlon and Tiernan and the fatal raid on the lodge in October.

Devan and his associates are censored for their brutality, even if their crime was born out of an unequal society, but the Louth magistrates are equally censored for their reactionary retribution. Devan's personality and his actions epitomise all that is senseless about violence and bloodshed; at one stage one of his followers exclaims that 'He has gone out of his mind.'[80] Some of the followers cry out to him to save the child only to be met with: 'Nits grow into lice. The whole family must be destroyed'.[81] After the execution of Shanley, Conlon and Tiernan, the narrator says: 'But in spite of alibis, in spite of many witnesses for the defence, in spite of the fact that no one in Wild Goose Lodge sustained serious injury, in spite of an attempt to invoke vice-regal clemency for mercy, the penalty had to be paid.'[82]

The production of this play coincided with the beginning of the civil and political strife in Northern Ireland. It sent out a very strong message in 1968 with parallels for the time; it is evidently intended as an analogy for the growing tensions between rival communities in Northern Ireland and a plea for those rival

79 Typescript of Jack McQuoid and Michael Duffy, *Wild Goose Lodge: a feature concerning a tragic happening on a farm in Co. Louth in the year 1816.* **80** Ibid., p. 10. **81** Ibid., p. 11. **82** Ibid., p. 7.

groups to practise restraint. It condemns social inequality, illustrates that violence begets needless violence and suggests the need for an equitable judicial system that provides confidence in the law rather than one that compounds grievances.

David Hayes' play, again simply entitled *Wildgoose Lodge*,[83] is another fascinating drawing together of historical evidence and local lore. In fact, his storyline begs the question, could it all have happened in the way he depicts as a result of a complex coincidence of events? Hayes' play opens during an escalating famine and shows a society ravaged by pestilence and disease. Lynch is again presented as an industrious, prospering farmer and weaver. He has reclaimed about five acres of land from the surrounding bogland and can afford the best sherry available in Dundalk. He is sycophantic in his relationship with his landlord, William Filgate, the latter presented as a hard-headed businessman who has little time for alleviating the plight of the impoverished (in contrast to John Foster who is presented as a friend of the impoverished). He detests the rise in local agitation, telling Lynch: 'By God, if I was young enough to lead the civil militia, I'd teach these ruffians a lesson. Flogging, Lynch, that's the answer.' He warns Lynch to disassociate himself from agitators or he will evict him 'without compunction'. Filgate is not in favour of giving the lower classes what they have not earned, whereas Foster sees danger in the fact that 'a starving man is a desperate man'.

Patrick Devan is presented as a *slíbhín*, a sly and in many ways weak character who is the puppet of a landed gentleman named McKeown who resides at Kilkerley Hall. At the start of the play Devan makes his way to the lodge and attempts to talk Thomas Rooney into playing a role in the secret society, warning him of the consequences if he refuses. He then approaches Lynch to see if he will allow meetings to be held at the lodge. Lynch is reluctant but Devan reminds him of where he came from: 'You're a smug man, Lynch, aren't you, with your house and your farm and your servants. Ya can afford to forget what you came from' and he warns him not to 'crow from the top of your dunghill.' When Lynch holds out, this results in the first raid during which Lynch and Rooney are badly beaten. Hayes, however, does not have Lynch report the raid to the authorities; instead Filgate arrives at the lodge the following day demanding information on the perpetrators.

This is the only literary work that draws on the folk tale that associates a member of the Catholic gentry McKeown family of Belrobin with the incident. According to tradition, Christopher McKeown is alleged to have been one of the leaders of the raid. Afterwards, he was so racked with remorse that he gave the single largest donation to the fund for the construction of Kilkerley Chapel. There

---

83 I am grateful to Sean Farrell and Brendan McCaul for making a recording of this play available to me.

is no historical evidence to support this theory. In the play McKeown is presented as a failed clerical student who witnessed the French revolution first hand and who drew inspiration from the storming of the Bastille on 14 July 1789. He sees the importance of the burning of Wildgoose Lodge, not in terms of retribution for Lynch informing on Shanley, Conlon and Tiernan but rather as a means of generating the type of violence necessary to bring anarchy to the countryside in which a more widespread uprising of the lower classes would flourish. He tells Devan that 'deliberate, calculated terror' is an irresistible force:

> It infuses fear and creates doubt. It makes every man suspicious of his neighbour for none can be sure that the hand that shakes his today may not strike him down tomorrow. Terror divides, it turns the young against old, the poor against the rich, the ignorant against the knowing, the idealist against the propagandist. It's a social infection more deadly and insidious than the plague. There's no immunity from it. Terror justifies the violest [sic] of remedies, the suspension of legal processes, summary arrests, cruel punishments, torture and judicial murder. It provokes the most extreme reprisals, burning, maiming, killing and forms of butchery that would not be performed on animals. The most moral of men, the most tolerant of governments are corrupted by it. Individuals purchase their own safety at the cost of betraying others, informers are paid from the public purse, retribution falls as heavily on the innocent as the guilty. Each one killed for expediency becomes a martyr for the opposing cause. Violence begets greater violence. What begins in a single self-justifying act sets off a train of reaction, counter reaction that ends in anarchy and chaos. From the thatch you fire tomorrow night, Devan, sparks will be wafted over this island igniting the peasant's hovel and the landlord's mansion setting barns, ricks, standing crops and forests alight. In that conflagration, nothing will escape but from the ashes a new Ireland will arise.

Thus, Hayes presents the burning as a deliberate ploy by a power greater than Devan, a man who has been inspired by the events of the French revolution, to set off a series of events that will lead to a general uprising of the lower classes.[84] Hayes' John Foster considers Devan not cunning enough to be able to plan an orchestrated raid on the lodge on his own; he believes that 'a hidden hand guided him'. It is an interesting inversion of another folk belief, still very current in areas of Co. Louth, that the burning of the Wildgoose Lodge was

---

84 See article in *Belfast Newsletter*, 15 Nov. 1816 where the reporter referred to crimes in Louth and the reputed boasts of agitators that 'We can murder faster than you can try'.

planned and carried out by forces hired by the Castle authorities in order to provide a pretext for the arrest of prominent local agitators who were proving a threat to the administration. The dating of this particular folktale is impossible to determine but it may also have gained credence post-1969 as something of an allegory for alleged MI5 and SAS activities along the border.

Finally, Hayes draws on William Filgate's 1867 version that Lynch had a second daughter who was not in the lodge on the night of the burning. In the play Devan has an affair with her. She becomes pregnant, leaves the family home but is soon deserted by a very callous Devan who threatens to have her condemned as a whore if she ever reveals the identity of the father. Following the death of her child from fever or starvation in the aftermath of the burning, she reveals the whereabouts of Devan to the authorities.

The third play based on the murders is Eamonn Smullen's *Terrorism,* read at the Project Arts Theatre in Dublin in 1971. Unfortunately, this author, despite much searching, has been unable to acquire a copy or a recording of this play but certain information regarding it is available in the public domain. The reading of the play received excellent reviews, one of which, in the *Irish Times,* described the dialogue as 'superb, sharp, fast, involving and deep' and commended the sophistication and intelligence of the plot which gave a degree of internationalism to the scene: 'so that one has the odd inclination to shout "stop, action, replay" in order to fully absorb the argument, so old and yet so relevant'.[85] The setting and argument were over 150 years old, but the reviewer's suggestion was that the latter had some relevance for 1971 as it hurled the audience into the contemporary political situation in Northern Ireland.

By that time, Eamonn Smullen was prisoner 647995 in Gartree prison in Leicestershire having been arrested on a charge of 'conspiring to purchase arms' in 1969 and sentenced, after an appeal, to five years' imprisonment.[86] He wrote to Benedict Kiely that he was attracted to the story of Wildgoose Lodge because he thought he could use it as 'some societies use the body of an unknown soldier'.[87] Smullen argued that Devan's secret society was one that set itself up as the protector of 'the people' in the face of persecution under alien rule and oppressive law. His Mat Lynch, a strong farmer who lives at Wildgoose Lodge, becomes the villain of the piece; Captain Rooney is a brutal landlord who capriciously evicts fourteen families in the one day and worse, practises the *droit de seigneur* on a terrorised and submissive tenantry. Devan is the only hope that 'the people' have to escape their oppression. Smullen later wrote that he presented Devan as the hero of the piece for a specific reason; he represented some-

85 *Irish Times,* 29 Nov. 1971. 86 Ibid., 29 Nov. 1971, 31 May, 12 July 1972. 87 Quoted in ibid., 21 Sept. 1972.

thing of a role model for himself in his own perceived political struggle:

> ... people like Devaun have made a certain contribution to the strug-
> gle for a better life, not only in Ireland but in many parts of the world.
> There is a tendency in some places today to withhold honour from
> those who give a full measure of devotion to the people's struggle ...
> my life has followed pathways which allow me to understand the rea-
> soning of the people in the play.[88]

Terrorism epitomised just how far Patrick Devan had travelled in some
nationalist/republican mythologies.

Conclusion

Even if William Carleton had never written the story that brought the atrocity
at Wildgoose Lodge to an international audience, the contemporary furore
caused by this episode – local, nationally and internationally – and the impact
it had on Dublin Castle's policy towards the better government of Ireland should
have singled it out for attention from historians. And yet, one will search in
vain to find even the most cursory reference to it in any of the standard historical accounts of pre-Famine Ireland. It is not mentioned at all in W.E. Vaughan
(ed.), *A new history of Ireland, vol. v, Ireland under the Union, 1801–70* (1989). It
is mentioned only fleetingly in Michael Beames' study of pre-Famine underground movements, *Peasants and power: the Whiteboy movements and their control in pre-Famine Ireland* (1983). S.H. Palmer in his comprehensive *Police and
protest in England and Ireland, 1780–1850* (1988) makes only brief mention of the
1816–18 turbulence in Louth as does Galen Broeker in his *Rural disorder and
police reform in Ireland, 1812–36* (1970). Even the biographies of the main players, such as A.P.W. Malcomson's *John Foster: the politics of the Anglo-Irish ascendancy* (1978) mention it only in passing, despite the fact that the Wildgoose
Lodge episode reveals much about Foster's dealings at local level and with the
Castle administration and, indeed, his personality. Only Norman Gash's *Mr
Secretary Peel: the life of Sir Robert Peel to 1830* (1985) acknowledges the influential role which the incident played in formulating Peel's policing policy. What
follows is therefore the first attempt by a professional historian to provide a full
account of the incident and the events surrounding it before and after. In order
to do so it is first of all necessary to understand the economic, political and
social milieux in which the crime was incubated.

---

88 Eamonn Smullen to Elgy Gillespie, n.d.; quoted in ibid., 31 May 1972.

PART TWO

CHAPTER TWO

The historical evidence, I:
the socio-economic context

Introduction

In 1816, Edward Lynch, the tenant of Wildgoose Lodge and its surrounding lands, was 'an old man' and a widower who was remembered by his landlord's agent as 'a very honest industrious farmer and weaver' who 'had a bleach green & paid his rent to the day'.[1] There are no surviving records of how much land he held but the fact that the house had at least three apartments on the ground floor – one of which was designated a parlour – and a spacious loft above, suggests he was in the strong farmer–weaver class and at least moderately prosperous.[2] The three servants in his house in 1816 bore testimony to the fact that his was a labour-employing household rather than a labour-selling one. He had benefited from diversifying into the domestic linen industry that had been an important part of the north Louth and surrounding borderlands economy during the Napoleonic Wars. There was at least one loom in the house,[3] which means that under the government scheme of 1796 Lynch had allocated up to five acres to the growing of flax to entitle him to a loom, reels or hatchels to the value of fifty shillings.

As already noted in chapter one Edward Lynch had at least one son, Michael; one daughter, Bridget, who was married to Thomas Rooney; and a five-month-old grandson, Peter. Michael was a bachelor. His age is not recorded in any contemporary document but oral accounts intimate that he was approached on numerous occasions to join the local secret society, so he may have been in his late teens at least. Oral accounts also allude to a second daughter who was not in the house on the night of the burning but there is no other corroborating evidence of her existence. It is difficult to ascertain the relationship between Lynch and his neighbours prior to the incident. His nearest neighbour, Patrick Halpenny, a cottier, had no direct social contact with him; it seems he merely knew the Lynch family by sight. James Butler, from nearby Aclint, declared that Edward Lynch was 'one of the best neighbours in the country …

---

1 William Filgate's 1867 account; Samuel Pendleton to Sir William Gregory, 12 Apr. 1816 (SOC, 1763/19). 2 Evidence of Alice Rispin, 3 July 1818; reproduced in *Dundalk Examiner*, 12 Nov. 1881. 3 *Belfast Newsletter*, 1 Aug. 1816.

He was a good doctor, and used to bleed his [Butler's] family and horses and cows and give them advice without charging them anything.'⁴ His wife, Mary 'was very fond of Lynch's people'.⁵ However, the Butlers' sentiments were revealed during the trial of their son, William, for the murder of Lynch and the others and so should be judged accordingly.

That is essentially as much as the surviving historical evidence tells about Lynch, his family and their personal circumstances but the evidence does allow for the reconstrution of the social world in which the Lynches and their neighbours lived in Co. Louth that illuminates on the conditions that contributed directly and indirectly to the burning of Wildgoose Lodge.

Dundalk economy and society, c.1816

Louth is a maritime county bordered on the east by the Irish Sea; on the north by Carlingford Lough and Co. Armagh; and on the south by Co. Meath which also forms a large part of its boundary to the west along with Co. Monaghan. Wildgoose Lodge was located less than a mile from the Monaghan border. Despite its marshy location this was, in general, rich agricultural territory: in the pre-Famine period the 'best land' in the county was said to have been around Ardee and the town of Louth; there were 'extensive tracts of rich soil at Tallanstown, Dundalk and Castlebellingham'; the soil was 'suitable to every kind of agricultural produce, being a rich, vegetable mould, based on marl, limestone or clay-slate'. Much of the land was under pasture (each year considerable numbers of cattle and sheep were purchased at the Ballinasloe fair in Galway to be fattened on the plains of Louth and then exported to the English market) but extensive tracts of land around Ardee were also devoted to wheat and around the town of Louth to barley. Every type of green crop was grown by the large farmers who predominated on the outskirts of the towns of Dundalk, Louth and Ardee and the villages of Tallanstown, Knockbridge and Mullaghcrew. Flax was also grown in great quantities in the region by weaver-farmers such as Lynch – flax mills were to be seen on all the smaller rivers and there were major bleach greens at Collon and Ravensdale – principally for the supply of the local industry and for the supply of spinners in Leeds, Bolton and other manufacturing towns in England. The rearing of pigs was an important part of the small farmer, cottier economy.⁶

4 Ibid., 7 Apr. 1818. 5 See chapter seven. 6 Samuel Lewis, *A topographical dictionary of Ireland* (London, 1837); consulted on www.jbhall.freeservers.com/lewis_county_louth.htm (28 Sept. 2006).

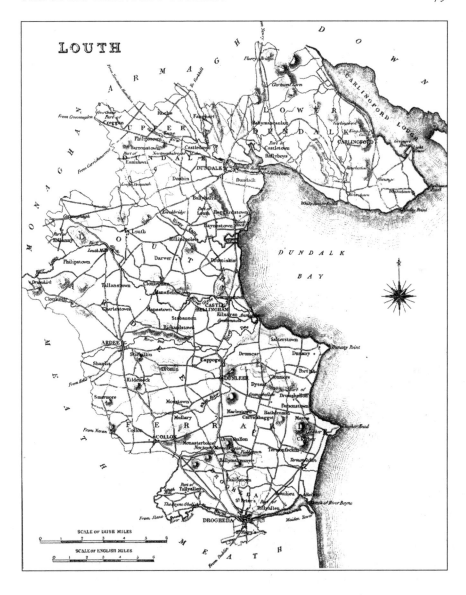

8 Contemporary map of Co. Louth and surrounding areas, taken from
Taylor and Skinner, *Maps of the roads of Ireland* (1783 ed.).

There were three places of export for the agricultural and manufacturing produce: Dundalk and Drogheda in Co. Louth, and Newry in Co. Down. For the purposes of this study, Dundalk is of most relevance for reasons that will become clear as this work progresses. It was a seaport, borough, market (held every Monday), fair (held six times a year) and post town in the barony of Upper Dundalk (the county was divided into the five baronies of Ardee, Ferrard, Louth, Dundalk Upper and Dundalk Lower for purposes of civil jurisdiction) with a population in 1816 of around 9,000 people. Situated on the south side of the Castletown River that runs into Dundalk Bay, the town consisted of two principal streets, each about a mile in length that intersected in Market Square and a number of smaller streets and lanes. The main streets were 'decently paved and flagged for the accommodation of carriages and foot-passengers'. When A. Atkinson arrived in the town in 1817, he was greatly struck by its appearance from Castletownmount:

> The buildings of the town, which form a magnificent group on the margin of the bay; the lofty spire of the church; the plantations of the neighbouring demesnes; the tall oaks and limes that wave their heads in awful grandeur above the plains; the bay at full tide, exhibiting as it were, that widening by degrees, at length embraces the blue horizon; and lastly, the chain of brown impending mountains which terminate the view; altogether form a group of objects so striking and so grand as to throw into confusion and almost rout from the field, the brilliant powers of the poet and painter.[7]

Atkinson was taken in particular by the architectural grandeur of St Nicholas's parish church that had recently been refurbished during the tenure of the Revd Elias Thackeray, cousin of the author William Makepeace Thackeray.[8] Likewise, he was impressed by the new courthouse, at that stage almost completed (the July 1818 trials of the Wildgoose Lodge suspects would be held there) which he described as 'an extremely handsome and perfect structure; it is composed entirely of hewn stone and then portico, which is formed on the model of the Temple of Theseus at Athens'.[9] For the previous seven years, the market house in Market Square had been 'applied to purposes so entirely foreign to its appellation and mercantile business ... as to render this appellation by no means descriptive of its present uses'; in other words it had been used as the temporary courthouse. On a visit to the county jail in Chapel Lane

7 Extract from A. Atkinson, *Ireland exhibited to England: a political and moral history of the population* (London, 1827) in *Tempest's Annual 1952*, p. 3. **8** Ibid., p. 4. **9** Ibid.

9 Late nineteenth-century photograph of Market Square in Dundalk,
showing the courthouse completed in 1818

Atkinson beheld a building that was 'inconveniently small' to house 'the vast
numbers of persons ... who, in the circumstances of this county, have been
unavoidably stowed in some of the cells'. They included over twenty men
accused of the burning of Wildgoose Lodge.[10]

Until the end of the Napoleonic Wars in 1815, Dundalk was a thriving town
that had been expanding from the 1730s when the old subsistence economy of
the south Ulster/north Leinster region began to give way to a commercial economy.[11] It had a major distillery owned by Malcolm Brown and Co. (which in
1816 employed 100 men, consumed up to 40,000 barrels of grain per annum,
produced more than 300,000 gallons of whiskey annually and paid £78,000 in
duties to the government),[12] extensive breweries owned by Bernard Duffy and
James McAlister (the latter became Macardle, Moore & Co.). There were two
considerable flour mills on the outskirts of the town owned by the Callan family
and another at Philipstown owned by James Kieran which had been built at a
cost of £30,000 and which could use up to 39,000 barrels of wheat in a season.

10 Ibid. 11 W.H. Crawford, 'The reshaping of the borderlands c.1700–1840' in Raymond Gillespie
and Harold O'Sullivan, *The borderlands: essays on the history of the Ulster-Leinster border* (Belfast,
1989), p. 93; idem, 'Economy and society in south Ulster in the eighteenth century' in *Clogher
Record*, 8:3 (1975), p. 249. 12 Revd Elias Thackeray, 'Statistical survey of Dundalk parish in 1816'
(unpublished); Lewis, *Topographical dictionary*; both consulted on www.jbhall.freeservers.
com/lewis_county_louth.htm (28 Sept. 2006).

There were a number of soap and candle factories, four large tan-yards, four tobacco factories and a very extensive iron foundry and forge owned by Alexander Shekleton. Dundalk market catered for meal, potatoes, vegetables, poultry, butter and eggs and was the most important corn market in the borderlands. The grand pillar of commercial prosperity in the town was the export trade. New quays, extensive stores and a customhouse had all been built in the previous decades. In 1812–13, before the economic downturn, exports of corn, beef, pork, bacon, butter, eggs, poultry, linen, flax and livestock had totalled almost £365,000.[13]

Nearly all of the land on which the town was built was owned by Robert Jocelyn, second earl of Roden (d. 1820) including most of the commercial heartland of Clanbrassil Street, Park Street, Dublin Street and Market Street.[14] In fact, he had long considered Dundalk to be *'his* town'.[15] He resided some of the time in Dundalk House (but mainly at Tollymore Park in Co. Down), located more or less in the centre of the town, amidst a richly planted demesne of just over 200 acres. In the environs of Dundalk economic prosperity in the decades before 1815 gave rise to the construction of 'many seats of respectability'. On the northern shore of Dundalk Bay, Francis Tipping lived in Bellurgan Park located on 300 acres of demesne and Lord Clermont lived in the two-storeyed Italianate early-nineteenth century Ravensdale Park. Atkinson noted there were also 'some farmhouses' that combined with the local big houses 'to give the stranger an impression of civilisation in this place'.[16] These belonged to the minor gentry, the middlemen, strong farmers and a few professionals or wealthy merchants (with the usual appellations of 'esquire'). John McNeill, for example, resided at Mount Pleasant on an estate belonging to Lord Clermont; his house was 'a pretty lodge in the villa style [situated on] 40 acres of a richly planted demesne'. Neale McNeale lived at Faughart in 'a small but neat dwelling house and 80 acres of demesne'. In Ravensdale valley were the neighbouring homes of Judge Baron McClelland (the judge in Patrick Devan's trial),[17] Robert Thomson, Thomas Lloyd and Robert Murphy esquires. A contemporary wrote:

> To these ... the valley is indebted for that health, plenty and vivacity which are inseparable from an extensive diffusion of the linen trade; while, in a picturesque point of view, their bleach greens glistening in

13 Atkinson, *Ireland exhibited to England* in *Tempest's Annual 1952*, p. 6.   14 Harold O'Sullivan, 'The eighteenth-century maps of the Clanbrassil estate, Dundalk' in *Journal of the County Louth Archaeological Society*, 15:1 (1961), pp 39–87.   15 A.P.W. Malcomson, *John Foster: the politics of the Anglo-Irish ascendancy* (Oxford, 1978), p. 247.   16 Atkinson, *Ireland exhibited to England* in *Tempest's Annual 1952*, p. 11.   17 See chapter five.

the sun, vying with the whiteness of the snow and blending with the evergreen foliage of the surrounding seats, complete the beauty of this valley. The most eminent, and we believe, the most highly elevated and extensively planted of these seats, is that of Baron McClelland [Annaverna], to whose finger of improvement Ravensdale is also said to be indebted for its best agriculture.[18]

Atkinson claimed that Dundalk in 1817 could be 'considered as the centre of the rank and fashion of that district of the Irish coast ... and some of the gentry of the surrounding country exhibit in their manners and appearance, a degree of taste and elegance that would not disgrace a court'. He went on to acknowledge that individuals in 'the decent ranks of society' preserved 'that attention to hospitality and letters for which this country was once eminently remarkable'.[19] It was, indeed, through hospitality that social relationships were consolidated between 'the decent ranks'. But it was through commercial prosperity that these relationships had first been developed and men of property in Dundalk, whether Protestant or Catholic, found common ground in the need to safeguard their newfound gains and to use them to build for a more socially prestigious and politically active future.

Between 1785 and 1809, the Church of Ireland population of the town had increased fivefold from 166 to 865. Many of the new families soon became the most prominent merchants, businessmen and professionals in the town including James Gillichan who established a distillery in 1799; the aforementioned James McAlister who established a brewery at around the same time; Alexander Shekleton who established the iron foundry; Paul Parks of the Stamp Office who also became county coroner; Laurence Tallan who was a wealthy general merchant; and Henry Hale who was an extensive timber merchant.[20] The settlement of these families and their subsequent rise in fortunes was very much dependent upon the patronage of the proselytising Lord Roden and his son, Viscount Jocelyn (1788–1870). As a minor, the latter had been returned as MP for Louth in 1806. His seat was taken over by his uncle until he reached his majority four years later. Jocelyn was a strong tory and regularly voted against Catholic relief in parliament. He was a staunch adherent of the evangelical movement in the Church of Ireland and strongly supported the 'second Reformation' in Ireland. Throughout his long political life he maintained 'a robustly anti-Catholic stance'. He became grand master of the Orange Order (having been dismissed from the commission of the peace by the whig govern-

---

18 Atkinson, *Ireland exhibited*, p. 14.   **19** Ibid., p. 10.   **20** Ua Dubhthaigh, *Dundalk*, p. 100.

ment in 1849 for partiality in dealing with the sectarian affray at Dolly's Brae in Co. Down).[21] But his patronage extended to the Catholic as well as the Protestant middle class. In 1799, Malcolm Browne leased his brewing premises from Roden for a period of three lives; it would be renewed by his son in 1827.[22] James McAlister had a long-standing lease since 1771 (originally with Roden's predecessor, Earl Clanbrassil) that was renewed in 1837 for a 'term of several lives'.[23] On 25 May 1811, Roden issued a 999-year lease to a conglomerate of Protestant and Catholic businessmen including Laurence Tallan, Malcolm Browne, Hugh McSherry and Bernard Duffy for the erection of a Buttermarket Crane and Stores in the town centre. The rent for the first four years was one peppercorn to rise to £37 10s. per annum thereafter.[24] Alexander Shekleton's iron works was very much dependent upon the local Protestant gentry and strong Catholic farmers who needed iron gates, ploughs, horse shoes and other farm implements.[25] (In 1816 Shekleton was an officer in the Dundalk yeomanry, which undoubtedly provided more of his business contacts.)[26] By the early nineteenth century, the Catholic large farmers who dominated the surrounding hinterland of Dundalk – an estimated 20 per cent of farms in the Dundalk and mid-Louth area at this time were over 30 acres in size with many, belonging to middlemen, well exceeding that acreage[27] – were dependent upon and benefited from the demands of the town's breweries, distilleries and flour mills owned predominantly by Protestants.

The men who dominated the commercial and social life of the town also dominated local governing bodies.[28] Shekleton and Laurence Tallan, for example, were members of the Vestry of St Nicholas' Church of Ireland parish in Dundalk and at different stages had been sidesmen, churchwardens and committeemen.[29] The vestry was essentially an assembly of parishioners which operated as a type of quasi-corporation and which enjoyed certain legal powers to raise funds through the parish cess – a local tax on householders – for the provision of local services such as poor relief, a fire brigade, town lighting, the repair

21 John Wolffe, 'Jocelyn, Robert, third earl of Roden (1788–1870)', *Oxford dictionary of national biography*, Oxford University Press, 2004 [http://www.oxforddnb.com/view/article/39661, accessed 5 Oct. 2006]. 22 Joseph Martin, 'Old title deeds of Co. Louth' in *Journal of the County Louth Archaeological Society*, 10:2 (1942), p. 143. 23 Ibid., p. 140. 24 Ibid., p. 139. 25 Ua Dhubhthaigh, *Dundalk*, p. 102. 26 Pádraig Ó Néill (ed.), *Journal of Henry McClintock* (Dundalk, 2001), p. 227. 27 P.J. Duffy, 'Geographical perspectives and the borderlands' in Gillespie and O'Sullivan (eds), *The borderlands*, pp 17–18. 28 See Toby Barnard, 'The eighteenth-century parish' in Elizabeth Fitzpatrick and Raymond Gillespie (eds), *The laity and the Church of Ireland, 1000–2000* (Dublin, 2005), p. 294. 29 The information that follows is taken from the minutes of the Vestry for the parish of Dundalk from 1803 to 1816 that are published in *Tempest Annual, 1938*, pp 42–52; *Tempest Annual 1939*, pp 42–54; *Tempest Annual 1940*, pp 8–22; *Tempest Annual 1941*, pp 44–54; *Tempest Annual 1942*, pp 5–8.

and cleaning of streets and the transfer of foundling children from Dundalk to the Foundling Hospital in Dublin. Following the abolition of the Penal Laws membership of the vestry was opened to Catholics although its administration continued to be controlled by Protestants. Hugh McSherry was one of a minority of Catholic merchants who served on the vestry. (There were other times when the Catholic clergy and Presbyterian clergy came together with members of the vestry to mark special events such as the retirement of the Revd Gervais Tinley in 1815.)[30]

The wardens were elected annually by the select vestry, a small committee which could levy taxes for the maintenance of the church and the payment of parish officers. It was a responsible position with important rights and privileges and it was considered an honour to be elected. Membership of the same was also important in terms of local patronage and the regeneration of local business interests. In 1812, the vestry commissioned the first public lighting installed in the town; 200 globes, double burners and irons had to be provided.[31] Shekleton secured the tender to supply the irons and Tallan was paid around £300 to light the 200 lamps with oil and wick.[32] As vestry officers in 1817–18, they both served under Lord Roden who had been chairman since 1815. (The gallery in the north transept of St Nicholas' church was reserved to Lord Roden and his family.)

Henry McClintock's (1783–1843) diaries from 1806 to the early 1840s provide an excellent insight to how the country gentry and the town merchants, professionals and clergymen of Dundalk socialised together. In January 1814, for example, besides doing the usual rounds of gentry houses belonging to the various branches of the Fortescues, Forsters, Fosters, Alexander and William Filgate, he spent time with land agents such as John Straton and John Woolsey; army officers stationed locally; merchants such as John Page and the Catholic Peter Coleman; clergymen including the Revd Elias Thackeray and the Revd Pilkington, while Fr Duffy (the Roman Catholic chaplain of Dundalk jail) was a frequent guest of McClintock's and they often rode out together. In April he attended dinner at Fair Hill, home of Lord John Jocelyn, where he met Robert Page (collector of excise in Dundalk), Charles Eastwood (gentry), Toby Purcell (retired army officer) and his sons Joe (a merchant) and Willy (landwaiter of

30 The vestry minutes recorded that Fr Edward McArdle PP, Fr Duffy (chaplain to Dundalk gaol) and the Revd William Neilson (Presbyterian minister) joined with the vestry committee in calling for 'a general meeting of the inhabitants of the parish' to organise a celebration to mark the occasion; minutes of Dundalk vestry, 4 Sept. 1815, in *Tempest's Annual, 1941*, p. 54. 31 'Minutes of the vestry for the parish of Dundalk, 1812–1816' in *Tempest's Annual 1941*, p. 44. 32 'Minutes of the vestry for the parish of Dundalk, 1807–1809' in *Tempest's Annual, 1939*, pp 45, 48; 'Minutes of the vestry for the parish of Dundalk, 1812–1816' in *Tempest's Annual, 1941*, p. 47.

the port of Dundalk), the Revd Gervais Tinley (Church of Ireland rector), Lennox Bigger (magistrate and Castle informer)[33] and Malcolm Brown (distiller). In February 1815, he dined again with Brown, the aforementioned Laurence Tallan and a number of other town merchants. At the end of March, Bernard Duffy ('my neighbour Barney', a Catholic brewer from Seatown Place) came to pass the evening at Drumcar.[34] In early October 1816, he stayed with Baron Judge McClelland at Annaverna. Years after the Wildgoose Lodge atrocity, in December 1830, McClintock attended the funeral of Laurence Tallan's wife and on 23 December 1832 he 'attended (as a bearer) the funeral of my worthy friend Malcolm Brown'.[35]

Most of the prominent Dundalk merchants, businessmen and strong farmers named above were to serve on one or more of the Wildgoose Lodge juries which was arguably another signal of their intent to monopolise local responsibility and authority and above all to safeguard their property interests. In a broader context they worked within a society where patronage was seen as a social perquisite and where individuals such as Lord Roden and John Foster[36] were the chief dispensers of such patronage, with the power to control social mobility. These two prominent local landlords exerted undue influence over the trading and commercial classes below them, while simultaneously presuming the privilege to influence the Dublin Castle administration.

The onset of economic depression

Edward Lynch lived within easy access of Dundalk. He was also only about four miles from Carrickmacross, the thriving market and post town in south Monaghan that provided the main outlet for pigs and butter and of which Sir Charles Coote wrote in 1801 there was 'no town which has a better appearance of wealth, and great business'.[37] The 'cold and deep clays' of the south Monaghan/north Louth area were ideal for the growing of flax. Coote emphasised that in Co. Monaghan 'every farmer possessing ever so little land, is engaged in the linen industry'.[38] Even the 5–10 acre farmers acted as middlemen charging two guineas per year in rent from the cottiers who supplemented their meagre wages with spinning.[39] By 1796 there were thirty-six weavers in the parish of Ardee owning sixty-nine wheels; 287 in the parish of Louth owning almost 400 wheels; eighty-four in the neighbouring parish of Killanny owning 170

33 See chapter four. 34 O Neill (ed.), *Journal of Henry McClintock*, pp 176, 178, 181, 196, 199, 204. 35 Ibid., pp 209, 210, 510, 606, 663. 36 See below. 37 Charles Coote, *Statistical survey of the county of Monaghan* (Dublin, 1801), p. 129. 38 Ibid., p. 44. 39 Ibid., p. 43.

wheels.[40] Writing of the south Monaghan, north Louth area in 1801, Coote announced:

> The men here are very industrious and manufacture is now pursued towards the borders of the barony [of Farney] where the land is poor … and nearer to Louth they are very much engaged in journey work; the merchants in Drogheda and also in the northern towns, give them yarn to weave at home, which they return in web. The linen trade has been increased twenty fold in twenty years.[41]

The growth in the linen industry had consequences for local agriculture. As it developed holdings became smaller; a weaver and his family could survive providing he had enough land for his annual potato crop and a supplementary income from weaving and so subdivision became a way of life, accommodating a rapidly growing population.[42] In Louth there was a dramatic increase in the number of houses subject to hearth tax from 7,741 in 1777 to 21,302 in 1821, a strong indicator of the extent of population growth and increased density.[43] Because the linen industry provided a supplementary income to smallholders, market demand caused by a growing population drove rents way above the levels that might have been sustained in the past through agricultural output alone.[44] Writing in 1857 William Brett recalled that during the Napoleonic wars 'the abundance of corn and cattle exported from Dundalk across the Channel was exceedingly great; and an excessive competition for the possession of land raised rents exorbitantly.'[45] The majority of farms in the two baronies of Dundalk were small, ranging from three to fifteen acres in size and were let from 16s. to £5 per acre. The upper levels were extraordinarily high but the relative absence of agrarian agitation in the area during the good years suggest that they were affordable (or at least being paid). The benefit to landlords at the top end of the scale was reflected in the big house-building boom in Louth from the 1770s: the Fosters built their home, Oriel Temple, in the 1780s and expanded it around 1812; the Filgate home at Lisrenny was built between 1788 and 1798; Louth Hall was built

---

40 A list of persons to whom premiums for sowing flax-seed in the year 1796 have been adjudged to the trustees of the linen manufacture (PRONI, Flax growers bounty list, T3419). 41 Coote, *Statistical of Monaghan*, p. 133. 42 Mary E. Daly, *Social and economic history of Ireland since 1800* (Dublin, 1981), p. 8. 43 David Dickson, Cormac Ó Gráda and S. Daultrey, 'Hearth tax, household size and Irish population change 1672–1821' in *Proceedings of the Royal Irish Academy*, section C, 82:6 (1982), pp 177–8. 44 J.W. O'Neill, 'Popular culture and peasant rebellion in pre-Famine Ireland' (PhD thesis, University of Minnesota, 1984: University Microfilms International version), p. 37. 45 William Brett, *Reminiscences of Louth: Being an authentic and truthful narrative of political and social events which occurred in the County of Louth* (Enniskillen, 1857), p. 6.

around 1760 with battlements added in the early nineteenth century; Castlebellingham, although dating to the late seventeenth century, was remodelled in both the late eighteenth and early nineteenth centuries; Glyde Court was built in the later eighteenth century and remodelled in Jacobean style in the early nineteenth century, while the Rathdonnell home at Drumcar was built in 1778.[46]

At the opposite end of the social scale, contemporary commentators had long argued that if the necessary supplementary income derived by the lower classes from the domestic linen industry was to be lost, the consequences would be calamitous. In his statistical analysis of Monaghan, Sir Charles Coote noted with caution that 'the weaver can never be a good farmer' – he simply spent too much time at his more profitable loom than he devoted to good husbandry – and so he advised the separation of farming from weaving for the mutual benefit of agriculture and the linen industry.[47] That would have been easier said than done for ultimately access to land, no matter how little, was the determinant of social status. Writing in 1836 G.C. Lewis contended that 'none but the very poorest of the Irish labourers are entirely without land, either permanently or as conacre' and perceptively concluded:

> They act on the general impression, prevalent among their class, that land is necessary to the maintenance of a poor man's family; and though they may not have at present, yet they have a future interest in the matter; though they may not be personally concerned, yet their kinsmen and friends and fellows are concerned.[48]

Thus, the rapid expansion of the population, the corresponding increase in the number of smallholdings, the marked increase in rents dictated by demand and market forces, the hunger for land and the dependence upon the linen industry left the long term future for the lower classes fraught with difficulty.[49] They were in danger of becoming sacrificial lambs to adverse weather conditions, poor harvests, diseased potato crops or cyclical slumps in the agricultural or linen markets. Cormac Ó Gráda is right to point out that the war years 'may have been prosperous for farmers and landlords, but high food prices and the government's ravenous appetite for revenue probably increased hardship for everybody else'.[50] In 1816, it was reported that on the small farms in the barony

46 Mark Bence-Jones, *A guide to Irish country houses* (London, 1988 revised ed.), pp 62, 112, 141, 189, 194, 229. 47 Coote, *Statistical survey of Monaghan*, pp 212–14, 239. 48 G.C. Lewis, *On local disturbances in Ireland and on the Irish church question* (London, 1836), pp 188–9. 49 'General Introduction' in Clark and Donnelly, *Irish peasants*, pp 4–5. 50 Cormac Ó Gráda, 'Poverty, population and agriculture, 1801–45' in W.E. Vaughan (ed.), *A new history of Ireland*, vol. v: *Ireland*

of Upper Dundalk: 'we have a great many poor in this district, especially when provisions are high'.[51] In most need were itinerant labourers and journeymen weavers. Coote wrote of the latter in Co. Monaghan in 1801:

> The houses of the third class, or manufacturers, are warm, and of tolerably comfortable appearance; but the poorer class of all, who are the journeymen weavers, and such as inhabit the environs of the towns and villages, are wretchedly bad indeed.[52]

Thus when the economic crash came after 1815 it had an immediate and dramatic effect on Co. Louth and surrounding areas where a high percentage of the population was dependent to a large extent upon the benefits of the linen industry.[53] This dependency was reflected in the 1821 census statistics for the four proclaimed baronies of Co. Louth.[54]

Table 2:1 Numbers employed in agriculture and in trade, manufacture and handcraft in four baronies of Co. Louth, 1821

Barony	Employed in agriculture	Employed in trade, manufacture and handcraft	Other
Ardee	4315	4514	1929
Dundalk Lower	3648	4918	1556
Dundalk Upper	3225	4875	2353
Louth	2540	3933	1020

Source: Census 1821

In eighteenth- and nineteenth-century Ireland, changing economic conditions had the habit of changing social relations. Economic downturns frequently gave rise to the growth of secret societies. What emerged in Louth in the years after 1815 was, on the surface, a protest that was concerned mainly with agrarian grievances and was similar in form and action to the earlier agrarian episodes of the late eighteenth, early nineteenth centuries. The most widespread of these earlier movements was the Whiteboy protests (they wore white shirts over their everyday clothes) of the 1760s–80s in large parts of Munster and Leinster concerned with grievances such as the enclosure of common land, tithes

under the union, 1801–70 (Oxford, 1989), p. 108. 51 Mason, A statistical account, vol. i, p. 207. 52 Coote, Statistical survey of Monaghan, p. 43. 53 Brett, Reminiscences of Louth, p. 6. 54 See below.

on potatoes and conversion of tillage land to grazing land. These protests led to the passing of the Whiteboy Acts (1766, 1776, 1787) that created numerous capital offences for the protection of property. In 1815 in Louth some contemporaries saw the agrarian protests there as an extension of the non-political Thresher movement that had emerged in Connaught in 1806–7 in response to the issue of tithes, priests' fees, the price of land and wages. This outbreak preceded the activities of the Caravats and Shanavests in parts of Munster and Leinster in 1809–11, which ranged farmers and shopkeepers against labourers and cottiers.[55] In the winter of 1812–13, there had been further outbreaks in a number of midland counties over issues such as the price of conacre, rising food prices and evictions.

The depression in agricultural prices was exacerbated by the harsh winter of 1815, followed by two further disastrous seasons in 1816 and 1817. These were exceptionally cold wet years with the result that grain harvests in Louth were late and scarce ('sadly unpropitious' as William Brett recalled in his 1857 mem-oirs), the potato crop was retarded by poor growing conditions and turf could not be sufficiently harvested because of the excessive rain.[56] On 7 April 1817 Fr James Marron (1764–1839), parish priest of Tallanstown, wrote to a friend that around Ardee 'the winter had been long and severe and the spring so winter-like that gardens were uncultivated and farmers unable to sow their crops'.[57] According to figures produced by Atkinson the value of exports from Dundalk plummeted from £346,000 in 1812–13 to just over £70,000 in 1816–17. This he put down to 'a dreadful specimen indeed of the effects of our sudden transition from war to peace, and of the calamitous effects of one eminently deficient har-vest'.[58] In Louth there were reports of corn merchants driven to bankruptcy.[59]

For the more numerous small farmer class rents that had been agreed during an extended period of prosperity became unaffordable. As was anticipated, it was the classes below the small farmers – the cottiers, labourers and linen weavers – who most felt the effects of depression. The fall in the price of pigs, for exam-ple, meant that a large proportion of cottier and labouring families struggled to secure the cash earnings necessary to make ends meet. Farmer-weavers went into decline and the industry 'faded rapidly' in Louth and neighbouring Monaghan and north Meath.[60] The cumulative effect resulted in near famine conditions. In 1817, the town and surrounding districts of Dundalk 'suffered

55 See P.E.W. Roberts, 'Caravats and Shanavests: Whiteboyism and faction fighting in east Munster, 1802–11' in Clark and Donnelly (eds), *Irish peasants*, pp 64–101. 56 Brett, *Reminiscences of Louth*, p. 6; see also Joseph Robins, *The miasma: epidemic and panic in nineteenth century Ireland* (Dublin, 1995), pp 38–9. 57 Fr James Marron to Mrs Margaret O'Reilly, 7 April 1818; quoted in Paterson, 'The burning of Wildgoose Lodge', p. 178. 58 Atkinson, *Ireland exhibited to England*, p. 98. 59 Brett, *Reminiscences of Louth*, p. 6. 60 Cullen, *Economic history of Ireland*, p. 120.

from scarcity of food'.[61] In several parts of the Louth countryside (and the bordering areas of Meath), Atkinson found cottages inhabited by 'men out of employment and ... women and children, from whose naked or famished appearance humanity revolts!'[62] James Anton later recalled that the people of Dundalk and its hinterland were 'borne down by sickness and famine'; the potatoes rotted in the fields and supply and demand dangerously dictated market forces. Provisions were so scarce that regular soldiers received an increase of three pence per day in their pay, but the less privileged were left to beg:

> The potatoes, which constitute the principal food of the inhabitants, are usually sold, in plentiful years, at two-pence or three-pence per stone, but this year [1817] the same quantity was selling at eighteen pence, and they were scarcely fit for the use of man or beast: frosted and bitter to the taste, the one half had to be cast to the ash-pit ... The mail and stage-coaches were surrounded, on their arrival and departure, by crowds of poor famishing families, with squalid children pulling at their milkless breasts, or tugging at the wretched rags that scarcely covered their mothers' nakedness. Every countenance was marked by affliction; the voice of the mother calling for charity, and the children imploring the mother for food, of which she had none to give.[63]

These social and environmental conditions were all too conducive to the spread of infectious diseases. On 30 June 1817, Blayney Balfour, a Louth landlord, recorded in his diary that on a trip from Townley Hall in Drogheda to Rostrevor in Co. Down he witnessed 'the greatest distress among the poor, everybody giving and selling rice meal'. And on the following day: 'dreadful scarcity & famine thro' the whole summer – dreadful fever rages in every part of the kingdom especially fatal at Armagh'.[64] By the end of 1817, a report in the *Dublin Evening Post* singled out Dundalk as the Irish town most severely hit by 'this pestilential calamity'.[65] Atkinson heard that in the back lanes around Ardee 'famine had made such rapid progress that the poor were dying of a noxious disease, and that it was not safe to visit them'.[66] In the House of Commons in 1818, Robert Peel, chief secretary for Ireland, was forced to admit that the fever that raged from early 1817 had resulted from:

61 D'Alton and O'Flanagan, *The history of Dundalk* (Dundalk, 1864), p. 223; Atkinson, *Ireland exhibited to England*, p. 97. 62 Atkinson, *Ireland exhibited to England*, p. 98. 63 Anton, *Retrospect of a military life*, pp 252–53. 64 Diary of Blayney Balfour, 30 June, 1 July 1817 (NLI, Balfour papers, MS 9554). 65 *Dublin Evening Post*, 30 Dec. 1817. 66 Atkinson, *Ireland exhibited to England*, pp 103–4.

the great poverty of the labouring classes, owing to a want of employment [that] had produced a marked depression of mind. The pressure of scarcity was also most severely felt, and an excessive wet season had deteriorated the quality and reduced the quantity of that species of food [potatoes] on which the people almost exclusively subsisted ... The causes therefore of the disease arose from want of employment and the poverty it engendered, from the defective quality and quantity of food, from the wetness of the season, and from want of fuel.[67]

K.H. Connell has estimated that perhaps as many as one million people contacted typhus during the period 1816–19 and up to 65,000 may have died.[68] But the endemic nature of poverty and disease in Ireland at this time meant that they were more or less regarded as a normal feature of Irish life and the Dublin administration made no significant efforts to address the problem.[69] One of Peel's biographers, Robert Shipkey, points out that the administration acted 'only in the most routine, unimaginative manner'.[70] When Lord Limerick presented a petition in the House of Lords stating that 'great distress' had arisen in Ireland because of agricultural depression, the petition 'having been read ... was ordered to lie on the table' while the members pressed on with what were obviously regarded as the more important issues of foreign policy.[71] James Anton was equally critical of the lack of effort made at local level; he claimed to have heard of 'no extraordinary exertions ... to raise subscriptions for the relief of the famishing' in Louth and remembered a distinct lethargy amongst the better off. When the mail and stage coaches arrived in the towns: 'So accustomed were passengers to those solicitations for alms that their hearts became callous to the voice of supplication; the exhausted hand of charity shrunk from relieving the poor.'[72]

Landlords and middlemen who had broken up their grazing lands during the Napoleonic wars to profit from rents payable by a rapidly increasing population of small farmers were not readily convinced when the wars ended that rent levels should be reduced.[73] Arrears in Louth began to accumulate as tenant farmers defaulted. On 24 June 1816, Blayney Balfour of Townley Hall recorded

67 *Hansard parliamentary debates, House of Commons,* 22 April 1818, vol. xxxviii, 288–9. 68 K.H. Connell, *The population of Ireland, 1750–1845* (Oxford, 1950), pp 230–3. 69 Robins, *The miasma* (Dublin, 1995), p. 35. 70 R.C. Shipkey, *Robert Peel's Irish policy, 1812–1846* (New York, 1987), p. 73. 71 *Hansard parliamentary debates,* 1816, vol. xxxii, 632–3. 72 Anton, *Retrospect of a military life,* p. 255. 73 George Sigerson, *History of the land tenures and land classes of Ireland with an account of the various secret agrarian confederacies* (London, 1871), p. 170; Atkinson, *Ireland exhibited to England,* p. 109; Mason, *A statistical account,* vol. i, p. 211.

in his diary that there was 'no rent to be had' in the whole of the county.[74] In 1825 Sir John Foster told a select committee of the House of Lords that rents in Louth became 'almost evanescent for two or three years' after 1815.[75] There are no reliable statistics available but it is probably safe to assume that as with later economic crises such as the Great Famine of 1845–51, the economic downturn of 1861–4 or the Land War of 1879–82, non-payment of rents led to a marked increase in evictions. From 1816, evictions were more easily facilitated by the passing of the Civil Bill Ejectment Act, which allowed landlords to obtain eject-ment decrees in local courts against defaulting tenants whose holdings were valued at less than £2.[76] Threat preceded eviction; in 1816, Henry Leslie, agent to Blayney Balfour, wrote to his employer: 'I am using every kind of threat to endeavour to get what I can from the tenants, particularly beyond the lake, where they are most behind but our markets are grown deplorable & no one to purchase the description of young cattle they [?tenants] have.'[77] The 1821 census figures tentatively suggest a rise in evictions in the general area of Wildgoose Lodge showing 339 uninhabited houses in the barony of Ardee. (Evicted families may have found shelter with families and friends as the number of families returned exceeded the number of houses inhabited by 326 but, of course, one always needs to guard against the inaccuracies there may have been in the collation of such statistics.)[78]

Table 3: Population figures for four baronies of Co. Louth, 1821

Barony	Houses inhabited	Families	Houses uninhabited	Male	Female	Total
Ardee	4748	5074	339	12550	13125	25675
Dundalk Lower	3224	3372	91	9029	9233	18262
Dundalk Upper	4001	4905	265	11055	11793	22848
Louth	2328	2440	82	6208	6399	12607
Totals	14301	15791	777	38842	40550	79392

Source: *Census 1821*

74 Diary of Blayney Balfour, 24 June 1816 (NLI, Balfour papers, MS 9554). 75 *Minutes of evi-dence taken before the select committee of the House of Lords appointed to inquire into the state of Ireland, more particularly with reference to the circumstances in that part of the United Kingdom*, HC 1829, vol. ix (181) 1. 76 56 Geo. III, c.88; O'Neill, *Popular culture and peasant rebellion*, p. 352. 77 Henry Leslie to Blayney Balfour, n.d. [1816] (NLI, Ainsworth report, no. 390). 78 Crawford, *Counting the people*, p. 15.

As noted earlier, there was also a move towards the consolidation of farms as landlords and middlemen contemplated the return to expansive grazing farms (livestock prices remained relatively stable in comparison to the prices of tillage products after 1815), which in turn, resulted in the unemployment of significant numbers of former tillage labourers.[79] Thus the conditions were ripe for an agrarian outbreak.

The rise in agrarian agitation and local secret societies

In 1814, when W.S. Mason visited the baronies of Dundalk (Upper and Lower) he observed of the lower classes:

> Where industrious exertion arises more from necessity than will, the lower orders never can be wealthy. It is so with the generality of the people here, who are therefore poor. Their usual food is potatoes: their appearance not superior to their wealth or food. They are perfectly contented and quiet, except when their bad passions are excited by the artifices of the designing, or by the harsh treatment of landlords and agent, of which, it is to be regretted, instances have been found.[80]

He continued that the people while of 'infinite good nature under a certain mode of treatment' could, when irritated, become 'cruel and treacherous, and but too easily led by the voice of faction and discontent'.[81] Nowhere was this cruelty more clearly observed than at Wildgoose Lodge.

Mason's interpretation of agrarian conflict was very much a traditional one that remained current until the 1970s, that conflict was determined by the relationship that existed between landlords and agents on the one hand and tenant farmers on the other. Since the 1970s historians have very much re-appraised this perception and it has become more generally acknowledged that agrarian conflict centred more on grievances between farmers and the classes below them than it concerned head landlords and tenants.[82] Large farmers or middlemen formed the buffer zone between the former and the lower classes, and the latter's access to land was usually more dependent upon the larger farmers than head

---

79 E. Margaret Crawford, 'Dietary considerations in pre-Famine Louth and its environs' in Gillespie and O'Sullivan, *The borderlands*, p. 121; for an incisive study of county Meath at this time, see Peter Connell, *The land and people of county Meath, 1750–1850* (Dublin, 2004). 80 Mason, *A statistical account*, vol. ii (1816), pp 71–5. 81 Ibid., p. 72. 82 Joseph Lee, 'The Ribbonmen' in T.D. Williams (ed.), *Secret societies in Ireland* (Dublin, 1973), pp 26–35.

landlords. When in 1815–16 this level of access in Louth was threatened by such things as a rise in the price of conacre, the threat of more land passing from small tillage farmers to expanding graziers, an increase in evictions, land grabbing (the taking over of evicted farms by farmers with progressive ideas who were willing to pay higher rents) and the taking in of outside (and invariably) cheaper labour, a broad rural alliance emerged between labourers, cottiers, small farmers and small farmer-weavers who organised themselves in secret societies or quite simply in local gangs with the objective of controlling the local economy through violence and threat directed at those they perceived to be in contravention of existing mores. Prosperous farmers such as Edward Lynch were to experience the fallout in social as well as economic terms.

It was in the spring of 1816 that agitation manifested itself in a virulent form in the north Louth/south Monaghan region, having been simmering for some months previously.[83] In March, a local magistrate, William F. Swann, reported that there existed 'a numerous association of persons calling themselves Threshers or Carders who have also taken an illegal oath.' These, he claimed, had been responsible for 'many enormities' and were attempting to purchase arms. They specialised in destroying houses and burning haggards of hay.[84] On 20 March 1816, Matthew Daly, a farmer from Clonturk in Killanny, a few miles from Wildgoose Lodge, received a threatening letter accusing him of land grabbing. On 2 April, a party of around 100 men armed with guns, pistols, swords, bayonets and at least one blunderbuss raided Daly's house. He was dragged outside, assaulted, robbed of his gun and informed that the raid was in response to 'his having taken poor people's lands'. Around the same time, large farmers in the barony of Ardee, including one of Edward Lynch's neighbours, James Fallon – referred to in a threatening letter as 'the extortioner of this county' – were warned to let their lands 'at the rate of the parish' or 'Jack the Carder' would visit them.[85] On 1 July 1816, Major General John Burnet sent his military superiors a report on the state of Co. Louth: 'Several outrages have occurred in the baronies of Dundalk in the course of the last month, perpetrated by a lawless banditti who attempt farmers & others from paying rent beyond the rate they fix upon.'[86]

W.F. Swann's assertion that the agitators were attempting to purchase arms merely reflected the local gentry's alarmed and alarmist reactions that there might be more sinister plans afoot for a general uprising of the lower classes as

83 See below. 84 Information of W.F. Swann sworn before John Foster, 9 Mar. 1816 (NA, SOC 1763/12). 85 Statement of James Fallon sworn before John Foster, 11 Mar. 1816 (NA, SOC 1763/14); *Newry Magazine*, 1816; Murray, *The burning of Wildgoose Lodge*, pp 136–7. 86 Report of Major General John Burnet, 1 July 1816 (NA, SOC 1776/60).

had happened in 1798. However, historical evidence suggests there was little likelihood that robbed arms were to be used for insurrectionary purposes. The target group and the motivations behind the crimes referred to above (as reported by the magistracy and military) emphasised that the main priority of the local societies was not open rebellion but rather to control the local agrarian market in a time of economic crisis. Robbed arms were more likely to have been acquired in order to provide local societies with a more formidable threat in later robberies or even for fowling purposes.

Significantly, in Swann's report he called these societies 'Threshers' or 'Carders' while Burnet called them 'banditti' at a time when it had become more popular with the authorities to refer to them in generic terms as Ribbonmen. W.E. Vaughan has made the valid point regarding the post-famine period that is just as applicable to the pre-famine period: 'There is no doubt that Ribbonism was used generically and carelessly to describe behaviour that seemed to result from conspiracies. The constabulary tended to use words like Ribbonism, Whiteboyism, and Rockism indiscriminately for the same actions.'[87] This is certainly true with regard to the contemporary reports generated by the so-called 'Louth conspiracy'. From the outset gangs operating out of north Louth and south Monaghan were certainly not members of a Ribbon Society as understood by historians in the present day; they had no formal structures and probably minimal contact, although there may have been an understanding regarding the territorial boundaries that had to be respected. Dr Jennifer Kelly's study of popular mobilisation in pre-Famine Leitrim clearly shows that the Ribbon Society, which had a strong, if illegal, formal organisation cannot be easily conflated with agrarian unrest.[88] Thus Major General Burnet's description of the Louth gangs as 'lawless banditti' captured more accurately the loose organisational structures of some of the gangs that were out for personal gain as much as for the general good of the lower classes and who certainly had very little political ambition, however loose, in mind.

For months, the propertied classes of north Louth were concerned at the growth in crime. In August 1815, Lord John Jocelyn chaired in Dundalk courthouse 'a numerous and respectable meeting of the gentlemen, clergy, landholders and inhabitants of the barony of Dundalk'. Both Catholics and Protestants were represented. The Church of Ireland rector of Dundalk, the Revd Elias Thackeray was there along with Fr Edward McArdle, the Catholic parish priest. Jocelyn spoke of depredations recently committed and 'the

87 W.E. Vaughan, *Landlords and tenants in mid-Victorian Ireland* (Oxford, 1994), p. 198. 88 Jennifer Kelly, 'An outward looking community?: Ribbonism & popular mobilisation in Co. Leitrim 1836–1846' (unpublished PhD thesis, University of Limerick, 2005), pp 21–2.

refractory spirit that has appeared among the peasantry'. A number of the smaller landlords such as Matthew Fortescue of Stephenstown, Francis Tipping of Bellurgan Park and the Catholic merchant-cum-landowner Thomas Fitzgerald of Fane Valley moved resolutions for the raising of a fund by private subscription that would lead to the apprehension and prosecution to conviction of perpetrators. They condemned the attacks that had been carried out on their tenantry, 'the houghing of Mr Denis Fitzpatrick's cows and the destruction of poor Hearty's wheat'. It was resolved that anybody connected with the agitators, relatives or sympathisers, should not be continued as tenants or servants and that 'every exertion should be made to prevent their being entertained as such elsewhere'. On the motion of the Revd Thackeray and seconded by Fr McArdle, books were to be opened in Protestant and Catholic churches to allow for people of all persuasions to show their abhorrence of crime by subscribing to the proposed private fund.[89]

During the harsh winter that followed, yeomanry patrols attempted to keep agrarian crime in check but inability to do so meant that magistrates throughout the borderlands became increasingly alarmed.[90] In December 1815, a meeting of the magistrates of Louth was called in Dundalk to see what could be done to restore order in face of the 'infatuated, barbarous and wanton acts that have lately been perpetrated in the neighbourhood of Dundalk'.[91] It was at this stage that the chairman of the meeting, John Foster (1740–1828), later first Baron Oriel, began to exert his considerable influence.[92]

John Foster and secret societies

John Foster, who resided at Collon, first became MP for the parliamentary borough of Dunleer in 1761.[93] Seven years later, he succeeded to his father's seat for Co. Louth and from then until his elevation to the peerage in 1821, he was to serve uninterruptedly as MP for Louth in first the Irish Houses of Commons and then Westminster. During that period, he held the most important political positions that an Irish politician could aspire to: in 1784 he was officially appointed Chancellor of the Exchequer and the following year Speaker of the Irish House of Commons, a position which he held until the Act of Union of 1800; he became a significant figure amongst the Irish MPs sitting in

---

89 *Belfast Newsletter,* 1 Sept. 1815. **90** For a selection of reports, see NAI, SOC 1815/1712/65–70. **91** Part of resolution passed at extraordinary session of Louth magistrates, 19 Dec. 1815 (PRONI, Foster papers, D562/3746). **92** See NAI, SOC 1815/1712/63–4. **93** For a comprehensive biography of Foster, see Malcomson, *John Foster* (Oxford, 1978).

10 John Foster, later first Baron Oriel (1740–1828).

Westminster until his retirement in 1821 and held the position of Irish Chancellor of the Exchequer for the periods 1804–6 and 1807–11.[94]

When Foster first entered the Irish Parliament, the Penal Laws were still in existence. Simply stated these were a series of discriminatory measures passed since the 1690s that represented the culmination of previously ad hoc attempts to exclude Catholics from landownership and positions of political and administrative influence and to repress Catholic worship. Catholics were debarred from direct political participation; they could not hold land for any longer than a thirty-one year lease; they could not practise their religion and so theoretically priests and bishops should not have functioned in Ireland during the period of their existence. While Foster supported the Irish Catholic Relief Acts of 1778 and 1782 (which were largely confined to property rights and rights of worship), he was totally opposed to full Catholic Emancipation and after 1801 he was a staunch supporter of the Union 'as an essential guarantee of the survival of Irish Protestants'.[95] He made his position clear in 1782 when, in a much quoted remark, he proclaimed: 'He would draw a line round the Constitution, within which he would not admit them [Catholics] while their principles were, he would not say hostile, but certainly not as friendly to the Constitution as those

---

94 Malcomson, 'Foster' (www.oxforddnb.com/view/article/9960).   **95** See S.J. Connolly, 'Aftermath and adjustment' in W.E. Vaughan (ed.), *A new history of Ireland*, vol. v, *Ireland under the Union, 1801–70* (Oxford, 1989), pp 3–4.

of Protestants.'[96] In 1793, Foster used his influence to ensure that the Relief Act did not extend to Catholics the franchise or the right to carry arms. He was, as Anthony Malcomson concluded, 'the Anglo-Irish ascendancy's most effective spokesman against Catholic Emancipation' who was determined that its position should not be undermined 'indirectly by weakening the British connection or directly by reforming the Irish representation or admitting Catholics to a participation in political power'.[97]

Foster had a long established reputation for dealing resolutely with any semblance of lower class (and almost exclusively Catholic) rural disorder in Louth. His biographer Anthony Malcomson points out that he was 'a leading advocate of tough measures of counter-insurrection in the period 1795–8'.[98] He had been even before that. During what was a particularly troublesome period for the landed class – 'a group whose social, political, economic, emotional, and physical well-being was under increasing pressure from a variety of directions'[1] – Foster seems to have been determined to show an increasingly sceptical government that landlords still had the ability to control their regions. His control of the local yeomanry – 'an overwhelmingly Protestant armed force which had originated in the counterrevolutionary frenzy of the mid-1790s'[2] – provided him with the manpower to assert order. (Moreover, when a proclamation issued at the end of April 1793 allowed for the raising of the Co. Louth militia, Foster used his influence to ensure that his eldest son, the Hon. T.H. Foster, was appointed commanding officer of the Louth Regiment with the rank of colonel.)[3] As J.S. Donnelly Jr points out: 'The past history of yeomen as super-loyalists and their local knowledge of the workings of agrarian combinations made their Catholic neighbours especially hostile towards them'; he quotes the Revd Ralph Stoney who in 1822 saw their importance in the fact that 'the disaffected dread them more than they do the regulars because they are well acquainted with their characters and know their haunts'.[4]

In the early 1790s, Foster's use of the Louth yeomanry inflamed local popular feeling. When the Defender movement began to make inroads in Co. Louth from its place of origin in neighbouring Armagh, Foster responded accordingly to stamp out any form of activity. In 1792, he controversially used the strong-arm tactics of ordering a party under his command to first fire into a crowd of people attending a pattern at Tallanstown (a short distance from Wildgoose Lodge) and

96 Connolly, 'Aftermath and adjustment', p. 23. **97** Quoted in Malcomson, *John Foster*, p. 66. **98** Ibid., p. xvii. **99** Malcomson, 'Foster' (www.oxforddnb.com/view/article/9960). **1** Allan Blackstock, *An ascendancy army: the Irish yeomanry, 1796–1834* (Dublin, 1998), p. 198. **2** Donnelly, 'Pastorini and Captain Rock', p. 127. **3** www.jbhall.freeservers.com/drogheda_militiamen.htm (22 Feb. 2006). **4** Donnelly, 'Pastorini and Captain Rock', pp 127–8.

then to charge them with drawn swords.[5] Two men were killed and a number seriously wounded. In the aftermath of the attack, Patrick Byrne, a local Defender leader, wrote a pamphlet as an appeal to the Presbyterians of Ulster to unite with Catholics against the ruling establishment in which he asked:

> Are they (the Catholics) attacked at Louth? Yes, by whom? Another placeman, the Speaker [Foster] and for assembling at patterns as has been the custom from time immemorial, the army is brought on the poor people, not the day before, or early in the morning to prevent their meeting, but in the evening when the people are warm with liquor and when resistance may furnish a pretext for military executions – and why all this? Because they think the Catholics are disposed to join you if you call upon them in demanding a reformed parliament.[6]

Foster was accused of goading Defenders into unrest so as to place the blame for popular disturbance on Catholic agitation. Following the Tallanstown affray, the *Morning Post* commented on his actions: 'Certain jobbing gentlemen … have for some days past taken much pain to magnify some petty quarrels in a country fair near Dundalk into open rebellion – and poor Popery! as usual, comes in for the principal blame.'[7] Around the same time Foster also came in for criticism for his actions in Co. Meath (where he owned a small estate and was a magistrate). From the beginning of 1793, Meath acquired the reputation of being 'the site of the most sustained Defender activity in Ireland'. In October of that year, Thomas Butler, founder of the Meath Association that was intended to counteract Defenderism, was murdered. The county magistrates, with Foster in attendance, met twice in quick succession and offered rewards for the arrest and conviction of the perpetrators. Contemporaries noted Foster's 'new-born influence' in Meath and when a few days later, John Foy, secretary of the Catholic committee in the county was arrested, Foster's role and the political implications of his arrest 'aroused a good deal of speculation (and suspicion)'.[8] John Keogh (1740–1817), the noted campaigner for Roman Catholic rights, and Francis Plowden (1749–1929), lawyer and historian, both accused Foster of being implicated in the false charging of Foy. When Foy was acquitted in March 1794 his arrest and trial were easily construed by the Catholic party 'as an exercise in political spite'.[9]

---

5 Kevin Whelan, 'The United Irishmen, the Enlightenment and popular culture' in David Dickson, Dáire Keogh and Kevin Whelan (eds), *The United Irishmen: republicanism, radicalism and rebellion* (Dublin, 1993), pp 294–5; Smyth, *Men of no property*, p. 68.   6 Quoted in Harold O'Sullivan, 'A history of Dundalk' in *Tempest's Annual 1968*, pp 60–1.   7 *Morning Post*, 7 July 1792; quoted in Smyth, *Men of no property*, p. 68.   8 Smyth, *Men of no property*, p. 106.   9 Ibid.

The following year, 1793, Foster and his son continued to lead numerous raids on fairs and patterns in Louth in order to prevent the gathering of Defenders and the spread of sedition. Scores of suspected Defenders were arrested and tried. At the Dundalk sessions alone, the calendar was so full that Judges Boyd and Downes were said to have been fatigued from alternating on the bench during the trials of 120 prisoners 'most of whom were Defenders'.[10] At the spring assizes in Dundalk and Drogheda twenty-one men were sentenced to execution and twenty-five more were transported for taking an illegal oath.[11] Foster's involvement in the so-called 'show trials' of prominent Catholics in Louth and Meath led to accusations that he was capable of using the law as 'an instrument of persecution'.[12] When the Defenders were more or less subsumed into the United Irish movement Foster again caused a great deal of controversy by making pre-emptive arrests of suspected leaders in Louth in March 1798. It was this type of local exertion that ensured the movement was broken before the outbreak of insurrection in 1798 and this assiduity was to once again characterise his actions when troubles broke out in Louth in 1815–16.

The barony of Ardee was squeezed between Foster's exertions in Louth and those of Andrew Thomas Blayney, eleventh Baron Blayney (1770–1834), in the south Monaghan/south Armagh areas. He had strong Louth connections; his mother was Elizabeth Tipping, daughter of Thomas Tipping of Beaulieu, a near neighbour of Foster's. In the late 1790s, Blayney acquired a notorious reputation for repressive counter-insurrection measures that lived long in local social memory.[13] His self-styled 'flying camp' of militia wrecked havoc in these areas; according to himself in May 1797: 'Nothing can really be effectual but retaliation in point of destroying property, burning houses and setting the inhabitants to the mercy of the elements, by which means you will either force them to action or make them surrender the arms'.[14] Blayney's over-zealous approach to suspected United Irishmen is captured in his letter to Lord Glentworth in June 1797 in which he boasted of his actions against rebels in Forkhill, along the north Louth/south Armagh border:

> I ... had information of three drills that night. Impossible to come across them but no person was in their houses at 3 o'clock in the morn-

---

10 For a record of these assizes from 1793 to 1799, see www.jbhall.freeservers.com/louth_assizes_1793–99.htm. **11** *FJ*, 16, 23 Mar. 1793; Smyth, *Men of no property*, p. 78; L.P.M., 'Dundalk assizes, 1793' in *Journal of the County Louth Archaeological Society*, 7:3 (1931), p. 47. **12** Smyth, *Men of no property*, p. 107. **13** See Brian MacDonald, 'Monaghan in the age of revolution' in *Clogher Record*, 17:3 (2002), pp 770–5. **14** Lord Blayney to Thomas Pelham, chief secretary, 22 May 1797 (NA, Rebellion papers, 620/30/148); quoted in ibid., p. 771.

ing so I burned 22 houses and one man I had strong reason to suspect saw returning from those associations so rode up and cut him down. I burned the house and property of a leading man named Donaldson. … I found a man had been attempting to corrupt a man of the Cavan Militia on parade … I sentenced the man to be flogged round the town [Forkhill]; suppose he received 300 [lashes]. It is useless crowding the jails. Advice – If you are disengaged and will take a trip down, you may see some amusement with those natives and I can give you a tent.[15]

When Blayney made an incursion into the Carrickmacross area, Norman Steele, agent to the extensive Shirley estate, wrote angrily to Thomas Pelham, the chief secretary that 'he should leave to me the curing of this district [Farney] as it does not accord with my feelings to practice the indiscriminate vengeance his lordship takes of the country'.[16] In a letter to Dublin Castle dated 21 July 1797, Blayney defended the reportedly brutal activities of the militia in south Armagh claiming that 'the Roman Catholics *alone* have universally been guilty of robbery and murder'.[17] While Blayney became a noted figure of hate amongst the United Irishmen, he was rewarded by the government in the aftermath of 1798 being given a regiment, the rank of major-general, the governorship of Co. Monaghan and a trusteeship on the Linen Board,[18] on which John Foster held the most influential position.

By 1816, Foster and Blayney were still very much concerned with the suppression of lawlessness. That year the Louth magistracy were faced with the added burden of secret societies from the Killanny and Inniskeen areas of south Monaghan carrying out raids and robberies in Co. Louth. On 25 March 1816, at a meeting of the Monaghan magistracy, Blayney, as chairman, warned the people of Inniskeen that if such activities continued he and his fellow magistrates would make application to the government to have the parish placed under the provisions of the Peace Preservation Act.[19] Threatening to make application to the government, as Blayney did, was effectively an admission that the local gentry had lost their grip on law and order in south Monaghan and that they required the assistance of the state apparatus. In the same month, Foster was instrumental in directing eighteen of his fellow magistrates in Louth to petition the Dublin administration for the extension of the Peace Preservation Act to the county, expressing regret that their ordinary powers were 'utterly

15 Lord Blayney to Lord Glentworth, n.d. (NA, SOC 620/34/45); quoted in ibid., pp 772–3. 16 Norman Steele to Thomas Pelham, 8 June 1797 (NA, Rebellion papers, 620/31/55); quoted in ibid., p. 773. 17 Quoted in ibid., p. 774. 18 Ibid., pp 774–5. 19 Notice issued by magistrates of Co. Monaghan, 25 Mar. 1816 (NA, SOC, 1816, 1765/64).

incompetent' to curb the growing anarchy that threatened the propertied class (which he later defined as 'Lords & squires, the gentry & farmers & graziers').[20]

By which time John Foster was seventy-five years of age but he still very much controlled the county. Since 1798, he had been governor of Co. Louth, an office he actually shared with his eldest son, Thomas, who, because he was a colonel in the local militia, was automatically elevated to the position under the 1803 Militia Act. Father and son remained joint governors until the former's death in 1828.[21] Foster was also foreman of the county's grand jury where his connections gave him added influence.[22] Malcomson has written that throughout his career (and that of his father): 'The one virtual constant is that issues in national politics were never allowed to upset the alliance between the Fosters and their county partners ... "the old interests" were always either on the same side of them or else agreed to differ'.[23] Lord Roden was amongst his closest political allies. They had joined forces in the election of 1806. That year the voting freeholders on the Foster estate, were informed by their landlord that 'the old interests went together'. Both Roden and Foster were returned again in the elections of 1807 and 1812. Despite the re-enfranchisement of Catholics in 1793, the electorate had risen insignificantly so that by 1815 there were still only around 900 registered electors in Louth reflecting what Malcomson claims was 'the unanimity of the [Louth] Protestant gentry against Emancipation'.[24] The outbreak of rural violence did little to persuade the gentry to raise the number of Catholic freeholders on their properties.

The arrival of the Peace Preservation Force in Louth, 1816

By 1816, Sir Robert Peel (1788–1850) had been chief secretary for Ireland for four years. Born in Bury, he was the eldest son of Sir Robert Peel (1750–1830), a printed calico manufacturer and landowner.[25] After successfully graduating with

20 Memorial signed by magistrates of Co. Louth, 12 Mar. 1816 (NA, SOC 1763/13); John Foster to Lord Norbury, 3 Feb. 1820 (PRONI, Foster papers, D562/3988). 21 Malcomson, *John Foster*, p. 260. 22 See chapter four. 23 Malcomson, *John Foster*, p. 154. 24 Ibid., pp 134–5, 136. 25 See, for example, Norman Gash, *Mr Secretary Peel: the life of Sir Robert Peel to 1830* (London, 1961); Norman Gash, *Sir Robert Peel: the life of Sir Robert Peel after 1830* (London, 1972); Donal Kerr, *Peel, priests and politics: Sir Robert Peel's administration and the Roman Catholic Church* (Oxford, 1982); R.C. Shipkey, *Robert Peel's Irish policy, 1812–1846* (New York, 1987); E.J. Evans, *Sir Robert Peel: statesmanship, power and party* (London and New York, 1991); John Prest, 'Sir Robert Peel' in H.C.G. Matthew and Brian Harrison (eds), *Oxford dictionary of national biography*, vol. 43 (Oxford, 2004).

11 Sir Robert Peel (1788–1850), chief secretary of Ireland,
later British Prime Minister.

highest honours from Christ Church, Oxford, in 1808 Peel decided to go into
politics instead of pursuing a career in the family business. Thanks to his father's
influence with the Portland ministry and that of Sir Arthur Wellesley, Peel was
elected for the rotten borough of Cashel in Co. Tipperary in 1809. A distinguished political career was to follow which would see him become under-secretary for war and the colonies in 1810 before becoming chief secretary of Ireland.
(He would later become home secretary (1822–7, 1828–30) and eventually prime
minister, 1834–5, 1841–6.) The office of Irish chief secretary had been increasing in importance even in the years prior to the Act of Union for, as S.J.
Connolly concludes: 'the chief secretary's status as the government's main
spokesman on Irish affairs, in direct contact with members of the cabinet, and
far enough away from his nominal superior to be guaranteed a considerable
degree of practical independence, inevitably enhanced his prestige relative to
that of the lord lieutenant'.[26]

John Prest has noted that 'Nothing in Peel's upbringing gave him the historical imagination to question the legitimacy of British rule in Ireland, and he
cheerfully joined a regime which was locked into reliance upon Penal Laws and
the Protestant ascendancy', opposing all measures for Catholic relief and being
influential in having the far from revolutionary Catholic Board dissolved in

26 Connolly, 'Aftermath and adjustment', p. 5.

1814.[27] Shortly after his arrival in Ireland, Peel very quickly struck up a strong working relationship with Foster that manifested itself in an almost continuous stream of correspondence between both men. Peel relied heavily on Foster's advice in such important local matters as the raising of the yeomanry, plans for the new jail in Dundalk (from around March 1814) and who should be appointed sheriff of Louth.[28] On the other hand, Foster used his relationship with Peel to strengthen his powers of patronage in Louth recommending, for example, freeholders on his estate for administrative positions in the county.[29] Both men shared a desire to prevent any measure of Emancipation well beyond Peel's chief secretaryship: in May 1821, for example, Peel wrote to Foster asking him to use his influence in Ireland to ensure Irish MPs would use their parliamentary powers to defeat it.[30]

In 1816, the other main players in the Dublin Castle administration were equally prepared to work to uphold Protestant ascendancy in Ireland. Peel's under-secretary, William Gregory (1762–1840), was staunchly opposed to Catholic Emancipation. The younger son of a wealthy Galway landowner, he had been educated at Harrow (Peel's school) and later Trinity College, Cambridge. He read law at the Inner Temple in London, after which he returned to Ireland where he held a series of minor administrative positions. He sat briefly in the Irish parliament (1798–1800) for the rotten borough of Portarlington, which was under the influence of the earl of Clancarty, another Galway landowner, whose daughter he had married in 1789. He was a vigorous supporter of the Act of Union and at local level had served as captain of the Galway militia and high sheriff of the county. From 1799 to 1806, he had been a commissioner responsible for examining the claims of loyalists who had suffered during the rebellion of 1798. In 1812 he was appointed civil under-secretary for Ireland, a position he held until 1830 (by which time the offices of civil and military under-secretary had been merged) and ultimately established a reputation as being 'the real ruler of Ireland'.[31] Peter Gray has concluded that:

> His intense political Conservatism as under-secretary owed much to his connection with the Trench family of Co. Galway, who were both leading tories and proponents of the evangelical campaign in Ireland known as the Second Reformation (Archbishop Trench of Tuam was

27 Prest, 'Sir Robert Peel', pp 407–8. **28** See for example Foster papers, PRONI, D207/39/1–11. **29** See for example, John Foster to Robert Peel, 29 Sept. 1816 (PRONI, Foster papers, D207/39/56). **30** Robert Peel to John Foster, 30 May [?1821] (PRONI, Foster papers, D207/39/63). **31** Peter Gray, 'William Gregory' in H.C.G. Matthew and Brian Harrison (eds), *Oxford dictionary of national biography*, vol. 23 (Oxford, 2004), pp 688–9.

Gregory's brother-in-law). Gregory's own evangelicalism was well known; he was a member of the Philanthropic Society and believed that the advance of Protestant proselytism would resolve many of the problems of the country. Like many of his generation he was deeply alarmed by the 1798 rebellion and resolved thereafter to oppose any further concessions to Catholic agitation, which he was convinced sought the destruction of the established church, the Protestant ascendancy, and eventually the union itself.[32]

One of his contemporaries, Lord Anglesey, summed him up as 'a determined intriguer. False as hell. A violent anti-Catholic – a furious tory – and quite ready to betray the secrets of any one whose confidence he obtains.'[33] Like Foster, Gregory achieved a reputation for a 'preference for harsh repression of social unrest and political opposition'.[34] He became a long time friend of Peel.

Of Manners, the lord chancellor, Norman Gash has written: 'Reputed a bad lawyer, he was by way of compensation a good Protestant and a devoted shooter of woodcock'.[35] The attorney general, William Saurin (1757–1839), had been appointed to the position in 1807 and was to retain it for an unsurpassed span of fifteen years.[36] David Huddleston tells us that 'in 1812 Saurin recognised that Robert Peel ... shared his views with regard to the maintenance and protection of the Protestant establishment. They worked closely together and Saurin was an influential adviser during Peel's tenure.'[37] In one famous case in 1813, where he faced Daniel O'Connell, Saurin prosecuted John Magee, editor and proprietor of the *Dublin Evening Post*, for libel. This newspaper was to be central to the reporting of the murders at Wildgoose Lodge and the subsequent trials but it is clearly obvious that the reportage suffered from Saurin and Peel's emasculation of the pro-Catholic press from around the summer of 1814 (around the same time that the Catholic Board was suppressed). During the Wildgoose Lodge trials, Saurin was to play a very prominent role advising Peel, Gregory and Samuel Pendleton on legal precedence.[38] Finally, Charles Kendal Bushe (1767–1843), the solicitor general, and third member of the Castle's legal triumvirate, was regarded as being more liberal than Saurin or Manners.[39] In conclusion, Norman Gash has noted:

32 Ibid. 33 Lord Anglesey to William Lamb, 17 Sept. 1827; quoted in Gray, 'William Gregory', p. 689. 34 Ibid. 35 Gash, *Mr Secretary Peel*, p. 99. 36 David Huddleston, 'William Saurin' in Matthew and Harrison (eds), *Oxford dictionary of national biography*, vol. 49, p. 59. 37 Ibid., p. 59; see also J. P. Casey, *The office of the attorney general in Ireland* (Dublin, 1980), p. 17. 38 On, for example, the use of the military to patrol the proclaimed areas along with the police see note appended by Saurin to letter from Samuel Pendleton to Robert Peel, 6 Dec. 1816 (NA, SOC 1763/46). 39 For an insight to his life and career, see Edith Somerville and Martin Ross, *An*

The central core of officials, from the lord lieutenant down to the Civil under-secretary, was composed of supporters of the Protestant estab-lishment ... Peel himself would hardly have been chosen for chief sec-retary had he not also belonged to that [Protestant] party. In his family, opposition to Catholic claims was almost a religious faith, and Peel entered on politics with convictions on that issue which had been formed in his earliest boyhood.[40]

When he arrived in Ireland, Peel was faced with what was in truth a vio-lent society or at least it was presented as such to Peel and the Dublin admin-istration in the scores of letters and reports on the 'state of the country' pour-ing in every month from landlords, magistrates (usually one and the same), military commanders, clergymen and so on. They testified to a distinct lack of respect for life or property and the dangerous conditions in which upholders of the law, enforcers of the law (including tithe collectors, revenue officers, bailiffs and so on), transgressors of local agrarian codes and informers had to live. Then there were the 'reports of singularly barbarous incidents which were verified by irrefutable evidence and which in their ugliness made a profound impression on his [Peel's] mind'.[41] One of these was the burning of Wildgoose Lodge.

To deal with such criminality (and social warfare) Peel believed that an army of police would be much more effective than the military. By the summer of 1814 he was convinced of the necessity to introduce some form of policing to counter the lawlessness he perceived to be endemic in the Irish lower classes, an observation he often made to his parliamentary colleagues. On Christmas Day 1816, for example, less than two months after the Wildgoose Lodge inci-dent, he wrote to Charles Abbot, speaker of the House of Commons:

There is, no doubt, the average proportion of murders and burnings and other atrocities, the acts of a set of human beings very little advanced from barbarism, unaccustomed to regard the law either as the protector from or the avenger of outrage, and subject, as far as the inter-ests of society are concerned, to the pernicious influence of the religion they profess. It is quite impossible for anyone to witness the remorse-lessness with which crimes are committed here, the almost total anni-hilation of the agency of conscience as a preventative of crime, and the

incorruptible Irishman: being an account of Chief Justice Charles Kendal Bushe, and of his wife Nancy Crampton and their times, 1767–1843 (London, 1932). **40** Gash, Mr Secretary Peel, p. 140. **41** Ibid., p. 171; for examples of these atrocities, see ibid., pp 171–4.

universal contempt in which the obligation of any but an illegal oath is held by the mass of the people, without being satisfied that the prevailing religion of Ireland operates as an impediment rather than an aid to the ends of the civil government.[42]

Thus in June 1814, the Peace Preservation Act[43] had come into being under Peel's astute stewardship. The act allowed for the establishment of a salaried, Dublin Castle-controlled police force that could be drafted into disturbed areas of Ireland when called for. The lord lieutenant was empowered to proclaim any county, barony or half-barony following a request from local magistrates. He could then send into the area a stipendiary magistrate (paid £700 per annum), a chief constable (paid £150 per annum) and a force of constabulary (paid £50 per man per annum). The stipendiary magistrate, usually referred to as the chief magistrate or chief police magistrate, assumed superiority over the local magistrates who now had to function under his direction. The burden of the expense of the force fell upon the ratepayers in the proclaimed areas by means of grand jury presentments, often to their resentment (it was not until 1817 that some of the costs were transferred to the central administration).[44] The police could only be withdrawn after the lord lieutenant announced the restoration of 'peace and good order' in the proclaimed area.[45] The ease with which the measure passed through parliament, inspired Peel to introduce a further bill less than three weeks later to try to secure a new Insurrection Act. Entitled 'A Bill to provide for the preserving and restoring of peace in … Ireland', the title was chiefly responsible for giving the new police their name, the Peace Preservation Force.[46]

As noted above, the Louth magistracy under Foster petitioned for the extension of the Peace Preservation Act to Louth in March 1816. As in the case of Blayney's petition for Monaghan this was a plea for state intervention because the local magistracy no longer had the machinery to deal with the escalating rural disorder. In response, Lord Lieutenant Whitworth (1782–1825) proclaimed the four baronies of Upper Dundalk, Lower Dundalk, Louth and Ardee. Notably Ferrard, where John Foster's residence was located in Collon, was not proclaimed which obviously speaks volumes for his control of the area. Foster was commanding officer of the Collon yeomanry that numbered around fifty men. In 1814 he had been mildly rebuked when it came to the attention of the

42 Robert Peel to Charles Abbot, 25 Dec. 1816; quoted in Parker, *Sir Robert Peel*, p. 236.   43 54 Geo. 3 c. 131.   44 M.R. Beames, *Peasants and power: the Whiteboy movements and their control in pre-Famine Ireland* (New York, 1983), p. 158.   45 Tadhg Ó Ceallaigh, 'Peel and police reform in Ireland, 1814–18' in *Studia Hibernica*, 6 (1966), pp 34–6; Palmer, *Police and protest*, pp 200–1.   46 Palmer, *Police and protest*, p. 202.

Castle that the Collon yeomanry were in possession of arms that had been illegally issued.[47]

After the proclamation Peel sent 100 members of the new police force to Louth headed by two superintending magistrates, Thomas D'Arcy (Co. Longford brigade-major of yeomanry who would eventually rise to inspector-general of Constabulary of Ulster in 1824) and Samuel Pendleton, a career military man.[48] The new police would have presented a curious sight to the people of Louth, dressed as they were in a motley collection of uniforms, wearing cloaks of many different colours, brass helmets and plumes.[49] Pendleton stayed on as chief police magistrate after D'Arcy was recalled. He was 'a coarse and garrulous man' who S.H. Palmer informs us 'had seen his brother-in-law, a clergyman, butchered in the 1798 rebellion'.[50] The extent to which this experience impacted upon his future attitudes and behaviour cannot be judged from the sources and it might be unfair to surmise but soon after his appointment to Louth he made himself unpopular with the lower classes and, indeed, with his Dublin Castle superiors largely because of his over zealous approach to the maintenance of law and order.[51] However, he had his supporters in Louth, most notably, John Foster.[52]

The arrival of the new force did little to quell local agitation. While the four baronies of Louth were proclaimed, they and the areas in their immediate vicinity remained in a state of terror. On 5 April 1816, for example, Monaghan magistrates issued a proclamation to the people of the parish of Killanny (half of which was in the proclaimed area of Co. Louth) following three nights of incessant raids on farmers' houses:

> We give this public notice to the inhabitants of said parish, that, if before the 25th instant (on which day a special session of the peace is to be holden at Monaghan, in this county) information is not lodged before either of us, or some other magistrates for this county against one or more of the persons engaged in the above mentioned felonies, we shall at such special sessions use our utmost endeavours to have an application made by the magistrates then assembled, to his excellency the Lord Lieutenant praying that he will be pleased to place under the provisions of the Peace Preservation Act, the part of said parish which is situated within this county, the part of which lies in the county of Louth, being at present subjected to the provisions of the act. And we hereby entreat

47 Robert Peel to John Foster, 11 Aug. 1814; Peel to Foster, 22 Sept. 1814 (PRONI, Foster papers, D207/39/5, 8). 48 Palmer, *Police and protest*, pp 211, 225. 49 Ibid., p. 227. 50 Ibid., p. 211. 51 See Lord Whitworth to Robert Peel, 17 Apr. 1817; Peel to Whitworth, 21 Apr. 1917; both quoted in ibid., pp 211–12; see also chapter four. 52 See chapters four and seven.

the householders of that parish, as they value character and property, diligently to enquire into the occupation of their dependents and inmates on the night of 2nd instant in the hope that the offenders above referred to may be so discovered.[53]

It is at this stage that the association of the crime at Wildgoose Lodge with formal Ribbonism becomes problematic. A formal Ribbon organisation was growing in the south Monaghan–north Louth area by 1816.[54] On 7 April 1816, a patrol of the Peace Preservation Force (which 'traversed a great part of the baronies of Louth and Ardee'), accompanied by Louth landlords William Filgate, Chichester Fortescue, Faithful Fortescue, Brabazon Disney Shiels (high sheriff of Louth), apprehended a man named Bryan Clarke on the Carrickmacross–Ardee road at 3 a.m., probably very close to the location of Wildgoose Lodge. When they searched him, they found several copies of an oath on his person – 'principally directed against Orangemen' – and later many more copies in his house, along with a number of threatening notices that were intended to be put on the doors of local farmers' houses. The reaction of the authorities was fairly typical of the time; they immediately concluded that Clark was a 'self-professed Ribbon organiser'.[55] In this case, he may very well have been, for later that month the authorities were alerted to a meeting of Ribbonmen that took place in the bustling market town of Carrickmacross. These were certainly not local agrarian agitators of the type who had been terrorising the surrounding countryside; these were described as parochial, county and provincial delegates, all of 'respectable appearances' who had come from 'a great distance', including two or three men allegedly from Mayo and Wexford.[56] At this stage Carrickmacross may have been a key town in terms of the organisation of a more formal Ribbon society; it and south Monaghan were eventually to become strong Ribbon territory. By then, there was, as one historian has concluded: 'a worrying tendency that growing awareness of the Catholic question, albeit crudely conceived locally, meant that traditional agrarian grievances were entangling with political and sectarian jealousies'.[57] This was undoubtedly true in areas were the local popu-

---

53 Proclamation issued by magistrates of Carrickmacross, 5 April 1816 (SOC, 1816, 1765/66A).
54 Tom Garvin, 'Defenders, Ribbonmen and others: underground political networks in pre-Famine Ireland' in C.H.E. Philpin (ed.), *Nationalism and popular protest in Ireland* (Cambridge, 1987), pp 227–8.   55 *Newry Magazine*, 1816; in Murray, *The burning of Wildgoose Lodge*, pp 136–7.
56 John Stacke to William Gregory, 29 April 1816 (SOC 1816, 1765/67); Tom Garvin has suggested: 'Ribbon societies of the period, usually described as a series of local and unconnected groups, showed distinct signs of politicisation and articulation over long distances, although no really effective central authority emerged'; Garvin, 'Defenders, Ribbonmen and others', p. 134.
57 Blackstock, *An ascendancy army*, p. 248; see also, Kelly, 'Ribbonism in Co. Leitrim', p. 2.

lation was divided along religious lines as in Carrickmacross, a town with a strong Protestant commercial aspect. It had been reported to a local magistrate in Carrickmacross in 1813 that

> the Catholics refuse to deal with Protestant shopkeepers. Peremptory steps should be taken or else the consequences to the loyal inhabitants of the district will be fatal. The principal production is hats which are made by Protestants. On the last fair day, very few hats were purchased but they were knocked off the stands and trampled in the mud.[58]

This, of course, suited the economic desire of Catholic shopkeepers (and may very well have been prompted by them) who were much more in evidence in the Ribbon Society than they were in agrarian societies.[59]

However, one fundamental difference between the Ribbon Society and the type of local agrarian societies (or gangs) operating out of north Louth and south Monaghan at this time is that the latter were completely indiscriminate in their choice of targets – Catholic farmers were as likely (in fact more likely because of their numerical superiority) to be attacked as Protestants. As the rural disorder gathered pace in Louth and south Monaghan in 1816, and local societies proliferated, the potential they offered for a more ambitious revolutionary movement may have captured the attention of Catholic radicals, the type of 'decent respectable-looking' gentlemen who 'rode good horses' and who gathered in Carrickmacross. Writing twenty years after the events of 1816, G.C. Lewis made the point that

> The connexion between Ribbonism and Whiteboyism (wherever any subsists) arises in one of the two following ways: either agents are sent from the Ribbon societies to the counties where the Whiteboy combination exist, in order to raise and extend their objects; or the secret oaths taken by the Ribbonmen are used by the persons to swear in the Whiteboys.[60]

Bryan Clarke was arrested in the vicinity of Wildgoose Lodge three nights before the first raid on it. The Ribbon meeting at Carrickmacross coincided with the climax of agrarian crime in south Monaghan and north Louth. Around the same time it was reported independently to William Gregory that several persons had come into the barony of Ardee from Monaghan, Cavan and other

---

58 Quoted in Peadar Livingstone, *The Monaghan story* (Enniskillen, 1980), pp 181–2. **59** Beames, *Peasants and power*, p. 144. **60** Lewis, *On local disturbances in Ireland*, p.161.

parts of Louth to swear men into the Ribbon organisation.[61] Therefore, some movements were afoot to change the character of local secret societies. This perturbed the local magistracy even further, which would be reflected in their determination to break the so-called Louth conspiracy in the weeks and months that were to follow.

In the meantime, the local societies carried on in their traditional ways. Samuel Pendleton reported to the under secretary, William Gregory, that eleven houses in the barony of Ardee were raided in one week in April. They all belonged to persons: 'of the better class who had signed the resolutions of Louth & Ardee binding themselves to co-operate with magistrates, to give information etc. etc.' He continued:

> The opinion as to the peaceable disposition of the vicinity of Ardee is so very much changed within the last few weeks, that I am now requested by the magistrates immediately thereabouts to represent to you the necessity of ordering a detachment of military there in the room of that lately withdrawn. From the well-known zeal and activity of those gentlemen, it is not likely that they would suggest such a want, if they did not feel it.[62]

One of the eleven houses raided was Wildgoose Lodge. This first raid set in motion a train of events that would have far-reaching consequences.

61 [?] Smyth to Sir William Gregory, 27 May 1816 (NA, SOC 1763/22).   62 Samuel Pendleton to Sir William Gregory, 12 Apr. 1816 (SOC, 1763/19).

CHAPTER THREE

The historical evidence, II:
the murders at Wildgoose Lodge, October 1816

'A crime barbarous beyond the power of expression, and scarcely credible to have been committed within the precincts of a country deemed
civilised.'

Part of resolution of Louth magistracy, Nov. 1817

Introduction

As police magistrate Samuel Pendleton reported, the raid on Wildgoose Lodge
was just one of eleven that took place in one week in April 1816 in the Ardee area
of north Louth. Therefore one could argue that there was neither anything
particular or personal to the motive; it was just one in a series of indiscriminate
robberies carried out on strong farmers' houses and instead of being singled out
for attention Edward Lynch and his family simply found themselves caught up
in all of the violence and social mayhem that characterised Louth at that time.

Local lore, as discussed in chapter one, would have one believe otherwise but
that is largely because it fails to take into account the other ten raids (and those
were only the ones reported to the authorities). Lore claims that Lynch was singled
out because he would not allow his son or son-in-law to join the local secret society
or that having once been a member himself Lynch decided to opt out as a result
of his increased prosperity. Having withdrawn, he then forbade any further
meetings in the lodge much to the anger of the society's leaders who saw the
advantages of using it because of its desolate location. It may be that over the
generations stories relating to different local families got woven together. For
example, on 21 January 1817 the haggard of a farmer named Leary (Lynch was often
referred to as 'Lynchy' by contemporaries) from the Mills of Louth (only a short
distance from Wildgoose Lodge) was maliciously set on fire. According to a
newspaper report of the time, his 'crime' was that he had refused to allow his sons
to join 'the confederated villains who infest the lower baronies of that county'.[1]

Nonetheless, there is one piece of important surviving historical evidence
that suggests Lynch's antipathy to secret societies that could have attracted unwel-

1 *Belfast Newsletter,* 31 Jan. 1817.

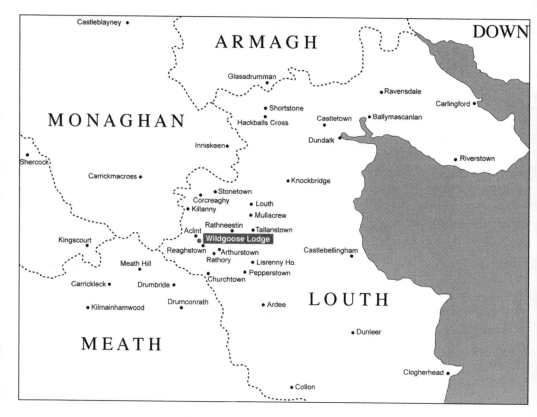

12 Map of the general area around Wildgoose Lodge.

come attention to him. In 1817, the aforementioned Fr Bernard Loughran, then Roman Catholic curate in Ardee, wrote to the *Newry Telegraph* outlining what had taken place a week before the first raid on Wildgoose Lodge:

> It is a well-known fact that the disgraceful catastrophe of Wildgoose Lodge was accelerated, if not occasioned, by the active and zealous interference of the Rev. Dr Marron, the parish priest of that place [Tallanstown]. Whilst remonstrating with his flock from the altar, on Sunday, whilst admonishing them to keep free from party, to guard against those who would attempt to bring them into any illegal combination, which he said was creeping into the neighbourhood, but which had not he hoped reached his charge, Lynch stood up and told him, 'he was very much mistaken, that the greater part of his auditors were [already] sworn Ribbandmen'. This imprudent, bold declaration was the cause of all the misfortune which has ensued and disgraced our

county, it drew upon Lynch the vengeance of the disaffected; they meditated revenge; his place was shortly after broken into and racked.[2]

There is hardly any reason to disbelieve Fr Loughran; one can perhaps
surmise that he heard the story directly from Fr Marron and certainly the latter
did not refute Fr Loughran's claims in the press. Lynch's bold statement in a
chapel full of his neighbours suggested a certain arrogant belief that he was
beyond punishment. It certainly reflected the gulf between aspiring strong
farmers such as him and the cottiers, labourers and smallholders who
predominated in the local societies. Lynch's public announcement may just as
easily have been borne out of the frustration of living in dread of continuous
attack or even suggestive of the fact that Lynch in his ambitions towards
respectability was adopting a modernist approach, looking to the apparatus of
the state as a means of protecting his property from those who would threaten
it. Lynch was no different in this respect to the majority of other respectable
farmers in his locality or the respectable classes of Dundalk who, as we shall
see, were content to use the machinery of the state's courts to prosecute social
miscreants. Analyses of the composition of secret agrarian societies show that
in general large farmers remained aloof of them, understandably, given that
in Louth and its surrounding areas in 1816–18 it was they who were
predominantly the targets of aggressors and who felt most threatened. Even if
there was a sectarian dimension to Ribbon (in its more generic term) activities,
Catholic farmers would still have feared for their own future, a point not lost
on a secret agent, identified only as 'M.G.', reporting to Dublin Castle in 1815:
'The thirst for the property of others has excited the fever of even the middling
classes of Catholics, and prevented them associating with Ribbonmen, as they
apprehend that when the poor get possession of Protestant lands, if they are
not sufficient to satisfy them they will help themselves without any religious
distinction.'[3] Lynch's accusation directed against the majority of his fellow
parishioners hardly added to his local popularity in an area deeply divided in
social class warfare.

The first raid on Wildgoose Lodge, 10 April 1816

On the night of 10 April 1816 Edward Lynch and his son-in-law, Thomas
Rooney, and a young servant boy, James Rispin (a neighbour's son whose home

2 The original appeared in the *Newry Telegraph* shortly after the raid; this version quoted in *Dundalk
Examiner*, 5 Nov. 1881. 3 Lady Gregory (ed.), *Mr Gregory's letter-box, 1813–30* (1898), p. 40.

was just across the bog), were in Wildgoose Lodge. None of the historical records make reference to Rooney's wife, Bridget, being there. She would have been heavily pregnant at the time given that her son was described as being five months old the following October. (Had she been in the house the prosecution lawyers at the trials would have undoubtedly drawn attention to her situation.) Nor it seems was Lynch's son, Michael, present when a gang of armed men forced their way into Wildgoose Lodge. The raiders demanded arms and when Lynch told them he had none, they retaliated by breaking a web in the loom and vandalising the furniture.[4] (Breaking a web in the loom was a deliberate means of causing a weaver's family a great deal of inconvenience, if not hardship.)[5] A scuffle ensued between Lynch, Rooney and the raiders. The details of this are all very sketchy but it seems that Lynch knocked one of the raiders down and somehow managed to grab a pitch-fork which he used as a weapon to defend himself. One of the raiders took a lighted coal from the fire and threatened to set the house ablaze. The mark of fire was seen the following morning in the thatch. Meanwhile, Thomas Rooney ran into a back bedroom. Some of the raiders followed him. He was knocked on to the bed and struck on the back with a sharp implement. He was then forcibly lifted from where he lay and brought back to where Lynch was fending off the other raiders. At this point Rooney seems to have escaped their grasp and both he and his father-in-law made their way up to the loft. Ranging above the raiders, Lynch was now in a much better position to fend off the attackers with his pitch-fork. After another brief struggle the raiders fled.[6]

The next day Lynch was faced with the dilemma of reporting the crime to the local magistracy, in which case he would have to prosecute and therefore endanger himself as an informer, or he could turn a blind eye to it and risk it happening over and over again. He decided to report the crime to William Filgate Sr of Lisrenny, who in his capacity as local magistrate was the link between the victim and the courts. Lynch must have been acutely aware of the dangers of informing. The majority of other farmers whose houses had been raided around the same time as Wildgoose Lodge did not come forward.[7] Besides the obvious fear of recrimination, the costs involved to the victim(s) who prosecuted a case at the assizes could run to between £10 and £20 which were prohibitive (costs depended on the number of witnesses called and court fees for such things as drawing up the indictment or paying the officers involved including clerks, bailiffs, doorkeepers and criers, although reimbursements were some-

4 Mathews, *The burning of Wildgoose Lodge*, p. 3. 5 Smyth, *Men of no property*, p. 47. 6 *Belfast Newsletter*, 1 Aug. 1816. 7 For examples of the punishment meted out to others who did see below.

13 The only known contemporary sketch of Wildgoose Lodge attributed to a niece of its owner, Townley P. Filgate. Note that it shows what looks like a barn close to the lodge. If this existed it may have been where the 'survivor' was in hiding.

times available). In Lynch's case, he not only had to find the ready money but he also had to calculate the loss involved to himself and his son-in-law by taking time away from work in order to attend the court (unless he was to be rewarded by the Castle). Certainly in the English example J.M. Beattie has found that there was an apparent reluctance of victims of property crimes to prosecute because of the costs and inconvenience involved.[8]

Because Louth had earlier been proclaimed, there was a police presence in the Ardee area. It was they who became responsible for the search and arrest of suspects (prior to this the work of detecting and apprehending suspects was very much left to victims and the posses that they could muster). The Louth magistrates collectively praised Lynch for having acted 'for the protection of himself and family, and had manfully discharged his bounden duty to the country that gave him birth' but he and his family had now to be protected.[9] On 12 April, Samuel Pendleton, the chief police magistrate for Co. Louth, reported to William Gregory that Lynch was 'an object worthy the attention of government ... In his present state I do not think the man safe. I offered him protection and support here, he preferred to [? venture] himself at home and has a

8 J.M. Beattie, *Crime and the courts in England, 1660–1800* (Oxford, 1986), pp 36, 47. 9 Part of resolution passed by Louth magistrates at Castlebellingham on 4 Nov. 1816; quoted in *FJ*, 11 Nov. 1816.

constable in his house to assist him.'[10] At the same time, Pendleton confirmed to Gregory that he had been given information on six men who were accused of the raid and that five of them had been arrested. Presumably the information had been supplied by Lynch and Rooney but Pendleton also identified an informer named Kelly who allegedly confessed his role in the raid to him. If Kelly's information was crucial in the naming of some of the men leading to their arrest, his evidence does not seem to have been used in court probably because, rather revealingly, Pendleton later admitted that he was 'not the man on whose confession I was disposed to rely'.[11] Pendleton believed that there would be no problem in convicting at least three of those arrested and that 'a few more [arrests] each night would make this county quiet.'[12]

But despite the arrests, raids on large farmers' houses continued for some months after. Between 10 April and 20 July 1816, Pendleton received thirty-three reports of house burglaries or raids for arms; seven cases of malicious burning of houses or haggards; five of destruction of property; four attacks on animals; five of riotous assembly and thirty reports of assaults.[13] Vigilante groups were being organised locally but Pendleton was not convinced that their function was the protection of property; instead he saw them as a pretext to break curfew. Towards the end of June, he had the following notices posted in Ardee:

> The inhabitants of the proclaimed districts of Louth are hereby required to take notice that any persons who shall be found at night assembled under the pretence of being safeguards or patrols for the safety of any village or townland therein, not being duly authorised by the law for such purpose, will be taken and detained in custody it being known to me that the persons composing such pretended safeguards and patrols are themselves in many instances active members of unlawful and treasonable associations.[14]

A month later, the first Wildgoose Lodge trial opened at the summer assizes at Dundalk. Less than a fortnight after the raid in April John Foster had written to fellow magistrate, William Ruxton, in relation to the other raids on farmers' houses in Reaghstown that the trial would 'show whether the outrage proceeded from any dangerous or illegal association to disturb the country, make rules for rent & the value of the produce of the land ... Should such a system

10 Samuel Pendleton to William Gregory, 12 April 1816 (NAI, SOC 1816, 1763/19). 11 Samuel Pendleton to Robert Peel, 1 Nov. 1816 (NAI, SOC, 1763/35). 12 Ibid. 13 Samuel Pendleton to William Gregory, 4 Aug. 1816 (NAI, SOC 1763/27). 14 Quoted in W.P. Ruxton to Blayney Balfour, 23 June 1816 (NLI, Balfour papers, MS 10,368 (6)).

appear to exist, how could the reduction of the police in that barony [Ardee] be justified?'[15] Unfortunately the lack of evidence sheds no light on whether a motivation for the crime was ever debated during the trial. Only minimal facts are available. Three men were tried under the Whiteboy Act – Michael Tiernan (sometimes Kiernan), Patrick Shanley and Philip Conlon (sometimes Conlan). Pendleton was impressed by the fact that despite his age Lynch's conduct and testimony was 'manly without appearing to be the result of any vindictive feeling'.[16] However, the report of the trial in the *Belfast Newsletter* suggests that Lynch did not or could not identify any of the raiders (rather than being manly, he had possibly lost his mettle) and that it was, in fact, Rooney who identified them all.[17] Rooney told the court that he recognised Michael Tiernan by his voice (obviously suggesting that they were not strangers to each other). Rooney also claimed to have seen Shanley and Conlon clearly, even though it was by candlelight in a dimly lit kitchen. James Rispin, the servant boy, corroborated this evidence.

Each of the accused had alibis (at least six were called) who swore that the three men were 'otherwise employed the night Lynch's house was attacked'. Shanley was from Tallanstown, three miles from the lodge and was married with a number of young children. His father swore that his son never left the house on the night of the raid. John Reg, steward to Henry Foster, said that he knew Tiernan, a herd on Lord Louth's Tallanstown demesne, to be an honest, law-abiding, hardworking man. James Breen (neighbour) and Peggy Tiernan (the prisoner's sister) swore that Tiernan could not have been at the raid because he had been seriously assaulted at the fair of Ardee the day before and was consequently unable to move out of his home. Peggy swore that she spent the night applying sheep's liver and vinegar to her brother's battered eyes. Rooney denied that on the night of the raid Tiernan showed any signs of having been previously beaten. Fr James Marron, parish priest of Tallanstown, who had been so condemnatory of Ribbonism, testified that he knew both Conlon (for fourteen years) and Shanley (for five or six years): 'and until this last business never heard they had been charged with any crime, but always bore an honest, peaceable and industrious character'.[18] Conlon's sister, Catherine, testified that her brother had spent the night in his own house with her, his wife and his children. Put simply, Rooney's testimony was accepted, while that of the prisoners' alibis was rejected.[19] The prisoners were all found guilty, even though the *Dublin Evening Post* contended that many circumstances seemed 'to corroborate the testimony

15 John Foster to William Ruxton, 20 Apr. 1816 (PRONI, Foster papers, D562/13093). 16 Ibid. 17 *Belfast Newsletter*, 2 Aug. 1816. 18 Report of July 1816 trial, reproduced in *Dundalk Examiner*, 24 Sept. 1881. 19 *Belfast Newsletter*, 1, 2 Aug. 1816.

given on their behalf' (at the time the *Post* had its own anti-establishment agenda and trials such as this were used to highlight the need to address the issue of Catholic civil liberties). They were all sentenced to execution.[20]

Just over one week later, there was a disturbing development reported in the *Post*: it was claimed that after the trial Shanley swore that while he was guilty Tiernan and Conlon were both innocent. There were also rumours in circulation that Rooney had tried desperately to retract his accusations against them but to no avail. The newspaper called for 'vice-regal clemency' to 'be invoked for mercy'.[21] According to John Mathews' 1897 nationalist account, the counsel for the accused, Mr Perrin, tried to obtain a commutation of the prisoners' sentence, that he went to Downpatrick where the trial judge was then in session but Judge St George Daly declined to sign the petition. The three men were executed on 21 August 1816 (bringing the total executed that month to six) and buried in the one grave in Dundalk jail that was then filled with nine barrels of lime.[22]

During the following months agitation died down presumably because of the multiple executions but also because of the availability of more employment opportunities for the lower classes during the summer and harvest months and partly to the success of Pendleton and the police (on 27 June Foster wrote to Pendleton congratulating him on his work to date and inviting him to dinner at Collon).[23] On 28 October 1816, a meeting of the magistrates of Louth, as anticipated by Foster in his letter to Ruxton, called for the removal of the police establishment from the barony of Ardee because it was proving too costly, especially at a time when the countryside seemed to be returning to more peaceful ways.[24] However, the magistrates decided that the parish of Louth should remain proclaimed, highlighting the fact that it continued to be a hotbed of activity. It was John Foster's responsibility to forward the resolution to Sir Robert Peel. Foster and three other magistrates – Viscount Jocelyn, Henry Brabazon and Samuel Pendleton – refused to sign the petition; they felt the four baronies were still too disturbed. Pendleton believed that 'a greater tendency to outrage' existed and pointed to the fact that of six men capitally convicted at the summer assizes for their parts in armed robberies and other crimes around Channonrock (between Louth village and Inniskeen) and Knockbridge (between Louth village and Dundalk), five were from the baronies of Ardee and Louth, including

20 Ibid., 1 Aug. 1816; the whole judicial procedure that operated at the time will be described in more detail in relation to the later trials for the burning of the lodge in chapters 4–6. 21 *Dublin Evening Post*, 10 Aug. 1816. 22 Mathews, *The burning of Wildgoose Lodge*, p. 3. 23 John Foster to Samuel Pendleton, 27 June 1816 (PRONI, Foster papers, D562/13114). 24 Sir William Gregory to Robert Peel, 29 Oct. 1816 (British Museum, Peel papers, MS 40,203).

Shanley, Conlon and Tiernan.[25] They were outvoted.[26] On the evening of the meeting, Foster wrote to Peel: 'It was my misfortune from the sentiment I entertain of the state of the country, not to be able to persuade myself to join in the opinion it expresses or in the prayer it concludes with [to exempt the baronies from the police establishment, with the exception of the parish of Louth].'[27] Ironically, it was the day before the fatal burning of Wildgoose Lodge.

Plans for revenge

The local society operating in the parishes of Louth and Killanny has traditionally been described as a Ribbon society, its members as Ribbonmen and its leader, Patrick Devan, as a captain of the same. The point has earlier been made that in 1816 Ribbonism was used very much in its generic sense by the Castle, the magistracy of Louth and Monaghan and later by writers such as William Carleton. In fact, the local society was just one of a number of inchoate gangs working out of the borderlands, some of which were agrarian societies, some criminal bands, others perhaps a mixture of both.

Patrick Devan had been born and reared near Tully in the parish of Louth, close to the crossroads of Corcreaghy (at the time described as a village in the parish of Killanny) along the Louth-Monaghan border.[28] On a clear day from above the Mills of Louth, a short distance from where he lived, he was able to see Wildgoose Lodge situated on a hill in the distance with its panoramic view of parts of Louth, Monaghan, Meath, Cavan and Armagh. There is no official record of Devan's family background in Corcreaghy, although it seems that his father was a small farmer in the area who was also involved in the domestic linen industry.[29] Devan had received enough of an education to 'qualify' him as a local hedge schoolmaster. This may have facilitated his rise to prominence in the secret society; as Tom Garvin points out: 'Hedge schoolmasters occasionally acted as scriveners for local secret societies. As learned men they acted as arbiters in internal disputes of these groups and were involved in the doings of the Whiteboy, Rockite and Ribbon gangs of the eighteenth and early nineteenth centuries.'[30] More particularly they could read and write English which, for one

25 Samuel Pendleton to Robert Peel, 29 Oct. 1816 (NA, SOC 1763/32). 26 John Foster to Robert Peel, 28 Oct. 1816 (NA, SOC 1763/31A); the other signatories to the petition were George Bellew, W.P. Ruxton, John McClintock, R. Thompson, Chichester Fortescue, Joseph Wright, Fitzherbert Ruxton, Faithful Fortescue, Philip Pendleton and Blayney Balfour. 27 Foster to Peel, 28 Oct. 1816, SOC 1763/31A. 28 O'Neill (ed.), Journal of Henry McClintock, 23 July 1817, p. 217. 29 See account of Devan's trial in chapter five. 30 Tom Garvin, The evolution of Irish nationalist

thing, had become by 1816 the accepted language of threatening letters. Devan was also clerk, or sacristan, of the Roman Catholic chapel at Stonetown in the parish of Louth, about two miles from Corcreaghy, for which he would probably have received a modest stipend.

William Carleton represented Devan as 'a man of slight build, probably no more than thirty. He was unremarkable in both dress and physical appearance, but he certainly commanded the respect of his men.'[31] The only surviving physical description from a contemporary newspaper account of his trial put him at about 25–30 years of age in 1817 (therefore born sometime between 1787 and 1792), about five feet seven inches tall and stout, with 'a forbidding countenance'. However, the 'forbidding countenance' was on the day of his trial, so it was unlikely that he would have presented any other appearance![32] Letters produced at Devan's trial written by him to his father and authenticated by his neighbour, Thomas Woods, an employee of the postal service in Carrickmacross, suggested another side to his character: six times he used the term 'dear father'; he signed off 'your loving and affection[ate] son' and 'your dutiful son'. The general content implied an affectionate bond between father and son and highlighted a certain respect that Devan had for his father and an inherent trust that he would not believe the rumours circulated about him after he left the neighbourhood.[33]

But there was also a more ruthless side to Devan. As far as he was concerned Edward Lynch and Thomas Rooney had to be punished; an example would have to be made to deter others from informing. Lynch and Rooney had been paid a £20 reward by the grand jury of Louth for prosecuting Shanley, Tiernan and Conlon and this information would have been generally known.[34] Moreover, following this initial payment Lynch seems to have continued to act as an informer; an entry dated 22 October 1816 in the Wildgoose Lodge reward payment books, a week before the second raid on Lynch's home, states: 'S. Pendleton Esqr for Lynch (Co. Louth), half year to 10 October: £7 10s'.[35] This was a climate in which informers were severely dealt with. In 1836, G.C. Lewis wrote:

> A man who has given information or evidence against a Whiteboy is doomed to certain death. If he attempted to return from the assizes to his house, he would be hunted through the country like a mad dog; every hand would be raised against him. A man who takes land over another's head may be spared; but a man who has given evidence to

politics (Dublin, 1981), p. 20; see also Smyth, *Men of no property*, p. 115. **31** Carleton, 'Wildgoose Lodge', p. 354. **32** *Belfast Newsletter*, 29 July 1817. **33** These letters are reproduced in chapters four and five. **34** Murray, *The burning of Wildgoose Lodge*, p. 98. **35** Ibid., p. 320.

convict a Whiteboy may (in the language of the threatening notices) 'make ready his coffin'.[36]

In the months that followed the July 1816 assizes, Thomas Rooney became the primary target of revenge. According to Fr Loughran:

> Rooney, who was son-in-law to Lynch, and joint prosecutor … felt a remorse of conscience for what he had sworn, between the time the unhappy convicts received their sentence, and the period destined for their execution, he communicated his uneasiness, and expressed a wish to retract his testimony, which he afterwards refused doing. This pre-varication incensed the friends of those who died, and prompted them to enter into the inhuman resolution of acting as they have done of set-ting fire to the house wherein Lynch, Rooney and their family lived.[37]

After the assizes, Rooney had been kept in Dundalk jail for a time for his own safety, a common practice in such circumstances. Samuel Pendleton wanted to move him to Kilmainham jail in Dublin but instead Rooney returned home and sought protection from local landlord, William Filgate, who along with 'other gentlemen of the neighbourhood' provided Rooney and Lynch with arms for their defence.[38] A constable continued to stay in the lodge for a time after the trial; a song that survived down to the late nineteenth century tells of the guard who: 'stood on Rooney's duty for 13d a day/And he couldn't wed his daughter till he received his pay'. (The significance of the second line seems to have been lost.) T.G.F. Paterson, while researching his 1950 account of the burn-ing claimed to have met an employee of the O'Reillys of Knockabbey Castle who told him that his ancestors had guarded Lynch and Rooney after the trials.[39]

According to traditional accounts, Devan harnessed local hostility towards Lynch and Rooney through the organisation of a series of meetings in various locations such as Ballykelly, Killanny and Corcreaghy (all areas on the Louth-Monaghan border where there were important crossroads). But the crucial meet-ing took place in Stonetown chapel on 29 October 1816. Much was to be made of the fact in contemporary newspaper accounts that a Roman Catholic place of worship was used, particularly by the anti-Catholic Emancipation *Belfast Newsletter*. However, when the Catholic Church came under attack for what was termed its involuntary compliance,[40] the pro-Emancipation *Dublin Evening*

36 Lewis, *Local disturbances in Ireland*, pp 264–5. **37** Quoted in *Dundalk Examiner*, 5 Nov. 1881. **38** Evidence of William Filgate; *Correspondent*, July 1817. **39** Mathews, *The burning of Wildgoose Lodge*, p. 4; Paterson, 'The burning of Wildgoose Lodge', p. 178. **40** See chapter five.

Post argued with some justification that nothing extraordinary, sinister or deeply symbolic should have been read into the location of the meeting place:

> It was a better rendezvous than a barn, because it was more detached, and because there was easy access to it, Devan having custody of the key. It was better than a cabin, because it was more private and commodious [even Carleton's Captain makes reference to this when he told his men: '… well for us it is that the chapel is in a lonely place, or our foolish noise might do us no good'.[41]] The fact of all the parties directly interested in the horrid league, the conspirators as well as those conspired against, being Catholics, keeps the circumstance of the meeting in the chapel free of all the importance which is sought to be attached to it. It could only borrow interest from a difference of religion existing between the murderers and murdered.[42]

What of the timing? Was the night of 29–30 October chosen for a deliberate reason? It was two nights before Hallow E'en, according to ancient custom 'the night of the dead', when recreational vandalism, to borrow a more modern term, was a feature of rural society as men, sometimes dressed in straw hoods and skirts (strawboys), broke windows, smashed doors, stole gates and carried out a variety of other malicious pranks often on despised neighbours. Moreover, there was an old proverb: 'Everyone has debts at Hallow E'en'.[43] These were not all material debts and there seems to have been some significance attached to the fact that this was deemed the appropriate time of the year for the local secret society to exact its dues from Lynch and Rooney. Alice Rispin, an approver, was to testify in the case of John Keegan that he had boasted to her 'he would be the first of 12 men who would stand forward to burn Lynch, his house and family to ashes, and they should not eat their supper on Holy-Eve night [1 November]'.[44] Other witnesses such as Mary Butler recalled the night of the burning so clearly because it was 'within one or two of Hollintide'.[45] One should not disregard the hold of superstition upon the mindset of the people of rural Ireland at this time (and indeed for a long time after).[46]

This was also a busy and important time of the year for farmers and labourers. The fair of Ardee had been held on 23 October that would have provided

41 Carleton, 'Wildgoose Lodge', p. 356.   **42** *Dublin Evening Post,* 16 Mar. 1818.   **43** Glassie, *Passing the time* (Dublin, 1982), p. 282; Kevin Danaher, *The year in Ireland: Irish calendar customs* (Cork, 1972), pp 200–27; E. Estyn Evans, 'Peasant beliefs in nineteenth century Ireland' in D.J. Casey and R.E. Rhodes (eds), *Views of the Irish peasantry, 1800–1916* (Hamden, CT, 1977), p. 53. **44** *Belfast Newsletter,* 7 Apr. 1818.   **45** Ibid.   **46** Evans, 'Peasant beliefs', p. 53.

an important opportunity for men from different surrounding parishes to meet and plan.[47] The fair of Ardee's catchment area included Reaghstown, Tallanstown, Killanny, Carrickmacross, Inniskeen, east Cavan, Drumconrath and Meath Hill, areas from where separate gangs were to converge on Wildgoose Lodge a week later.

As well as market time, 1 November signified the end of the farming year when all livestock had to be secured for the winter, all crops had to be harvested and stored; wages and rents had to be paid (1 November and 1 May were traditionally the two gale days) and all conacre had to be settled. It was therefore an important time for an agrarian society to make a statement of its intent towards those who might transgress in the future, those, for example, who might agree to pay more for conacre than the local economy could sustain in a time of deepening economic crisis. 1816 had been a particularly bad season. An agricultural report for the end of August concluded: 'In Ireland … the harvest has been retarded by cold unnatural weather and perpetual rains.' The report which followed in October recorded the destruction to the wheat crop, the prevalence of mildew and blight, the inferior nature of oats, 'much of the lying corn had vegetated before it was completely fit for reaping', potatoes were abundant but deficient in quality and concluded: 'It is to be dreaded that during the ensuing winter the poor will suffer most severely from want of fuel.'[48] All during October Peel had attempted to ascertain the state of the country from local correspondents. The news was not good. B.T. Balfour of Townley Hall near Drogheda told him that 'the probable effects of combined disaffection and starvation upon millions cannot be contemplated without something more than apprehension', while Major General Burnet reported that in Louth, Monaghan, Armagh and Cavan: 'scarcely any of the crops of grain has been got in and that which is in the low grounds I fear will not be saved. The poor are suffering more from the rising prices of meal and potatoes and want of work as no harvest work can be done in this weather'.[49] Large farmers and the magistracy anticipated that crime would accompany distress. Thus on 9 October 1816, W. H. Trotter wrote to Sir Robert Peel:

> Horror and dismay appear in the countenances of the landholders and the labouring poor are much worse. Great apprehensions are entertained

47 Jennifer Kelly has noted that 'the timing of at least some Ribbon meetings seems to have been deliberately organised around fair days in the northern half of Ireland': Kelly, 'Ribbonism in Co. Leitrim', p. 144. 48 'Agricultural report, 30 Aug. 1816, 26 Oct. 1816' taken from *Newry Magazine, 1816*; quoted in Murray, *The burning of Wildgoose Lodge*, pp 29–30. 49 B.T. Balfour to Robert Peel, 9 Oct. 1816; Major General Burnet to Peel, 10 Oct. 1816; both quoted in Murray, *The burning of Wildgoose Lodge*, pp 31–2, 33.

amongst the farmers and the latter will resort to violence and robbery during the winter, and no doubt many of the idle and profligate will take advantage of the public distress for the purpose of plunder.[50]

John Mathews suggested another reason for the timing of the raid – Lynch and his family had got so tired of living with fear and under protection that they decided to quit the lodge and move into the town of Dundalk. The date they fixed was 1 November, after the potatoes had been harvested. If the move was planned it was probably generally well known but as Mathews concluded: 'to the carrying out of this arrangement there was an awful interruption'.[51]

Devan convened the meeting in Stonetown chapel about an hour after nightfall, which would have meant it was late evening rather than midnight as Carleton depicted.[52] The night has usually been described along the lines first represented by Carleton. In his 1897 account John Mathews, for example, wrote:

> It was indeed a violent, troubled night for a rendezvous; one of those nights when the fir trees writhe and struggle with the wind, the oaks rock angrily, and the elms lash the air in desperate despair ... If ever the devils wander in the darkness prompting hopeless men to despair, urging bad men to murder and to cruelty, and rejoicing at the growth and progress of wickedness wherever planning or accomplishing, this is the night that should bring them on such ghastly journey, such is the storm that should shroud and cover them in their exulting search, leaving behind a wake of wreck, death and destruction.[53]

But there is no historical evidence to suggest that it was such a night. According to the journal of Henry McClintock (1783–1843) who resided a few miles from Dundalk at Drumcar, 28 October 1816 was a 'fine day'; Tuesday 29 October was 'a showry [sic] day'; and Wednesday 30 October was a 'very cold day'. Thursday 31 October was once again a 'fine day', as were the two following days.[54] In her diary, Marianne Fortescue recorded on 6 November that 'there was a large meeting of magistrates here to talk over the horrid business at Wildgoose Lodge ... the weather very fine & mild'.[55] One of the approvers, Patrick Murphy, also recalled that it was 'a dry night', while one of Thomas Gubby's statements described it as 'not a very windy night'.[56] This, of course,

50 W.H. Trotter to Sir Robert Peel, 9 Oct. 1816; quoted in Murray, *The burning of Wildgoose Lodge*, p. 31. 51 Mathews, *The burning of Wildgoose Lodge*, p. 4. 52 *Kilkenny Moderator*, 12, 19 Mar. 1818. 53 Mathews, *The burning of Wildgoose Lodge*, p. 4. 54 O'Neill (ed.), *Journal of Henry McClintock*, pp 210–11. 55 Noel Ross (ed.), *The diary of Marianne Fortescue* (Dundalk, n.d.), p. 502. 56 *Drogheda Journal*, 4 Apr. 1818; Statement of Thomas Gubby, 12 Apr. 1817 (NA, SOC

probably makes sense as it would be hard to see the purpose of setting out to torch a thatched house on the type of extremely wet, stormy night as described by Carleton and others for obvious melodramatic effect.

Carleton's description of the power and control that Devan exerted over his followers is less fictional (and Carleton would have sensed this from having lived amongst Devan's neighbours). An estimated forty men assembled in the chapel.[57] They came from the surrounding districts of Stonetown, the town and rural hinterland of Louth (these would most likely have travelled down the Barnamaaher road that linked Louth with Ballykelly and then travelled the short distance on to Stonetown), Corcreaghy and Killanny. They were joined by a contingent from Inniskeen including a blacksmith named Bryan Lennon from the townland of Drumass, who came armed with a sledge. Others were armed with pistols and pitchforks.[58]

What is not known is who orchestrated the other gangs from within about a ten miles radius to converge simultaneously on the lodge. While the Stonetown meeting was taking place groups of men were preparing to leave from south Monaghan, north Meath, east Cavan as well as the rural hinterland of Ardee. For example, a gang left from Meath Hill and proceeded to the crossroads at Ballinahone where they met about seven other men. This gang went on to Churchtown where they procured three horses.[59] Another group left from Kingscourt.[60] A party that left Carrickleck met with other gangs at Ballyvorneen, Drumbride and Churchtown. Their passage to Wildgoose Lodge was facilitated by the extensive road network that by 1816 stretched across the region. The important trade route that was described in a survey of 1736 as 'the great road from Monaghan to Drogheda' cut through Killanny and Corcreaghy on its way towards Ardee.[61] This route also linked the other important market and export town of Dundalk with east Cavan – a lease in the Filgate papers refers to 'a lane running into the turnpike road leading from Kingscourt to Dundalk'.[62] Close to Devan's home was Corcreaghy crossroads where a number of roads converged that led to the post towns of Louth, Dundalk, Tallanstown, Ardee and Carrickmacross and then on to Newry, Drogheda and Dublin.

One coincidence that is very much worth noting is that all the areas from which the different groups left had lands owned by William Filgate Sr of Lisrenny or else his son, William Jr, acted as agent on behalf of local landlords

1828/15). **57** *Kilkenny Moderator,* 12, 19 Mar. 1818. **58** *Dublin Evening Post,* 10 Mar. 1818; *Kilkenny Moderator,* 19 Mar. 1818. **59** *FJ,* 6 Apr. 1818. **60** *Kilkenny Moderator,* 12 Mar. 1818. **61** E.P. Shirley, *Some account of the territory or dominions of Farney* (London, 1845), p. 204. **62** Lease between A.J. Foster and trustees of Rocktate schoolhouse [parish of Killanny], 4 April 1844 (Dundalk Museum, Filgate papers, PO14/55).

(including members of his own family) in one or more of them. People who lived on an estate formed their own community and even if in the case of the Filgate estate it was fragmented over a geographical area that included parts of Louth (Tallanstown, Reaghstown, Dromin and Lisrenny), Monaghan (in the parish of Inniskeen) and Meath (around Carrickleck), with agency concerns in all three counties as well as possibly Cavan, the tenantry were tied together by the common bonds of estate management policy.[63] It was not unknown in the early nineteenth century for a wave of agrarian crime to be sparked by the management policy of an individual landlord or his agent. Shunsuke Katsuta has argued that the Rockite movement that began in west Limerick in 1821 can be traced to Alexander Hoskins' harsh management of the Courtenay estate.[64] It has already been concluded in chapter two that the 1821 census figures show 339 uninhabited houses in the barony of Ardee, tentatively suggesting large-scale evictions on the Filgate (as well as other landlord) estates in the recent past and they suggest a move towards the consolidation of farms as landlords and middlemen contemplated the return to pasture farming which in turn, resulted in the unemployment of significant numbers of former tillage labourers.[65] The Filgates were also magistrates in both Louth and Monaghan and it was, of course, to William Sr that the first raid had been reported. Therefore, the attack on the lodge could be construed as an attack on the ailing William Filgate Sr (he died in December 1816 a few weeks after the burning) and his land agent son; and Ribbon involvement, while still a distinct possibility given the activity around Carrickmacross and Ardee at this time, was not necessarily the facilitator of the conjoined efforts of gangs from different locations. The fact that Wildgoose Lodge was Filgate property and tenanted by Lynch made it doubly attractive to avengers.

Certainly in the aftermath of the burning and later executions the unpopularity of the Filgates stretched physically from south Monaghan to mid-Louth, at least, and mentally from before the burning to well into the twentieth century. Pat Malone is said to have shouted after Wildgoose Lodge collapsed: 'All is well now, if we only had Filgate.'[66] In the trial of three conspirators for the attempted murder of the rector of Killanny, Sir Harcourt Lees, in 1820, one of the accused was alleged to have said in a public house in Carrickmacross, 'he

63 National Library of Ireland, Ainsworth reports on private collections, no. 24, pp 465–8. 64 Shunsuka Katsuta, 'The Rockite movement in County Cork in the early 1820s' in *IHS*, 33:131 (May 2003), p. 279. 65 E. Margaret Crawford, 'Dietary considerations in pre-Famine Louth and its environs' in Gillespie and O'Sullivan (eds), *The borderlands*, p. 121; for an incisive study of Co. Meath at this time, see Peter Connell, *The land and people of county Meath, 1750–1850* (Dublin, 2004). 66 Mathews, *The burning of Wildgoose Lodge*, p. 7.

would shoot Filgate and Sir Harcourt Lees for they were not worthy to live'.[67] In 1822, John Deery, a prisoner at Dundalk jail recalled how in November 1816, a Ribbon plot was hatched in a shebeen house belonging to Mary Clinton in Carrickmacross to murder William Filgate Sr.[68] When Bernard McIlroy was arrested around February 1817, he is supposed to have provided F.D. Hamilton, a magistrate, with information on the 'attempt on the life of William Filgate.'[69] Around the same time, William Jr had the protection of two army privates stationed at his residence in Kiltybegs, near Inniskeen.[70] By the middle of the same month, he was calling for the stationing of more soldiers on parts of his estates around Kiltybegs and Corcreaghy.[71] In January 1820, the governor of Dundalk jail, John Crowe, reported to him that 'a conspiracy has been formed by some people between Dunleer and Collon to take advantage of you when hunting in that part of the country ...'[72] Over 100 years later, in February 1922, at a Sinn Féin meeting in Knockbridge, James Filgate, a bailiff from Dundalk, was met with cries of 'Gripper' and 'Wildgoose Lodge'.[73] He was perhaps related to a junior branch of the landlord family who once owned the lodge or it may simply be that the coincidence of surname and occupation was tantamount to attracting hostile attention.

Returning to the night of 29 October 1816, it should first of all be pointed out to the reader that much of what follows is drawn from the accounts of the incident given by approvers, whose unreliability as witnesses will be discussed in the following chapters. However, the point should also be made, as will become clear later in this work, that they were presenting information gathered by the authorities over a period of months from local informers and so the facts as represented in court should not be readily dismissed.

When the men gathered at Stonetown chapel, whiskey was distributed liberally, as Carleton suggested, and the men were later 'topped up' near Reaghstown (Arthurstown) chapel. Bernard McIlroy claimed he drank as much as he wanted at Reaghstown from a jug passed round, having already had his quota at Stonetown. Patrick Murphy in his 'voluntary confession' claimed: 'The body attacking the house were more or less drunk.'[74] Whether men drank to

67 *The Times*, 2 Aug. 1820. 68 Notes of a confession made by John Deery, a prisoner in Dundalk gaol on 5 June 1822 and initialled by William Filgate Jr (Dundalk Library, WGL papers). 69 F.D. Hamilton to William Filgate, 5 June 1817 (NA, SOC 1817, 1828/13). 70 Lt-Col Ramsay to Sir William Gregory, 2 Feb. 1817 (NA, SOC, 1813/38). 71 Lt-Gen Lord Forbes to William Gregory, 18 Feb. 1817 (NA, SOC 1817, 1828/3). 72 John Crowe to William Filgate, 1 Jan. 1820 (Dundalk Library, WGL papers); for other attempts on Filgate's life, see Thomas Kidd to William Filgate, 14 Aug. 1821; Ibid. 73 *Dundak Democrat*, 23 Feb. 1918. 74 'Voluntary confession' of Patrick Murphy taken by John Pollock, A.H.C. Pollock and Samuel Pendleton, 12 Mar. 1817 (in private possession).

give themselves courage or simply for enjoyment is largely irrelevant; what is significant is the fact that despite McIlroy's admission in court that he had overindulged, the authorities and the courts readily accepted his evidence and did not doubt his ability to identify suspects who had been strangers to him before that night, some of whom he only saw scurrying about in the mayhem of shadows.[75] Moreover, illicitly distilled poteen, which is most likely what the men had to drink, is extremely potent and undoubtedly played a crucial role in heightening men's passions during the raid.

The men who left Stonetown chapel divided into two groups before they reached the Mills of Louth, not far from Tallanstown. There was a watchman's tower at the Mills, so they had to be careful to avoid detection.[76] As they neared Wildgoose Lodge they met the various other gangs. Amongst these were thirty men mounted on fifteen horses who had come a distance from the Carrickleck area of Co. Meath. Another group came by boat, presumably down the River Glyde, which at that stage had burst its banks flooding the plains at the foot of Wildgoose Lodge.[77] The gangs became more rowdy and boisterous. A man named Carroll, who lived in one of the houses nearest the lodge, opened the door of his cabin only to be told by one of the gang: 'Shut up, or I'll blow out your brains.'[78]

At that stage Devan took control of the arriving parties. He ordered a circle of men to cordon off the lodge.[79] The most pertinent question is what was their intention? Did Devan and his followers set out to massacre all in the house including the women and an infant or did they set out to assault (and possibly murder) Lynch and Rooney alone? Did they even set out to burn the house? Shortly after the arrests of Tiernan, Shanley and Conlon, Samuel Pendleton had been secretly informed that all of the others involved in the raid on Wildgoose Lodge had gathered together and swore that if any more of them were appre-hended those who remained free would 'put to death the witnesses and burn them'.[80] Notably the only other farmer who seems to have reported a raid on his house around the same time as the raid on Wildgoose Lodge was John Reath, a wealthy farmer from Irishtown near Ardee, who was robbed of £200 and a number of arms. One man was subsequently tried and executed on the evidence

75 Evidence of Bernard McIlroy; *Kilkenny Moderator,* 12 Mar. 1818; see also evidence of Thomas Gubby in *Drogheda Journal,* 4 Apr. 1818. 76 *Belfast Newsletter,* 7 Apr. 1818. 77 *Papers relating to disturbances in the County of Louth,* H.C. 1817, vol. viii (263). 491. 78 Extract of an anony-mous letter, addressed Ardee, 1 Nov. 1816; *FJ,* 4 Nov. 1816. 79 Samuel Pendleton to Robert Peel, 30 Oct. 1816 (NA, SOC 1763/34); evidence of Bernard McIlroy in *Kilkenny Moderator,* 12 Mar. 1818; *Dublin Evening Post,* 2 Nov. 1816; *FJ,* 4 Nov. 1816; see also evidence of Patrick Halpenny at Devan's trial in *Enniskillen Chronicle and Erne Packet,* 31 July 1817. 80 Samuel Pendleton to Robert Peel, 7 Nov. 1816 (NA, SOC 1763/35).

of Reath. In January 1817, Reath was shot dead while having supper with his family, a blunderbuss fired through the window blew his head to pieces.[81] His family was not harmed. Around the same time as the first raid on Wildgoose Lodge, the house and outoffices of a farmer named Treanor near Ball's Mills in south Armagh were set on fire: 'in revenge, as is supposed, for a prosecution carried on by him against some person' at the previous assizes. Towards the end of March, in the same area, the house of Arthur Harrison was also fired in revenge for him having prosecuted two men at Armagh assizes.[82] In neither case were attempts made by the raiders to ensure that the target or his family could not escape.

According to Carleton's account, the men who left Stonetown chapel took with them 'a live coal' in a small pot.[83] The intent, he suggested, was therefore to burn the house, which would have fitted in with his overall agenda to highlight the callousness of Ribbonmen (as he described them.) However, according to Patrick Murphy's original deposition taken on 12 March 1817, the raiders did not have fire with them when they arrived at the lodge. Instead four or five men rushed to the door and called on Lynch and Rooney to open it. Those inside panicked and bolted the doors. Lynch and Rooney loaded four guns they had been given for their protection following the April raid.[84] They probably feared another raid at worst. One of them shouted at the raiders that they would shoot anybody who dared enter. John Kieran attempted to do so and was wounded by a gun blast in the face.[85] According to Murphy it was at this stage some of the raiders ran off in search of fire to a nearby cabin belonging to Patrick Halpenny.[86] Thus it may be that their reactions to the shooting of Kieran were impassioned by their drunkenness. It was not until the trials that Murphy changed his account and stated in court that some of the men had carried fire with them in a pot to the lodge.[87] This later version suggested to the jurors the deliberate intention of the raiders to carry out a premeditated heinous plan and so the burning could not be interpreted then or later as the spontaneous act of a group of drunken men whose passions were excited by the shooting of one of their number.

The lodge was thatched which for obvious reasons left it particularly vulnerable to incendiaries. (Richard Griffiths, of primary valuation fame, was to

81 Samuel Pendleton to William Gregory, 29 Dec. 1816; Samuel Pendleton to Robert Peel, 17 Jan. 1817; both in *Papers relating to disturbances in the County of Louth*, H.C. 1817, vol. viii (263), 491; *Correspondent*, 20 Jan. 1817. 82 Ibid., 19 Mar. 1816. 83 Carleton, 'Wildgoose Lodge', p. 357. 84 Extract of an anonymous letter, addressed Ardee, 1 Nov. 1816; *FJ*, 4 Nov. 1816. 85 *Dublin Evening Post*, 10 Mar. 1818; *Kilkenny Moderator*, 12 Mar. 1818. 86 Statement of Patrick Murphy, 12 Mar. 1817 (NA, SOC 1829/15). 87 *Kilkenny Moderator*, 19 Mar. 1818.

conclude in the early 1820s that 'no farmer who resides in a thatched cottage dare oppose anything he is directed to do, and consequently they are quite under the control of the disturbers of the peace'.)[88] The majority of men stood back while the few with the lighted turf set about firing the lodge.[89] None of the historical evidence provides the explicit details of Carleton's version but even its sensationalism hardly captures the horror of the night. Eye witnesses later claimed that as the flames leapt across the roof of Wildgoose Lodge, Thomas Rooney called out for mercy for his child but Devan shouted at him: 'Rooney, these are not old times – this night is your doom.'[90] A number of witnesses agreed on this exchange, which suggests that Devan and Rooney had been acquainted in the past and perhaps had even been comrades in the secret society. At that stage the fearful cries of the women and the child could be clearly heard. Patrick Clarke recalled: 'the shrieks of the people inside would terrify anyone'.[91] Clarke claimed that there were those present who wanted to save the 'innocent', presumably meaning the servants, women and child, but Devan was having none of it.[92] A woman called out: 'I am the servant girl. I have no call to the house. Let me out.' A member of the gang coldly replied: 'You did not take warning in time'.[93] According to the informer, Thomas Gubby, those who wanted to save the women and children were told by Devan: 'the nits should be burned and destroyed as well as the louse'.[94] Even though Gubby is the most unreliable of the informers and was almost certainly not even at the Lodge on the night,[95] it is this phrase that has remained synonymous with the cruelty associated with the burning of Wildgoose Lodge; there are few published or oral accounts that do not attribute it to Devan.

As the cry of no mercy went up, Bryan Lennon, the blacksmith from Inniskeen, sprang forward with a sledgehammer and broke in the door of the lodge. More and more flax and unthreshed straw was then piled inside to fan the flames.[96] As John Mathews put it: 'The hay yard furnished the funeral pile for its unhappy owner.'[97] All signs of life inside the house soon dissipated. Some of the raiders shouted and huzzaed and threw their hats in the air in celebration as the roof finally collapsed. Patrick Murphy later recalled some of them 'wishing Lynch joy of his hot bed'. Another man allegedly turned to a comrade and asked him: 'Do you think the goose will be soon well done?' – a darkly humorous

88 Quoted in Beames, *Peasants and power*, p. 78.   **89** *Enniskillen Chronicle*, 31 July 1817; *FJ*, 6 Apr. 1818.   **90** *Dublin Evening Post*, 10 Mar. 1818.   **91** *Correspondent*, 28 July 1817; *Dublin Evening Post*, 10 Mar. 1818.   **92** *Correspondent*, 28 July 1817.   **93** Statement of Patrick Murphy, 12 Mar. 1817 (NA, SOC, 1829/15).   **94** Statement of Thomas Gubby, 9 Apr. 1817 (NA, SOC 1828/15).   **95** See chapter four.   **96** *Enniskillen Chronicle*, 31 July 1817.   **97** Mathews, *The burning of Wildgoose Lodge*, p. 7.

14 'Another word' said the Captain 'an you're a corpse',
taken from William Carleton, *Traits and stories* (1833 ed.).

reference to the name of the house – to which the other replied, 'Yes, and the gander too', and both men burst into laughter.[98] Devan then gave the final order to the men to scatter and return to their homes. According to McIlroy: 'Every man before they separated took an oath never to divulge the proceedings of the night, under pain of suffering the same torture which Rooney did.'[99]

How long the horror lasted is difficult to determine: Patrick Halpenny, Lynch's nearest neighbour, suggested it might have been as long as two hours.[1] This was a densely populated area and the location of the Lodge on a hill would have meant the flames from it would have been seen for miles around. Mary Butler lived at Aclint, across the bog from the lodge. She was up late baking bread – 'it was late when she got the word from her husband to bake' – and when she saw the fire at around 2 a.m. she alerted her husband who, in turn, went to three other neighbours to raise the alarm. The Mohans, Taafes and Butlers all gathered near the latter's house but ventured no further; they were all afraid they would be killed if they went to the rescue. James Butler said: 'he heard firing of guns and a great noise of bloody war there'. Patrick Butler claimed: 'they heard several shots and were afraid'; the shots suggested to him that the fire was not accidental, otherwise: 'it would have been his duty to have

98 *FJ*, 8 Apr. 1818. **99** *Correspondent*, 28 July 1817; *Belfast Newsletter*, 7 Apr. 1818; *Dundalk Examiner*, 22 Oct. 1881. **1** *Correspondent*, 28 July 1817.

gone to help put the fire out'. Michael Mohan's brother was married to Edward Lynch's sister but instead of getting his family to go help, he stood: 'all about the street ... trembling about the fire'.[2]

In the cold light of day, the eight bodies were found in the ruins. According to Patrick Halpenny: 'all was burned, the roof had fallen in, and nothing remained but the walls and a few old rafters'.[3] One eyewitness, Alice Rispin, mother of the servant boy, James, claimed the infant Rooney was found between his father's knees as if the latter had been attempting to shelter the child from the devouring flames.[4] If Rispin's evidence is correct, then Thomas and Bridget Rooney must have huddled together with their child before they died which casts doubts on the authenticity of the various stories regarding the mother's attempts to save her child by thrusting it out the window only to have it thrust back at her on a pike, or of the appearance of Rooney on the wall of the gable end of the house where he, too, was supposedly piked and thrown back into the flames.

Unfortunately, all that survives of the coroner's report is a brief reference to it in the local newspapers stating that within hours of the outrage, H.M. Blackwell went to the lodge to hold an inquest. His verdict was rather predictable: 'wilful and malicious murder of the eight persons, by being burned in their house by persons unknown'.[5] Most of the bodies were burned beyond recognition. When Samuel Pendleton arrived at the scene the following morning, he found the bodies 'to be so far consumed as to be barely distinguishable from each other'.[6] William Filgate said at Devan's trial in July 1817 that 'he could not positively say that the objects he saw at Wildgoose Lodge next morning were dead bodies, except one in which a small vestige of human form remained'.[7]

The mysterious survivor

Before leaving this account of the burning, it is important to deal with what is probably the most mysterious aspect of the story. T.G.F. Paterson in his account refers to a local folk tale that 'most of those concerned in the attack were identified by a woman who was brought into Dundalk and placed in a house for that purpose'.[8] Local tradition claims that this woman survived the fire and

2 *Belfast Newsletter*, 7 Apr. 1818. 3 *Correspondent*, 28 July 1817. 4 *FJ*, 12 Mar. 1818. 5 Copy letter John Foster to Robert Peel, 30 Oct. 1816; *Papers relating to disturbances in the County of Louth*, HC 1817, vol. viii (263), 491; original in PRONI, Foster papers, D207/39/59. 6 Copy of letter from Samuel Pendleton to Robert Peel, 30 Oct. 1816; *Papers relating to disturbances in the County of Louth*. 7 *Enniskillen Chronicle*, 31 July 1817. 8 Paterson, 'The burning of Wildgoose Lodge', p. 59.

came back to wreak revenge. What of the historical evidence? On 9 March 1817, Under-Secretary William Gregory wrote to Sir Robert Peel:

> I have the girl in Dublin who was saved from the massacre at Lynch's; she has been wonderfully tutored, & as yet has told of no one, but I hope from this kind manner in which she is treated & removed from her mother and friends, the truth may yet come out. Had Pendleton immediately on her discovery taken possession of her, we might have had [?some] information.[9]

Gregory identified her only as 'a survivor'. About two years after the atrocity, Sir Robert Peel corroborated her existence at a dinner at Moresfield House in England, hosted by Lady Frances Shelley, who later recorded in her diary:

> Mr Peel also told us that in the county of Louth a house was surrounded, set fire to, and burned to the ground. Thirteen people, who were living in it, were supposed to have been killed, but afterwards it was found that a girl of fifteen had escaped. She was brought up to Dublin. Although every means were employed to tempt her to give evidence, nothing they could say or do could induce the girl to utter a word on the subject. She said she had been saved; but by whom or in what manner, she firmly refused to say. She told the court that she could not possibly live in her own country if she spoke out, and, as she would not live anywhere else, she was determined to hold her tongue.[10]

The notion of a survivor from the holocaust seems scarcely credible given the rest of the evidence that survives to suggest that absolutely no mercy was shown on the night. That a five-month-old infant was not spared might imply the improbability of anyone else being released from the house. Unless there were outoffices at Wildgoose Lodge, which is probable given that Lynch was a progressive farmer (see illustration 13, page 111), and a servant girl was in hiding in one of them during the raid observing all that happened. Peel's story as recorded by Shelley (and its inaccuracies regarding the number killed, for example, should be noted) suggests that she was reluctant to give any information to the authorities, knowing full well what the consequences of her actions might be. Shelley's account further implies she was called as a witness in court but there is no reference in any of the surviving historical records to verify this.[11]

9 William Gregory to Robert Peel, 9 Mar. 1817, 9 Apr. 1817 (British Museum, Peel papers, MS 40,203). 10 Richard Edgcumbe (ed.), *The diary of Frances Lady Shelley* (London, 1912), p. 19. 11 See conculsion regarding payments to informers.

On the other hand, given both Gregory's communication and Peel's dinner conversation, it is difficult to discount the possibility that there was a survivor, not necessarily a young girl who was released from the house on the night, but one who was fortunate enough to have remained undetected in an out-office, possibly where she usually slept. Perhaps Peel was simply being guarded with his dinner comments given that the Wildgoose Lodge trials had just recently concluded. The evidence shows that Gregory's communication regarding the young survivor was dated 9 March 1817. She had been in police custody for some days. From October 1816 to March 1817 the authorities had made no arrests.[12] It is something of a coincidence that less than a week after the young woman was taken into custody the first wave of arrests began. Traditionally these captures were seen to have been the result of information and names provided by approvers from 12 March 1817 onwards, but as this work will suggest names were more likely to have been fed by the authorities to the approvers rather than the other way around and so it may very well have been this young woman who provided the authorities with their major breakthrough, at least regarding the facts of what happened on the night.

There is one other interesting piece of historical evidence that suggests a young woman with some connection to the events at Wildgoose Lodge was given safe passage from Ireland. In one of the Wildgoose Lodge informer payment books for 1819, there is an entry for 17 August stating that £28 7s. 8d. was paid to the Honorable Colonel Robert Le Poer Trench for the 'expense of sending Judith Lynch home from New Brunswick'.[13] Robert Trench (1782–1823) was a son of William Trench, first earl of Clancarty. His sister, Ann (d. 1833), was married to William Gregory. (Another sister, Elizabeth, was married to John McClintock of Drumcar in Louth, parents of the aforementioned diarist, Henry McClintock.) The highly decorated Trench (KCB, KTS), a lieutenant-colonel in the 74th Regiment, had played a prominent role in the Peninsular War 1808–14, and in 1818, the same year the Wildgoose Lodge trials ended, was sent to New Brunswick.[14] Was Judith Lynch the young survivor referred to by Gregory? Did he send her to New Brunswick with his brother-in-law out of harm's way in the knowledge that it was expedient to provide her with safe passage from Ireland for even if she had not provided the information required, the fact that she was taken into custody was enough to arouse communal suspicion of her as an informer particularly when the arrests of suspects began so shortly after her detention. If she was sent with Trench did she then decide to

12 See chapter four.   13 A transcript of the payments are to be found in Murray, *The burning of Wildgoose Lodge*, pp 320–1.   14 http://glosters.tripod.com/allwot.htm (4 Jan. 2007).

return the following year to Ireland and take her chances? The fact that a mother is mentioned in Gregory's letter meant she was not a daughter of Edward's as he was a widower but Lynch was a common name in the area at the time. She could have been a relative or a neighbour possibily employed as a servant.

Who was involved in the burning of Wildgoose Lodge?

Most of the participants cannot now be identified, and as later chapters will show not all of those subsequently tried were present on the night. But by using the historical evidence available on those suspected and/or tried we can at least deduce the social backgrounds of those likely to have been involved in the local society. The occupation of thirteen tried suspects has been identified, including that of Devan, schoolmaster and parish clerk. Of the other twelve, three were labourers, three were weavers, two were hacklers (flax combers), one was a stonemason (on Lord Louth's estate), one a blacksmith, one was described as a turfman's son and one, Thomas McCullough, was a wealthy weaver-farmer. The fact that six of those identified were associated with the linen industry hints at the significance of its collapse. Some of the men may have fitted Carleton's stereotypes – Hudy McElearney, for example, was described during his trial as 'an old malignant convict'[15] – but the majority were probably of the same class backgrounds as the others described above, reflecting the social composition of most secret agrarian societies of this nature at that time. McCullough was not necessarily an exception. Even though there are serious question marks over whether or not he was actually at Wildgoose Lodge on the night,[16] he had nevertheless come to the attention of the authorities probably as a Ribbonman of the type who had met in Carrickmacross in April 1816 and so he was fairly typical of 'the kinds of people who later became prominent in the activist ranks of later Irish political parties and militant nationalist movements'.[17]

The authorities it seems used the Wildgoose Lodge incident as their chance to arrest and convict McCullough. James Campbell was another who was later arrested on suspicion of involvement in the Wildgoose incident. At the end of May 1816, a month after the aforementioned Ribbon meeting at Carrickmacross, the authorities were alerted to another Ribbon meeting to be held at

15 FJ, 12 Mar. 1818. 16 See chapter six. 17 Lee, 'The Ribbonmen', p. 27; Beames, Peasants and power, pp 53–62; idem, 'The Ribbon societies: lower class nationalism in pre-Famine Ireland' in Past & Present, 97 (Nov., 1982), p. 263; Garvin, 'Defenders, Ribbonmen and others', p. 151; see also Kelly, 'Ribbonism in Co. Leitrim', p. 6.

Castleblayney. On a scrap of paper attached to the report of an informer was a note identifying Campbell as a leading organiser of this meeting.[18] Again this implies there may very well have been recent attempts at Ribbon infiltration of the local societies in an effort to reorganise them for a wider conspiracy; Wildgoose Lodge may have been seen as a rallying point; and Campbell may have been involved in that respect. (Patrick Murphy, an approver, would later claim that the leaders who brought the different gangs to Wildgoose Lodge knew each other through their association in the 'Ribbon organisation' but it is not clear what Ribbonism meant to him.)[19] While McCullough would later plead his innocence, Campbell reportedly admitted to his involvement.[20]

Many of those implicated in the attack on Wildgoose Lodge were the Lynches' parochial neighbours, and would certainly have known them and some may even have been related to Edward Lynch or Rooney. Andrew Rooney (in this case no relation of Thomas) in a sworn statement to Samuel Pendleton named Bryan Malone of Harmonstown 'a near relation of [Thomas] Rooney' as one of the perpetrators and commented: 'it was a barbarous thing of him [Malone] to have anything to do with such a business against his own flesh and blood'.[21] (Rooney's statement contains the names of almost thirty men who were supposed to be at the lodge; all were obviously known to Rooney and so had to be local to the Ardee area. Two were blacksmiths, one was a broom maker and one a servant. None of those on this list seem to have been brought to trial, although some may very well have been members of one or other of the gangs that met at the lodge.) Of those arrested, Hugh McCabe was a near neighbour; the back of his house looked towards the lodge.[22] Thomas McCullough and James Smyth both lived at Arthurstown, about a mile from the lodge. William Butler lived a short distance away at Aclint. It was Butler's father, who, as already noted, claimed that Edward Lynch 'was the best neighbour in the country'.[23] James Smith, John Keegan and Thomas Sheenan were all from the parish of Tallanstown. There were two sets of brothers tried – Laurence and Owen Gaynor and George and Edward McQuillan – from the parish of Louth.[24] Another father and son both named Pat Malone and two brothers-in-law – James Smith (who worked as a wrought-mason for Lord Louth on his Tallanstown demesne) and John Keegan – were also tried. Michael Tiernan and his son, cottiers who lived in a one-room mud cabin near Tallanstown, were father and brother respec-

18 [?] O'Neill to John Stacke, 28 May 1816 (NA, SOC 1816, 1765/68). 19 Affidavit of Patrick Murphy, 12 Mar. 1817 (NA, SOC 1829/15). 20 See chapter five. 21 Statement of Andrew Rooney, 21 April 1817 (NA, SOC 1817, 1828/15). 22 Report of trial of 3 Mar. 1818 from *Faulkner's Dublin Journal*, reproduced in *Dundalk Examiner*, 24 Sept. 1881. 23 Ibid., 29 Oct. 1881. 24 Statement of Peter Gollogly, 14 Apr. 1817 (NA, SOC 1829/27).

tively of Michael Jr who had been executed for the first raid.[25] It is quite likely, as Carleton suggested, that there were others related to Tiernan, Shanley and Conlon who gathered at Wildgoose Lodge. The 100 or so men had a very wide network of family connections and friends. That is essentially why so many were summoned on the night: those who planned the crime knew that they would be sought out by the authorities so a large crowd (as opposed to a handful of men who undoubtedly could have carried out the same act) became their insurance policy that people would be reluctant to inform least one's own son, father, uncle, nephew, cousin, or neighbour might be later arrested.

Whether the 100 or so men went to Wildgoose Lodge willingly or not is a matter of conjecture. Carleton's claim in his autobiography, already noted, that 'when there was no apprehension of legal proceedings against any others than those who had been convicted, several whom Devan had summoned without disclosing to them the frightful object in view, actually admitted that they had been present' is probably a legitimate one.[26] Details from 'Wildgoose Lodge' hint at the fact that the word on the ground during Carleton's time in Killanny was that men had been summoned who knew nothing of their leader's plans; the Captain stated in the chapel: 'I knew if I had told yez the sport, that none of you, except my own boys, would come.'[27] Many of those who gathered on the night possibly did so for reasons of conviviality. Some would have contemplated at worst another raid, hardly considering involvement in a crime of such a heinous nature. Historians who have studied the Ribbon Society or later revolutionary organisations such as the Fenians of the nineteenth century or the IRA of the early twentieth century have pointed to the recreational aspects attached to volunteering.[28] But for many, willingly joining a society and willingly partaking in the more violent crimes were two very different issues: sending threatening letters was one thing; carrying out the threats contained therein was something that required a much stronger constitution. As noted above, the historical evidence suggests that there were those at the lodge who did not have the stomach to see women and children murdered. But once members were summoned and gathered there were few places to hide. A strong indication of this is seen in Carleton's account where the Captain swears vengeance on those

25 Report of trial of 3 Mar. 1818 from *Faulkner's Dublin Journal,* reproduced in *Dundalk Examiner,* 8 Oct. 1881. 26 Carleton, *Autobiography,* p. 116. 27 Carleton, 'Wildgoose Lodge', p. 359. 28 Kelly, 'Ribbonism in Co. Leitrim', p. 209; R.V. Comerford, *Charles J. Kickham: a biography* (Dublin, 1979), p. 58; Peter Hart, *The IRA and its enemies: violence and community in Cork, 1916–1923* (Oxford, 1998), pp 165–83; Elizabeth Malcolm, 'Popular recreation in nineteenth-century Ireland' in Oliver MacDonagh, W.F. Mandle and Pauraic Travers (eds), *Irish culture and nationalism, 1750–1950* (London, 1983), p. 51.

who have refused to turn up at the chapel on the night and he reminds those present that if they shirk their responsibility they, too, will be punished.[29] This was no mere fiction; members of secret societies such as the Whiteboys, bound by oath, regularly intimidated those who refused to join their ranks, sending threatening notices warning destruction of property, personal violence, and even murder.[30] Thus on 10 November 1816 Foster claimed in a letter to Peel that 'the influence of terror' had prevented the waking of the corpses of Rooney and his child in Reaghstown chapel and that notices were posted around the area threatening vengeance and destruction on anyone who prayed for the souls of the victims.[31] This was the outcome of being associated with informing. According to the evidence of the aforementioned Andrew Rooney, a man named Malone, a neighbour of Lynch's, had boasted to him in a public house in Ardee: 'Didn't we destroy Lynch and Rooney so that as long as the world lasts, there will never be a stag [informer] in Ireland again.'[32]

Conclusion

It would be easy to conclude that a crime of this nature engendered a great deal of fear in the rural areas of Louth and its bordering counties amongst a wide cross section of the population. This was undoubtedly true of the gentry class and particularly the large farmer class who bore the brunt of the agitation and whose sense of fear and panic was palpable. Less than three weeks after the murders, John Foster claimed that both social groups were 'living in fear of long winters' nights.'[33]

However, in the case of the lower classes it would be too simplistic to look at it in terms of fear alone. Amongst them there was often a very thin dividing line between fear of the perpetrators (especially in terms of retribution for informing) and actual moral support for them (particularly in face of drastic measures used by the police and yeomanry under the Peace Preservation Act). In 1836 Sir G.C. Lewis commented on the former:

> it is to be remarked that the Whiteboys find in their favour already exist-
> ing a general and settled hatred of the law among the great body of the

---

29 Carleton, *Traits and stories*, ii, pp 351, 353.   **30** Lewis, *On local disturbances in Ireland*, pp 14, 16; see also, Garvin, 'Defenders, Ribbonmen and others', p. 150; Garvin, *Irish nationalist politics*, p. 41; Broeker, *Rural disorder and police reform*, p. 9.   **31** John Foster to Robert Peel, 10 Nov. 1816; *Papers relating to disturbances in the County of Louth*.   **32** Information of Andrew Rooney given to Samuel Pendleton, 21 April 1817 (NA, SOC 1828/15).   **33** John Foster to Robert Peel, 17 Nov. 1816 (NA, SOC 1763/36).

peasantry. The Irish peasant has been accustomed to look upon the law as an engine for oppressing and coercing him, administered by hostile persons and in a hostile spirit.[34]

It is impossible to quantify but equally difficult to avoid surmising that the lower classes retained ancestral grievances in relation to the over zealous actions of the likes of Foster and Blayney in the relatively recent troubles of the later 1790s, early 1800s. In the early nineteenth century, the hostility to the law and those who administered it was not just symptomatic of the perception that a Protestant dominated administration was too favourably disposed to discrimination in judicial and other matters;[35] there was what Tom Garvin has termed a more general (and less sectarian) 'upper-class contempt for the activities of a despised social class'.[36] On 1 November, having received reports on the murders at Wildgoose Lodge, Sir Robert Peel wrote to Lord Sidmouth, secretary of state for Home Affairs (1812–22):

> I do not often trouble you with the detail of individual outrages – but one has been committed in the county of Louth of so atrocious a nature that I cannot help reporting it to you ... It is entirely to be attributed to revenge against the prosecutor – and is but one of many proofs of the wretched depravity and sanguinary disposition of the lower orders of this country.[37]

Like his fellow politicians and administrators Peel considered it his responsibility to protect the propertied classes against 'the wretched depravity' of the lower orders. He made no mention of the fact that this was a crime carried out by Catholics upon Catholics. That was largely incidental – although in some respects he may have perceived this crime to be an opportunity to deal with the 'sanguinary disposition' of the lower classes without having to face any charge of sectarianism – but Peel was not beyond blaming atrocities such as what happened at Wildgoose Lodge on obstacles placed to the better state administration of Ireland by the Roman Catholic Church as evidenced in his letter to Charles Abbott of 25 December 1816 where he concluded 'that the prevailing religion of Ireland operates as an impediment rather than an aid to the ends of the civil government'.[38]

34 Lewis, *Local disturbances in Ireland*, p. 250. 35 Oliver MacDonagh, *States of mind: a study of Anglo-Irish conflict, 1780–1980* (London, 1983), p. 87; see also Gearoid Ó Tuathaigh, *Ireland before the famine, 1798–1848* (Dublin, 1972), pp 87, 89. 36 Garvin, 'Defenders, Ribbonmen and others', p. 244. 37 Peel to Sidmouth, 1 Nov. 1816. 38 See Peel to Abbot, 25 Dec. 1816, quoted above.

In neither letter is there any word of sympathy for the victims but this merely reflected the distance that the upper classes kept from the lower orders. Townley Patten Filgate, the owner of the lodge and Lynch's landlord, simply recorded in his diary on 31 October: 'I received a letter with an account of the murder of the Linchy [sic] family at Reaghstown eight in number, by burning them in their dwelling house Wildgoose Lodge on Tuesday night October 29th.'[39] He made his way to Reaghstown on 4 November and remained there for around ten days. Unfortunately, or perhaps revealingly, he leaves no account of what he witnessed there during this time.[40] Marianne Fortescue, a cousin of John Foster's, recorded in her diary on 31 October: 'We sat at home all morn[in]g – Mr Thursby visited us – Doct[o]r John is here and thank God we are all well – Emily's cold almost gone – we heard of Wildgoose Lodge being burned & eight souls in it – done maliciously – how truly dreadful.'[41] 'Emily's cold' was as significant an event as the murder of eight members of the lower classes.

Lower class disregard (or arguably ignorance of) the state system could manifest itself in support for criminality directed against the landlord and by extension governing classes or those, like Lynch and Rooney, who supported the state apparatus by informing on their lower-class neighbours. In the same letter of 10 November 1816 quoted above, Foster told Peel that 'in some instances an appearance of exultation has shown itself [since the murders]' amongst the wider community.[42] The following day, the Louth magistrates meeting under the chairmanship of Foster reported 'a general apathy' amongst the mass of the people, which made them nervous given that the natural response to such a crime should, he contended, have been one of horror.[43] It could be argued that Foster was attempting to convince Peel once again of the need for state intervention but he was not the only one to report events in this light.[44] A farmer named Brabazon, who lived about seventeen miles from the lodge, alleged that when the news of the burning reached thirty of his labourers working in the fields, 'they received it with a shout of joy'.[45] There is also evidence of masses having been said in local chapels for some of those who were later executed for their suspected role in the burning, but no word of masses for the victims.[46]

That some form of moral support for the perpetrators existed is undeniable.[47] Some regarded Devan a communal hero just as he was regarded a villain

39 Farm diary of T.P. Filgate, 29 Oct. 1816 (NLI, Filgate papers, MS 19,963).   40 Ibid., 4–14 Nov. 1816.   41 Ross (ed.), 'Diary of Marianne Fortescue', p. 495.   42 Foster to Peel, 10 Nov. 1816; *Papers relating to disturbances in the County of Louth*.   43 Resolutions of Louth magistrates, 11 Nov. 1816 (NA, SOC, 1763/36).   44 Copy of letter from John Foster to Robert Peel, 10 Nov. 1816; *Papers relating to disturbances in the County of Louth*.   45 Samuel Pendleton to Robert Peel, 14 Nov. 1816 (NA, SOC 1763/39).   46 Samuel Pendleton to Robert Peel, 28 July 1818 (SOC, series, ii, box 168).   47 See Carleton, *Autobiography*, p. 118.

by others.[48] As the century progressed to a close, he was certainly more cele-
brated in nationalist Ireland than he was condemned.[49] Thus, fear and intimidation alone does not explain why virtually a whole community, the majority
of whose members were law-abiding, at least in the sense that they did not
actively and openly participate in secret societies, should effectively condone
such a crime by their silence. It is better explained as a mixture of fear and sympathy which conspired to make it difficult for the authorities to bring the perpetrators of the murders at Wildgoose Lodge to trial as quickly as they would
have wished.

48 See chapter one. **49** K.T. Hoppen has adjudged such communal sympathy to be widespread:
'the very fact … that there existed within rural society at least a tendency, even if a fluctuating
one, towards sympathy with violence in general suggests that in the popular mind the perpetrators of outrages were not simply criminals and were in no deep sense separated from their local
communities'; K.T. Hoppen, *Ireland since 1800: conflict and conformity* (London, 1999 ed.), p. 55.

CHAPTER FOUR

The arrest of the suspects

'Now, boys,' said the Captain, 'all is safe – we may go. Remember, every man of you, what you've sworn this night, on the book an' altar of God – not on a heretic bible. If you perjure yourselves, you may hang us; but let me tell you, for your comfort, that if you do, there is them livin' that will take care the lase of your own lives will be but short.'

William Carleton, 'Wildgoose Lodge', p. 362.

Introduction

On 3 November 1816 the *Freeman's Journal* referred to the massacre at Wildgoose Lodge as 'a deed of the most savage enormity that the malignity of wickedness could devise for the destruction of humanity'.[1] The *Annual Register* for 1816 decried the murders as

> one of those atrocious acts of vengeance, the frequency of which brings shame upon the country, has been again committed, and under such tremendous circumstances as beggar all the power of words to describe them in their full enormity ... Human nature sickens at the contemplation of such an act of horror, and language sinks under the task of expressing the emotions which it raises.[2]

All reports were in general agreement that this was a crime of vengeance. The evidence of Alice Rispin, whose son, James, was one of those murdered, was the most blunt. James had given evidence in the first trial and Alice recalled that 'he had been much threatened in the country on this account'. Hugh McCabe had warned her that 'if her son's oath had been taken, that, by his Maker, he would make him dance in the fire with Lynch and Rooney yet.'[3] Four days after the incident, the writer of a piece in the *Freeman's Journal* referring to the three men, Tiernan, Shanley and Conlon, executed for the initial raid back in April stated: 'It is supposed that it is some of the friends or adherents of these three unfortunate men, who regardless of the injunctions of religion,

1 *FJ*, 3 Nov. 1816. 2 *Annual Register 1816*, pp 175–6. 3 *Kilkenny Moderator*, 12 Mar. 1818.

15 William Filgate's home at Lisrenny, Co. Louth, taken from
Encumbered Estates Rental of 1854.

and the dictates of moral obligations, listened to the suggestions of an implacable revenge …'[4] The Castle authorities and the Louth magistracy categorised the burning in the same way and therefore firmly assigned the murders to the category of a crime against the state instead of simply another agrarian outrage. That is the way it was to be presented by the Crown prosecutors, magistrates such as William Filgate and Castle informers in the trials that were to follow.[5] In the meantime, the heinous nature of the outrage and the outcry occasioned by it in government and propertied circles made it incumbent upon the government to act swiftly and retributively.

Calls for the Insurrection Act

Early on the morning of 30 October 1816, a few hours after the bodies had been removed from Wildgoose Lodge, Bob Shiels, steward on the Filgate estate at Lisrenny, rode out to William Filgate Jr's residence at Kiltybegs, near the south Monaghan village of Inniskeen, and reported to him the events of the previous night. Filgate immediately made his way to the Lodge.[6] He then made a report

4 *FJ*, 3 Nov. 1816. 5 Ibid.; *Newry Telegraph*, 4 Apr. 1818; *Kilkenny Moderator*, 12 Mar. 1818. 6 William Filgate's 1867 account.

to the governor of the county, John Foster, who had already heard the news in a hurried correspondence from the coroner, H.M. Blackwell, a resident of Collon. Foster was the first to report the incident to Sir Robert Peel claiming that 'he was mortified and ashamed for the country to have such a barbarity to state to you' and notably remarked that this 'most shocking murder' took place only 'about ten miles from hence' [Collon].[7] Foster's decision a few days earlier to oppose the withdrawal of the Peace Preservation Force from the four Louth baronies had been vindicated. Samuel Pendleton had also refused to sign the petition and in his report to Peel a fortnight after the incident he stated that no act of 'such barbarous atrocity' had occurred in the whole of the United Kingdom since 1641. With some justification he argued not even the massacre at Scullabogue compared to it, for while Scullabogue happened during 'the ferment of mutual animosity, and actual civil war', the burning of Wildgoose Lodge had 'the aggravation of being meditated for months, and deliberately executed'.[8]

Foster immediately began to lobby his fellow Louth magistrates to convene a meeting to address the escalating crisis. To date the only barony not proclaimed in Louth was Ferrard, which was effectively policed by Foster and the local yeomanry. Wildgoose Lodge was only ten miles or so from his home in Collon, less than an hour's ride away. The eye of the storm was getting too close for his comfort. A week after the atrocity the magistrates of Louth assembled at Castlebellingham where in common resolution they described the burning as a 'horrid and never-to-be-forgotten crime, staining the annals of our country'; 'a crime barbarous beyond the power of expression, and scarcely credible to have been committed within the precincts of a country deemed civilised'.[9] The rhetoric was very similar to that used by Foster in his earlier report to Peel.

In a separate communication Foster warned Peel that the atrocity had been perpetrated by Ribbonmen and had 'resulted from a system of illegal association, united by oaths of secrecy and obedience.'[10] This was suggesting something more than the vengeful attack of a local secret society whose numbers were boosted by outside gangs. Peel took this on board, and a short time later while reporting on Irish affairs in the House of Commons he ascribed the murders to 'the effect of a general confederacy in crime – a systematic opposition

---

7 Copy letter from John Foster to Robert Peel, 30 Oct. 1816; *Papers relating to disturbances in the County of Louth*, HC 1817, vol. viii (263). 491. **8** Samuel Pendleton to Robert Peel, 14 Nov. 1816 (NA, SOC, 1763/39); for events at Scullabogue, see Tom Dunne, *Rebellions: memoir, memory and 1798* (Dublin, 2004), pp 247–64. **9** *FJ*, 11 Nov. 1816; resolutions enclosed in correspondence from John Foster to Robert Peel, 30 Oct. 1816 in *Papers relating to disturbances in the County of Louth*. **10** In John Foster to Robert Peel, 30 Oct. 1816, ibid.; see also part of resolution passed by Louth magistrates at Castlebellingham on 4 Nov. 1816; quoted in *FJ*, 11 Nov. 1816.

to all laws and municipal institutions' and claimed that the proliferation of raids were attempts to provide arms for Ribbonmen with the political agenda of arming the lower classes for all out rebellion. He was clearly intending to convince the Commons that Ribbonism, as he and Foster and the other magistrates of Louth understood it, posed a political as well as a social threat to the powers of the state and that extraordinary measures would have to be taken to prevent it spreading, but as of yet this did not include the extension of the Insurrection Act to Louth.[11]

The agitation was certainly not waning at this stage – if anything it seems as if the burning of the lodge provided impetus to the local secret societies – but despite the authorities' fears of something more sinister and seditious, the local societies continued to focus their attentions primarily on agrarian issues. In November 1816, Samuel Pendleton reported that 'unlawful assembling by night has recommenced in many parts of this district, and in some, to a greater extent, than at any time since I have been in it'.[12] Pendleton had received 'threatening letters of a savage tendency'; so had members of the local gentry and large farmers.[13] Gangs estimated at 200–300 persons continued to carry out agrarian crimes particularly against those who took up evicted farms. On 17 November 1816, notices were posted on chapels in the Dundalk/Carlingford area, threatening that 'if any person or persons offered to take land, out of which any person had been dispossessed, or had left, that the person taking such land [and] his property would be consumed by fire and his life taken the first opportunity'. The following night, the home of a man named Coulter, a middleman on the Tipping estate near Drogheda (the family estate of the eleventh Lord Blayney's mother) was burned because he allowed an under-tenant to take over an evicted holding.[14] In December a large farmer named James Feehan made a statement to Pendleton which, the latter told Peel, was 'more descriptive than many others of the same tendency, which I have, of the principle endeavoured to be established, namely that no change in the occupancy of land is to be suffered'.[15] Later that month, a party of disguised men plundered the houses of two Ardee farmers named Ekins and Mullins of arms and money. As already mentioned, John Reath, a farmer from Irishtown near Ardee, was murdered in January 1817 in revenge for having prosecuted a man for a raid on his home the previous

11 Copy letter John Foster to Robert Peel, 10 Nov. 1816; *Papers relating to disturbances in the County of Louth*; *Annual Register, 1816* (London, 1817), p. 48; also see below. 12 Samuel Pendleton to Robert Peel, 18 Nov. 1816 (NA, SOC 1763/38). 13 Samuel Pendleton to Robert Peel, 10 Nov. 1816 (NA, SOC 1763/37). 14 Paul Parks to John Foster, 18 Nov. 1816 (NA, SOC 1763/41); Samuel Pendleton to John Foster, 18 Nov. 1816 (NA, SOC 1763/41). 15 Samuel Pendleton to Robert Peel, 22 Dec. 1816; quoted in Murray, *The burning of Wildgoose Lodge*, p. 149.

month.[16] Around the same time, the home of another neighbouring farmer, Arthur McCabe, was raided.[17] Towards the end of January, Pendleton wrote to William Gregory: 'the disposition to disturbance ... has shown itself to an increased degree in this district [Ardee]'. There had been attacks on eight houses by large groups of men and: 'from the terror produced by the horrid acts which have been committed, the persons suffering will not give information voluntarily'.[18] In February, the home of James Byrne at Channonrock near the town of Louth was burned. Byrne's daughter died in the blaze.[19] In nearby Knockbridge, the property of Neal McCann had been attacked so often Pendleton could only conclude that 'he seems an object of peculiar enmity.'[20] Notably, the areas of Ardee, Knockbridge and Channonrock (both in the parish of Louth) were very much within the raiding area of Devan's gang and rather significantly levels of violence there did not diminish until he went on the run in March 1817.

At this stage the Louth magistrates had called on the government on several occasions to place Louth under the Insurrection Act.[21] In early November 1816, they informed Peel that this was the only way to tackle crimes 'unknown but to the savage tribes of Indians when in open war':

> we cannot expect information to enable us to act with effect, nor evidences to come forward voluntarily, while the system of intimidation, which is the object of the illegal associations in these baronies, and many parts of the adjoining counties, not only exists, but must receive increased strength from the late barbarous murder of a prosecutor, Lynch, and his witness Rooney, with their families, unless we are able to counteract that intimidation and these associations by the provision of the Insurrection Act.[22]

The act, which had been renewed in 1814, allowed for a minimum of seven magistrates to request the lord lieutenant and the Irish privy council to proclaim a county or a part thereof to be in a disturbed condition. The powers given to magistrates under the act were far-reaching: persons found outside their homes after sundown, if not on lawful business, could be deemed idle and dis-

16 Samuel Pendleton to Robert Peel, 17 Dec. 1816; *Papers relating to disturbances in the County of Louth*. 17 Samuel Pendleton to Robert Peel, 14 Jan. 1817; ibid. 18 Samuel Pendleton to William Gregory, 21 Jan. 1817; ibid. 19 Samuel Pendleton to Robert Peel, 7 Feb. 1817; ibid. 20 Ibid. 21 54 Geo. 3 c.180. 22 Copy of letter from John Foster to Robert Peel, 10 Oct. 1816; Copy of memorials forwarded to Robert Peel, 30 Oct. 1816; both in *Papers relating to disturbances in the County of Louth*.

orderly; magistrates were empowered to enter houses between sunset and sunrise and anyone absent could later be arrested; so could persons who took illegal oaths, who were found in possession of arms, who were in public houses after 9 p.m. and before 6 a.m., as well as any persons 'tumultuously assembled in the day time' or found in possession of seditious papers.[23] The act gave magistrates in Ireland considerably more power than they had in England.[24] Contemporary commentators warned of its dangers; J.B. Trotter claimed that the act had 'none but injurious consequences ... and tends to alienate this country from Great Britain more than most measures that could be devised'. It was, he argued, 'inquisitorial instead of administrative, despotic instead of constitutional'.[25] Later historians looked at it in a similar vein; J.W. O'Neill concluded with some justification that the Insurrection Act 'contained provisions which were antithetical to the tradition of civil liberties enjoyed by freeborn Englishmen, and it may be surmised that they would have provoked a loud and persistent outcry had they been proposed in the mother country.'[26]

These were exactly the type of powers Foster craved for the resident magistracy; he told Peel that it was regrettable that the Louth magistracy and the police did not have the authority to 'keep people at home in the night time, pay domiciliary visits, search houses and take up arms'.[27] But despite the pleas of the Louth magistrates and the persistent encouragement of Foster, Peel procrastinated. He was willing to continue to keep a police presence in Louth but he was not convinced of the benefits of extending the Insurrection Act. Since his arrival in Ireland he had been wary of magistrates who became alarmist, preferring to use the Insurrection Act as a last resort. On 15 April 1815 he wrote: 'we receive so many false alarms that we ought not to be very much blamed if when the wolf were really there we should disbelieve the story'.[28] In January 1816 he offered an explanation:

> I have no hesitation in giving a decided opinion against an application for the Insurrection Act. We are determined to reserve this strongest and last remedy for occasions of great emergency ... Depend on it, however, that nothing will be half so effectual as an active stipendiary magistrate patrolling by night with thirty or forty mounted constables, and occupied by day in detecting and preparing evidence for the trial of offenders.[29]

23 Geo. III, C. xiii, [1 Aug. 1807]; 54 Geo III, C. clxxx [30 July 1814]; 57 Geo. III, C.L [27 June 1817]. 24 5 Geo III, c. 8; 15 & 16 Geo III, c. 21. 25 J.B. Trotter, *Walks through Ireland in the years 1812, 1814 and 1817* (London, 1819), pp 324–5. 26 O'Neill, 'Popular culture and peasant rebellion', pp 208–9. 27 John Foster to Robert Peel, 10 Nov. 1816; *Papers relating to disturbances in the County of Louth.* 28 Quoted in Shipkey, *Robert Peel's Irish policy*, p. 138. 29 Quoted in

As Peel procrastinated, Foster, despite his solid relationship with the chief secretary, could not help expressing his frustration in a letter of 19 November 1816 which he concluded: 'You have given the insurgents a long day. I wish you could give us the like.'[30] In the meantime, the Louth magistrates subscribed to a private fund for the purpose of obtaining information leading to the prosecution of the perpetrators of the crime. Offering rewards for evidence was a fundamental and often a necessary strategy adopted by an association of local gentry to secure the evidence necessary to lead to the arrest and conviction of offenders.[31]

Table 4: Amount subscribed to Wildgoose Lodge fund by
Co. Louth magistrates and others, November 1816

Name	Sum [pounds]	Name	Sum
John Foster	50	John McClintock	50
Lord Jocelyn	50	Robert Thompson	50
T.H. Foster	50	Chichester Fortescue	50
John Jocelyn	50	Faithful Fortescue	50
Blayney Balfour	50	Lenox Bigger	50
Edward Bellew	50	Samuel Pendleton	50
Francis Tipping	50	Matthew Fortescue	50
Wallop Brabazon	50	W.P. Ruxton	50
Rev Dr Little	50	William Filgate	50
Alexander Dawson	50	Philip Pendleton	50
Neal McNeal	20	Fitzherbert Ruxton	50
Hugh Moore	10	Nicholas Coddington	50
James Read	10	Henry Coddington	50
John Dawson	10	T.P. Filgate	50
George Evans	20	F. W. Fortescue	50

Source: Handbill, 4 Nov. 1816 (Wildgoose Lodge papers, Dundalk Library)

As table 4.1 shows over £1,300 was pledged to the fund. The treasurer appointed was John Straton (1763–1821) of Dundalk, collector of customs for the town who was married to Lady Emily Jocelyn, youngest daughter of the earl of Roden. Straton was charged with paying a sum of £400 to the person who gave the first information leading to prosecution and conviction; four rewards

Broeker, *Rural disorder and police reform*, p. 95. **30** John Foster to Robert Peel, 19 Nov. 1816 (NA, SOC 1763/41). **31** Beattie, *Crime and the courts in England*, p. 48.

of £200 to each of four persons who would next inform; £50 to other informants after the first five had been made; and rewards of £25 for further information from others. Informers were to be protected by anonymity and promises of pardons were held out to prospective informers who had been involved in the burning. Notices were posted 118 times in the *Drogheda Journal* alone.[32]

On 18 November 1816, a proclamation was issued by the lord lieutenant and the council of Ireland ('being determined in so far as in us lies to bring the persons concerned in the said most barbarous and most inhuman outrage, to speedy and condign punishment') that offered further rewards of £200 and a pardon (more specifically immunity to prosecution) to approvers or discoverers, 'for each and every of the persons so apprehended and prosecuted to conviction'.[33] Rewards offered by the government were another fundamental part of public policy long established in the system of criminal administration. The promise of a royal pardon was a major incentive, particularly as a pardoned suspect could use the reward money to leave the locality, thereby avoiding the threat of revenge from the convicted men's associates. But offering substantial rewards and pardons could, of course, have undesired repercussions. As Beattie contends regarding the situation in England: 'such massive sums encouraged malicious prosecutions.'[34] To put this into perspective: in the rural hinterland of Dundalk in 1816, labourers earned ten pence to one shilling per day.[35] If we take the higher figure of one shilling, then a man would have to work for 8,000 days in order to earn the £400 on offer from the Louth magistrates' fund.

The continued efforts of John Foster to restore order to the Louth countryside and to capture the perpetrators should not be underestimated: hours before the Wildgoose outrage he had warned his fellow magistrates and then Chief Secretary Peel of the dangers of withdrawing the police from the proclaimed baronies; he was the first to communicate the news of the atrocity to Peel; in the days and weeks which followed, he chaired a succession of meetings of the Louth magistracy in Dundalk, Ardee and Castlebellingham (where he 'commented in forcible language on the horrible murder of Lynch and his family'),[36] and in the meanwhile kept Peel abreast of local developments in a flurry of letters. He became something of a thorn in Dublin Castle's side,

---

32 Casey, 'Wildgoose Lodge: the evidence and the lore', p. 143. 33 Proclamation issued by the lord lieutenant and council of Ireland, 18 Nov. 1816 (Dundalk Library, WGL papers). 34 Beattie, *Crime and the courts in England*, p. 53; it should be noted, however, that in the Irish case, at least by the 1830s, records were it seems rarely claimed; see Brian Griffin, 'Prevention and detection of crime in nineteenth-century Ireland', in N.M. Dawson (ed.), *Reflections on law and history* (Dublin, 2006), pp 99–125; R.J. McMahon, 'Homicide. the courts and popular culture in pre-Famine and Famine Ireland' (unpublished PhD thesis, UCD, 2006), p. 323. 35 Mason, *A statistical account*, ii, p. 74. 36 *Belfast Newsletter*, 15 Nov. 1816.

REWARDS.

The Magistrates of the County of Louth offer the following Rewards, to be paid by John Stratton, Esq. Dundalk, Treasurer to the Fund, raised by Subscription for discovering and bringing to punishment the Perpetrators of the late horrid Murders at Reaghstown, in this County, on the 30th of October last.

A REWARD OF

Four Hundred Pounds,

To the Person who shall give the first information against any one concerned in the late horrible Murders at Reaghstown, so as he be prosecuted and convicted thereof.

FOUR REWARDS OF

Two Hundred Pounds each,

To each of the four Persons who shall next inform against any Persons so concerned so as they be prosecuted and convicted.

A REWARD OF

Fifty Pounds,

To each Person who shall inform against any further or other Persons so concerned, after the foregoing five Informations shall have been made, so as such further or other Person be prosecuted to conviction.

REWARDS OF

Twenty-five Pounds each,

For Private Information leading to the discovery, apprehension or conviction of any Person concerned in planning, concerting, or perpetrating the said Outrage and Murders, or being in any way accessory thereto, and a strict secrecy will be observed.

The MAGISTRATES of the Head Office of Police, in Dublin, have given Notice by advertisement in the *Hue and Cry,* that if any Person shall within six Calendar Months, from 1st Nov. inst. apprehend and prosecute to conviction any of the Persons concerned in said Outrage, they shall receive a Reward of £50 for each so apprehended and convicted, and that they will give a further Reward of £20, for any Information leading to the apprehension and conviction of any of the Persons concerned.

16 Poster, printed after 4 November 1816, offering rewards for the capture of the perpetrators of the Wildgoose Lodge murders (Louth County Library, Dundalk).

CASTLEBELLINGHAM, *November* 4, 1816.

At a Meeting of the Magistrates of Louth, called by the Governors of the County.

Right Hon. JOHN FOSTER, in the Chair.

Lord Jocelyn,
Right Hon. Thomas H. Foster,
Honourable John Jocelyn,
Blaney Balfour,
Sir Edward Bellew,
Francis Tipping,
Wallop Brabazon,
John M'Clintock,
Robert Thompson,
Chichester Fortescue,
Lenox Bigger,
Mathew Fortescue,
Samuel Pendleton,

Fitzherbert Ruxton,
William P. Ruxton,
Reverend Doctor Little,
Alexander Dawson,
Neal Mc.Neal,
Hugh Moore,
James Read,
John Dawson,
George Evans,
F. W. Fortescue,
Faithful Fortescue,
William Filgate,
Philip Pendleton.

The following Resolutions were unanimously agreed to :—

THAT a Crime barbarous beyond the power of Expression, and scarcely credible to have been committed within the precincts of a Country deemed civilized ; appears to have been perpetrated at Reaghstown, in the Barony of Ardee, within this County, during the Morning of the 30th October last ; by the deliberate and systematic Assault, of a number of Persons upon the House of Edward Lynch, and the wilful burning of the same —consuming no less than Eight Persons, including three Women and one Child.

THAT it appears the same House had been attacked and broken into, in the course of the last Spring, and that the unfortunate Lynch, supported by the evidence of his Son-in-Law, Rooney, had appealed at the last Assizes to the Laws of his Country, for the protection of himself and Family, and had manfully discharged his bounden Duty to the Country that gave him birth ; in prosecuting to conviction, three of the Robbers that had attempted to plunder his House of Arms.

THAT this horrid and never to be forgotten Crime, staining the annals of our Country, has resulted from a system of illegal association, united by oaths of secrecy and obedience.

THAT it does appear the ordinary Laws of a free Country, calculated to be met and forwarded by a People impressed with a due sense of moral and religious Feeling, are not those adapted to contend with Crimes such as the present one ; unknown but to the savage Tribes of Indians when in open War.

THAT not having witnessed that general feeling of indignation, which such an atrocious act was calculated to call forth in aid of the Magistracy, a Special Sessions of the Peace be appointed to be held, in pursuance of the Insurrection Act, on the speediest day ; and that we solicit a continuation of the operation of the Police Act of the 54th of the King, within the Baronies of Ardee and Louth.

THAT application be made to the Lord Lieutenant, to offer such Rewards for the apprehending and convicting of the Persons concerned, together with such offers of pardon, as may by His Majesty's Government be deemed expedient.

THAT Subscriptions be immediately entered into, for the purpose of procuring such Information as may lead to a Discovery, and to the Prosecuting to Conviction of those concerned in this terrific Crime.

THAT the Right Hon. JOHN FOSTER, be requested to communicate to Mr. PEEL, the result of this Meeting.

JOHN FOSTER.

THAT the Sheriff be requested to call a Meeting of the County, for the purpose of communicating to them the foregoing Resolutions, on the earliest day most convenient.

JOHN FOSTER.

WE, the undersigned, severally agree to pay the Sums subscribed with our Names, in order to form a fund, for the purpose of obtaining Information and Prosecuting to Conviction the Persons concerned in the late horrid and atrocious Outrage at Reaghstown.

JOHN FOSTER, ...	£50	JOHN M'CLINTOCK,	£50	Rev. Doctor LITTLE,	£50	WILLIAM FILGATE,	£50
JOCELYN, ...	50	ROBERT THOMPSON,	50	ALEXANDER DAWSON,	50	PHILIP PENDLETON,	50
THOMAS HENRY FOSTER,	50	CHICHESTER FORTESCUE	50	NEAL MC.NEAL, ...	20	FITZHERBERT RUXTON,	50
JOHN JOCELYN, ...	50	FAITHFUL FORTESCUE,	50	HUGH MOORE, ...	10	NICHOLAS CODDINGTON,	50
BLAYNEY BALFOUR,	50	LENOX BIGGER, ...	50	JAMES READ, ...	10	HENRY CODDINGTON,	50
EDWARD BELLEW, ...	50	SAMUEL PENDLETON,	50	JOHN DAWSON, ...	10	TOWNLEY P. FILGATE,	50
FRANCIS TIPPING, ...	50	MATHEW FORTESCUE,	50	GEORGE EVANS, ...	20	
WALLOP BRABAZON,	50	W. P. RUXTON, ...	50	F. W. FORTESCUE,	50	

17 Poster showing the outcome of the meeting of Louth magistrates on 4 November 1816 (Louth County Library, Dundalk).

badgering the administration to extend the Insurrection Act to Louth as a matter of urgency. He also went after the large farmers for support of the act, thereby shaping an alliance of the propertied against lower class agitators. In a letter to Dublin Castle on 17 November 1816, he wrote: 'the farmers and landholders, who are to pay the expense of it [Insurrection Act], concur with us & they will have a cheap bargain, even if it exists till April [1817] which I trust will not be necessary.' The rate of 8 pence per acre was, he argued, a small price to pay for their security.[37] On 10 November he assured Peel that thirty of the county's thirty-one resident magistrates were in favour of the Insurrection Act as the only means of restoring more peaceful ways to the countryside (the other magistrate was ill).[38] Foster also met regularly and at length with Samuel Pendleton to advise him on such matters as 'the most desirable stations in the disturbed baronies for troops' to be billeted. He had great regard for the chief magistrate and in a letter to Peel in mid-November 1816 he complimented Pendleton for adding 'the great weight of his decided opinion' to the meetings of the Louth magistrates.[39]

But for months Peel continued to refuse to yield on extending the Insurrection Act to Louth.[40] When he sought advice from his under-secretary, a sceptical William Gregory replied that he did not believe the extension of the act would have 'some magic ... sufficient to tranquillise a county.'[41] Instead, police reinforcements were sent to Louth and Samuel Pendleton, acting on Foster's advice, immediately established stations of 30–40 men in the town of Louth and at Corcreaghy, Hackballscross, Manfieldstown and Riverstown.[42] Concurrently, additional military detachments were sent to the area towards the end of November and beginning of December 1816. Pendleton took charge, as he was entitled to do as chief police magistrate, and instructed the army officers to send their men out in small groups every night: 'at uncertain hours and in such directions as under circumstances might seem most expedient.' Each patrol was to make contact with the others and to ensure that a continuous patrolling system was in operation. The soldiers were warned not to incite further crime: they were not to enter houses either in search of men or arms. But they were to detain any person found breaking the curfew until they were questioned by a magistrate the following day and they were to deal resolutely with armed gangs should they encounter them.[43] At this stage,

37 John Foster to Dublin Castle, 17 Nov. 1816 (NA, SOC 1763/36). **38** John Foster to Robert Peel, 10 Nov. 1816; *Papers relating to disturbances in the County of Louth.* **39** John Foster to Robert Peel, 15 Nov. 1816 (NA SOC 1763/36). **40** *Hansard parliamentary debates, House of Commons,* 21 May 1817, vol. xxxvi, 838. **41** Sir William Gregory to Sir Robert Peel, 18 Nov. and 17 Dec. 1816 (British Museum, Peel papers, MS 40,203). **42** Samuel Pendleton to Robert Peel, 18 Nov. 1816 (NA, SOC 1763/38). **43** Copy letter from Samuel Pendleton to Robert Peel, 6 Dec. 1816; *Papers relating to disturbances in the County of Louth.*

Pendleton believed that it would be necessary to arrest 'many men on suspicion or defective information.'[44]

Eventually in February 1817 Peel succumbed to pressure from the Louth magistracy for the extension of the Insurrection Act. He did so for three reasons: firstly, agrarian outrage in early 1817 had led to the deaths of at least two more people in the baronies of Louth and Ardee (John Reath and James Byrne's daughter) as well as a situation bordering on rural anarchy in which agrarian grievances remained the underlying cause ('the endeavour' as Pendleton put it, 'to control at their will the occupancy of lands'); secondly, the authorities had failed to charge anybody in connection with the Wildgoose Lodge murders; and thirdly Foster continued to barrage him with warnings that lawlessness and housebreaking was a prelude to a general insurrection for which the lower classes were becoming increasingly well armed.

The act was extended to four of the county's five baronies, Ferrard being once again the exception. (In June 1817 it was also extended to baronies in adjoining Co. Meath, including Morgallion from where participants in the Wildgoose Lodge raid had come.)[45] When in May 1817, Peel had to call on the government to renew the Insurrection Act for a further year he cited the situation in Louth and the case of Wildgoose Lodge, in particular, as evidence of its requirement.[46]

Rounding up the suspects

From the end of October 1816 until almost the middle of March 1817 the suspects in the Wildgoose Lodge outrage remained elusive. All that is, except Michael Tiernan and his son, Thomas, who were arrested by Samuel Pendleton on the morning following the raid. They were picked up on suspicion because they were father and brother of one of those hanged for the April 1816 raid. Pendleton wrote: 'There are some circumstances of suspicion which attach to them, and they are of infamous character.' However, he feared that 'any evidence to affect them is rather to be hoped for than expected'.[47] The Tiernans were subsequently released without charge, before being later rearrested in cat-and-mouse type tactics.

Those involved in the atrocity had slipped back quietly into their local communities the next day. During the trials which were to follow in 1817–18, wit-

44 Samuel Pendleton to Robert Peel, 7 Nov. 1816 (NA, SOC 1763/35). 45 Murray, *The burning of Wildgoose Lodge*, p. 158. 46 *Hansard parliamentary debates, House of Commons*, 21 May 1817, vol. xxxvi, 837–8; 13 June 1817, vol. xxxvi, 967. 47 Samuel Pendleton to Robert Peel, 30 Oct. 1816 (NA, SOC 1763/34).

nesses including employers such as Lord Louth from Tallanstown and members of the large farmer class vouched that some of the prisoners were back at their workplace early the morning after the burning.[48] Even Patrick Devan returned to his everyday routine. In a letter which appeared in *The Times* of 27 March 1818, one of many received (but the only one published) 'from respectable individuals in Dundalk and its vicinity', the correspondent wrote:

> It is known that Devan was clerk of the chapel of Stonetown. Mr McCann the parish priest [of Louth, 1799–1822] occasionally officiated there. On the Sunday after the burning of the Lynches, he proceeded to that place of worship, penetrated with the most indescribable horror and concern. He ascended the altar robed in his vestments, and with accents which will never leave my ear, cursed the author, abettor, and assistants of the crime! He then came down from the altar, took from his feet his shoes and stockings, desired his congregation to follow him, and he and they went in procession round the chapel, calling aloud to heaven for vengeance on the murderers. Guess who was next the minister of religion in the awful procession? Devan, the clerk! – the planner – the instigator – the mover – the commander in this horrible transaction! And, of the whole congregation, he appeared to be the person who reiterated Amen with the most vehement devotion.[49]

It seems that the author of the letter was from the parish of Louth. Because Stonetown was part of the same parish, it was usual (which remains the case to this day) for the parish priest to officiate in Louth and Stonetown. Rather than being intended as a condemnation of any complicity on the Catholic clergy's behalf, voluntary or otherwise, the letter was intended 'to exhibit at once the unparalleled obduracy of the desperados over whom it was so strangely imagined that their priests had an unbounded influence'.[50] No doubt there were others in that procession who had been at the lodge with Devan and who had been able to separate religious practice from Christian morality. Fr McCann's sermon and his actions suggested his abhorrence of the crime; yet, he would testify on Devan's behalf at his trial the following year and offer an impressive character witness.[51]

Investigations in Louth by the police and magistracy began directly after the atrocity. Witnesses were questioned by Samuel Pendleton as well as by a number of local magistrates including Foster, William Filgate and Chichester Fortescue. Two weeks after the incident, Pendleton reported:

48 See chapter six. 49 *The Times*, 27 Mar. 1818. 50 Ibid. 51 See chapter five.

These circumstances were not however stated upon oath, because we studiously avoided anything that could give the appearance of a formal examination, being convinced that no direct information could be at present expected, and that the best means of obtaining any clue leading to such, would be by carefully watching for what might unconsciously fall in an unguarded and apparently undesigned conversation.[52]

There were undoubtedly those who had been at Wildgoose Lodge who were more garrulous than guarded, suggested in Carleton's afore-quoted claim that 'others than those who had been convicted, several whom Devaun had summoned without disclosing to them the frightful object in view, actually admitted that they had been present, and had no hesitation in giving full details of the deeds which were done.'[53] Like members of the United Irishmen in 1798 (and, indeed, later nineteenth-century secret societies), 'their longing for sociability and conviviality, made them and their secrets open to penetration, infiltration and discovery', which is probably what Pendleton had hoped for in his early flush of enquiries.[54] The police could hope to pick up on 'unguarded and apparently undesigned conversation' in public houses such as Byrne's of Corcreaghy where Carleton heard much about the incident.

Complaints by the Louth magistracy and the Castle administration that it was difficult to get people to come forward with information questions the widespread prevalance of informers, but there was always going to be a few willing to take a chance.[55] Since his arrival in Louth Pendleton had built up his own ring of informers. As noted already, one of these after April 1816 was Edward Lynch who, it seems, continued to give information after the first raid on Wildgoose Lodge, glad of the £20 he received in the first place and then the half yearly payment of £7 10s. received on 22 October 1816, exactly a week before his murder. In the months of May and July 1816 the Castle had reimbursed Pendleton the sum of £19 for the subsistence of another informer and £7 10s. for 'information and guides'. In the meantime Dublin Castle was kept informed of events in Louth by the likes of Lennox Bigger Esq., a magistrate from near Dundalk, who got frequent payments for 'reimbursement of expenses for information' received from others or simply for his own information (usually around £30). Pendleton's informers after October 1816 included neighbours of Edward

52 Samuel Pendleton to Robert Peel, 14 Nov. 1816 (NA, SOC 1763/36).   53 Carleton, *Autobiography*, p. 116.   54 Thomas Bartlett, *Revolutionary Dublin, 1795–1801: the letters of Francis Higgins to Dublin Castle* (Dublin, 2004), p. 19.   55 See Bartlett, *Revolutionary Dublin*; for a more contemporary account see W.J. Fitzpatrick, *The sham squire: and the informers of 1798, with jottings about Ireland seventy years ago* (Dublin, 1866); for a reappraisal see McMahon, 'Homicide, the courts and popular culture', p. 323.

Lynch such as Patrick Halpenny and Alice Rispin, neighbours of Devan's such as Thomas Woods and longstanding informers such as Terence Cassidy who seems to have worked a radius from Castleblayney to Castlebellingham on the Castle's behalf.[56]

Within a month of the extension of the Insurrection Act to Louth the authorities at last made some progress in identifying and arresting suspects. The reasons for this were a combination of the powers of the act, good fortune and Castle scheming. First of all, fear of retribution amongst the strong farmers in the affected baronies was replaced by an anxiety to bring perpetrators to justice much more quickly in order to avoid the tax on their districts.[57] The act gave the police arbitrary powers to search houses and to arrest or threaten to arrest anybody breaking curfew. It became extremely difficult to hold unlawful assemblies and so more intense pressure was brought to bear on those who were previously active. Therefore the authorities' powers of intimidation came to at least match those of the secret societies. The tensions may have become all too much for some of the innocents caught in between and information may have become more readily available. It was, of course, around this time that Gregory reported to Peel the existence of the young woman who had reportedly survived the fire. Pendleton made the most of the new opportunities that presented themselves under the act and, it seems, he was anything but discreet. Rather revealingly, Lord Lieutenant Whitworth and Chief Secretary Peel accused him of fabricating 'cases from any materials' and too zealously jailing men 'when in fact the poor creatures ought to be set at large'. In April 1817, Peel, despite his knowledge of Foster's support for Pendleton, admitted to Whitworth that 'we made a bad choice ... I wish he would resign his situation ... the credit and character of the Peace Preservation Bill depends so much upon the instruments who are entrusted with the execution of it ... The mischief done by a [police] magistrate who conducts himself improperly is far more extensive than the district within which he acts.' Lord Lieutenant Whitworth responded: 'Would to God we could recall Willcox [Richard Willcocks, first chief magistrate to be appointed in 1814] from Tipperary and send him to Louth in the room of this horrible fellow!'[58] But while Peel and Whitworth expressed their reservations about Pendleton's tactics to each other, they did not interfere. The overriding concern was to break the perceived conspiracy in Louth and to reassert the authority of

56 See chapters five and six. 57 William Gregory to Robert Peel, 29 Oct. 1816 (British Museum, Peel papers, MS 40,203); see also letter of Alexander Duff, a Protestant farmer from Magheracloone, Co. Monaghan, quoted in report of Walter Dawson for Dublin Castle, 1 Mar. 1817 (NA, SOC 1817, 1828/6). 58 See Lord Whitworth to Robert Peel, 17 Apr. 1817; Peel to Whitworth, 21 Apr. 1917; both quoted in Palmer, *Police and protest*, pp 211–12.

the state. By the time Peel wrote to Whitworth, over twenty men had been arrested. And in the process, if Pendleton was guilty of impropriety he was not the only one; he had the moral as well as the physical support of the Louth magistracy, notably Foster whose reputation for using the law as 'an instrument of persecution' preceded him.[59] Foster would later highly commend Pendleton for his efforts in bringing the Wildgoose Lodge suspects to trial.[60]

Before Pendleton and the police could have made their arrests they obviously had to have names, a book of evidence and the prospective approvers who would present this evidence on behalf of the Crown prosecution. When the breakthrough finally came it was as a result of Pendleton's use of informers, the Castle's intelligence network quarrying furiously to gather information and to locate the leaders of the secret society through the Irish Post Office (see below in the case of Devan), vastly experienced Castle spies who had been adept at this type of work since the days of the Defenders and United Irishmen of the late eighteenth century, and some magistrates outside Louth, most notably Meath. More tantalising is the fact that connections made as far back as the 1790s were still evidently working together in similar ways in 1816 to bring about a similar result – the break up of 'a conspiracy' which was, and had been for a long time, a favoured term of John Foster.

The barony of Morgallion in Meath was equally as disturbed as Louth (it was as noted above proclaimed in June 1817 and the Insurrection Act extended to it). On 19 February 1817, during a raid at John Sillery's of Carrickleck one of his employees was murdered. Sillery was an extensive farmer and local merchant and so the raid was seen in terms of a robbery.[61] But he was also a tithe proctor who a few weeks before had been ordered by John Foster to proceed against tithe defaulters in the Drumconrath area of Meath, about four miles from Wildgoose Lodge, for the recovery of arrears.[62] This would undoubtedly have compounded local grievances and may, therefore, have provided an ulterior motive for the raid. At any rate, Sillery gathered a posse and five men were arrested, including Peter Gollogly, a former tailor from Carrickleck who, according to himself, turned to crime when he became unemployed,[63] and Patrick Murphy, a hackler (flax comber) from Meath Hill. On 10 March 1817, Lord Norbury sentenced Murphy, Gollogly and the three others to death at the Trim assizes. Their executions were to be carried out two days later. In the meantime they were to be housed in Trim jail where the governor, Philip Pendleton, was a nephew of Samuel.

59 Smyth, *Men of no property*, p. 107; see also chapter two. 60 See below. 61 See for example poem entitled 'The first race for the Ardee Hunt Cup' (dated 28 March 1808) in *Tempest's Annual*, *1953*, pp 8–9. 62 John Foster to John Sillery, 31 Dec. 1816 (PRONI, Foster papers, D562/13145). 63 *Correspondent*, 11 Mar. 1818; *Drogheda Journal*, 4 Apr. 1818.

The prisoners had been unsuccessfully defended by Leonard MacNally (1752–1820).[64] Over twenty years before, MacNally, then a United Irish barrister, had been 'turned' by John Pollock (d. 1825), clerk of the Crown for Leinster, who worked out of offices in Jervis Street in Dublin. Besides a number of sinecures Pollock made considerable financial gain himself as an informer in the secret war against the United Irishmen. With his new-found wealth he purchased Mountainstown House and estates in the barony of Morgallion in Meath in 1796. Pollock was the first to arrange payment for MacNally who specialised in defence briefs representing the opponents of government and along with John Philpott Curran was regarded during his lifetime as the great legal nemesis of the Castle administration.[65] He and Pollock sometimes worked as a double act, so to speak. Thus MacNally 'wormed out of the United lawyers the line of defence to be adopted' during the 1798 trial of Arthur O'Connor, a member of the Irish Directory, while Pollock 'briefed the British prosecutor with discreditable details about the Irish witnesses'.[66] MacNally's disreputable conduct has been most associated with the period from the mid 1790s to 1803 (from June 1801 McNally was in receipt of a secret pension of £300 per annum),[67] but he continued in a variety of ways to be of use to the Castle, not least of which was providing the illusion that a reputable defence was being offered to those on capital charges (including later some of the Wildgoose Lodge suspects).[68] During all of this time, MacNally was very much 'controlled' by John Pollock,[69] who as clerk of the Crown for Leinster was responsible for framing and recording all indictments against offenders and drawing up Crown pardons for those who turned approver.[70]

Early on the morning of 12 March 1817, three days after Gregory informed Peel of the anonymous survivor, John Pollock's only son, Arthur, magistrate for Morgallion, was, according to his own information, awakened at his town lodgings in Trim by William Ogle Sallery, chief constable of the barony. Pollock had been staying there during the trials of Murphy and the others. His annoyance at being disturbed soon dissipated when Sallery told him that Murphy wanted to make a confession about his role in the burning of Wildgoose Lodge. Pollock dressed and immediately made his way to Trim. William Smart, the jailer, brought in the prisoner. Pollock explained:

> The said jailer then brought the said Patrick Murphy before me, and desired him to make such confession as he had signified his intention

64 *Newry Telegraph*, 4 Apr. 1818. 65 Bartlett, *Revolutionary Dublin*, pp 18, 40–1. 66 Thomas Pakenham, *The year of liberty: the great Irish rebellion of 1798* (London, 1978 ed.), p. 148. 67 Bartlett, *Revolutionary Dublin*, pp 40–1. 68 See chapter five. 69 Bartlett, *Revolutionary Dublin*, p. 18. 70 See chapter six.

of doing, and accordingly the said Patrick Murphy did make a confession of his own guilt and of the names, occupations and places of residence of many other persons whom he stated to have been present and acting in the said arson and murders at Wildgoose Lodge ...[71]

Murphy was no stranger to crime, prison or even acting as an approver. Some time before the burning of Wildgoose Lodge he had been arrested for a robbery at Barkford's outside Carrickmacross. He turned approver on that occasion and was examined as a prosecution witness in the trial that followed and subsequently pardoned.[72] It seems remarkable and hardly credible in light of this that Murphy would have returned to the Carrickmacross area, given what frequently happened to informers, and therefore it is questionable that he could have joined the local society and therefore unlikely that he was at Wildgoose Lodge. However, the authenticity of the facts revealed in his signed statements or his court evidence should not be easily dismissed; the point has already been made that the police and magistracy had accumulated information about what had happened on the night and they had identified their suspects before they had secured the services of approvers such as Murphy. Samuel Pendleton, for example, later wrote to a friend that at the time of taking Murphy's confession he had been gathering independent information from an unidentified informer (perhaps the young woman).[73] It was crucial for the prosecution that Murphy's evidence would be seen to be credible and so at the spring assizes in 1818, Arthur Pollock tried hard to convince the court that Murphy's decision to turn approver was in the interest of justice:

> The man expected to be hanged in half an hour and did not expect the least hope of reprieve; nor did witness [Pollock] hold out any to him; he seemed much affected when giving his information; and when told afterwards by Mr [John] Pollock that he had got a respite of a few days for him, he fainted away.[74]

In reality, Murphy was willing to act as an approver in exchange for a pardon for the Sillery crime, immunity from prosecution for the Wildgoose Lodge murders and a generous reward and the police and magistracy had enough local-based information to feed him and the others to construct a case.

71 Affidavit of A.H.C. Pollock, 2 Sept. 1817 (NA, SOC, 1828/17). 72 Report of trial of 3 Mar. 1818 from *Faulkner's Dublin Journal,* reproduced in *Dundalk Examiner,* 17 Mar. 1881. 73 Samuel Pendleton to Alex Mangin, n.d. [1818] (NA, SOC, series ii, box 168). 74 *Kilkenny Moderator,* 12 Mar. 1818.

Murphy's original affidavits are still in the possession of the Pollock family of Mountainstown. The first of these dated 12 March 1817 originally began 'The information of Patrick Murphy …' but the word 'information' was struck out and changed to 'voluntary confession'. This 'confession' was taken in the presence of John and Arthur Pollock and Samuel Pendleton.[75] Those named by Murphy are underlined and numbered: Patrick Malone, Hudy McElearney, Thomas Tiernan, Terence Marron, Patrick Meegan, James Campbell, George and Edward McQuillan and Michael Kearnan. All would be later arrested. At the end of the statement is a list of other names appended in different handwriting: John Bray, Pat Barber, Pat Floody, Owen McGinny, Pat Scanlon and Peter Gollogly. Except for Gollogly, there is no other mention of these men in any of the later records. In a further statement taken from Murphy and dated 13 March, the same names as underlined and numbered in the first affidavit appear once again and another list is again appended: Campbell, Kearnan, Marron, Malone, McElearney all appear along with Michael (*not* Pat as in the above list) Floody, Patrick Craven, Hugh McCabe and Patrick Devan. All on this list would be convicted. It seems likely that the authorities were feeding the names to Murphy rather than *vice versa*.

In this respect two other points are worth noting. When the Louth magistrates issued their aforementioned memorial at Castlebellingham in November 1816, less than a fortnight after the atrocity, they made mention of such facts as it was carried out by persons from 'various & distant quarters' and fifteen horses were involved carrying two persons each. According to Murphy's version of events on 28 October 1816 Patrick Malone, a neighbouring weaver from Meath Hill, told him that Lynch and Rooney were to be punished for having 'prosecuted the boys at Dundalk'.[76] Malone enticed Murphy to join the raiding party with the promise of 'plenty of whiskey'. That night they met up with a gang of men which included the aforementioned Hudy McElearney (a labourer from Meath Hill), Patrick Meegan (Meath Hill), Terence Marron (a weaver from Drumbane in Monaghan), George and Edward McQuillan (a stone mason and a hackler from Parknamuddagh, near Louth town) and Thomas Tiernan, brother of one of the three hanged in Dundalk. Murphy's statement also placed James Campbell, the previously identified local Ribbon leader, at the scene and claimed that he too enticed Murphy to take part with the promise of 'lashings of drink'. The following night the men met up at a house in Meath Hill where there were two jars of whiskey.[77] From a geographical perspective this was an unusual meet-

75 'Voluntary confession' of Patrick Murphy taken by John Pollock, A.H.C. Pollock and Samuel Pendleton, 12 Mar. 1817 (in private possession). 76 Ibid.; see also report of trial of 3 Mar. 1818 from *Faulkner's Dublin Journal*, reproduced in *Dundalk Examiner*, 17 Mar. 1881. 77 Ibid.

ing place. Louth town was around ten miles from Meath Hill and seven or eight from Drumbane. It would have made infinitely more sense for the McQuillans, for example, to join Devan's gang at Stonetown chapel. Moroever, Murphy's statement made reference to his party having taken the Drumbride road and en route picking up a number of horses grazing in fields; his statement read: 'In all there were 14 men mounted, and each man had one behind him'.[78] Murphy's statement(s) therefore very much reflected what the authorities had already known for four months (the same would apply to the statements of the other approvers).[79]

On the same day that Murphy gave his statement Patrick Malone, James Campbell, Hugh [Hudy] McElearney, Terence Marron, Michael Kearnan and Patrick Meegan were all arrested by Pendleton and his constabulary.[80] That day the Louth police also arrested James Smyth, John Keegan, Hugh McCabe, Thomas McCullough, George McQuillan, Edward McQuillan and Thomas Sheenan. On 16 March, Patrick Craven, Pat Malone, and John Kieran were arrested by the police at Louth. On 31 March, James Loughran from Louth and Pat McQuillan from Meath were arrested by the Louth police. Murphy had named only nine of these eighteen men but according to Pendleton's reports Pat Craven and Thomas Tiernan when arrested allegedly 'named many others'. Michael Kearnan and Terence Marron allegedly confessed their guilt and agreed to be admitted as approvers but Kearnan would later deny his confession during his own trial and Marron would die, according to Pendleton, 'declaring himself innocent'.[81]

By the time the police arrived at the home of Patrick Devan he had already escaped the net.[82] Presumably he had been tipped off and thus went on the run. On 28 April 1817, he wrote to his father from Dublin that he had 'been very ill sometimes since I left home but is [sic] in employment at present and in hopes of better with the assistance of God.'[83] He wrote a second letter, dated 4 May 1817:

> Dear Father,
> All the news you have sent me about me being an informer is false, thanks to God for it. Dear father, I have travelled a very great deal since I left home and never got any employment until I came to Dublin. I have had the severest work, by all accounts, that ever was in Dublin, I am wheeling a barrow in the new docks this two weeks back, at the

78 Ibid. 79 See McIlroy's evidence below. 80 Return of all persons apprehended and committed for the burning and murders at Wildgoose Lodge (NA, SOC, 1828/16). 81 See Appendix II. 82 *Enniskillen Chronicle and Erne Packet*, 31 July 1817. 83 Quoted in *The Times*, 1 Aug. 1817.

small wages of ten shillings per week; there was many a good man cast by my side. I expect a job something easier next week and, in short, when I can buy a pair of shoes I will seek for some sort of place teaching school in the county of Kildare. Dear father, I have often lasted on a pennyworth of bread in the twenty-four hours, so I was very happy to get work where I had got it for I was very much in need of it. I was getting a very good place in the Queen's County for teaching so as I would get a character from my parish minister [Fr McCann], so I don't intend to write to him until I travel more. No more at present from your dutiful son, Pat Devan.[84]

Devan had found employment on the Customs House docks.[85] The coincidence of his sudden departure and the sweeping arrests gave rise to suspicion around Corcreaghy that he had turned informer. There are a couple of things in this letter that suggest possible Ribbon involvement – employment on the docks and contemplating using the traditional Ribbon route along the canal to Kildare[86] – but nothing more substantive. Nor is there anything in the letter that could have implicated him in agrarian activity. But it did lead the authorities to where he was.

Meanwhile, the men who were rounded up in Louth and elsewhere were housed in the very cramped county jail at Dundalk.[87] Like most contemporary jails, it was an unhealthy, noisome place at the best of times; sanitation was poor, the stench was often unbearable and nauseating and it incubated infectious diseases. In the spring of 1817, A. Atkinson found in one of the tiny cells on the ground floor, twelve or fourteen of these men: 'unfortunate victims of the law … unavoidably huddled together … a few days previous to their trial in the spring of 1817'.[88] He concluded:

> The vast number of persons, however, who, in the circumstances of this county, have been unavoidably stowed in some of the cells of that prison, and the inadequacy of the courtyard, to afford them a sufficient measure of air and exercise, clearly evidence the necessity of a new prison.[89]

(In fact, preparations were in train for the construction of a new jail for which the grand jury had voted £1,600 the previous year.)[90]

84 Quoted in ibid. 85 See also *Dublin Evening Post*, 22 July 1817. 86 Kelly, 'Ribbonism in Co. Leitrim', p. 136. 87 Atkinson, *Ireland exhibited to England*, p. 92. 88 Ibid., p. 106. 89 Ibid., pp 92, 106. 90 Revd Elias Thackeray, 'Statistical survey of Dundalk parish, 1816', quoted on

Patrick Murphy was allegedly kept in the magistrate's room attached to Trim jail, away from the general jail population and away from Peter Gollogly. An immediate benefit of turning state's evidence was that their prison conditions were made more comfortable and promises were held out that their families would be better cared for. Pollock instructed the Revd Wainright, inspector of the jail, to 'procure for them [Gollogly and Murphy] some sort of covering & to provide for their wives and children' but Wainright replied that it was impossible for him to find lodgings for the families: 'it being known to whom they belong'.[91]

Pendleton continued to gather corroborating evidence. On 2 April 1817, he formally interviewed Alice Rispin and took a written statement from her. She was to become one of the Crown's key witnesses in each of the trials that were to follow. Her affidavit gave information on the raid of 10 April 1816 and not on events of 29–30 October. She claimed to have been in Wildgoose Lodge that night, asleep in the parlour, when the raid took place. Yet she had not been called as a witness in the first trials nor was there any reference to her presence in the house given in the evidence. Rispin's statement for Pendleton named Hugh McCabe, John Keegan, William Butler, Owen Dickie and Ruck Sheenan,[92] all of whom with the exception of Dickie had by that time already been arrested.

Thomas Gubby

On 8 April, in an unrelated, but subsequently significant development, Sub-constable George Wright raided a number of houses in the townland of Cadian near Dungannon, Co. Tyrone. In the home of James Gubby he found a letter addressed to his son, Thomas, a former linen weaver, with an address at Peter St., Drogheda. Wright, knowing that Gubby, who had been using the alias of Hughes, was wanted for felony, confiscated the letter and passed it on to the police at Drogheda. The chief constable there (and for the un-proclaimed barony of Ferrard) was John Armstrong who owed his position to the patronage of John Foster. The latter wrote of him in July 1817:

> I have long known Mr John Armstrong, Chief Constable of Drogheda
> & Constable for Ferrard in this county, the barony in which my resi-

www.jbhall.freeservers.com/clonmore_1815.htm. **91** Revd M. Wainright to [?], 10 Apr. 1817 (NA, SOC 1829/19). **92** Copy of statement of Alice Rispin given before Samuel Pendleton, 2 Apr. 1817 (Louth County Library, WGL papers).

dence gives me frequent opportunities of knowing his merit which is very eminent on all occasions for activity, great zeal, determined resolution & the most prompt & vigorous exertion accompanied with a sharp understanding & great moderation.[93]

The Drogheda police arrested Gubby the following day and detained him in the town jail where he was interviewed by Foster and Samuel Pendleton.[94] Gubby was a full-time criminal – Samuel Pendleton described him as a 'notorious robber'[95] – who admitted the same in court. He was carrying forged notes when he was arrested in Louth, a felonious crime that carried a capital sentence. He had previously been arrested in Tyrone for 'taking up arms' but ironically released because 'the informant had before accused others of the offence'.[96] In the Wildgoose Lodge trials, the defence counsels time and again attempted to discredit Gubby as a witness by detailing his past criminal record and, indeed, his previous reputation as an approver. In Gubby's cross-examination by Leonard MacNally, for example, he claimed never to have 'witnessed at Armagh',[97] which suggested that the defence had evidence to the contrary. If he had approved in the past, the authorities would have been very much aware of this, certainly the likes of Pendleton and the crown solicitors who travelled the north-east circuit. Thus, when he was arrested in Louth for robbery and forgery, he would immediately have been recognised as a prospective approver.

Six statements were taken from Gubby, no two of which were identical. The main information proffered by him can be summarised as follows: Devan was the leader of the October raid on Wildgoose Lodge; Bernard McIlroy [sometimes Gilroy] was also present; the planning meeting was held at Stonetown where it was agreed 'to set fire to said Lynch's house and burn them therein' (they, therefore, could be said to have set out with intent); about twenty men came from Inniskeen; some of the raiding party wanted to save the children and innocent but the leaders were having none of it declaring that 'the nits should be burned & destroyed as well as the louse'; Devan and McIlroy were the first to fire the house; the other leader of note on the night was a man named McKeever (later identified as McCullough) who along with Devan swore those present to secrecy. Of five others named by Gubby, only James Smyth from Stonetown was brought to trial.[98]

93 Affidavit of John Foster on behalf of John Armstrong, 27 July 1818 (NA, SOC 1828/17). 94 Memorial of sub-constable George Wright, [?] July 1817 (NA, SOC, 1828/17). 95 Report of Samuel Pendleton on information supplied by Thomas Gubby, 21 Apr. 1817 (NA, SOC 1828/15). 96 Letter of G.R. Golding, 16 Apr. 1817; quoted in Murray, The burning of Wildgoose Lodge, p. 185. 97 Drogheda Journal, 4 Apr. 1818. 98 Statement of Thomas Gubby, 9 Apr. 1817 (NA, SOC

A close reading of Gubby's statements suggests that the interrogators were careful to ensure that information on key points emanating (allegedly) from Gubby corroborated the information they had already taken (allegedly) from Murphy and Gollogly. That the authorities wanted someone to implicate Devan as the leader is also evident: 'the plan of burning Wildgoose Lodge was first proposed to him by Pat Devan, schoolmaster at Stonetown'; 'Devan was the first to light the fire'. Gubby's statements also clearly implicated himself and Devan in Ribbonism which again was important from the point of view of Foster and the other magistrates wishing to break what they perceived to be a seditious conspiracy. The State of the Country Papers now on deposit in the National Archives of Ireland clearly demonstrate that 'the general confederacy of crime' suggested to the mindset of the local magistracy the dangers of another uprising like that of 1798. It has already been argued in this work that William Carleton and later writers such as James Anton were also aware of this mindset when they borrowed heavily from accounts of atrocities in 1798 to embellish their graphic descriptions of the terror at Wildgoose Lodge.[99]

In his second statement Gubby alleged that when he met Devan for the first time on the road, Devan 'threw him a sign' by stroking underneath his chin, which Gubby replied to by stroking the back of his left hand. He then produced a certificate to Devan that showed he was 'a true made member of the Defender Society' and that he had taken the oath.[1] Gubby's stated objective of the Ribbonmen –

> that they might be ready and know each other when some favourable opportunity would arise, to fight for their religion and in defence of their faith, and to overcome, and put down all those who were oppressing and persecuting them, namely all enemies to the true Roman Catholic religion, or friends to a Protestant monarchy

1828/15); Ralph Smyth to William Gregory, 14 April 1817 (NA, SOC 1817, 1828/9); Memorial of John Armstrong, chief constable of Drogheda, 26 July 1817 (NA, SOC, 1828/17). **99** See chapter one. **1** The oath read as follows: 'I, A. B., in the presence of Almighty God and his Blessed Son Jesus Christ do swear that I will be true to my brother on all lawful occasions, and that I will not fight a challenge with my brother or see him struck, without espousing his cause, that I will attend when and where I am called by my committee, and spend what is just and proper on the occasion. That I will not hear my brother ill spoken of without giving him information, that I will not buy any article from a Protestant, while a man of my own religion has one at the same rates, that I will not drink to be drunk and that I will not know a brother to be in distress without giving the aid of myself and my pocket'; Statement of Thomas Gubby, 12 Apr. 1817 (NA, SOC 1828/15).

– was more symptomatic of the alarmism of the magistracy and the anti-emancipationist views of his interrogators such as John Foster than reflective of the
local society's agrarian aims.[2] Ralph Smyth, deputy mayor of Drogheda and a
Louth magistrate, wrote to William Gregory on 14 April 1817 that after Pendleton
and Foster had interviewed Gubby in Drogheda jail they 'found him to corre-
spond with other approvers' and on the system of Ribbonism concluded: 'There
cannot however be a doubt that if those he has mentioned and their papers were
seized it would be a death wound to this system and bring to light all the leading persons concerned.'[3]

As noted above Gubby's six affidavits are littered with inconsistencies. In
one, for example, he claimed he was living in the house of Manus Callan
[Caulan] at Loughan in Co. Louth where he met Devan. In another, he says he
first met Devan on the road when, as also noted above, they threw each other
Ribbon signs.[4] If Gubby had been accepted so readily into the local secret society, it would have been exceptional. As Galen Broeker contends: 'It was next to
impossible for outsiders to enter an organisation whose members were all known
to each other.'[5] Broeker has also found that 'suspicion of all outsiders, even those
bearing the credentials of other societies, was a normal attitude amongst the
banditti'.[6] When one considers how difficult it had been for the authorities to
break the secret society, one can surmise that Devan would have been extremely
careful regarding initiating a stranger such as Gubby so freely.

The rest of the surviving historical evidence shows that Gubby's testimony
should never have been accepted.[7] Following his arrest there was a flurry of correspondence from the authorities in Louth attempting to ascertain the reliability of him as an approver. In late April 1817, after Gubby's statements were forwarded to the governor of Trim jail, William Gregory was told: 'This day I had
the honour of yours with the enclosed information of Gubby. I have gone
through it very particularly with Murphy who declares that he knows not one
of those people who are herein mentioned nor this Gubby.'[8] It was one thing
not to know Gubby but Murphy effectively now denied any knowledge of
Patrick Devan who was named in Gubby's statement and who Murphy was supposed to have named in the affidavit witnessed and signed by John and Arthur
Pollock and Samuel Pendleton.

On 19 April 1817 Samuel Pendleton wrote to William Murray, a landlord
magistrate from Drumfields in Tyrone. Murray was extremely sceptical of using

2 Ibid. 3 Ralph Smyth to William Gregory, 14 Apr. 1817 (NA, SOC 1828/9). 4 Statement of
Thomas Gubby, 9 Apr. 1817 (NA, SOC, 1828/15). 5 Broeker, *Rural disorder and police reform*, p.
18. 6 Ibid., p. 11. 7 See also discussion below regarding Bernard McIlroy. 8 William Murphy
to [?William Gregory], 25 April 1817 (NA, SOC 1817, 1829/27).

Gubby who he described as a man of the 'worst description' and so he advised Pendleton: 'I have reviewed Gubby's case in every way that I am capable of doing and am still of my former opinion that his testimony would not be believed'. There was nothing to be gained, he claimed, from using Gubby as an approver.[9] Pendleton forwarded this opinion to William Gregory with an appended note in which he admitted that Gubby's identification of suspects was dubious.[10] In July 1817, after Devan's trial but before the others, Pendleton wrote to Lord Caledon:

> There is no judicial knowledge of his [Gubby] having been concerned in the offence with respect to which the reward is offered – his own confession to that effect is of such description that it was judged not only useless, but dangerous to produce him as a witness, nor has he been at all used as such. As his confession then has not (at least as yet) been available to the publick [sic] for any beneficial purpose, it ought not (I conceive) to be admitted for the purpose of aggravating expense by conferring a reward, more especially where the claim of it rests on accident ...[11]

In September, he reiterated his remarks to William Gregory:

> I do not conceive that any reward can yet with propriety be claimed for apprehending Thomas Gubby. Wright (the Tyrone constable) is misinformed as to having contributed by his [Gubby's] testimony to the conviction of any persons. He has neither been used, nor yet admitted as an approver. It has not yet judiciously appeared that he was 'concerned' in the crime, neither is it certain that any publick [sic] advantage will ever be derived from his confession.[12]

Pendleton's letter to Lord Caledon is the most illuminating: he quite specifically stated that the authorities had no proof that Gubby was involved in the burning of Wildgoose Lodge and that he and others were acutely aware that Gubby's confessions were extremely dubious. Yet, he would become central to the Crown prosecutions.

---

9 William Murray to Samuel Pendleton, 15 April, 20 Apr. 1817 (NA, SOC, 1828/15). 10 William Murray to Samuel Pendleton, 20 Apr. 1817 (NA, SOC, 1828/15). 11 Samuel Pendleton to Lord Caledon, 29 July 1817 (NA, SOC 1828/17). 12 Samuel Pendleton to Sir William Gregory, 23 Sept. 1817 (NA, SOC, 1828/16).

The arrest of Patrick Devan

On 14 April, the aforementioned the Revd Wainright, inspector of the jail at Trim, took a separate statement from Peter Gollogly who named six men he had allegedly seen at the burning: Laurence and Owen Gaynor, James Campbell, Hudy McElearney, Patrick Meighan and Patrick Murphy. It was important for him to have named Murphy for now they could claim to corroborate each other's evidence. The Gaynors were arrested shortly afterwards; the others had already been taken into custody. Around the same time James Morris and William Butler were arrested by the Corcreaghy police. The remainder of the arrests took place on 1 July when Michael Floody from Co. Monaghan was arrested at Hackballscross in Co. Louth (his name had been appended to one of Murphy's affidavits); on 8 October, Bryan Lennon, the blacksmith, was arrested in Inniskeen; and on 22 December Michael Tiernan was re-arrested by the Louth police.[13]

By now Under-Secretary William Gregory was anxious to ensure that an example be made in Louth to put an end to the rural disorder sweeping the borderlands. On 25 April, in light of Murphy having turned approver and the arrest of Gubby, he offered the hope to Foster that there would 'soon be a well connected chain of evidence to prosecute the perpetrators of that horrid massacre'.[14] What was notable in the sweeping arrests that had taken place is that suspects had been lifted predominantly in north Louth, the heartland of the agitation, but also in Meath, south Monaghan (the barony of Farney) and along the south Armagh border near Hackballscross. In March 1816, Foster had written to Dublin Castle (drawing on information provided to him by William Foster, a strong farmer from Barronstown) naming all of these very areas as places where 'a numerous association of persons calling themselves Threshers or Carders' existed and he noted that gangs from Armagh and south Monaghan, notably Inniskeen where Lennon was arrested, had raided into Louth and warned that 'his information lead him to believe [that such raids] will be persevered in these counties unless put a stop to'.[15] The arrests were, therefore, intended to send out a strong message across a wide geographical region.

All this time, Patrick Devan had eluded capture. The authorities obviously knew he had fled, so they kept a watchful eye on the mail, knowing that it was probable that he would try to make contact with his family. In the late eighteenth century, Thomas Bartlett contends: 'The Irish Post Office ... was, apart

13 Memorials of those claiming rewards, 12 Mar. 1818, 21 Jan. 1819 (NA, SOC 1828/16). 14 William Gregory to John Foster, 24 April 1817 (PRONI, Foster papers, D207/42/9). 15 John Foster to [William Gregory], 9 Mar. 1816 (NA, SOC 1763/12).

from its letter-dispatch function, an information-gathering institution.'[16] Letters were regularly opened and copied and in that way used to monitor the movements of suspects. Interestingly, the man who spearheaded this form of espionage during the period of the United Irish threat was the 'vigilant and energetic' Sir John Lees (1739–1811), secretary to the Irish Post Office from 1784, who was father of Sir Harcourt Lees, the Church of Ireland rector of Killanny.[17] In the 1790s radicals such as Wolfe Tone and Arthur O'Connor avoided using the ordinary mail, preferring to dispatch their letters with somebody they could trust.[18] Devan's first letter suggested he knew of the dangers of his mail being intercepted (which, of course, begs the question as to why he continued to communicate) when he asked his father to write 'an answer to me by Biddy Cully when she is coming to Dublin. Let no person know where I am unless Thomas Hasty or Pat McGough.'[19] Who the three named persons were is unknown. None of them seems to have been arrested in connection with the Wildgoose Lodge incident.

Then sometime after 4 May 1817 the second letter from Devan to his father arrived at Carrickmacross post office. This time his handwriting was recognised by Thomas Woods (he would identify the letters and handwriting at Devan's trial and state that he had known the prisoner 'these four or five years')[20] and reported to the police. The morning after its delivery Pendleton's police raided Devan's home.[21] Constable William Leary found the letters concealed somewhere in the house – one account suggests in an old waistcoat that had been hidden under the bed tick, another in his sister's shoe.[22] They revealed Devan's whereabouts. A warrant was issued for his arrest which was then forwarded to George Payne, a constable of the 3rd Division of the Dublin Metropolitan Police, in the hope that him 'being a known city police officer [his presence] might prevent any attempt at rescue when he [Devan] should be arrested'.

Samuel Pendleton ordered Constable Leary and another of his officers to proceed to the Custom House docks in Dublin where Devan was working (and living at number 6 Bridgefoot Street). Leary arrived at the docks on the evening of Wednesday 21 May, a short time before the men were due to quit work. He examined the wages' book where he found a man named 'Devine' listed and assuming this was Devan he was directed to a squad of labourers under a gaffer named Cody. Leary walked up to Devan who 'was so much altered in appear-

16 Bartlett, *Revolutionary Dublin*, p. 14.   17 Ibid., p. 16; see chapter one.   18 Ibid.   19 Quoted in *The Times*, 1 Aug. 1817.   20 *Correspondent*, 28 July 1817.   21 Wallop Brabazon to [?] Ellis, 27 July 1817 (NA, SOC 1828/17).   22 William Filgate's account, 1867; Mathews, *The burning of Wildgoose Lodge*, p. 8.

ance since he had seen him' – he was therefore known to the police before he left Corcreaghy – that to be sure he called out, 'Devine, Mr Cody wants you.' When the labourer replied, 'I'll go to him when I put by my shovel', but then proceeded to head off in the opposite direction, Leary moved to arrest him.[23] There was no struggle. Leary took his prisoner into the back room of a nearby public house and waited there until Constable Payne and others arrived.[24]

Devan was brought to Kilmainham jail and was remanded there until about a week before his trial at the beginning of July.[25] According to John Mathews' account, news of his arrest soon reached Dundalk and this 'produced a dreadful panic … it being rumoured that he would turn informer and hang half the county'.[26] The Castle authorities were now sure that they had the leader of 'the conspiracy'. They decided to try him on his own – usually in the case of multiple arrests prisoners were tried in batches – to make a public statement of the government's intent to quell the rural disorder. But how were they to build up a case against him? William Gregory and others recognised that they needed a more reliable approver than Gubby to corroborate Murphy's evidence.[27]

Bernard McIlroy

In his statements taken before Pendleton, Foster and John Armstrong, Gubby had mentioned another notorious criminal by the name of Bernard McIlroy (once a journeyman weaver from Meath who had settled for a time around Reaghstown).[28] The two of them, it seems, worked out of the same criminal gang (as opposed to local agrarian secret society) at some stage. In April 1817 Pendleton wrote to G.R. Golding, the Tyrone magistrate who had sent the warrant to Drogheda for Gubby's arrest. He made enquiries about the latter and Bernard McIlroy who had been named by Gubby in his statements taken earlier that month. Golding's reply of 16 April 1817 is illuminating: 'There is also another reason to believe that he [Gubby] was guilty of stealing a horse from a person in this neighbourhood … of the name of Pat[ric]k McSorley, as a mare perfectly answering the description has been sworn before me by the Kilroy [McIlroy] alluded to in your letter, as having been in the possession of a brother of his [Gubby's] who also fled at the time of Dixon's robbing'.[29] Thus McIlroy

---

23 Memorial of William Leary, 15 July 1817 (NA, SOC 1828/17). 24 Ibid. 25 Memorial of George Payne, 1 Aug. 1817 (NA, SOC 1828/17); *Belfast Newsletter*, 25 July 1817; *The Times*, 1 Aug. 1817; *Dublin Evening Post*, 29 July 1817. 26 Mathews, *The burning of Wildgoose Lodge*, p. 9. 27 William Gregory to Robert Peel, 9 Apr. 1817. 28 William Murray to Samuel Pendleton, 20 Apr. 1817 (NA, SOC, 1828/15). 29 G.R. Golding to Samuel Pendleton, 16 Apr. 1816; quoted

had sworn against Gubby and his brother and so Gubby exacted his own wicked revenge. (McIlroy was forced to admit during Devan's trial that he was aware Gubby had implicated him in his statements.) Meanwhile, John Foster had already decided that McIlroy could be 'a most material witness' in Devan's trial and so a description of him was taken from Gubby and published in the local newspapers with a reward offered for his arrest.[30] On 27 May 1817, less than a week after Devan's capture, McIlroy was arrested in Navan at a place called the Factory when he was recognised by the local postmaster, John Shore (who would have handled the circulated reward posters).[31]

Unfortunately McIlroy's statement does not seem to have survived but his version of events can be taken from newspaper reports of his evidence presented at the various trials. His evidence epitomised the type of fabrication of which Pendleton stood accused by Peel. Firstly his testimony was constructed so as to suggest his repentance for his role in the Wildgoose Lodge atrocity and therefore give it some credibility. In court McIlroy claimed that for months after the night of the burning his conscience had been haunting him. He alleged that in April 1817 (notably dated to before Devan's arrest) he sent a message to William Filgate to meet him at Slane so that he could confess his role. According to Filgate he had just left for Dublin when the message arrived, and so it was some time later before he received it.[32] From Slane McIlroy made his way to Navan; if he was so remorseful why did he not continue on a few miles north from Slane to Foster's home at Collon or to Filgate's house at Lisrenny? Then one day after his arrest he was looking out the window of Trim jail when by sheer coincidence Mr Charleton, captain of the Meath militia company to which he had once belonged, walked by. McIlroy called out to him and in a desperate attempt to purge his conscience he told Charleton of his active part in the burning of Wildgoose Lodge. At least this is the way the sequence of events were divulged in court and yet in his first statement given to the Revd F.D. Hamilton, McIlroy denied having been at the lodge on the night of the burning although he did claim to have been at the earlier meeting in Stonetown chapel to plan the raid.[33] Hamilton impressed this upon William Gregory, so the under-secretary was clearly aware of his unreliability.[34]

McIlroy was transferred to Dundalk where he made another statement to Samuel Pendleton and local magistrate, Wallop Brabazon, this time allegedly stating that he had been at the lodge on the night of the burning.[35] However, it later emerged in the trials that McIlroy was threatened during his interrogation by Pendleton that he would be tried and executed for the Sillery robbery unless he agreed to turn approver in the Wildgoose Lodge trials.[36] It is very difficult, therefore, not to conclude that there was a wider conspiracy being enacted by the authorities and an alarmed Louth magistracy. That any of these men – McIlroy, Murphy, Gollogly or Gubby – could be depended upon as reliable and conscientious witnesses is questionable. And yet, beginning with the trial of Patrick Devan, they were the key to the prosecution of the Wildgoose Lodge suspects.

35 *The Times*, 1 Aug. 1817. 36 See chapter seven.

CHAPTER FIVE

The trial of Patrick Devan

Hanoverian judges worked within a criminal justice system which quite purposefully upheld propertied hierarchy first and delivered justice second, in which respectable patronage, perceived character, and local tensions were *meant* to affect sentences and appeals, in which judges and home secretaries *had* to placate great men even if not to capitulate to them, in which juries were often timid, mercy grudging, pardons rare, and compensations for wrongful punishment unthinkable.

V.A.C. Gatrell, *The hanging tree*, p. 515.

Introduction

By the summer assizes of July 1817 Patrick Devan had been in gaol for around six weeks, most of the time in Kilmainham. There was nothing unusual in this; bail was a rarity before 1826 and hardly ever allowed in felonies or any crime of a serious nature. Prisoners might become physically and mentally drained from incarceration in grim, overcrowded prison conditions for a period of months before their trials, but there is no evidence to suggest that Devan's prison experience left him in any worse a physical or mental state than when he had been arrested, and there is little point in speculating otherwise.

As a prisoner, Devan had few rights at this stage of the legal process.[1] He had, for example, not been present when the depositions from approvers were taken and most likely had not been informed of the evidence that had been gathered against him. This was very much part of the legal strategy which also prevailed in the English court system. J.M. Beattie has written that 'this ... fitted a particular form and conception of trial in which it was believed that the truth would be most clearly revealed if the prisoner was confronted with the evidence only in the courtroom so that the jury could judge the quality of his immediate, unprepared response'.[2] It was a strategy that put the defendant at an obvious disadvantage, particularly one not represented by a lawyer.

---

1 Much the same procedures were to be gone through in the trials of his alleged co-conspirators the following year. There will, therefore, be no need to repeat a description of these procedures in the next chapter. **2** Beattie, *Crime and the courts in England*, p. 271.

18 A late nineteenth-century sketch of Kilmainham jail in Dublin
to where Devan was taken following his arrest in May 1817.

The pomp and ceremony of the assizes

Saturday 19 July 1817, the first day of the summer assizes, was a 'very fine day'.[3]
By 9 a.m. crowds of people drawn from a wide cross section of society – urban
and rural – thronged the Market Square in Dundalk waiting for the arrival of the
presiding judge, Mr Baron James McClelland (1768–1831), from his home at
Annaverna on the outskirts of the town. McClelland was born and reared in
Banbridge in Co. Down. In 1790 he was called to the Irish bar and eight years
later became MP for Randalstown. Following his support for the Union, he was
appointed solicitor-general in 1801. He was one of the leading crown prosecutors
in the trials of those implicated in the Robert Emmet rebellion of 1803, for which
he received 'high encomiums from the Irish government' and became a baron of
the exchequer in the same year.[4] In 1790, the year he had been called to the bar,
he married the daughter of Acheson Thompson of Annagassan, a Louth landlord.
By 1807 their home at Annaverna had been completed. It was a plain late-

---

3 O'Neill (ed.), *Journal of Henry McClintock*, p. 229.   4 F. Elrington Ball, *The judges of Ireland
1221–1921*, vol. ii (London, 1926), pp 244–5.

Georgian house designed by James Gallier (later renowned for his design of many significant buildings in New Orleans).[5] The house and surrounding estates represented McClelland's initiation into the Louth landed ascendancy.

The pomp and ceremony of the assizes had begun the previous day. Twice a year in the spring (Lent assizes) and July (summer assizes) Dundalk witnessed what could best be described as: 'the most visible and elaborate manifestation of state power to be seen in the countryside apart from the presence of a regiment'.[6] For the gentry it was an occasion to be noted in their social diaries as they paraded from one country house to another on a round of dinners, balls and other forms of entertainment.[7] The gentry, in their capacity as grand jurors, saw the necessity to nurture a strong working relationship with the assize judges; thus, prior to the summer assizes of 1816, John Foster wrote to Brabazon Disney Shiels, the high sheriff of Louth, informing him that the judges would dine and sleep at his home in Collon before moving on to Dundalk.[8]

For the less well off, the assizes provided a carnival atmosphere especially when they coincided with fairs and markets. For the thousands who crowded into Dundalk that fine summer morning the trial of Patrick Devan was an occasion in its own right.

At shortly after 9 a.m. Baron McClelland handed his commission to the clerk of the crown, John Pollock, as was customary, who read it aloud thereby announcing the formal opening of the court and ensuring the legality of the proceedings. Depositions and statements were then presented to the clerk for him to prepare bills of indictment for the grand jury. The latter institution had its roots in the medieval period. It played a central role in the criminal justice process as it was the responsibility of its members to examine the bills and the depositions which had been taken by the magistrates and to decide who of the accused would be set free or brought to trial. Invariably, John Foster's influence once again came to have a major bearing on proceedings as the composition of the jury reflected his long nurturing of a strong working relationship with many of the county's most powerful families. Twenty-one of the maximum number of twenty-three jurors were present, an obvious statement of intent by the Louth ascendancy to put an end to the widespread criminality. In 1817 Foster was chairman of the jury as he had been for a number of years. His eldest son, Thomas, joined him on the jury. Thomas' wife was the only child of the fourth earl of Masserene and Harriet Jocelyn, daughter of the first earl of Roden, which made him a brother-in-law of Viscount Jocelyn who also sat on the jury.[9] William

5 Bence-Jones, *A guide to Irish country houses*, p. 4.   6 Gattrell, *The hanging tree*, p. 532.   7 O'Neill (ed.), *Journal of Henry McClintock*, p. 229; see also Garnham, *Criminal law in Ireland*, p. 105.   8 John Foster to B.D. Shiels, 15 July 1816 (PRONI, Foster papers, D562/13120).   9 Harold

Filgate and Alexander Filgate were nephews of Townley Filgate, owner of the Wildgoose Lodge, and both were sons of William Sr of Lisrenny (died December 1816) to whom the first raid on the lodge had been reported by Lynch. The Filgates had long been political supporters of John Foster and close friends; in the previous December 1816 Foster wrote: 'I am afraid my good old friend Filgate is dangerously ill & his family much alarmed for him.'[10] There were further ties of a financial nature: in the late eighteenth century, William Filgate was just one of a number of fellow landlords and middlemen/strong farmers from whom Foster borrowed money at a time when his own debts stood at £72,000 on a rent roll of £10,000 per annum.[11] Thomas Foster was colonel of the Louth Militia; Alexander Filgate was lieutenant-colonel, as was Chichester Fortescue. John Foster's mother was Fortescue and so he was kinsman to Chichester, Mathew (Stephenstown) and Faithful (Corderry), all of whom sat on the jury. Indeed, Foster, Viscount Jocelyn, the three Fortescues, William Ruxton (Red House, Ardee) and John McClintock (brother-in-law of William Gregory) all belonged to families that had intermarried over successive generations. Of the other jurors, Thomas Lloyd was agent to Lord Clermont (elder brother of Chichester Fortescue). John Woolsey was agent to Mrs J.W. Foster. John Taafe resided at Smarmore Castle and William H. Richardson at Prospect House. At least twelve of the jurors had held or would hold the prestigious office of high sheriff of Louth one of whose functions was to select the grand jury on an annual basis. With the exception of Thomas Fitzgerald (who had made his fortune as a merchant and only recently had purchased Fane Valley House and estate as a means of access to social and political respectability), all of the 1817 grand jury were of 'old landed stock'.[12] Very little had changed from the eighteenth century when the 'packing' of the grand jury in Louth illustrated the way in which it was dominated by powerful family interest groups.[13]

The decision regarding who was to be tried was now in the hands of the jurors. Before they retired to a private room in the Market House to deliberate

O'Sullivan, 'The courthouse Dundalk and the contract for its erection, dated 30th April 1813' in *Journal of the County Louth Archaeological Society*, 15:2 (1962), p. 132. **10** John Foster to Samuel Pendleton, 13 Dec. 1816 (PRONI, Foster papers, D562/13145); Malcomson, *John Foster*, pp 260–1. **11** The rental and account ledger for 1780 records £80 for one year's interest paid to Filgate; H.G.T., 'Rental and accounts of Collon estate, 1779–81' in *Journal of the County Louth Archaeological Society*, 10:3 (1943), p. 225; Malcomson, 'Foster' (www.oxforddnb.com/view/article/9960). **12** The grand jury was comprised of John Foster (foreman), Viscount Jocelyn, T.H. Skeffington, Blayney Balfour, Chichester Fortescue, Mathew Fortescue, Alexander Filgate, Nicholas Coddington, Wallop Brabazon, John McClintock, W.P. Ruxton, J.F. Ruxton, John Taafe, F.W. Fortescue, Thomas Tisdal, John Woolsey, Thomas Fitzgerald, Philip Pendleton, William Filgate, Thomas Lloyd and W.H. Richardson. **13** Garnham, *Criminal law in Ireland*, p. 126.

in private whether the prepared bills of indictment represented *prima facie* cases or not, they were addressed by McClelland in what was more or less a set-piece, the standard fare of which has been described by Neal Garnham:

> This [charge by the judge] was essentially a judicial 'pep-talk' designed to inculcate the appropriate sentiments in the grand jurors. In general, the charge extolled the virtues of trial by jury and the national constitution, before moving on to remind the jury of the onerous burden of their responsibilities, and highlighting the particularly heinous nature of recent prevalent offences. The charge could additionally hold a political significance.[14]

Several bills of indictment for the murders of Lynch, Rooney and Rispin as well as for the burning of the lodge were sent for Patrick Devan who was to appear alone before the court on the following Monday, 21 July. The government's intention to break up the so-called conspiracy by striking right at the heart of it was further emphasised when it sent its most powerful team of prosecutors to Dundalk. The solicitor-general, Charles Kendal Bushe (1767–1843), and Serjeant Henry Joy (1763–1838) were both nominated by the attorney general, William Saurin, to lead the crown prosecution. Sir Robert Peel held that Bushe, often referred to as the 'incorruptible Irishman',[15] who had successfully prosecuted members of the Catholic Committee in 1811, was 'one of the most distinguished sons of Ireland' while Joy was the son of Henry Joy, proprietor of the *Belfast Newsletter*, an ardent anti-emancipationist.[16] The latter had been called to the Irish Bar in 1788 and for twenty years had travelled the north-east circuit. In 1808 he became king's counsel and in 1817 was elevated to the position of first serjeant.

The composition of the petty jury

On the following Monday morning the Market House was packed to capacity and beyond when Patrick Devan entered a plea of 'not guilty' (one reporter found it difficult to hear because of the bustle around him).[17] This meant he had to be tried by a petty jury that had to be constructed by the high sheriff

14 *Drogheda Journal*, 4 Mar. 1818; Garnham, *Criminal law in Ireland*, pp 106, 109. 15 Edith Somerville and Martin Ross, *An incorruptible Irishman: being an account of Chief Justice Charles Kendal Bushe, and of his wife Nancy Crampton and their times, 1767–1843* (London, 1932). 16 Ball, *The judges of Ireland*, vol. ii, p. 260. 17 *Belfast Newsletter*, 25 July 1817.

unless he delegated responsibility for the same to a sub-sheriff. In April 1816 Brabazon Disney Shiels, high sheriff of Co. Louth that year, had accompanied the patrol of the Peace Preservation Force that policed the disaffected baronies of Louth and Ardee. William Filgate was part of the same patrol and the close relationship of both with John Foster has already been noted. According to the law, Protestant or Catholic freeholders – men who owned property outright (in fee) or who held it by lease for one or more lives of people named in it and with a freehold worth at least forty shillings a year – were entitled to act as jurors. In other words, these were men of property who had been susceptible to outrage and attack from agrarian societies over the previous two years or so. In total there were seven Wildgoose Lodge juries and fifty-seven jurors were used (a number were repeat jurors.) The properties which most of these held were considerably more in excess of forty-shilling freeholds. Of thirty-four for whom the valuation was identified only two were forty-shilling freeholders (Owen McKenna and Robert Getty); one was a £100 freeholder, twenty-five were £50 freeholders and six were £20 freeholders. On the Devan jury the freeholds of seven were identified and six of these were £50 and one £20.[18] Of the English case in the early nineteenth century, Douglas Hay has written:

> The cottager who appeared in court charged with theft had no illusions about being tried by 'his equals and neighbours', whatever the writers of law books claimed. The twelve men sitting opposite him were employers, overseers of the poor, propertied men, in most cases they were the equals and neighbours of the prosecutor, not the accused, and this was especially true in cases of theft. The point is not that such juries convicted against the evidence, but rather that a more democratic jury might not have convicted at all.[19]

There is no doubt but that the sheriffs responsible for the choice of panels could abuse their powers and easily pack juries.[20] There are very few details about the choosing of jurors in any of the Wildgoose Lodge trials. One newspaper noted that Devan, who defended himself, used up his twenty peremptory challenges (challenges without cause), which he was entitled to do, but

---

18 The Louth sources used for identifying the jurors are available at www.jbhall.freeservers.com.
19 Douglas Hay, 'Property, authority and the criminal law' in Douglas Hay et al. (eds), *Albion's fatal tree: crime and society in eighteenth-century England* (London, 1975), p. 39.   20 D.S. Johnson, 'The trials of Sam Gray: Monaghan politics and nineteenth century Irish criminal procedure' in *Irish Jurist*, 20 (1985), p. 132; see also J.F. McEldowney, 'The case of the Queen v. McKenna (1869) and jury packing in Ireland' in *Irish Jurist*, 12 (1977), pp 338–54.

unfortunately that is all the information available. It is unlikely that these challenges made any significant impact as the Crown had a corresponding right to
challenge (without showing just cause) and to request a potential juror to 'stand
aside' until the whole panel of names chosen by the high sheriff had been gone
through. The implication of this process was that from the Crown's point of
view favourable jurors down the list would then comprise the jury, therefore
effectively allowing the Crown to hand pick who sat on it.[21] Other than the
Devan trial, the only insight into this process was given in the *Freeman's Journal*
in respect to the spring trials of 1818 when the Crown prosecutors unsuccessfully questioned the right of the defence counsels to issue its challenges before
the prosecution set aside the jurors called, citing as precedence a trial held in
Derby, England.[22]

   If Louth landlords were dominating local politics and society, they were
doing so with the tacit support of their freeholders, in the main men who were
strong farmers in the rural areas or prosperous businessmen in the towns (the
propertied urban classes of Dundalk accounted for at least twenty of the jurors
whose occupations were positively identified), the majority of whom also shared
their Protestant religion (although one jury was comprised entirely of Catholic
gentlemen),[23] and all of whom were tied to each other through an intricate web
of socio-economic relationships that were more rather than less often moulded
by patronage.[24] These businessmen, merchants and strong farmers had all made
considerable social and economic gains during the modernisation and commercialisation era that had preceded the ending of the Napoleonic wars and as
McClintock's diaries suggest Dundalk was an example of a town and rural hinterland where instead of religion dividing communities, socio-economic bonds
tied them together. A. Atkinson in his report on Dundalk in 1817 explained that
'in former years a considerable proportion of the money which the landholder
received for the purpose of his farm was expended in this town in purchasing
the necessary articles and comforts that his farm would not supply; the money
was thus returned to its former channel and the consequence was wealth and
prosperity'.

   Devan and his gang had worked out of an area within a radius of about ten
miles of Dundalk. The point has already been made that Judge Baron
McClelland lived at Annaverna right on the outskirts of the town; the high sheriff in 1817, Turner Macan from Greenmount, lived a few miles away. By the time
the jury was selected it was evident that Macan had used the panel in such a
way as to ensure compliance. All of the jurors were from the proclaimed bar-

21 My thanks to Niamh Howlin for her advice on this subject.   **22** *Freeman's Journal*, 3 Apr. 1818.
23 See chapter six.   **24** See chapter two.

onies of Dundalk. Half (at least) were officers of the Dundalk vestry and therefore shared responsibility for major areas of the town's administration. They
were William Foster, Alexander Shekleton, Malcolm Browne, Laurence Tallan,
John Scott and John Barrett.[25] (Fourteen out of the twenty-seven petty officers
named in the minutes of the vestry for the period 1812–16 served on one or more
of the Wildgoose Lodge juries.) As noted in chapter two, Shekleton owned the
iron foundry; Browne owned the distillery; Tallan was a successful merchant
and a juror of long-standing experience: he was listed as far back as 1777 in the
names of the jurors 'to try the prisoners and traversers at the assizes and general gaol delivery, to be held at Dundalk for the said county, on Tuesday, this
12th day of August 1777'.[26] The strength of Tallan's business was to a large extent
based on the patronage of the local governing elite. In March 1816, for example, he entered into negotiations with John Foster regarding the supply of lamps
and other merchandise to be used for the proposed new Dundalk jail.[27] In
February 1819, Alexander Shekleton would write to Foster that his firm would
have the railings ready for the new courthouse in time for its opening and further stating that another Dundalk merchant, William Hale (who would sit on
later Wildgoose juries), would have the furniture ready.[28] Of the other jurors,
William Foster, a landlord from Barronstown, had, as referred to above, corre-
sponded with Foster in March 1816 telling him of the 'numerous association of
persons, calling themselves Threshers or Carders who have also taken an illegal
oath & who under that oath have committed many enormities, and intend further to commit (if not checked in time) various others of a more serious nature',
and warning of the dangers of raiding parties from south Monaghan and south
Armagh to the future peace of Louth.[29]

The others who made up the twelve-man jury were Henry McNeale, John
Baillie, Alexander Donaldson, George Eyre, John Corry and Robert Wynne.[30]
Henry McNeale, John Baillie and Alexander Donaldson were all £50 freehold-
ers and extensive farmers or middlemen. Baillie was a near neighbour of Judge
McClelland at Annaverna and held hundreds of acres. MacNeale also appears
time and again in the correspondence with Dublin Castle from amongst those
seeking protection from the spread of agitation from 1815 onwards.[31] George
Eyre was a shopkeeper in Dundalk. One of the two jurors not positively iden-

25 See footnote 29, chapter 2.   26 Anon., 'Jurors of Co. Louth in 1777' in *Journal of the County
Louth Archaeological Society*, 6:4 (1928), p. 276.   27 John Foster to Laurence Tallan, 12 Mar. 1816
(PRONI, Foster papers, D562/13092).   28 Alexander Shekleton to John Foster, 7 Feb. 1819
(PRONI, Foster papers, D562/13234).   29 William Foster to John Foster, 9 Mar. 1816 (NA, SOC
1763/12).   30 *Correspondent,* 28 July 1817.   31 See for example, NA, Official Papers, 1712/60–4,
referred to in Murray, *Burning of Wildgoose Lodge*, p. 134.

tified was John Corry (the other was Robert Wynne) but there is a strong possibility that he was a close relation of James Corry, secretary of the Linen Board of Ireland, who had been appointed to this position as a result of Foster's patronage. A.P.W. Malcomson writes of James Corry: 'John Foster's strongest card was that he could count on the unswerving loyalty of the secretary of the board, James Corry. Corry and his father before him had been appointed secretary through Foster's influence, and both had served under him as clerks in the Irish House of Commons and in other key situations.'[32]

The jury was thus comprised of men of substantial property and so their impartiality and independence should therefore not be overstated. By the early nineteenth century upholding the law through the state apparatus was very much a concern of such men. The first raid on Wildgoose Lodge had been an attack on property. For that three men had forfeited their lives. But the second raid was seen to be an attack on the laws of the state; men had deliberately taken the lives of those who had aided and abetted the state in prosecuting the suspects. This was of particular concern not only to the local governing elite such as the county MPs, Foster and Lord Roden, but also Dublin Castle.[33] The trial scenario that presented itself was, therefore, very different to a later period. Devan was to be tried in Dundalk in the heart of the disturbed area of Louth, by a jury who were all most likely personally acquainted with each other, presided over by a judge who was also from Dundalk and who knew most of the jury. Judge and jury were all familiar with the history of agrarian crime in the area and all had been undoubtedly affected in some way by the activities of societies such as that led by Devan. In the eighteenth century it was commonly held that this situation was completely acceptable because juries who came out of the neighbourhood were regarded as the 'best judges of the witnesses and local circumstances'.[34] Overall, the selection of petty jurors, the strength of the prosecution team sent to Dundalk, the length of the addresses to the jury and the tone and the content of the same suggested that the authorities saw Devan's trial as their best chance to break the chain of violence once and for all that had existed in Louth for over two years.[35]

The solicitor-general, Charles Kendal Bushe, opened the Devan trial for the Crown prosecution in a speech that lasted an estimated two and a half hours. He delivered it 'in his usual eloquent strain' (it was noted by F. Elrington Ball

32 Malcomson, *John Foster*, p. 271. 33 *Newry Telegraph*, 4 Apr. 1818; *Kilkenny Moderator*, 12 Mar. 1818; *FJ*, 3 Apr. 1818. 34 *The office and authority of a judge in Ireland* (Dublin, 1756), p. 5; quoted in Garnham, *Criminal law in Ireland*, p. 120. 35 On how the authorities set about doing this elsewhere, see Padraig Ó Macháin, *Six years in Galmoy: rural unrest in County Kilkenny, 1819–1824* (Dublin, 2004).

he usually 'exhibited in his speeches, no less legal knowledge than forensic elo-
quence').[36] Bushe was highly experienced in this type of trial; he had, for example, acted as counsel for the Crown in the prosecution of the Threshers in 1806.
His speech was as much directed to the packed courtroom as to the jury. He
began by describing the original raid on the lodge in April 1816 and praised the
Lynch family for their courage 'to convict three unfortunate delinquents'. He
then 'continued to reprobate the spirit which prevails in this country, where, if
a man comes forward to complain of the destruction of his family, he is exe-
crated'.[37] It was in vain, he told the court that 'the judges are learned and impartial, that juries are upright and honest; whilst the present turbulent spirit prevails, a man must almost despair of the country'. He spoke of 'infuriated mobs'
and 'secret oaths' and described the accused as 'the principal commander and
a most ferocious character':[38]

> [Wildgoose Lodge] stood in a morass, flooded almost all the year round
> in that season of the year, and near to which a number of roads meet;
> that the parties assembled at an appointed hour at that spot with mil-
> itary precision and they were so numerous that some of them, when
> they met, did not know and had never seen one another before that
> period. When the house was consumed they gave three cheers, and took
> an oath of secrecy! What species of education these people had received
> he could not conceive when, after having dipped their hands in inno-
> cent blood, they had the audacity to take a solemn oath to conceal their
> crime, in the presence of almighty God.[39]

Bushe finished with instructions to the jurors that conviction based on
the evidence of informers should not be used 'unless corroborated by other
evidence or other circumstances'.[40] But what exactly did that mean and how
did his warning translate in the context of the trial and the findings of the
jury? Seven years later, in 1824, a legal pamphlet justified the use of approvers
as a matter of 'necessity and good sense' by drawing on the Wildgoose Lodge
trials; after Bushe the point was made by Serjeant Joy to the jury that as all of
the people in Wildgoose Lodge had been murdered on the night (there were
no more references to the survivor reported by Gregory to Peel): 'it must be
naturally suggested that the testimony of accomplices must be reverted to, in

36 Ball, *The judges of Ireland*, vol. ii, p. 342. 37 Newspaper clipping, untitled, July 1817, (PRONI,
T2354/2/7). 38 *Enniskillen Chronicle and Erne Packet*, 31 July 1817; Charles Bushe to William
Saurin, 21 July 1817 (NA, SOC, 1828/14). 39 *Correspondent*, 28 July 1817; *Dublin Evening Post*,
29 July 1817. 40 *FJ*, 23 July 1817; *Enniskillen Chronicle and Erne Packet*, 31 July 1817.

order to bring the perpetrators of this most nefarious deed to condign punishment'.[41] In this (and every) case approver therefore equalled accomplice. The 1824 pamphlet contended that the burning was one of those crimes in which the evidence of accomplices was 'peculiarly admissable' because the crime had been planned and executed in such a meticulous manner and the oath-bound society had so quickly closed ranks that it baffled the ordinary means of detection.[42] Time and again during the remainder of the trials Joy emphasised to the juries that 'in such cases when the testimony of accomplices is supported by incontestable evidence the law allows such testimony to be sufficient to rest a verdict of guilty upon [the accused].'[43]

In their prefatory remarks the prosecution in the Devan case was therefore careful to acknowledge the legal boundaries within which the case should proceed but then they moved those boundaries so as to accommodate the use of approvers who were dependent for their lives upon the evidence they would give. Any attempts to discredit the approver system by the defence was preempted by Bushe's remarks to the effect that the law assumed that an accomplice had to be regarded as a competent witness if his/her evidence could be corroborated.[44] The principle of corroboration was based on testimony concurring with evidence or with facts that could not have resulted from mere coincidence or prior collusion between the witnesses. Corroboration, the 1824 pamphlet maintained, had to come from witnesses who were not accomplices and who were not dependent for their own lives on providing evidence.[45] Two types of witnesses were thus called in the Wildgoose Lodge trials: the approvers and the corroborators. The latter were men of standing such as William Filgate or Samuel Pendleton or neighbours of the Lynches such as Alice Rispin or Patrick Halpenny who were not implicated in the crime. In order to enhance the credibility of those Crown witnesses Bushe extolled their bravery to the jury by relating the story of a widow who had come forward to prosecute for the murder of her husband and a father who prosecuted for the murder of his son who both subsequently found themselves in need of military protection.[46] The prosecution made a protracted and grave address and, as Desmond McCabe contends: 'A tone of urgency in court could well have affected the more impressionable petit, or petty, jurors, who would actually try the case.'[47]

---

41 *Drogheda Journal*, 4 Apr. 1818. 42 E.N., *A full report of the important trial and execution for the burning of the Wildgoose Lodge* (hereafter *Wildgoose Lodge trial*) (Drogheda, 1824), p. 44. 43 *Drogheda Journal*, 4 Apr. 1818. 44 E.N., *Wildgoose Lodge trial*, p. 5. 45 Ibid., p. 10. 46 *Enniskillen Chronicle and Erne Packet*, 31 July 1817. 47 McCabe, 'Crown prosecution and jury trial', p. 162.

The case for the prosecution

In her study of Ribbonism Jennifer Kelly has made the point that very often 'witnesses' evidence would be questioned by the police and magistrates because the conduct of the witness was so incredible that it was not worthy of serious consideration, or else because the character of the witness was so notorious that no jury would be found to believe his story'.[48] The Wildgoose Lodge trials, beginning with that of Patrick Devan, were exceptional in that respect.

First called to the witness stand was William Filgate Jr.[49] He was a respectable member of a prominent local gentry family who at the time of the murders was agent to his uncle Townley Patten Filgate (also present at the trial) who owned the lodge; the jury were bound to take on board his evidence. He described the location of the lodge, remarked that Lynch was 'a brave old man' who had been given arms to protect himself after the first raid on his home. He said that he had gone to the lodge on the day following the burning where he saw 'the fragments of several dead bodies'.[50]

The next witness was another corroborator, Patrick Halpenny, who lived near Lynch's and whose home was raided for a burning turf on the night of the murders. He claimed he was the first to arrive at the lodge the morning after to find it still smouldering.[51] Alice Rispin, who lived about a mile from the lodge across the bog, informed the court about how unfortunate her son had been; the night after the April raid he had come home to stay with her and had only returned to Lynch's the very day of the burning. She saw eight corpses taken from the house, including that of her son. Rispin's testimony held an emotive appeal. Next called was Dr Henry Munro Blackwell, the county coroner, a resident of Collon. He does not seem to have had much to say except that when he arrived at the lodge the morning after he examined eight corpses that had by then been removed from the house. He had known Lynch for some time and was able to identify his corpse.[52]

The scene was now set for the introduction of the approvers. The first called was Bernard McIlroy who stated he sought no reward, he merely wanted 'to do justice'.[53] He began by identifying Devan in court whom he claimed to have known since the summer of 1816 when he had moved from Meath to live at

48 Kelly, 'Ribbonism in Co. Leitrim', p. 94.   **49** Unless otherwise stated the information on the trial is taken from *Freeman's Journal*, 23 July 1817; *Belfast Newsletter*, 25 July 1817; *Correspondent*, 28 July 1817; *Dublin Evening Post*, 29 July 1817; *The Times*, 1 Aug. 1817.   **50** *The Times,* 1 Aug. 1817.   **51** Ibid.   **52** *Belfast Newsletter*, 25 July 1817.   **53** His evidence as presented is taken from *Belfast Newsletter*, 25 July 1817; *Correspondent*, 28 July 1817, *Dublin Evening* Post, 29 July 1817; *The Times,* 1 Aug. 1817.

19 The taking of the oath at Stonetown Chapel. Taken from Carleton, *Traits and stories*. Note that Devan's followers are much more respectable looking than in the earlier sketch in figure 3, above.

Farly in the parish of Louth. McIlroy testified that he was a Ribbonman and that he had been persuaded under duress – 'he dared not refuse to do so or he would be probably shot himself' – to participate in the crime by Devan and Thomas Gubby. The prosecution made the most of this confession; he had to describe at length what it meant to be a Ribbonman and to reveal that the oath he took – 'an obligation he made on his knees and not on a book' – swore him, amongst other things, 'not to deal with a Protestant if they could get what they wanted from a Catholic'. In the context of the burning of Wildgoose Lodge this part of the oath had little if any bearing on what happened but it would have impacted strongly on a Protestant propertied jury most of whom were Dundalk businessmen. His examination on the subject hinted more at the authorities' alarmism regarding the so-called Louth conspiracy than their understanding of the working of a local agrarian society.

According to McIlroy, Gubby had brought him to an earlier meeting at Stonetown chapel on Friday night 25 October 1816 at which it was decided: 'there must be a gathering as quickly as possible of the boys to go and set fire to Lynch's house for the purpose of burning him and his family for prosecuting the three men at Dundalk'. (Gubby's statements do not corroborate this.) Therefore, McIlroy testified there had been intent from the start and that what happened on the night had been planned with malicious design. He also testified to the presence of a gang of twelve men from Inniskeen. The only other reference to Inniskeen men before this came in one of Gubby's statements of 12 April 1817, which again hints that the authorities were feeding information from one approver to another.[54] Moreover, on 5 June 1817, the Revd Francis Hamilton, described as the portreeve of Navan (an archaic term to describe the chief officer, possibly mayor, of a town or borough) had written to William Gregory that 'Kilroy [McIlroy] admits he was present amongst the party at the chappel [sic] of Stonetown upon the occasion of one of their meetings to prepare for the accomplishment of the burning and murders but was not present at the perpetration of them …'[55] Yet during Devan's trial, McIlroy gave extended details of what happened on the night including that he had been ordered by Devan to carry unthreshed corn to the house to fuel the flames. According to newspaper evidence McIlroy claimed during cross-examination that he had 'got acquainted with Gubby in Drogheda'.[56] The evidence of G.R. Golding, the Tyrone magistrate, quoted above shows that McIlroy and Gubby had long been acquainted as partners in crime and that McIlroy had previously

---

54 Gubby statement, 12 Apr. 1817. 55 F.D. Hamilton to William Gregory, 5 June 1817, (nA, SOC 1828/13). 56 *Belfast Newsletter*, 25 July 1817.

implicated Gubby in the theft of a horse with the result that when Gubby was arrested he named McIlroy in a fit of pique. The Revd Francis Hamilton said in court that when he arrested McIlroy the latter replied that 'he knew what the charge was; it was for the burning and murder at Wildgoose Lodge and said he was sure it was through Gubby's malice that he had been charged with it and he declared his innocence'.[57] The latter part of Hamilton's statement was very much in keeping with his earlier written report to Gregory; it adds to the scepticism as to how McIlroy could have been regarded in the first place as a reliable witness.

The authorities had been warned about the unreliability of Gubby and so decided against using him as the second approver. They also chose to ignore Murphy and Gollogly and opted instead for a surprise choice, a man named Patrick Clarke from Churchtown, close to the lodge, in the opposite direction to Stonetown. Clarke's testimony was straight forward: on the night of the burning he heard a great deal of noise outside his house, he went out to investigate and was then called over by a party of men who took him along with them and made him swear on 'a book' that he would never reveal what was about to happen. He claimed he was not an active participant in the raid. He never saw Devan before the burning and not again until he met him in Dundalk jail. However, he was sure that Devan was the leader on the night; it was he who refused to let the girls and child out saying: 'Did they [the raiders] want their lives to be taken, by letting any out to inform against them?' Therefore Devan was represented as the leader of a secret society, who showed callous disrespect for life on the night by someone who could clearly identify him.

The use of Clarke as the second approver is perplexing simply because the existing evidence throws up more questions than it provides answers. First of all, the historical evidence tells us that Devan defended himself during his trial and according to Mathew's nationalist account he did so 'with extraordinary ability until a man named Clarke came up ... As soon as Devan saw him coming on the witness table he let fall a handkerchief he held in his hand.'[58] This piece of lore suggests there was an acquaintanceship between the two and that Devan knew he was doomed the moment he saw Clarke was about to approve. But there is no further evidence to authenticate an acquaintanceship, unless one was struck up on Devan's arrival in the jail only days before, on the Wednesday prior to the trial.

It was Clarke's own confession that implicated him in the crime. Until the trial there had been no mention of him in official circles, and certainly not in any of the statements of the approvers. He had not been arrested during the March

1817 round up or later in connection with Wildgoose Lodge; in fact in his evidence during Devan's trial Pendleton stated that 'Clarke was taken up under no particular charge'. Why then within a week of Murphy's statement did Pendleton take one from Clarke on 19 March? A pardon for his crimes and a substantial monetary reward were obvious inducements for Clarke to agree to testify if a pardon for his own crimes could be procured but was he encouraged to do so by the authorities or even by his fellow inmates, McIlroy or Murphy? Was there something in Devan's line of enquiry when cross-examining the chief magistrate that forced the latter to deny he had heard that Clarke was a relation of Murphy's?[59] What did Devan know or suspect? More pertinently, why did Clarke choose to make a statement to the police implicating himself in the Wildgoose Lodge affair and thereby essentially signing his own death warrant if the crime he had been arrested for was totally unrelated? Initially he seemed to know very little about Devan. According to Pendleton's evidence, Clarke's March statement 'did not at all implicate Devan', 'never mentioned anything respecting Devan' and that 'up to Devan's committal to this jail [Dundalk] Clarke did not implicate him, but McIlroy did.'[60] According to Constable James Corrigan, one of Pendleton's police who was called to corroborate, Clarke only recognised Devan after he arrived in Dundalk – 'he knew his features but not his name' – and only then reported him to the jailers as 'a man that was at the burning of Wildgoose Lodge'.[61]

For six weeks or so one can surmise that Clarke had been unavoidably in contact with Bernard McIlroy in the cramped conditions of Dundalk jail and yet when Devan cross-examined him Clarke swore he did not know a man named McIlroy although he had 'heard of such a man being in jail'; he denied ever hearing that Murphy had sworn against him; and stated that he had 'never spoke to the prisoner [Devan] about Lynch's business'. From these scraps of testimony one can conjecture what Devan was implying: that the prisoners had co-existed for some time in the same jail where information could have passed freely from one to another; Devan had spoken to Clarke about the burning of the lodge before the latter identified him as being one of the leaders; Clarke had communicated with the other approver, McIlroy, which was against regulations; and that the police had forced Clarke to approve by threatening that Murphy had testified against him and so he could be tried for the murders at Wildgoose Lodge if he refused to co-operate. James Corrigan was quick to refute some of these charges by asserting that when he 'got charge of the prisoners [Clarke and McIlroy] after their communications to Mr Pendleton, he was desired to keep them asunder which he did placing one in the gaol and the other in the guard

59 *Correspondent*, 28 July 1817; *Belfast Newsletter*, 25 July 1817.   60 *Correspondent*, 28 July 1817.
61 Ibid.

20 A late-Victorian photograph of the Market Square in Dundalk (National Photographic Archive, Lawrence Collection).

room'.[62] William Filgate likewise emphasised in his 1867 account that McIlroy and Clarke's statements were taken separately but he went a stage further by stressing that they had been kept in separate prisons.[63] His statement seems a case of trying too hard to show that due legal procedures had been adopted.

This was the only case in which Clarke acted as an approver. The defence closed its case with corroborating evidence from Constable Leary who had searched Devan's house around 12–13 March (when he found nothing) and in May when he found the two letters previously referred to, and by George Paine, the chief constable of the 3rd Division of Dublin police who assisted in the arrest of Devan.[64]

The case for the defence

Defence counsels were not yet an integral part of criminal trial procedure particularly if the defendant could not afford a lawyer.[65] (In 1800 at the Old Bailey

62 Ibid.; *Dublin Evening Post,* 29 July 1817. **63** William Filgate's account, 1867. **64** *The Times,* 1 Aug. 1817; for other accounts of the trial see *Enniskillen Chronicle and Erne Packet,* 31 July 1817. **65** Garnham, *Criminal law in Ireland,* p. 114.

in London, seven out of every ten defendants, including many on trial for their lives, had no defence lawyers.)[66] Had Devan been a prominent Ribbonman as the prosecution claimed, it is likely that the society would have raised the necessary money to provide a defence counsel.[67] When Devan chose to defend himself whether out of pecuniary want or not, it may have been that neither he nor his associates anticipated the show of legal strength that would arrive in Dundalk.

Prior to the Prisoner's Counsel Act of 1836, the defence could cross-examine as the primary means of asserting its case. Devan certainly availed of this course of action, but as was usual for the time he relied primarily on character witnesses as his best means of encouraging the judge and jury to believe in his trustworthiness and by extension innocence. The general belief was that if an employer or a member of the local gentry or aristocracy could be secured it improved chances of acquittal.[68] James Devan, the prisoner's brother, when called told the court that Patrick had not weaved for quite some time and that the whole family 'were in hard circumstances' as they had 'not a spot of ground'.[69] It was perhaps a revealing statement as to why his brother had involved himself in the local agrarian society. His brother also alleged that Patrick had made little money from school teaching during the spring of 1817 as the children were hired out to local farmers or kept at home to help with the spring labour and with few alternative employment opportunities available as a result of the economic crisis he had migrated to Dublin. James contended that Patrick was at home the night of the burning, that he had been more or less bedridden for about a month because of sickness. The judge suggested calling 'the medical person' from Carrickmacross who supposedly administered medicine to the prisoner, but this course of action was not followed. James was questioned regarding the content of the two aforementioned letters written by his brother and produced in court: under cross-examination he admitted that neighbours, whom he refused to identify, had called his brother 'an informer' but claimed he did not know why. Philip Devan, the prisoner's father, gave similar evidence, explaining that his son went to Dublin 'through pecuniary wants'.[70]

Fr Thomas McCann, parish priest of Louth, with responsibility for Stonetown chapel, then took the stand. He had known the prisoner for a number of years as 'hardworking' and 'industrious'; he 'never heard of his being concerned in riots or trouble'; he trusted him enough to charge him with the

66 Beattie, *Crime and the courts in England*, p. 375. **67** This was often the case at Ribbon trials in the post-famine period when funds were raised for the defence of Ribbonmen; Vaughan, *Landlords and tenants*, pp 195–6. **68** Beattie, *Crime and the courts in England*, p. 350; my thanks to Richard McMahon for advice on this subject. **69** *Enniskillen Chronicle and Erne Packet*, 31 July 1817; *The Times*, 1 Aug. 1817. **70** *Belfast Newsletter*, 25 July 1817; *Enniskillen Chronicle and Erne Packet*, 31 July 1817.

keys of the chapel.[71] He did not know McIlroy. Devan's father and brother were undoubtedly telling lies but what about Fr McCann? Was this his genuine estimation of Devan's character? The point has already been made that the Sunday following the burning Fr McCann had censured all those involved and likewise during Devan's trial he asserted that he had made strenuous efforts to prevent his congregation from involving themselves 'in these troubles'.[72] But the whole role of the local Catholic clergy in contributing to or even in nurturing disaffection is a good deal ambiguous. Some like Fr Marron, parish priest of Tallanstown, and Fr Duffy, chaplain of Dundalk jail, undoubtedly tried to ingratiate themselves with the local gentry.[73] But while Fr McCann railed against agitation he obviously did not disown his parish clerk who practised the same. Perhaps much of what G.C. Lewis astutely concluded in the 1830s applied to this case: 'It may be remarked, that the dependence of the Irish priest on the alms of the poorest of his flock, naturally indisposes him to take any part which may offend their feelings, however objectionable those feelings may be.'[74] Fr Marron's evidence closed that part of the trial.

There is one other issue worth commenting on before leaving the trial. The point has earlier been made that Devan and his associates came from areas where the Irish language was still very much alive.[75] Devan was obviously proficient in English. He was a hedge schoolmaster whose role was, amongst other things, to teach literacy in the English language. He had written both letters to his father in English suggesting that it had become at least the language of written correspondence and suggests that literacy in English was regarded as being of much greater value than literacy in Irish in the more mobile world of the nineteenth century.[76] But in terms of the spoken word, were some of the Crown witnesses such as Patrick Halpenny and Alice Rispin completely proficient? There is no evidence to suggest that Irish was used at any stage during the trials and so perhaps one should not read too much into this but language barriers (even in the case of the flashy rhetoric of the prosecution) may offer one possible explanation as to why so little of what happened there has survived in local lore. (Language difficulties were a controversial part of the 1882 trial of the ten men accused of the infamous murder of five members of the Joyce family in the predominantly Irish-speaking Gaeltacht area of Maamtrasna in Co. Galway. The suspects had no English at all and an inspector of the Royal Irish Constabluary had to be drafted in as an interpreter.)[77]

71 *The Times*, 1 Aug. 1817. 72 *Correspondent*, 28 July 1817. 73 See letter of Fr James Marron, quoted in chapter six. 74 Lewis, *Local disturbances in Ireland*, p. 145. 75 See chapter one. 76 Cullen, *Modern Ireland*, p. 132. 77 Jarlath Waldron, *Maamtrasna: the murders and the mystery* (Dublin, 1992), pp 56–8.

Devan's trial ended at 8 p.m. It was unusually long, even for a murder trial. The judge them summed up for the jury. McClelland was acutely conscious of the fact that the court provided him with a platform to address the lower orders. A correspondent for the *Freeman's Journal* wrote:

> Baron McClelland gave really a very luminous and acute charge. Coming to speak of illegal associations in reference to the Ribbonmen's oaths which had been given in evidence, and which appeared to be an obligation 'to stand by each other and not to deal with Protestants' – he became truly eloquent – said that it was a feature in the state of this country of the most lamentable description that associations of exclusion of different religious descriptions existed. That they were alike illegal whether Protestant or Catholic, equally deserved reprobation and should equally be made to feel the vengeance of the law.[78]

McClelland's stated criticism of Protestant and Catholic secret societies might suggest that politico-religious differences were not a consideration in the eyes of the law. But religion had not been a factor in the murders at Wildgoose Lodge, and his references were therefore irrelevant. Furthermore, whether McClelland was ever totally objective in trials such as this is debatable. His subsequent performance on the northeast circuit raises some questions. In 1826, McClelland presided over another (in)famous trial in the borderlands, that of the notorious Sam Gray of Ballybay in Co. Monaghan, possibly the only man ever to have been tried five times for the same offence (for which he was eventually found guilty, sentenced to transportation for life, but released 'as a matter of legal interpretation as a result of a ruling of the House of Lords').[79] Gray was a farmer-publican in Ballybay and by the 1820s, district master of the Orange Lodge. In 1824, he was tried for the murder of the Catholic Bernard McMahon during a sectarian brawl on market day in Ballybay. The Catholic Association financed the costs of his prosecution. At the end of the trial, McClelland stated: 'Of all the cases that ever came before him, more opposite testimony he had never heard than on the present trial.'[80] Nevertheless, his charge to the jury was strongly in favour of Gray, with the result that the Protestant jury took a mere two minutes to acquit him.[81] McClelland was, of course, a judge of his time who had to work within the system that gave him his standing. Judges, in Ireland as in England, depended on patronage for their rise through the ranks and it

---

78 *FJ*, 23 July 1817.   79 Johnson, 'The trials of Sam Gray', pp 109–10.   80 *FJ*, 10 Aug. 1824; quoted in Johnson, 'The trials of Sam Gray', p. 111.   81 Johnson, 'The trials of Sam Gray', p. 111.

was the landed classes who primarily bestowed it.[82] The favourable reaction of the Castle administration to McClelland's address at the end of Devan's trial, which undoubtedly reflected that of the Louth magistracy, was epitomised in Charles Bushe's praise of the same to William Saurin: 'you cannot conceive a more useful and powerful charge or a more impressive & awful exhortation on passing sentence than Baron McClelland's'.[83]

The petty jury did not leave the courtroom to carefully consider their decision; they huddled together in public view, possibly only a short distance away from the prisoner and within minutes delivered their unanimous verdict of guilty.[84] The authorities were relieved. Charles Bushe wrote immediately to William Saurin: 'Devan was … found guilty after a long trial by a verdict which has left no doubt of his guilt in any man's mind. He appears to have been the principal character & a most ferocious character.'

The courtroom was jammed to hear the passing of sentence. In these circumstances, judges tended to act in a fairly stereotypical manner. In 1785, Martin Madan described the actions and intentions of judges passing the death sentence at English assizes:

> With a countenance of solemn sorrow, adjusting the cap of judgment on his head … his lordship then, deeply affected by the melancholy part of his office, which he is now about to fulfil, embraces this golden opportunity to do exemplary good – He addresses in the most pathetic terms, the consciences of the trembling criminals … shows them how just and necessary it is, that there should be laws to remove out of society those, who instead of contributing their honest industry to the public good and welfare have exerted every art, that the blackest villainy can suggest, to destroy both … He then vindicates the *mercy*, as well as the *severity* of the law, in making such examples, as shall not only protect the innocent from outrage and violence, but also deter others from bringing themselves to the same fatal and ignominious end … He acquaints them with the certainty of speedy death, and consequently with the necessity of speedy repentance – and on this theme he may so deliver himself, as not only to melt the wretches at the bar into contrition, but the whole auditory into the deepest concern – tears express their feelings – and many of the most thoughtless among them may, for the rest of their lives, be preserved from thinking lightly of the first steps to vice, which they now see will lead them to destruction.[85]

82 Gattrell, *The hanging tree*, p. 515. **83** Charles Bushe to William Saurin, 21 July 1817 (NA, SOC 1817, 1828/14). **84** *Correspondent*, 28 July 1817. **85** Martin Madan, *Thoughts on executive justice*

And so it was in Devan's trial. The scarlet-robed Judge McClelland put the black cap of death on top of his full-bottomed wig and in front of Devan's family, friends, neighbours and possibly some of his associates in crime ordered him to be executed by hanging two days later, 23 July, at the Wildgoose Lodge and afterwards to be gibbeted at Corcreaghy crossroads, near his home-place.[86] McClelland exhorted Devan to 'atone to his country' by revealing who were his associates. Devan remained impassive only raising his eyes on hearing the words: 'The Lord have mercy on your soul.' Charles Bushe wrote on the evening of the trial:

> On passing sentence … the wretch [Devan] was not only unmoved but displayed a firmness to which nothing can account for except the persuasion which I am convinced he feels that he is to die in support of a just cause & that the burning of the house and family of an informer was not only not criminal but meritorious.[87]

It was perhaps a more instructive observation than he intended. Devan's demeanour very much captured what one commentator later felt in 1824 was what distinguished those tried under the Insurrection Act from those tried for other offences: 'those that are convicted under the Insurrection Act … think themselves heroes and patriots'.[88] Ironically, in Devan's case, newspaper reporters may very well have been responsible for beginning the myth of heroic martyrdom. According to one report of his trial, Devan very audibly uttered on his way back to the dock: 'He wants me to disclose my secrets, but he is mistaken if he thinks I will.'[89] More likely, the spectators poured out of the market house, each to their several homes, to carry news of the sentence to friends and neighbours.

The hanging and gibbeting of Patrick Devan

Nineteenth-century governments in much of the western world regarded hanging as the most effective way to deal with felonious crimes. V.A.C. Gattrell argues with some justification that the death sentence and the gallows were central to authority in Georgian Ireland.[90] The almost stage-managed affair of a

with respect to our criminal laws, particularly on the circuit (1785), pp 26–30; quoted in Hay et al. (eds), Albion's fatal tree, pp 17–18. **86** FJ, 24 July 1817; Mathews, The burning of Wildgoose Lodge, p. 9. **87** Charles Ruskin to William Saurin, 21 July 1817 (NA, SOC 1828/14). **88** M. Blacker quoted in Lewis, Local disturbances in Ireland, p. 255. **89** FJ, 28 July 1817; The Times, 1 Aug. 1817. **90** Gattrell, The hanging tree, p. 32; see also Kelly, Gallows speeches, p. 11; Michel Foucault,

public execution affirmed in the public mind the power of the state to punish those who transgressed and was intended to impress upon the same mind what would happen to anyone else foolish enough to attempt to emulate the criminal activities of the offender.[91] Thus the gallows was both a deterrent and a device to deliver terror.

Wednesday 23 July 1817 was another 'very fine day'.[92] At 9 a.m. the Dundalk yeomanry under Viscount Jocelyn and the Louth police under Samuel Pendleton assembled in front of Dundalk jail to escort Patrick Devan to his place of execution at Wildgoose Lodge. At 10 a.m. the procession got under way. Two carts with the gibbets led the way. Alexander Shekleton, a member of the Devan petty jury, who participated in the procession as an officer in the Dundalk Yeomanry, had been paid £238 by the Louth grand jury for the manufacture of the gibbets in his Dundalk iron works.[93] They were of the iron cage variety mainly used for displaying the bodies of the most hardened criminals. The cage went over the head, torso and upper legs and was then suspended by a chain from a high wooden beam.

The gibbets were followed by another cart that contained the prisoner, dressed in a long loose black stuff gown and cap, and the Catholic chaplain of Dundalk jail, Fr Patrick Duffy. Back in 1811, Duffy's appointment as chaplain by the Louth grand jury without the consent of his superiors had caused some consternation in hierarchical circles and Archbishop Reilly subsequently forbade him from carrying out his duties until he had granted his permission.[94] It is clear from the diaries of Henry McClintock that Duffy was very much on friendly terms with many of the local Protestant and Catholic gentry. (The Catholic gentry such as the Taafes of Smarmore employed their own chaplains on Sundays and holy days.)[95] One of Fr Duffy's functions was to solicit some form of repentance from the condemned. He was later to be commended and financially rewarded by the Dublin Castle administration for his role in offering spiritual comfort to the condemned.[96] In a 'trying scene' during one of the later executions he was said to have 'patiently and fervently implored the wretched men to meet their God as penitent sinners, and to forgive their prosecutors'.[97] Perhaps the authorities believed that some form of public contrition

Discipline and punish: the birth of the prison (London, 1979). **91** See Malcolm Gaskill, 'Reporting murder: fiction in the archives in early modern England' in *Social History*, 23 (1998), p. 5. **92** Ó Néill (ed.), *Journal of Henry McClintock*, p. 229. **93** Grand jury presentments, Louth, 1818 (National Library of Ireland); cited in Murray, *The burning of Wildgoose Lodge*, p. 322. **94** Most Reverend Richard Reilly, archbishop of Armagh to Dr Conwell, vicar general, 2 Apr. 1811 (O'Fiaich Memorial Library, folder 3). **95** Reilly to Conwell, 4 Feb. 1811; ibid. **96** See chapter seven. **97** *Correspondent*, 14 Mar. 1818.

or repentance would have as desirable an effect as the execution. When Devan 'fully confessed his guilt on the gallows', Henry McClintock considered his scaffold confession significant enough to record in his diary.[98]

The anonymous executioner followed behind Devan in another cart surrounded by foot police and the Dundalk yeomanry. It was not unknown for either attempts at rescue to be made or for executioners to be stoned by an angry mob.[99] In his 1867 account, William Filgate claimed that 'to the last moment he expected a rescue, but, though immense crowds were collected on the surrounding hills, no attempt of the kind was made'.[1] But in this case the large yeomanry and police presence was an obvious deterrent.

The procession passed through the town of Louth where it was joined by the Louth yeomanry under Colonel Fortescue. At the hill of Mullacrew they were joined by the Ardee yeomanry under Lieutenant Young; at Arthurstown by the Collon yeomanry under Captain Shekleton of Pepperstown and the Louth Regiment of the militia under Captain Rickby. There were no regular soldiers present. (Their absence from executions was common practice in England, which Gattrell contends was 'an index less of an incapacity to produce ceremonial than of a simple confidence that they were not needed.')[2] John Foster and most of the members of the county's grand jury were also present. Lord Louth joined the procession at Tallanstown. Townley P. Filgate, the owner of Wildgoose Lodge, was also there.[3] This was an occasion that few of the Louth gentry wanted to miss.

The middle classes and upper classes – urban and rural – were much like their English counterparts in their reactions towards executions of this nature. V.A.C. Gattrell contends that in England 'most middle class diaries, letters and newspapers reveal an extraordinary detachment about the spectacle [of execution], or else they reveal defences, denials, and rationalisations which spoke for anxiety at the least'.[4] The diary entry of Henry McClintock on the day of Devan's execution suggests the same casual attitude and an extraordinary detachment:

> Very fine day – I attended a yeomanry parade at eight o' clock in the morning & at ten we escorted a prisoner [Devan] to Wildgoose Lodge at Rheastown in this county, where he was hanged inside the walls of Wildgoose Lodge from a board that was placed on the two chimneys

98 Quoted in Ó Néill (ed.), *Journal of Henry McClintock*, p. 227.   **99** Lewis, *Local disturbances in Ireland*, p. 251; Kelly, *Gallows speeches*, p. 39; Kevin Boyle, 'Police in Ireland before the union: I' in *Irish Jurist*, 7 (1972), p. 125.   **1** William Filgate's account, 1867.   **2** Gattrell, *The hanging tree*, p. 97.   **3** *FJ*, 25 July 1817; Belfast *Newsletter*, 29 July 1817; *Dublin Evening Post*, 29 July 1817.   **4** Gattrell, *The hanging tree*, p. viii.

of the house – his crime was being the commander of a party of near a hundred men who on the night of 31 October [*sic*] had set fire to Wildgoose Lodge & burned eight people in it – men, women & children – he fully confessed his guilt on the gallows – after he was hanged his body was put into iron chains & conveyed to Corcria (about four miles from Rheastown) & hung there on a gibbet – Corcria was his native place & a party of soldiers are stationed there which will prevent the gibbet being taken down – this Divan was a school master & clerk to the popish chapel at Stonetown very near Corcria – this chapel was the place where he and his associates met at night to plan their diabolical act – almost every gentleman in the county attended the execution – Mr Foster, Lord Jocelyn, Lord Louth, Mr Balfour &c, &c – no regular soldier attended the execution, merely the different yeomanry corps & the staff of the Louth militia – the Dundalk, Collon, Louth and Castle Bellingham corps attended & also some of the police – we did not get back to Dundalk until ten o' clock at night when we (the officers of the Dundalk corps) dined with our captain Lord Jocelyn.[5]

Sometime between 3 and 4 p.m. the procession reached the place of execution.[6] The journey of less than twenty miles had taken five hours or more. The authorities had not taken the direct route from Dundalk to Ardee; instead it had wound its way through Knockbridge, the town of Louth, Mullacrew and Tallanstown, right through the heart of the most troubled area of Louth, deliberately chosen to make a clear statement of intent. As Filgate's account suggests, there were crowds of people lining the country roads from Dundalk to Wildgoose Lodge and crowds more must have followed on foot, no doubt including Devan's relatives, friends and neighbours. During the entire of the journey, the only place that Devan reputedly showed 'signs of trepidation' was passing through Tallanstown. Was this simply because he was almost in sight of Wildgoose Lodge or was it because it was one of the nearest points to his own home?

An estimated 30,000 people had gathered near the lodge by the time the procession arrived, spread out across the surrounding hills.[7] Crowd estimates are notoriously unreliable but crowds of this magnitude at public executions in England and Ireland were by no means rare. Executions in London could attract crowds of 100,000, and crowds of 10,000 and more were not unknown in Dublin.[8] The high profile nature of the Wildgoose Lodge trials meant that the execution of Devan would have attracted a sizeable audience from Louth and

5 Quoted in Ó Néill (ed.), *Journal of Henry McClintock*, p. 227.   6 *Belfast Newsletter*, 29 July 1817; *FJ*, 28 July 1817.   7 *Dublin Evening Post*, 29 July 1817.   8 Henry, *Dublin hanged*, p. 27.

the surrounding counties and given the relatively close proximity of populous towns such as Dundalk, Newry, Carrickmacross and Drogheda, 30,000 may not be overly exaggerated. Many turned out to see justice done; others to pay their last respects; and not a few to witness the spectacle: Edmund Burke once argued that public executions offered a free and irresistible drama without equal in urban or rural life:

> Choose a day on which to represent the most sublime and affecting tragedy we have; appoint the most favourite actors; spare no cost upon the scenes and decorations, unite the greatest efforts of poetry, painting and music; and when you have collected your audience, just at the moment when their minds are erect with expectation, let it be reported that a state criminal of high rank is on the point of being executed in the adjoining square; in a moment the emptiness of the theatre will demonstrate the comparative weakness of the imitative arts, and proclaim the triumph of real sympathy.[9]

Unfortunately, we do not know who made up the bulk of the crowd. Were, for example, men and women there in equal numbers? (Henry McClintock turned up but his sister stayed at home.) Were children present? The criminal's family, friends and neighbours were probably there. We can only surmise that the executions impacted differently on different people with a variety of consequences for the future. The execution of Mat Kavanagh, the Ribbon hedge schoolmaster in Carleton's 'The hedge school' is worth quoting at length (it may even have been inspired as much by Devan's story as was his 'Wildgoose Lodge'):

> On Tuesday morning, about six weeks after this event, the largest crowd ever remembered in that neighbourhood was assembled at Findramore Hill, whereon had been erected a certain wooden machine, yclept – a gallows. A little after the hour of eleven o'clock, two carts were descried winding slowly down a slope in the southern side of the town and church … As soon as they were observed, a low suppressed ejaculation of horror ran through the crowd, painfully perceptible to the ear – in the expression of ten thousand murmurs all blending into one deep groan – and to the eye, by a simultaneous motion that ran through the crowd like an electric shock. The place of execution was surrounded by a strong detachment of military; and the carts that conveyed the convicts were also strongly guarded.

9 Quoted in Gattrell, *The hanging tree*, p. 73.

As the prisoners approached the fatal spot, which was within sight of the place where the outrage had been perpetrated, the shrieks and lamentations of their relations and acquaintances were appalling indeed. Fathers, mothers, sisters, brothers, cousins and all persons to the most remote degree of kindred and acquaintanceship, were present – all excited by the alternate expression of grief and low-breathed vows of retaliation; not only relations, but all who were connected with them by the bonds of their desperate and illegal oaths. Every eye, in fact, coruscated with a wild and savage fire that shot from under brows knit in a spirit that seemed to cry out blood, vengeance – blood, vengeance! The expression was truly awful; and what rendered it more terrific was the writhing reflection, that numbers and physical force were unavailing against a comparatively small body of armed troops. This condensed the fiery impulse of the moment into an expression of subdued rage that really shot like livid gleams from their visages.[10]

Contemporary newspaper reports claim that when Devan reached the lodge, he was allowed into one of the ruined rooms to pray.[11] (Other reports stated that he prayed 'with the utmost fervency' during the journey.)[12] Two of the chimneys of the house were still standing. A wooden beam was erected from one to the other and a rope thrown over it so that it acted as the gallows. *The Times* reported:

At his coming out of the room, he [Devan] coolly looked up at the beam and turned to the executioner and said: 'How am I to get up there?' He was informed by a ladder, and on going up the ladder the low part of his gown caught his foot and impaired his progress; he very deliberately stooped down and lifted the gown high enough up not to prevent his proceeding. At last, having gone up several steps of the ladder [he] asked: 'Am I high enough?' He was desired to proceed two steps further, which when he did he again acknowledged his guilt, the justness of his sentence, forgave his prosecutors and said he died in charity with all men.[13]

According to newspaper reports Devan 'addressed the people around him in an audible voice, and said: "Good people, I die guilty. I forgive my prosecutors – (good Christians) pray for me."' Another report claimed he 'evinced not

10 William Carleton, 'The hedge school' in *Traits and stories*, vol. i, pp 322–3. 11 *FJ*, 28 July 1817; *The Times*, 1 Aug. 1817. 12 *FJ*, 28 July 1817. 13 *The Times*, 1 Aug. 1817.

only the most cool and steady firmness all through, but the utmost degree of piety and resignation'. The only thing that supposedly gave him concern was the fact that he was to be gibbeted opposite 'his father's door' near Corcreaghy crossroads. 'Would not a fortnight be long enough to remain on the gibbet?' were supposedly his last words before he was launched into eternity.[14]

It is extremely difficult to determine how much truth there was in these accounts of Devan's last minutes. It is all fairly standard fare for execution reporting at the time. He may have prayed fervently and for a lengthy period; even the most hardened criminal would look for some spiritual solace in the midst of great fear. His 'cool and steady firmness' would seem to suggest that his months of incarceration, the exhortations of Fr Duffy or the horror of what faced him had not affected his mental equilibrium. On the other hand, his placidity and his reputed last words may have been a reporter's implied criticism of the barbaric usage of gibbets to display a decaying body for months. His admission of guilt and his plea for forgiveness was characteristic of the last words from the gallows invariably attributed to criminals to convince of the immorality of the crimes for which the likes of Devan was convicted (especially at a time when Dublin Castle very much controlled the dissemination of news in papers such as the *Freeman's Journal*).[15] Thus the general reportage may simply have conformed to a formula made familiar in England during the previous century – a profession of guilt, the acceptance that justice was being done, the forgiveness of his prosecutors and the impression of penitence.[16] As a comparison, the *Belfast Newsletter* report of the hanging of Michael McDaniel indicted for burglary and felony in January 1817 and hanged in front of Dundalk jail on 4 April 1818 read as follows:

> On mounting the scaffold he seemed much agitated and continued in prayer, with apparent fervour, for about fifteen minutes. He inquired of the Rev. Mr Duffy, chaplain, who attended him until the last moment, if the gibbets which he saw hanging against the wall were for him? On being told that they were not, he replied, 'Well I will die easy.' He inquired if his friends would get his body, and seemed much satisfied on being answered in the affirmative. He then stood up and addressing the few who stood round him, acknowledged his guilt, said he had been a Ribbonman, and that drunkenness and bad company had brought him to this untimely end, adding that he hoped his awful death would serve

14 *FJ*, 28 July 1817; *Belfast Newsletter*, 29 July 1817; *Dublin Evening Post*, 29 July 1817. 15 This was certainly the case in the late eighteenth century; see Bartlett, *Revolutionary Dublin*, p. 18. 16 Kelly, *Gallows speeches*, p. 15.

21 A nineteenth-century gibbet pole
from which the iron cage was
suspended by chains.

22 The type of iron cage gibbet,
manufactured in Shekleton's foundry
in Dundalk, in which Devan and
the others were hanged.

as a warning to others. Agreeable to his request, he was suspended so low
that he could scarcely be perceived by the populace. He met his fate with
much resignation, and died without a struggle.[17]

If he 'died without a struggle' he was fortunate. Execution by hanging in
the early nineteenth century was by no means an exact science. People did not
die neatly on a scaffold as basic as that prepared for Devan – nothing more than
a knotted rope thrown over a beam between two chimneys in a rather medieval
fashion. Samuel Haughton, the Trinity College Professor of Anatomy, had not
yet devised the knot that broke the neck immediately nor had the means of cal-
culating the precise ratio of body weight to distance dropped been established
that would in a later era increase the chances of death on the scaffold being
instantaneous. And so victims often strangled slowly and painfully rather than
dying instantaneously. Raymond Gillespie vividly describes the tortuous death
experienced by many:

17 *Belfast Newsletter,* 10 Apr. 1818.

The face would swell, especially the ears and lips, the eyelids would turn blue and the eyes red, and sometimes they were forced from their sockets. A bloody froth or mucus might escape from the mouth or nose and, very often, urine or faeces might be involuntarily expelled at the point of death. All this could happen even when the hangman was knowledgeable and efficient, but bungled executions were not unheard of. An incompetent hangman could either decapitate the victim or, alternatively, leave him or her dangling in the air for up to half an hour before death came.[18]

Devan would have dropped only inches so his death was a slow, painful one from asphyxiation. Newspaper reports stated that 'he was with some difficulty launched into eternity (having got hold of a rung of the ladder). After hanging half-an-hour he was lowered down and the body fixed in chains.'[19] None of the historical evidence points to any crowd response.

When his body was taken down, it was covered in pitch to ensure that it would be preserved for longer and then encased in the iron cage before being taken to Corcreaghy crossroads where it was gibbeted on a pole that was 'fifteen feet above the reach of any man'.[20] It was not unusual for such poles to be around thirty feet high, with the chains or cages riveted to the top of them, and the poles were sometimes spiked with nails to prevent nocturnal raiders attempting to climb them to claim the body.[21] Corcreaghy crossroads, as noted already, was an important junction and trade route through which masses of people passed on their way between Carrickmacross, Ardee, Dundalk, Tallanstown, Killanny, Inniskeen, Louth and on to Newry, Drogheda and Dublin. Some of the later suspects were also to be gibbeted there for the same reason that the maximum number of people would see them and be deterred from wanting to join them. Carleton's recollections of the gibbets (more precisely Devon's gibbet) were vividly described in his autobiography:

> The autumn was an unusually hot one; the flesh of the suspended felons became putrid, and fell down in decomposed masses to the bottom of the sacks; the pitch which covered the sacks was melted by the strong heat of the sun, and the morbid mass which fell to the bottom of the sacks oozed out and fell, as I have stated in Devaun's case, in slimy ropes,

---

18 Raymond Gillespie, '"And be hanged by the neck until you are dead": Introduction' in Frank Sweeney (ed.), *Hanging crimes: when Ireland used the gallows* (Cork, 2005), p. 1; see also Gattrell, *The hanging tree*, p. vii.   19 *Belfast Newsletter*, 29 July 1817.   20 *Dublin Evening Post*, 29 July 1817.   21 Gattrell, *The hanging tree*, p. 87.

at the sight of which I was told, many women fainted. Every sack was literally covered with flies, which having enjoyed their feast, passed away in millions upon millions throughout the country.[22]

The prevailing belief amongst the authorities was that gibbeting, dissection or burial in the jail grounds would prevent wakes and the hatching of further conspiracies.[23] It was the worst fate a criminal or, by extension, his family could meet. In 1772, a judge at the sentencing of a murderer at Gloucester in England told the latter that his gibbeted bones would never enjoy Christian burial but would remain 'as a dreadful spectacle of horror and detestation, to caution and deter the rest of mankind'.[24] J.W. O'Neill has wryly concluded that 'the state as well as the peasantry knew the value of symbolic action as a form of terrorism'.[25]

A party of soldiers was placed at Corcreaghy crossroads to prevent Devan's body being removed.[26] The extent to which the 'stealing' of a corpse was a common occurrence is difficult to gauge. It was certainly the case in London in the late eighteenth century that members of the Irish community there frequently found themselves in conflict with the authorities regarding who should have the rights to the hanged body.[27] Likewise in Ireland in the second half of the eighteenth century where James Kelly tells us: 'bodies left in gibbets or hung in chains were taken for reviving … gibbets were pulled down; and attempts were made to rescue condemned men'.[28] If there were attempts to remove Devan's gibbets, they were unsuccessful for he was left hanging for almost eighteen months. The remains of his body were then taken to Dundalk jail for interment. Local lore has it that his gibbets were kept until recently in a house near the gibbet site.

Conclusion

After Devan, over twenty more men were awaiting trial, possibly as many as twenty-seven.[29] The night after his trial, Charles Bushe consulted with Samuel

---

22 Carleton, *Autobiography*, p. 117. **23** Lewis, *On local disturbances in Ireland*, p. 266. **24** Hay, 'Property, authority and criminal law', p. 30. **25** O'Neill, 'Popular culture and peasant rebellion', p. 300; see also Gattrell, *The hanging tree*, p. 90. **26** Ó Néill (ed.), *Journal of Henry McClintock*, p. 229; in his memoirs James Anton also referred to the fact that 'detachments were posted at the respective gibbets to prevent any of their criminal associates from consigning the bodies to the graves'; http://www.jbhall.freeservers.com/1816_wildgoose_lodge.htm, 23 Oct. 2004; Anton, *Retrospect of a military life*. **27** Peter Linebaugh, 'The Tyburn riot against the surgeons' in Hay et al. (eds), *Albion's fatal tree*, pp 83–5. **28** Kelly, *Gallows speeches*, p. 39. **29** *FJ*, 24 July 1817.

Pendleton on the wisest course to follow. The evidence of the approvers in Devan's trial had been corroborated but counsel and Pendleton were not so confident of the next cases. They decided not to proceed immediately with the prosecution of the remainder of the Wildgoose prisoners but instead 'to postpone the trials to the next assizes without bailing the prisoners'. They were unconfident about going to trial because they still required more corroborating evidence and were hopeful that 'perhaps even in that interval something may turn up in consequence of the spirit of the confederacy being much broken by this conviction of their leader'.[30] Something did turn up – famine and fever – that raged through the region for the rest of the year, offering a respite from agitation to the authorities before the next assizes in March 1818.

30 Charles Bushe to William Saurin, 21 July 1817 (NA, SOC 1828/14).

CHAPTER SIX

The trials of 1818

'I know something of the laws of other countries and I have grown old in the study, the practice and the administration of the laws of this – and I tell you all, there is not a country upon earth whose criminal code is founded upon principles so humane and so benevolent; there is no country upon earth but this [Ireland] where the first duty of the judge is to act as counsel for the prisoners!'

Judge William Fletcher, spring assizes, Dundalk, March 1818.

Introduction

The day after Devan's trial, Alice Rispin was back in the witness box. This time she was giving evidence against eight men accused of riotous behaviour in incidents unrelated to Wildgoose Lodge. Her evidence was interesting. She knew seven of the accused but did not recognise the man identified as James Durnan. He was not, she insisted, the Durnan she knew: 'she had a good right to know him, as he was the captain of the party, and always exercised them ... they exercised as soldiers do, marching etc. etc.' (Perhaps worth noting was the fact that a publican named Pat Durnan from Reaghstown was accused by Murphy of having 'topped up' Devan's men with whiskey near Arthurstown chapel.)[1] Under cross-examination she said: 'it was not through malice or revenge she swore against these men, as God was kindly merciful to her, and she was able to bear her misfortune with fortitude but she considered it could have been a mortal sin to have hid it [evidence] on them'.[2] She was obviously being cross-examined about the death of her son at Wildgoose Lodge at the hands of what the prosecution preferred to call Ribbonmen. But this trial suggested that there was no so-called conspiracy in Louth. Durnan was simply the leader of another local society or perhaps more accurately gang (even though they were represented as insurgents in military training) that was responsible for outrages independently of Devan's cohort.

Baron McClelland was much more lenient than he had been the previous day: the man supposed to be Durnan was acquitted because he could not be

1 'Voluntary confession' of Patrick Murphy taken by John Pollock, A.H.C. Pollock and Samuel Pendleton, 12 Mar. 1817 (in private possession). 2 *Dublin Evening Post*, 30 July 1817.

positively identified; six of the others were sentenced to one year's imprisonment: 'and all, excepting the younger McAneaney, to be whipped several times
during that period through the streets of Dundalk'. The latter was then extended
the mercy of the court and discharged on the grounds of his youth. The prisoners 'evinced the greatest joy by repeated thanks to the court' for the leniency
of their sentences.[3]

This batch of prisoners were arguably lucky – their punishments were relatively moderate particularly given that they had been accused of drilling as well
as riotous behaviour. It was as if McClelland had decided on a mixed policy of
coercion in the Devan case and conciliation the following day. That Rispin gave
evidence in this trial implies that she was exploited by the authorities in their
search for witnesses to local disorder. She was also taking her life into her hands.
There is no evidence to substantiate this but given that she was a key witness
in the trials that ensued the following spring and summer, Alice Rispin most
probably was kept under lock and key in the local jail for her own protection
from the summer of 1817 to the spring and beyond of 1818.

The two approvers in the Devan case were not so fortunate. On 29 July
1817, less than a week after Devan's execution, Samuel Pendleton reported to
William Gregory that Bernard McIlroy and Patrick Clarke 'are no longer admitted inmates in to any house. They are for the present kept and with much inconvenience in the police barrack and if out of the way of protection would unques-
tionably be destroyed.'[4] Shortly afterwards, Clarke was, in the words of Samuel
Pendleton to William Gregory, 'spirited away', never to be seen again.[5] According
to John Mathews' nationalist account:

> Immediately after Devan's execution Clarke became ill of the yellow
> fever, which then prevailed to a fearful extent, and was sent to the large
> store opposite the Steampacket Quay (known at that time as Taylor's
> store), where such patients were treated, and from here he disappeared
> in the most mysterious manner. Be this as it may, to the great joy and
> satisfaction of many, he was never afterwards heard of. He never
> informed on any man but Devan.[6]

Bernard McIlroy was also murdered but not before he acted as approver in
the later trials. According to traditional accounts, he was spotted by a carman
from Dundalk at a wake house near Ballymahon in Co. Longford some time

3 Ibid.   4 Samuel Pendleton to Robert Peel, 29 July 1817 (NA, SOC, 1817, 1828/17).   5 Samuel
Pendleton to William Gregory, 3 April 1818; Mathews, *The burning of Wildgoose Lodge*, p. 9; see
also, Paterson, 'The burning of Wildgoose Lodge', p. 179.   6 Mathews, *Wildgoose Lodge*, p. 9.

after the trials. This would have been after September 1819, for he was paid his £200 around the beginning of that month.[7] This carman was going with a cargo of whiskey from the Dundalk distillery to Boyle in Co. Roscommon when his cart broke down and seeing light and hearing noise in a nearby house, he went in to seek help. He recognised McIlroy immediately and told some of the locals who he was. A gang then allegedly forced McIlroy into a nearby field where some young horses were grazing, tied his limbs to four of them and chased the horses in opposite directions.[8] Because Bernard McIlroy was chiefly responsible for the execution of Devan and at least seven others, it is likely that he was forced on the run. If he was found as far away as Longford, it may not have been by accident.

Interestingly, in 1825 a report appeared in *The Times* of a libel case in London taken by Richard Martin (1754–1834) better known as 'Humanity Dick', the noted animal welfare campaigner, social reformer and Catholic emancipationist, against the *Morning Chronicle.* An earlier report in the newspaper had more or less decried Martin's attempts to penalise those responsible for cruelty to animals and so the plaintiff told the judge: 'I wish to call your Worship's attention to the temper with which I have been pursued and assailed by that part of the press called the *Morning Chronicle,* for conduct which has called forth the general approbation of the country', claiming that the intention of the article 'was to stir up the populace to murder me'.[9] The author did this in an oblique manner that reminded Martin

> of something that happened in Ireland some time ago at a place called Wildgoose Lodge where the most horrible murders were committed, nine persons being deprived of life and, I believe, the house burned to the ground. On the return from the trial, the approver was pointed out to the crowd by a man who said: 'There is the man who has the means of hanging your 19 poor boys – there is the man who has brought them to the gallows; but don't touch him, don't shed blood … pray don't murder him!' The witness was murdered and the fellow who thus addressed them, in spite of his ingenious side-wind mode of arguing … was tried, convicted and executed for the offence.

It is not clear which approver Martin had in mind and he obviously got details wrong regarding numbers murdered and executed but his drawing on

7 Report of meeting of Louth magistrates at Castlebellingham, 23 Aug. 1819 (PRONI, Foster papers, D562/3786). 8 *Dundalk Examiner,* 26 Nov. 1881; Mathews, *The burning of Wildgoose Lodge,* p. 14. 9 *The Times,* 22 Sept. 1825.

the story almost a decade later was a reminder of the widespread resentment at the conduct of approvers amongst the communities affected by prosecution.

The Louth magistracy were much relieved when Patrick Devan was executed. While Samuel Pendleton was none too popular with his superiors at Dublin Castle because of the tactics he adopted in securing arrests and convictions, the same could not be said of the local magistracy and in particular John Foster. Following Devan's trial, the grand jury lavished praise on the chief police magistrate:

> We the grand jury ... having witnessed not only the ability and perse-verance by which you have succeeded in bringing to justice a principal perpetrator of the horrid murders at Reaghstown but also your judi-cious and indefatigable exertions in all the other duties of a magistrate, deem it incumbent on us, publicly to express our approbation of your conduct and the high opinion we entertain of your talents, which have been so fully displayed in this county.
>
> It is to a continuance of your exertions we look for a speedy restora-tion of tranquillity; and should our hopes be realised, we have no doubt in whatever situation you may then be placed, that the same eminent qualities that have distinguished you here, will contribute to confirm to the public the justice and propriety of the high opinion which your condition in this county has impressed on our minds.[10]

The day after Devan's execution Foster wrote personally to Pendleton from his home at Collon: 'No man can feel more strongly than I do, what the coun-try owes to your unwearied exertions, supported by your very distinguished tal-ents and legal knowledge; nor is any man more sensible of the good fortune of this county in the choice which government has made in placing you at the head of our police establishment.'[11] Foster's praise was reciprocated the following day when Pendleton replied: 'For having so far succeeded I am materially indebted to the suggestions of your eminently superior knowledge and experience and to my having always before me the example of your energy and decision.'[12]

The Insurrection Act continued in force until the following year. At the beginning of March 1818 it was reported in the editorial of the *Dublin Evening Post* that 'among country gentlemen [of Louth] generally there exists a strong conviction that it has proved salutary in its operation'. This was about a week before the beginning of the spring assizes.

---

10 *Correspondent*, 28 July 1817.   11 John Foster to Samuel Pendleton, 24 July 1817; quoted in ibid.
12 Samuel Pendleton to John Foster, 25 July 1817; quoted in ibid.

Judge William Fletcher and the opening of the spring assizes, 1818

On Monday morning 3 March 1818, at about ten minutes before eleven, the Hon. Judge William Fletcher (1750–1823) took his place on the bench in Dundalk. It was only his third time to travel the north-east circuit. The eldest son of a Dublin physician, Fletcher had been called to the Irish Bar in 1778. He became king's counsel in 1795 and was elected MP for Tralee in the same year.[13] In the post-Union period, Fletcher acquired a reputation of being a firm supporter of Catholic Emancipation and a champion of lower-class grievances. In his most famous charge to a grand jury delivered at the Wexford summer assizes of 1814, he condemned the sensationalism of newspaper reports which exaggerated the extent of disturbances in the country and the threat of conspiracy and collusion between 'internal rebels or foreign foes'; he criticised landlords and middlemen for their greed for profit making at the expense of displaced tenants and warned of the dangers of bringing in outsiders to populate evicted holdings; and he attacked the government for its coercive policy in Ireland: 'Is there no remedy but act of parliament after act of parliament, in quick succession, framed for coercing and punishing? Is there no corrective but the rope and the gibbet?'[14] The answer, he argued, lay not in coercion but in addressing sympathetically the plight of the lower classes and in this respect he charged absentee landlords with responsibility:

> to promote the establishment of houses of refuge, houses of industry, school houses, and set the example upon their own estates, of building decent cottages, so that the Irish peasant may have at least the comforts of an English sow; for an English farmer would refuse to eat the flesh of a hog, so lodged and fed as an Irish peasant is ...[15]

There was very little that Fletcher left untouched in this address – religion, tithes, education – 'Where have you ever heard of a people desirous of education, who had not clothes to cover them, or bread to eat?' – Peel's Peace Preservation Bill, the Insurrection Act, factionism, oath-taking, perjury and, in particular, the incompetence of local magistrates: 'Of these I must say, that some are over zealous, others too supine; distracted into parties they are too often governed by their private passions, to the disgrace of public justice, and the frequent disturbance of the country.'[16] They were, he argued, too quick to crowd jails with members of the lower classes arrested for the most innocuous crimes, and he denounced 'the hideous but common picture' of many an acquitted pris-

13 Ball, *The judges in Ireland*, vol. ii, p. 338. 14 *Annual Register*, 1814. 15 Ibid. 16 Ibid.

oner returning 'a lost man, in health and morals, to his ruined and beggared family'. He believed 'equal and impartial administration of justice' was the only way to 'greatly reconcile the lower orders of the people with the government under which they live'.[17] But he concluded:

> I do not hesitate to say, that all associations of every description in this country, whether of Orangemen or Ribbonmen … all combinations of persons bound to each other (by the obligation of an oath) in a league for a common purpose, endangering the peace of the country, I pronounce them to be contrary to law. And should it ever come before me to decide upon the question, I shall not hesitate to send up bills of indictment to a grand jury against the individuals … whenever I can find the charge properly sustained. Of this I am certain, that, so long as those associations are permitted to act in the lawless manner they do, there will be no tranquillity in this country; and particularly in the north of Ireland.[18]

Fletcher was essentially a liberal whig who espoused civil liberty, progress and toleration but who was still prepared to repress any danger of civil conflict in the most brutal way. He may have been condemnatory of the propertied class' negligence of duty and he may have sought answers to the underlying causes of lower class discontent, but he still perceived it to be his function as a judge to protect the propertied from lawless associations. He had illustrated this eight months prior to the Dundalk assizes when at the summer assizes in Omagh in 1817 (at the same time as Devan's trial) he sentenced twenty-six men to death (which he declared 'a most painful duty') for crimes 'arising out of the pressure of the times,'[19] in other words for the same type of agrarian crimes that had been prevalent in Co. Louth.

It was perhaps Fletcher's willingness to deal so resolutely with such a large number of agrarianists simultaneously that suggested to Dublin Castle he was the best choice from their point of view to try the Wildgoose suspects. Or possibly the chief secretary, Sir Robert Peel, and the Castle administration had an ulterior motive. Fletcher's address to the Wexford jury had incensed Peel largely because it had satirised the new Peace Preservation Act 'as a measure for providing jobs for government supporters'[20] and particularly as it received widespread publicity in the national and local newspapers, as well as the *Annual Register* in 1814. It was also widely distributed in pamphlet form throughout Britain. In a letter to Lord Desart in September 1814, Peel described Fletcher

17 Ibid. 18 Ibid. 19 *FJ*, 23 Aug. 1817. 20 Gash, *Mr Secretary Peel*, p. 182.

as 'a shabby fellow' and told Lord Sidmouth that 'it was a gross violation of the duty of a judge to animadvert in the manner and language used by Judge Fletcher, upon the Acts of the Legislature'.[21] Peel felt so personally insulted by what he considered a poisonous assault that was tantamount to encouraging a breach of the Union, that he not only prepared an elaborate reply but even went so far as to bring up at cabinet level the possibility of proceeding against Fletcher in parliament. The British prime minister, Lord Liverpool, dissuaded him from doing so and in the end Peel allowed the whole affair to pass over without any official action.[22] While Fletcher felt the backlash of his fellow judges and was forced to mellow his criticism of the government in the years which followed, Peel did not forgive nor forget and given the government's intense interest in the Wildgoose case some consideration must have been given by the Castle to Fletcher as choice of judge. The Castle knew from the Omagh example that Fletcher was unlikely to flinch in his duty (as Fletcher would have defined it) and that being the case he would break the so-called Louth conspiracy. On the other hand, if Fletcher did not perform as expected then the onus of blame would fall on him rather than on Peel and his administration, so the latter would have a ready-made scapegoat to hang out to dry. The same conclusion applies to Fletcher as was made regarding McClelland in the last chapter: he was a judge of his time who had to work within the system that gave him his standing and had to be mindful of those who provided the patronage on which that standing was contingent. His temporary fall from grace in the aftermath of his charge to the Wexford jury had arguably taught him a valuable lesson.

Besides, the nomination of a supporter of Catholic emancipation would give the impression that the state had provided even handed justice to all. This may explain the preclusion of Baron McClelland in the multiple trials. He was never far from controversy particularly, as we saw in the last chapter, accusations of party discrimination. In fact, less than twelve months later, in February 1819, he became the subject of censure on a number of occasions in the House of Commons including for malpractice in cases dating back to 1814–15 when he was accused by the above-mentioned Richard Martin of 'corruption ... weakness and incapacity'.[23] Meanwhile, in Louth, Fletcher was held in some esteem by the Catholic party. During the spring 1818 assizes, 'A Louth Catholic Priest' (Fr Bernard Loughran) in a letter to the *Newry Telegraph* reflected that:

21 Both quoted in Parker, *Sir Robert Peel*, pp 153–4. 22 See ibid., pp 153–4; Gash, *Mr Secretary Peel*, pp 132, 182. 23 *Hansard*, 12 Feb. 1819, vol. 39, cols 437–39, 1491–1504; 2 June 1819, vol. 40, cols. 849–53.

his [Fletcher's] fair even handed distribution of justice, without favour to person or sect, since he first stepped into office, has invariably distinguished him as an upright, incorruptible judge, as a friend to virtue, and a foe to vice, in whatever shape he may meet either in his judicial capacity.[24]

At the same assizes, Faithful Fortescue of Corderry, a kinsman of John Foster, was appointed high sheriff of Louth replacing Turner Macan who then became a grand juror. John Foster was still foreman of the latter and its composition had hardly changed since the previous year.

Over the course of the next three assizes six petty juries were used to try the suspects indicted by the grand jury bringing the total of jurors used in all of the trials (including that of Devan) to eighty-four. Of these, there were eighteen who appeared on at least two juries. There was nothing in law to prevent this (as there was in England).[25] Henry McNeale (£50 freeholder) sat on four. He was, as noted earlier, a Dundalk strong farmer who had been in constant contact with Dublin Castle since the outbreak of tensions after 1815. Alexander Donaldson (£50 freeholder, farmer), Lawrence Tallan (£50 freeholder, merchant/publican), Ben Atkinson (£50 freeholder, farmer), Neal Coleman (£50 freeholder, merchant) and Robert Getty (a forty-shilling freeholder, farmer with a Dundalk town address at Clanbrassil Street) all sat on three.[26] At least fourteen of the jurors were committeemen, churchwardens or sidesmen of the vestry of the St Nicholas parish of Dundalk. These were Alexander Shekleton, William Hale, Malcolm Browne, Laurence Tallan, Robert Getty, Neal Coleman (a Catholic), Hugh McSherry (also a Catholic), James McAlister, Paul Parks, Robert Moritz and John Barret. The occupations or social credentials of fifty-seven jurors were found. Twenty-one were strong farmers (or middlemen) with freeholds of £50 or in excess of the same in the vicinity of Dundalk. The other thirty-six were Dundalk businessmen, merchants, shopkeepers, brewers, publicans and professional. At least seven of them had substantial businesses in Lord Roden's Clanbrassil Street alone (William Hale, Robert Getty, Thomas Byrne, Neal Coleman, Laurence Tallan, and Alexander Shekleton).

The composition of each individual jury once again reflected the determined ambition of the authorities to put an end to the rural disorder (while the willingness to participate reflected the Louth propertied classes' – rural and urban, Protestant and Catholic alike – ambitions to put an end to the threat to

24 'A Louth Catholic Priest' to editor of *Newry Telegraph,* n.d. [Mar. 1818]; quoted in *Dundalk Examiner,* 5 Nov. 1881. 25 Garnham, *Criminal law in Ireland,* p. 144. 26 The unidentified Robert Sheddon and James Johnson also sat on three juries.

their position). Back in November 1816, one of the jurors, Paul Parks, postmaster of Dundalk and coroner, had written to Foster deploring the state of agitation (a letter that Foster subsequently forwarded to Peel): 'If the Insurrection Act is not introduced into this county and these fellows kept within doors at night, I fear many burnings will happen, and some lives lost.'[27] Over the previous two years some of these Dundalk businessmen such as the Catholic brewer Bernard Duffy (who sat on two of the juries) had experienced the effects of agitation first-hand. On the night of 12 December 1815, during the very severe winter of that year, his stockyard was set on fire 'by some malicious evil disposed persons and before sufficient help could be collected the fire had got to such an extent as almost to frustrate every exertion' with the result that between 200 and 300 barrels of oats and barley were destroyed. An extraordinary meeting of the county magistracy took place in Dundalk a few days later attended by John Foster, Lord Jocelyn and 'an immense number of the magistrates and gentlemen of rank and file' of Louth. The local yeomanry under Lord Jocelyn later 'brought in' nine men and a division of the Fifeshire militia arrived around the same time in the town to offer protection from further raids.[28]

At the commencement of the spring assizes of 1818, Judge Fletcher set the tone of the proceedings when he launched an uncharacteristic stinging tirade against the Roman Catholic clergy.[29] Almost as if he was pandering to the Dublin Castle administration (which he may very well have been doing) he focused on 'the evils of Ribbonism' and vilified the Catholic bishops and clergy for not having acted to prevent combinations and criminal outrages. He concluded by asking why they had not used their power to: 'deny the rites of the church to all who participate in such crimes, or who refuse to discover the conspirators':

> If the priests of this and the neighbouring counties ... possessing as they do, and everybody knows they do, the most unbounded influence, and means of information respecting the conduct of their several congregations – had done their duty, it is impossible such a conspiracy could have existed, without coming to their knowledge.[30]

He highlighted the fact that the 'diabolical scheme' was planned in a Catholic chapel and masterminded by the chapel's clerk. He denounced the dead Devan as 'a monster' who had been facilitated in his evil actions by being given the responsibility for 'forming the morals and minds of the rising gener-

27 Paul Parks to John Foster, 18 Nov. 1816 (NA, SOC 1763/41). 28 *Belfast Newsletter*, 22 Dec. 1815. 29 *Kilkenny Moderator*, 19 Mar. 1818. 30 Ibid.; see also *FJ*, 12 Mar. 1818.

ation' and concluded: 'It was incumbent on the Catholic clergy of Louth Monaghan, Cavan and Meath to vindicate their sacerdotal character.'[31]

To those who had commented favourably on Fletcher in the past his address came as a surprise. The pro-emancipationist *Dublin Evening Post* considered his speech to be an unmerited attack upon the Catholic clergy.[32] Fr Bernard Loughran, then curate in Ardee, responded to Fletcher's attack contending that it resulted not from any bigotry on Fletcher's behalf but rather an ignorance of the exertions that had been made by the Catholic clergy in the locality to stem the flow of agrarianism. Fr Loughran argued that the priests had seen 'the gathering storm and cautioned their respective flocks to guard against it'. They communicated the dangers to their bishops who 'reprobated their nefarious system by passing their ecclesiastical censures on any person connected with such associations': the bishops forbade the priests to grant absolution to any member of a secret society and an undertaking from the confessor that he would immediately withdraw from the society. Fr Loughran did admit that all too often 'nominal Catholics' went to confession and concealed membership of secret societies from their confessors.[33] Peter Gollogly, one of the principal approvers, was later to admit that he 'did not confess to a priest this long time' and that as a Catholic he had 'given up attending confession since he began such business'.[34] In such circumstances, as Loughran argued, the clergy were largely helpless.

In contrast to his Wexford address, Fletcher clearly defended the men of property and particularly commended them for having embraced the laws of the state while the lower classes continued to ignore them in favour of lawlessness and violence. Those Catholic farmers such as Edward Lynch (who resorted to 'the laws of the country for redress') were, he remonstrated, unfortunate victims of diabolical schemes and any continuation of attacks on 'the men of property' would have calamitous consequences:

> Do the deluded people of this county consider to what their conduct tends? I will tell them, it will drive from it every man of property – every man of mild and peaceable disposition – every man of kind and humane feeling; all those who by their property, or from inclination, would be likely to improve it, or ameliorate their condition; in short, every man who is not boldly determined to risk his safety, to set them at defiance, and stand ever watchful, and on his guard. To this wretched state would they reduce this country.[35]

31 *FJ*, 12 Mar. 1818. 32 *Dublin Evening Post*, 14 Mar. 1818. 33 'A Louth Catholic Priest' to editor of *Newry Telegraph*, n.d. [Mar. 1818]; quoted in *Dundalk Examiner*, 5 Nov. 1881. 34 *Drogheda Journal*, 4 Apr. 1818; *Dundalk Examiner*, 22 Oct. 1881. 35 Ibid.

The first trial

The trial procedure in the spring assizes was much the same as that described in the previous chapter for the Devan trial, except that in all but one case, that of Thomas McCullough, the prisoners were tried in batches of three or more. The first ten for whom bills of indictment were returned were: Hugh McCabe, John Kieran, James Campbell, Terence Marron, Patrick Craven, Patrick Malone, Michael Floody, Patrick Meighan, Hugh [Hudy] McElearney and Bryan Lennon. All were arraigned together.

This time the prisoners had the benefit of defence counsels. How this came about is unclear. There is no evidence that money was raised on behalf of the prisoners so perhaps the potential public exposure attracted some lawyers who perceived an opportunity to raise their profiles by working *pro bono publico*. However, there was some scepticism later attached to the fact that in some of the trials the prisoners' leading counsel was Leonard MacNally who the *Freeman's Journal* proclaimed 'was brought down specially for the prisoners'.[36] As recently as 2003, a speculative commentary conjectured that MacNally was a deliberate plant by the Castle administration to ensure that the Wildgoose prisoners would receive nominal justice only.[37] Given his track record in the past, there may have been some element of truth in this.[38]

Sergeant Henry Joy opened the case for the prosecution. In preparation for these multiple trials, he and William Gregory had gathered documentary evidence from the famous Special Commission held in York in January 1813 at the height of the Luddite agrarian agitation in Yorkshire. English contemporaries had compared that outbreak to Irish Whiteboyism largely because of the Luddite obstruction to economic change.[39] The Special Commission was designed to crush the Yorkshire agitation and resulted in the execution of seventeen men. Lord Sheatfield had sent Gregory a comprehensive file a few days before the Dundalk assizes began, which unfortunately does not seem to have survived, but the Castle administration had evidently considered what could be learned from the Luddite trials.[40]

On 4 March, McCabe, Kieran and Campbell were the first three prisoners to be tried. McCabe was a near neighbour of the Lynches; the back of his cabin looked towards the lodge.[41] Kieran had been arrested near Louth town so was

36 *FJ*, 3 Apr. 1818. 37 Paddy Martin to editor; *Dundalk Democrat*, 4 Oct. 2003. 38 See Bartlett, *Revolutionary Dublin*, p. 42. 39 Palmer, *Police and protest in England and Ireland*, p. 51. 40 William Gregory to Lord Sheatfield, 27 Feb. 1818 (PRO, Peel papers, ADD 40205). 41 Report of trial of 3 Mar. 1818 from *Faulkner's Dublin Journal*, reproduced in *Dundalk Examiner*, 24 Sept. 1881.

212   THE MURDERS AT WILDGOOSE LODGE

also from the locality. Campbell was the most high profile of the first batch, in that he had come to the attention of the authorities as a Ribbonman (as distinct from simply a member of one of the local agrarian societies) present at the Carrickmacross meeting in April of 1816.

Bernard McIlroy was called once again by the prosecution as the chief approver. He provided much the same evidence he did in the Devan trial, except this time he claimed that near Reaghstown chapel his party 'met about twenty persons who had fire in a small pot'. This was the Stonetown contingent who he was suggesting had set out under Devan with the deliberate intention to burn the lodge. McIlroy identifed Kieran as having been present; he recalled seeing him blasted in the face by gunpowder. Thomas Gubby, despite the reservations that had excluded him from the Devan trial, was used as the second approver. It is clear from the cross examinations that attempts were made to discredit him (and the other approvers) in the hope of getting an acquittal for the prisoners. Gubby had to surmise as to why he had not been called in the Devan case – 'does not know the reason why he was not used as a witness in Devan's trial, but supposes it was because they could do without him' – and answer allegations that he had been a member of a Drogheda gang guilty of a series of robberies.

Peter Gollogly and Patrick Murphy were then called and both gave 'lengthy depositions, all tending to fix the guilt imputed upon the prisoners'.[42] Murphy, like Gubby, had to answer questions relating to his criminal past and accusations that this was not the first time he had turned approver to save his life – 'was under sentence of death, but did not know his deposing as to Lynch's murder would save his life'; 'was concerned once in a robbery at Harkford's near Carrickmacross. Became approver on that occasion, and was examined as a witness in the trial which followed'. During these trials a brother of John Sillery's, the man whose property he had raided, exposed him as 'a noted rogue'.[43] Gollogly, under cross-examination, admitted 'that the desire to save his life was the most predominant incentive' to his having turned approver.[44]

One of the other prisoners, Michael Kearnan, was also called as an approver. Pendleton's notes on the Wildgoose Lodge arrests and trials (summarised in table form in appendix II) reveal that after his arrest he had agreed to provide state evidence but when he took the stand he had a dramatic change of mind. The trial notes as they appeared in the *Belfast Newsletter* read as follows:

---

42 *Belfast Newsletter*, 6 Mar. 1818; *Dublin Evening Post*, 10 Mar. 1818. **43** Clipping from *Enniskillen Chronicle and Erne Packet*, n.d. [April 1818] (Louth Library, WGL papers); see below. **44** *Belfast Newsletter*, 6 Mar. 1818.

[Kearnan] Knows nothing of Wildgoose Lodge. Except what he has heard. Has been a year in gaol. A policeman had told him he would be hanged in front of the gaol, if he did not discover. Another offered him money. He has seen Mr Pendleton before and told him a false story in his examination lodged before him, which implicated the prisoners. Witness was not of the party at the burning. McIlroy, a prisoner, put him up to saying he knew of the circumstances of the business. He told witness to be led by him, and they would get a great deal of money, which they would divide, and go to distant countries. McIlroy told him what he should say about Kieran being blasted in the face and Bryan Lennon breaking in the door with a sledge. McIlroy told him the reward was £7,000, a great part of which they would get.[45]

His evidence – at least as reported – raises a number of serious questions regarding the nature of the tactics used by Pendleton and the police to secure 'confessions'. It also points to the fact that information regarding the burning of the lodge was in the public domain and was fed to potential approvers; that the temptation of monetary reward was a major temptation to approve; that some of those arrested had been falsely accused; that McIlroy was represented to the court as being capable of deceit and craft and yet the court was still willing to accept his evidence as legitimate. Kearnan's testimony also suggested that contrary to due legal procedure, approvers had been kept together (and for a very lengthy time before the trials) allowing them time to concoct stories and corroborating evidence.

In defence of the prisoners, Bryan Greenan testified that the night before the burning he went to McCabe's house to take home a load of turf he had bought earlier from the prisoner's father. Greenan alleged that McCabe was confined to his home all of the night of 29–30 as he was incapacitated with a sore knee, a lump on the kneecap which the country people called 'a touch me not'. Peter Keenan corroborated the sore knee story. So did James McGahan and McCabe's father who further claimed that his son had not been able to work for some days either side of the burning. James Coleman, a local Catholic strong farmer: 'never heard anything to the prejudice of his [McCabe's] character before this'. But Alice Rispin effectively destroyed these alibis by claiming that she saw McCabe vault a ditch two days after the burning, showing no signs whatsoever of being lame.[46]

Margaret Donaldson swore that Campbell came to her house, about five miles from the lodge, at 7.30 p.m. on the night of the burning to attend the wake

45 Ibid.   46 Ibid.

of one of her children. He did not leave until 7 a.m. the following morning. She was positive about the times because 'she examined a neighbour's watch both at the time of prisoner coming and going from her house'.[47] No character witnesses were called on Kieran's behalf; he admitted his guilt during the trial.[48]

The trial of Kieran, McCabe and Campbell lasted six hours.[49] Judge Fletcher then spent one hour summing up for the jury but apologised that due 'to the confined place where he sat to administer justice that his strength would not permit him to comment upon the evidence in the copious manner he could wish'.[50] The jury went out at five p.m. and returned their verdict of guilty at seven.[51] When the jury did so, some of the prisoners acted with 'astonishing effrontery' and cried out: 'We are innocent; our prosecutors are all false and perjured.'[52] Two hours to return a unanimous verdict was a very long time in contemporary terms suggesting there was at least some element of doubt and dissension amongst the jurors compared to the Devan case. Perhaps the jury had considered Kearnan's evidence or maybe they had considered Kieran's confession of guilt to which he had added regarding the ten men arraigned: 'My lord, there are three of us guilty, the other seven are innocent of the charge'.[53] Judge Fletcher pronounced that the prisoners were to be executed at Wildgoose Lodge on Saturday 7 March. This was later postponed to 9 March, so that others arraigned could be executed on the same day.

The second and third trials and executions

On 5 March, Terence Marron (Carrickmacross), Patrick Craven (Castlering, near Louth town) and Patrick Malone (Meath Hill, Co. Meath) were arraigned.[54] This time the Castle had a different point to make. A few days after the trial, William Gregory impressed upon Sir Robert Peel that the jury was comprised entirely of members of the Catholic propertied middle class.[55] Similarly, it was highlighted in the newspapers that this was 'a most respectable and truly impartial jury consisting of the following Catholic Gentlemen': Hugh McSherry, Thomas Byrne, James Hampton, Philip Boylan, John Norris, Bernard Duffy, Arthur Sherry, James Carraher, John Coleman, John Carroll, Neal Coleman Jr,

47 Ibid.   **48** *Dublin Evening Post,* 10 Mar. 1818.   **49** What follows is drawn from *Belfast Newsletter,* 6 Mar. 1818; *Dublin Evening Post,* 9, 10 Mar. 1818; *Faulkner's Dublin Journal,* 3 Mar. 1818 (reprinted in *Dundalk Examiner,* 17, 24 Sept. 1881).   **50** *Dublin Evening Post,* 10 Mar. 1818.   **51** Ibid.   **52** *Dublin Evening Post,* 10 Mar. 1818.   **53** Mathews, *The burning of Wildgoose Lodge,* p. 10.   **54** *Correspondent,* 11 Mar. 1818; for these trials see also *Dublin Evening Post,* 11 Mar. 1818; *Drogheda Journal,* 7 Mar. 1818.   **55** William Gregory to Robert Peel, 7 Mar. 1818 (British Library, Peel papers, ADD 40205).

Joseph Kelly.[56] James Hampton was a £100 freeholder and gentleman farmer from Castlebellingham; Philip Boylan (Harristown), James Carragher (Cardistown, also a member of Ardee Dispensary Committee)[57] and John Coleman (Rathory) were all £50 freeholders and farmers from north Louth; Bernard Duffy, the Dundalk brewer had sat on the previous jury; John Carroll and Neal Coleman (who sat on three of the juries) were £50 freeholders and merchants from Earl Street and Clanbrassil Street respectively in Dundalk; Thomas Byrne was also a Clanbrassil Street merchant whose property had a valuation of £20; Arthur Sherry and Hugh McSherry were merchants in Dundalk (no valuation was found for either) and the latter, as noted previously, was a committeeman of the vestry of St Nicholas' parish in Dundalk. No information on the social backgrounds of John Norris and Joseph Kelly was found.

These men may not have been the first choice of the prosecution. According to one newspaper account: 'In forming the jury, the challenges were so frequent that the panel was nearly exhausted,'[58] but the fact that they had turned up in such numbers to fulfil their panel obligations suggested once again the Catholic propertied class' determination to throw in their lot with the Protestant propertied classes. In many respects these jurors exemplified the social and economic gains made by Catholics following the relaxation of the Penal Laws (or perhaps even during them.) They had prospered as a result of increased access to lands on longer leases, or were part of the growing Catholic middle class in Dundalk who had made their money from the improved market conditions during the Napoleonic Wars. The point has earlier been made that their growth in social respectability divided them from the Catholic lower classes while the circles in which they moved drew them socially and commercially closer to the Protestant propertied middle class. The real controlling factor in the selection of jurors was ultimately social class over religion.[59]

The trial procedure was now very much according to formula. McIlroy identified Craven, Gollogly and Murphy identified Malone and Marron, while Gubby identified Craven and Marron. Patrick Murphy testified that Malone, his neighbour, came to his house and revealed to him the plan to murder Lynch and Rooney. Murphy elevated Malone to the position of 'captain' and alleged that he gave important orders on the night, including one to Murphy to go to Halpenny's house to get fire. Murphy recalled Malone say after the burning: 'all was well now if only they had Filgate'.[60] All four were found guilty; this time

56 *Correspondent*, 11 Mar. 1818.   57 Harold O'Sullivan, 'Ardee Dispensary minute book, 1813–1851' in *Journal of the County Louth Archaeological Society*, 16:1 (1965), pp 5–27.   58 *Correspondent*, 11 Mar. 1818.   59 On this point see Garnham, *Criminal law in Ireland*, p. 144.   60 *Correspondent*, 11 Mar. 1818.

there was no delay in reaching a verdict. Dramatic scenes ensued. Marron and Malone were said to be 'clamorous in declaring their innocence to the court and on their way to the gaol'.[61] In the courtroom, Malone made a grab for a bible and holding it up proceeded to swear his innocence. The 'ungoverned rage, vented in execrations' against the police and the jury supposedly 'struck the spectators mute with astonishment and horror'.[62] Judge Fletcher was incensed. When order was restored, he sentenced all three to be hanged and gibbeted on 9 March, but not before he berated the prisoners:

> Wretched men, I am sorry to say that you appear to be the most obdu-
> rate and hardened miscreants that ever came before me. I thought I
> should not be able to pronounce the sentence of the law upon you. I
> feared that my feelings would not be able to sustain the task my duty
> imposed upon me; but your obduracy has strung my nerves and I do
> feel myself now able, without any feelings for your fate to pronounce
> the awful sentence of the law that awaits you.[63]

On 7 March, the next batch tried comprised Hudy McElearney ('an old malignant convict' from Meath),[64] Patrick Meighan (Monaghan), Michael Floody (Meath) and Bryan Lennon (the blacksmith from Inniskeen). All four were found guilty and sentenced to be executed with the other six men two days later. A reporter in the *Freeman's Journal* who described McElearney as 'a hard-ened and inhuman miscreant' added that when sentenced he shouted: 'I don't care! I don't care what you do with me!'[65] More revealing, as a reflection of the attitudes of the Castle and its supporters to the outcome of these trials, was a report that appeared in the *Correspondent* on 11 March 1818 that is worth quot-ing in length. It laid bare the injustice felt by some of those sentenced to death, a point ironically lost on the author:

> The trial has exhibited as melancholy an instance of deep depravity and
> wickedness as has ever come under our observation. The same ferocious
> and inhuman spirit which instigated them to the commission of an act
> of almost unparalleled cruelty, displayed itself at that awful moment,
> when the law exacted a terrible retribution for the abominable act they
> had been guilty of – and instead of being impressed with the slightest
> sense of sorrow or contrition for what they had done – or with the fear
> of God, or of his eternal and immutable justice – or with a shadow of

61 Ibid. 62 Ibid.; *Kilkenny Moderator,* 14 Mar. 1818. 63 *Dublin Evening Post,* 10 Mar. 1818. 64 *FJ,* 12 Mar. 1818. 65 Ibid.; *Correspondent,* 11 Mar. 1818.

religious or moral sentiment they broke out into blasphemous imprecations, and horrible curses, against their accusers, and all those who
had been in any manner concerned in their prosecution. The solemn
tone and aspect of the judge, in passing sentence, had no effect upon
them. They continued in the same obdurate disposition, unawed and
unaffected by their fate, all the time his Lordship was passing the fearful denunciation of the law upon them, and even after they were taken
out of the court to be remanded to the gaol until the period of execution. The mind recoils from the contemplation of such a scene as this
...

  Where such things occur, the magistracy and the loyal and orderly
portion of the community cannot be supine or indifferent to the duty
which they owe to society. Such a system of atrocious co-operation as
that which united the barbarians who burned Wildgoose Lodge, must
be broken up effectually – and care must be taken that if it have any
ramifications, or extends beyond the part of the country where it has
first displayed itself with such horrible effects, it must be followed vigorously and unceasingly, until not a link of it is to be found or a trace
of it suffered to the peace of society.

The morning of Monday 9 March 1818 was a very wet one. A little after 6
a.m. the ten convicted prisoners were placed on two sociables to begin their
final journey from Dundalk jail to Wildgoose Lodge. They were escorted by a
company of the 14th Light Dragoons accompanied by Samuel Pendleton, John
Foster, Lord Jocelyn, most of the grand jury and members of the Louth gentry.
Incessant rain over a number of days had made the road to Wildgoose Lodge
impassable. It was therefore impossible to erect a makeshift gallows within its
walls. Instead the prisoners were taken a short distance to Reaghstown Hill
where the gallows overlooked the lodge. An estimated 20,000 people crowded
the surrounding hills. The men were executed in two groups of three and a
group of four.[66] Only Kieran, Craven, Lennon and Campbell confessed their
guilt on the scaffold although William Gregory was to exaggerate in a letter to
Robert Peel: 'it is a great satisfaction that six of the murderers confessed their
guilt at the place of execution'.[67] The fact that he ignored the pleas of innocence
of the others makes a point in its own right. After Craven confessed his guilt
he proclaimed to the crowds that some of the other prisoners were innocent.
He was about to continue his address with the noose around his neck when,

66 Ibid., 16 Mar. 1818 [taken from *Drogheda Journal*]; *Belfast Newsletter*, 13 Mar. 1818. 67 William
Gregory to Robert Peel, 11 Mar. 1818 (British Library, Peel papers, ADD 40205).

according to one report: 'the platform accidentally gave way and he dropped into eternity'.[68] Was the newspaper in which it appeared – the *Drogheda Journal* – suggesting the timely interference of officialdom? A letter from an Ardee correspondent which appeared in the *Dublin Evening Post* and the *Freeman's Journal* was more explicit in its reportage that the other six men 'declared in the most solemn and impressive manner' that 'they were as innocent as the child unborn of the crime for which they were about to suffer; and that they never in their lives were at the burning of Wildgoose Lodge'. Even when Fr Duffy entreated of them 'to confess their guilt and not to leave the world with a lie in their mouths his admonitions had no effect and these miscreants endeavoured to inflame the minds of the populace by declaring their innocence'.[69]

The *Dublin Evening Post* also observed that the convicted prayed fervently before ascending the scaffold but noted that a Catholic priest did not attend all of them. The chaplain did not have any preordained right to accompany the condemned. There had been precedents – a number of agrarian agitators had been denied services of a priest before their execution at Clonmel in 1776. James Kelly argues that this could be due to the fact that some Protestant officials believed that spiritual comforts offered by the clergy enabled offenders to face the gallows with less trepidation, thereby negating the terror of the gallows but he also more pointedly concludes that while what happened at Clonmel was exceptional: 'The fact that it happened at all bears vivid witness to the fact that whilst the clergy of the main Christian denominations were granted preferential access to offenders and a prominent place at the scaffold, the rules were determined increasingly by the state.'[70] Following enquiries the *Post*'s reporter had been told that at Reaghstown 'the narrow prejudice of the unlettered minds of two magistrates dictated the uncharitable policy of preventing the attendance of several respectable Catholic clergymen on the unfortunate prisoners'. Fr Duffy, the prison chaplain, was there but 'it was morally impossible for him to administer spiritual consolation to ten wretched victims'.[71] Some time after the executions, Fr James Marron (1764–1839, parish priest of Tallanstown, 1802–39) corroborated these allegations in a letter to Margaret O'Reilly (wife of Matthew O'Reilly, a Catholic landlord and a member of the Louth grand jury in 1818, who lived close to Wildgoose Lodge at Knockabbey). He wrote: 'for though I was at the place of execution, I would not be permitted to go near them [the prisoners] – of this they bitterly complained'.[72] It was later maintained that it was Faithful Fortescue, the new high sheriff of Co. Louth, and Samuel Pendleton who had intervened to prevent

---

68 *Drogheda Journal*, 14 Mar. 1818. **69** *Dublin Evening Post*, 11 Mar. 1818; *FJ*, 11 Mar. 1818; *Kilkenny Moderator*, 19 Mar. 1818. **70** Kelly, *Gallows speeches*, p. 44. **71** *Dublin Evening Post*, 11 Mar. 1818. **72** Letter cited in Paterson, 'The burning of Wildgoose Lodge', pp 179–80.

priests other than Fr Duffy attending the prisoners.[73] In this action the authorities were compounding the suffering of the prisoners and their families by denying them access to a priest as well as to a Christian burial. As a result there was a palpable change in the attitudes of the masses witnessing the executions: a growing unrest amongst the lower classes was reported with the *Drogheda Journal* stating that the crowd was much more hostile than at Devan's execution.[74] The simultaneous execution of ten men had undoubtedly a disconcerting influence on the lower class communities to which these men belonged, particularly when so many swore their innocence on the gallows or their innocence was proclaimed by those who admitted their own guilt.

Marron, Campbell and Meighan were gibbeted at Corcreaghy, close to Devan. McCabe, Malone, Kieran and Craven were gibbeted in the town of Louth; Floody, Lennon and McElearney were gibbeted at Hackballscross on the Castleblayney–Dundalk road. Corcreaghy, Louth and Hackballscross marked the three points of the geographical triangle within which the authorities intended to make a statement regarding their determination to restore peace and stability.

Shortly after the trials had finished, Serjeant Joy wrote to William Saurin, the attorney general, and suggested that the Crown should accept a plea of guilty from the remainder of the prisoners on condition that they would then be transported for life. He may have sensed the growing disaffection. Saurin communicated this to the under-secretary, but William Gregory was having none of it: 'Certainly not,' the latter responded, 'if there is any chance of them being convicted; such a dreadful act of cruelty merits the most severe punishment'.[75] The assizes had now ended and Gregory feared that the remaining prisoners in Dundalk jail would move to be brought up under the Habeas Corpus Act and subsequently discharged. To prevent this, he called the chief justice, the chancellor, the attorney general and the chief crown prosecutor to a meeting in his Dublin offices. A decision was reached to write to Judge Fletcher, who by then had moved further north to the Downpatrick assizes, and request him to return to Dundalk and establish a Special Commission at the end of the month to finish the work of the spring assizes. Gregory concluded: 'they can open this commission on the 30th or 31st and clear the gaol before the first day of term'.[76] In general these commissions, as in the York case noted above, were used 'when exemplary hangings or at least exemplary trials were deemed necessary for the public peace. Magistrates often petitioned

73 *Belfast Newsletter*, 13 Mar. 1818; *Correspondent*, 14 Mar. 1818. 74 *Drogheda Journal*, 14 Mar. 1818. 75 William Gregory to Robert Peel, 7 Mar. 1818 (British Museum, Peel papers, MS 40,203). 76 William Gregory to Robert Peel, 11 Mar. 1818; ibid.

for them when riot in their counties was becoming too serious or when the violence associated with popular crimes … verged on insurrection against their authority.'[77] Accordingly, on 10 March 1818 Gregory wrote to Judge Fletcher congratulating him on his work so far in the Wildgoose trials – 'executed by you so much to the satisfaction of His Excellency and so much to the advantage of your country'[78] – and asked him to convene the commission. Fletcher duly obliged and the commission sat on 31 March 1818 and succeeding days in Dundalk for the trials of James Smith, Patrick McQuillan, George McQuillan, Thomas Sheenan, John Keegan, Thomas McCullough, William Butler, Laurence Gaynor, Owen Gaynor and Michael Kearnan.

The Special Commission

James Smith (from Arthurstown, about a mile from the lodge), Patrick McQuillan (from Meath) and Laurence Gaynor (from the parish of Louth) were the first to be tried. Joy opened proceedings with his usual oration on the need to punish the perpetrators of such a heinous crime. His description of events was now firmly based on the evidence provided by the approvers in the earlier trials: the jury was reminded that up to 100 men on foot and horseback had converged at the Lodge from Louth, Monaghan, Cavan and Meath 'for the express purpose of sacrificing to their resentment these unfortunate men, with the whole of their family'; the main party had met at Stonetown chapel; they spread themselves around the lodge to prevent anybody escaping; they threw lighted flax and unthreshed oats into the house to fan the flames; and they 'completed the scene of horror with three huzzas'.[79]

McIlroy placed Smith at Wildgoose Lodge; on the night he recognised him from having seen him once before at a football match in nearby Tallanstown. Leonard MacNally accused McIlroy of lying, that in fact he had never seen Smith until the authorities brought him to the cell in Dundalk jail where Smith was being kept. McIlroy refuted McNally's allegations and claimed that he had mentioned Smith in the statement he gave to the magistracy before he was taken to Dundalk jail. But it was only in Gubby's statements that Smith's name appeared. Gubby then corroborated McIlroy's evidence by testifying that he had seen Smith carry unthreshed oats to the lodge in order to fan the flames. Significantly, this was the type of accusation that had become more regular

77 Hay, 'Property, authority and the common law', p. 31.   78 William Gregory to Judge Fletcher, 10 Mar. 1818 (PRO, Peel papers, ADD 40105).   79 Drogheda Journal, 4 Apr. 1818; Belfast Newsletter, 7 Apr. 1818; see also accounts reproduced in Dundalk Examiner, 22 Oct. 1881.

during the course of the trials which was used in order to implicate a suspect (but not to be found in any of the depositions taken from the approvers).

Smith's defence produced the most eminent character witness to date – Lord Louth of Louth Hall, Tallanstown – who testified that Smith and his father both worked as wrought-masons for him on his estate. He had known Smith for a considerable time as a 'very honest man'.[80] The defence also produced two other highly respectable character witnesses in John Coleman and Robert Hamilton, two gentlemen farmers from nearby Rathory, the former a Catholic, the latter a Protestant. Like Lord Louth, Coleman testified that he had known Smith for ten years: 'his character stood as fair as any other poor boy in the country until this accusation'. He maintained that he had 'frequently cautioned [the] prisoner against entering into any of those dangerous associations, which were then said to prevail in the country, and he seemed to make a due impression on him'.[81] Robert Hamilton also commended Smith's character while both the latter's father and brother swore that he had not left the house on the night of the burning.[82]

Gollogly, McIlroy and Murphy identified McQuillan (whose brother, Edward, was also a prisoner) and Gaynor. These three approvers had all been arrested for the Sillery robbery. Sillery's brother was called as a character witness for McQuillan. He told the court that he had known the prisoner for eight or nine years as an employee. On the night of the burning McQuillan had left work after dark and returned 'as soon as any other man next morning'. Sillery also knew the approver, Patrick Murphy, whom he believed 'to be a villain who would say and swear anything'. Most notably, he then told the court how McQuillan had been part of the posse that arrested Murphy after the Sillery robbery.[83] The insinuation was apparent: Murphy had clearly moved to implicate in the Wildgoose murders at least one of those who had been responsible for his own capture. McQuillan was still found guilty.

The same scenario ensued when Gollogly testified that he was told of the plans to burn the lodge by Laurence Gaynor, another member of the Sillery posse that had captured him. Gaynor was a labourer whose employer, Philip McGuire (or Patrick in other accounts), was married to Gaynor's wife's sister. McGuire attested that on the night of the burning, Gaynor stayed in his home, about seven miles from the lodge. There was a tailor, Patrick Ward, also in the house that night who slept in the same bed as McGuire and his wife, a type of arrangement that was not unusual in rural Ireland when there were often more guests than beds. (An attempt to provide an alibi in this way had famously been

80 *Newry Telegraph*, 4 Apr. 1818. 81 Ibid. 82 Ibid.; *Drogheda Journal*, 4 Apr. 1818. 83 *Drogheda Journal*, 4 Apr. 1818.

used in a mid-eighteenth century robbery case that had led to the release of the suspect.)[84] McGuire testified that his brother-in-law did not leave the house all night; he had seen him up on several occasions 'watching his master's turnips' (presumably meaning that a turnip field was a primary target of starving people during the course of a famine.) Ward corroborated this evidence as did McGuire's wife, Biddy. She had been up until 4 a.m. smoothing linen for her employer, Tom Murran. She often had to do this chore when, as she put it: 'hurry required exertion'. Gaynor, it seems, acted as his own defence counsel. He asked permission of the court to cross-examine Gollogly. During this cross-examination Gollogly remarkably admitted that he had falsified his evidence in revenge for Gaynor's role in his arrest.[85] Thus this was the second time in this particular trial that separate approvers actually disclosed that they had implicated in the Wildgoose murders men who had been responsible for their own capture. Gaynor was more fortunate than Smith and was given the benefit of the doubt and found not guilty by the jury. (According to Pendleton's chart in appendix II, he was not acquitted until April 1818.) Pendleton expressed his surprise to William Gregory: '[Gaynor] was not the one that we thought might possibly have been acquitted', but he assured him that 'the acquittal which took place did not go in any material degree to affect the credit of your witnesses'.[86]

The trial of Thomas McCullough

On 1 April 1818, Thomas McCullough was tried alone, the only one other than Devan to be accorded this dubious distinction. The apparent reason was that he was no lower class agitator and so the authorities wanted to make a separate example of him. The *Drogheda Journal* described this as 'a most important trial' of 'a man of most interesting appearance, possessed of considerable property ... six feet in height, well proportioned, and though like a country man was genteely dressed'.[87] The *Freeman's Journal* reported that he 'exceeded all those heretofore brought forward in point of respectability',[88] while according to Louth landlord, Henry McClintock, McCullough was 'a wealthy farmer & a decent well-dressed man.'[89] When Serjeant Joy addressed the jury, he told them:

> The prisoner at the bar was different from all those who had been indicted for this most nefarious transaction; he was a man possessed of

84 Garnham, *Criminal law in Ireland*, p. 139.   85 Ibid.   86 Samuel Pendleton to William Gregory, 1 April 1818 (NA, SOC, series ii, box 168).   87 *Drogheda Journal*, 4 Apr. 1818.   88 *FJ*, 6 Apr. 1818. 89 Ó Néill (ed.), *Journal of Henry McClintock*, p. 246.

a considerable property; he could not plead what many of the deluded
wretches that had appeared before them on former trial might do –
ignorance – his situation in life gave him an opportunity of knowing
better and if he was found guilty it would considerably aggravate his
offence.[90]

    McCullough's guilt, according to Joy, was all the greater because 'he who
should have known and acted better is certainly the more criminally flagitious.'[91]
The editor of the *Newry Telegraph* opined that it was 'astonishing that such a man
should have been so weak in intellect, so depraved in morals as to associate himself
with a nefarious gang of assassins, at the hazard of losing the advantages which
he possessed in society, and even life itself'.[92] McCullough had been arrested on
12 March 1817 in the first flush of arrests. In Pendleton's notes he (along with Pat
Malone, James Campbell, Pat Craven and Bryan Lennon, by then all tried and
executed) had come to the notice of the police long before the incident at
Wildgoose Lodge. The point has already been made that he may have been an
actual Ribbonman of the gentlemanly type who had met in Carrickmacross in
April 1816, as opposed to a mere local agrarian agitator and therefore that was the
reason he had been singled out for attention in the past. The authorities were
offered the pretext to arrest and try him after the incident at Wildgoose Lodge.
    Samuel Pendleton later reported to William Gregory that there was 'extreme
difficulty' in 'getting a proper jury' to try McCullough.[93] What he meant by
this is unclear but in the end most of those chosen were repeat jurors. Henry
McNeale, Malcolm Browne, Alexander Donaldson and Laurence Tallon had
all sat on the Devan jury. James Johnson, Ben Atkinson, Robert Sheddon had
all sat on the second trial jury and would again sit together on the seventh trial
jury. Neal Coleman had sat on two earlier juries, including the previous one.
Of the remainder, Robert Thompson from Ravensdale was a substantial landholder and linen manufacturer and brother-in-law of Baron McClelland. John
McNeale was another large gentleman farmer who lived at Mount Pleasant and
was, therefore, a neighbour of Thompson and McClelland. M.B. Taylor was a
£20 freeholder and merchant from Red Barnes in Dundalk and Robert Getty
a prosperous merchant from Clanbrassil Street in Dundalk. Browne, Coleman,
Getty and Tallon were functionaries in the Dundalk parish vestry.
    The drama in this trial began when Patrick Murphy was called as an approver
and 'pandemonium' broke out in the courtroom. For the first time in the
Wildgoose trials one of McCullough's counsels, Mr Murray, questioned the

90 Ibid. 91 *Newry Telegraph,* 4 Apr. 1818. 92 Ibid. 93 Samuel Pendleton to William Gregory,
1 April 1818 (NA, SOC, series ii, box 168).

validity of using Murphy as an approver (according to Judge Fletcher, McCullough employed 'the talents of the most able counsels in his defence'). Murray began by asking Murphy if he had been convicted of the robbery and murder at Sillerys, to which Murphy replied that he had. Murray then argued that in point of law Murphy should first have been pardoned of his own crimes before he could be eligible to give evidence in any of the trials. Murray demanded proof from John Pollock, clerk of the Crown, that this had actually happened but Pollock was not on hand and therefore 'much altercation took place and points of law [were] debated'. Pollock finally arrived with the necessary pardon and another legal debate ensued which lasted for over one and a half hours centred on whether the pardon was for the crime of robbery as well as murder. It transpired to be for murder only. Once again, the liberalities which had been taken with the law were highlighted but once again the authorities easily circumvented any obstacles put in their way; Pollock literally drew up another pardon on the spot 'for all offences whatever that he [Murphy] had ever committed'.[94] The legal technicality that could have precluded Murphy giving evidence in the earlier trials was obviously of little comfort to those he had already assigned to the gallows. Moreover, Murphy admitted during the trial that he had spent the previous night in a 'police office' along with Gollogly. The latter corroborated this statement.[95]

When he was eventually cleared to give evidence, Murphy alleged that on the night of the murders Patrick Malone (who had been one of the first prisoners executed for the crime) pointed McCullough out to him and identified him as 'Captain McCullough'. Gollogly then testified that he had reached the lodge with another of the accused, James Campbell (by this time also executed) who led a small group from the Meath Hill area. Gollogly identified McCullough as the leader of a group he met at Reaghstown chapel and said that the prisoner gave him a jug to drink from as much as he pleased, and told him that he had a group of men that 'would not fail to do anything they were desired'. The prosecution's case rested on the fact that, after Devan, McCullough was the most prominent leader on the night.

McCullough's brother, James, was the first witness called by the defence. He told the court that he and his brother lived about a mile from Ardee where they kept looms and a bleach green of yarn that was worth up to £200 at any given time. On the night of the burning, they had kept watch over the green, as usual, in order to prevent it being attacked. James recalled that his brother had a knee injury at the time which left him lame and suggested that this would have inhibited his movement on the night (much the same story as had been used by Smith in

94 *Drogheda Journal*, 4 Apr. 1818. **95** Ibid.

his earlier trial).[96] James Carragher was then called as a character witness. He was an extensive farmer (a £50 freeholder) from Cardistown in the parish of Arthurstown who had sat on the third Wildgoose Lodge jury. Carragher said he had known the prisoner for eight to ten years as 'a very good man'. The next character witness, Henry Blackwell, a Protestant farmer, said he knew McCullough the same length of time and claimed that the prisoner and the murdered Thomas Rooney were schoolfellows who 'were on good terms'. He also claimed they were related.[97] Even Halpenny, the Crown's corroborator, admitted under cross-examination, that he knew McCullough for 'many years' as a 'very good character'. Fr James Marron told the court that McCullough was 'a peaceable, industrious man'. Newspaper notes are sketchy, but it seems that at this stage Serjeant Joy questioned Fr Marron's integrity based on the fact that he had also given a character reference for three other of his parishioners, Shanley, Conlon and Devan, all of whom had by then been found guilty and hanged for their roles in one or other of the two raids. When Fr Marron said he hoped the three had repented, Joy retorted: 'Indeed, and I hope you will repent too, Sir.'[98] Joy's insinuation was clear.

Summing up, Judge Fletcher addressed the jury for almost an hour and a half. This, he claimed: 'was a more important case than any of the former. The peculiar situation of this man required their most serious consideration … The prisoner appeared to be a man that could not be induced from low circumstances in life or such causes to enter into this conspiracy … his motives must be of the most diabolical nature'. Once again, he returned to the importance of protecting men of property: 'it was wisely ordained by providence that ranks and degrees among men should exist, and it was impossible for one to subsist without the other'. If men of property were driven from the county, the lower classes would 'like voracious wolves cut each other's throats and quickly put an end to the community'. He could not understand McCullough's motivation to involve himself in a conspiracy of 'a band of ruffians, a conspiracy formed against all those who would dare to defend their property … It had appeared to them in evidence that he was a man who had a considerable property to defend and consequently it was more natural to expect that he would have supported the laws than enter into this foul conspiracy to oppose the distribution of justice.' Only then, did he direct the jurors to scrutinise carefully the evidence of the approvers: 'the testimony of one bad man must go for nothing, the testimony of two bad men can be no better than that of one, nor is that of three or four of any more weight, if not corroborated by some other facts'. The witnesses, he admitted, were 'men stained with the foulest crimes' but the law could allow of their evidence because of 'irrefutable corroboration'. He then explicitly con-

96 Ibid. **97** Ibid. **98** Ibid.

demned what he considered the 'palpable perjury' in James McCullough's evidence: 'a crime almost equal in magnitude to the murder in question'.[99] The heavy ironies in his address are now just as palpable.

The jury took just three minutes to return a verdict of guilty.[1] Then followed: 'a scene of the greatest confusion imaginable'. McCullough who had persistently attempted to interrupt Judge Fletcher during his summation in order to deny his guilt suddenly plunged his hands into his pockets. A panicked roar of 'a pistol, a pistol' echoed through the chambers. According to one report, Judge Fletcher 'retreated precipitately from the court' and 'the lawyers fled *pari passu*' into the grand jury room. In a moment the police had surrounded the dock and McCullough was restrained. When he was searched, the feared pistol was discovered to be a bible that McCullough wanted to use to swear his innocence. McCullough was placed in chains and removed to Dundalk jail to await execution.[2]

The following day, 2 April 1818, William Butler (from Aclint), John Keegan (from around the same area) and Thomas Sheenan (from Tallanstown) were brought to trial, just over a year after they had been arrested in March 1817. In early April 1817, when Samuel Pendleton interviewed Alice Rispin she named all three of them as having been present at the lodge during the first raid a year earlier.[3] All three were her neighbours. After the execution of Shanley, Conlon and Tiernan, both Keegan and Sheenan had warned her to take her son out of Lynch's employment; Keegan had told her that 'Lynch and Rooney were rogues and had turned traitor to their country'. This was the only comment that appeared in trial evidence that suggested the suspects might have had a different view of what constituted 'their country'. (In closing these assizes Judge Fletcher spoke of his love for 'his country' in which he saw no place for 'those illegal societies which have brought several of their fellow men to an ignominious death and has entailed disgrace and affliction on their unfortunate families and friends.')[4] Under cross-examination, Rispin said she had never told Lynch 'precisely' what was being said about him in the area, but she did warn him that his life was under threat. When she warned her son, he replied that 'people could not be murdered so easily as she seemed to fear' and so he returned to work in the lodge.[5] Thomas Gubby identified all three prisoners at the bar as having been at the lodge the night of the murders, so they were accused of being party to both raids.

There was little of note in Sheenan's defence. His chief alibi, Daniel Murphy, stated that he and his sister, Catherine, had stayed in Thomas Sheenan's house

99 Ibid. **1** Ibid. **2** *Newry Telegraph,* 4 Apr. 1818; *Belfast Newsletter,* 7 Apr. 1818. **3** Statement of Alice Rispin given before Samuel Pendleton, 2 Apr. 1817 (Louth County Library, WGL papers). **4** *Belfast Newsletter,* 10 Apr. 1818. **5** Ibid., 7 Apr. 1818.

the night of the murders. Sleeping arrangements were again used in evidence as in the Gaynor trial. Murphy alleged that he had slept in the same bed as Sheenan and his wife. There was another woman staying in the house, Nelly Reilly (who seems to have been employed as a spinner by the Sheenans), who went into labour. Murphy told the court that her childbirth had kept him awake as only a hanging sheet separated her bed from theirs. When asked why he had not stayed in his own house that night, which was only a short distance away, Murphy replied that his own wife had gone into labour that evening and he 'always left the house' during the birth of his children.

Butler, as noted already, was a near neighbour of Edward Lynch's who lived a mile or so across the bog from Wildgoose Lodge. He was one of five sons of a weaver/shopkeeper, four of whom were weavers while the youngest was still a boy. Butler's mother told the court that on the night of the murders the boys were all asleep in a room off the shop while she was up late baking (it was supper time, she claimed, before she thought to do so, remembering that a crowd of men would be gathered the following day to take out the potatoes). At around 2 a.m., she first noticed the fire at the lodge. She called her husband who, in turn, alerted some of the neighbours. They were all 'very fond of Lynch's people' but everybody was afraid to go to their assistance least they too be killed. Michael Mohan (a sister of Edward Lynch's was married to Mohan's brother-in-law) and Thomas Halpenny (Mohan's labourer) corroborated the evidence of the Butler family. (Mohan's extended relationship to Lynch serves to highlight how the local community came in time to be so divided by the incident.)

The most noteworthy defence witness called was James Lynch, a brother of Edward's. He had known William Butler since birth and acknowledged that the Lynches and Butlers were always on extremely good terms: 'he did not believe Butler would hurt his brother [Edward] more than himself'.[6] Then, there was a further twist – though not an unusual occurrence in early-nineteenth century trials – when the defence called one of the jury, the aforementioned John Coleman, the strong Catholic farmer from Rathory, to give a character reference for Butler. Coleman commended the young prisoner: 'he never knew a man … bear a better character'.[7] Before leaving the stand he gave a similar character reference for Keegan. During the McCullough trial Coleman's near neighbour, James Carragher, also a strong Catholic farmer, had testified similarly on behalf of the prisoner. Carragher had served with Coleman on the all-Catholic jury. Both of these were highly respected members of their local communities; for years after Carragher and Coleman would continue to serve on local bodies such as the Charlestown and Clonkeen Board of Health along

6 *Drogheda Journal,* 4 Apr. 1818.   7 *Belfast Newsletter,* 7 Apr. 1818.

with landlords such as William Filgate, Thomas Lee Norman and strong Protestant farmers such as Joseph Shekleton and Alexander Henry. In 1828 Coleman was amongst the most prominent residents of Dundalk and its surroundings areas to petition the government for the Extension of the Lighting of Towns Act 1828 to the town. His fellow petitioners included others of the Wildgoose Lodge jurors such as Alexander Shekleton, James McAlister, Henry Hale, as well as Robert Jocelyn, then third earl of Roden, and John Straton, the latter's agent and former secretary to the Louth Wildgoose Lodge fund. They would all work together as harbour commissioners in the years following that saw the development of Dundalk Harbour.[8] By the 1840s Coleman and his son, also John, were ardent Repealers and prominent members of other local bodies such as the Dundalk Famine Relief Committee.[9] The Wildgoose Lodge trials highlighted the ambiguous position in which some members of the Catholic propertied classes such as Coleman and Carragher found themselves. On the one hand, their economic standing had drawn them into the social world of the Protestant propertied classes. As part of the all-Catholic jury that had earlier tried Marron, Craven and Malone on 5 March 1818 they were prepared to defend property rights. On the other hand, their political outlook was different to the majority of the other Protestant jurors and the prominence of the Catholic question possibly made them challenge the working of the state's legal apparatus on the basis of widespread Catholic grievance with the legal and judicial system that became increasingly apparent as the Wildgoose Lodge trials progressed. In the aftermath of the spring assizes of 1818 the self-styled *Poplicola* (presumably deriving from Publius Valerius Publicola, or Poplicola, the Roman consul who died in 503 BC whose surname translated meant 'friend of the people') asserted: 'Everybody must know, and the Roman Catholic clergy amongst others, how frequently the people are told by the public speakers and by the writers of the day … that the law is not their friend – that it is their oppression, if they are not immediately emancipated.'[10]

   In Coleman's case, the popularity of his stance was later intimated in the fact that his was the only juror's name that appeared in later nationalist accounts. This stemmed from the outcome of Butler's acquittal. The jury (most of whom had sat upon former trials) retired at 3 p.m. and the court was adjourned until 9 p.m. when they returned a verdict of guilty for Sheenan and Keegan but stated they

8 See Harold O'Sullivan, 'Dundalk Harbour improvements in the nineteenth century' in *Journal of the County Louth Archaeological and Historical Society,* 24:4 (2000), pp 504–30. 9 O'Sullivan, 'Ardee Dispensary minute book', p. 9; see also Georgina Clinton, 'Relief committee membership in the Union of Dundalk during the Great Irish Famine' in *Journal of the County Louth Archaeological and Historical Society,* 24:1 (1999 for 1997), pp 51–9. 10 *Correspondent,* 21 Mar. 1818.

could not agree in the case of Butler. They were sent back to the jury room where they remained until 11.30 p.m. Still they failed to agree because Coleman refused to find Butler guilty, allegedly claiming that he would rather eat his own boots than do so. (He must, however, have been prepared to find Keegan guilty despite the fact that he had also provided a character reference for him.) According to John Mathews' nationalist retelling, Coleman was recognised at Ballinasloe fair the following October (his presence there was credible enough as according to Samuel Lewis 'considerable numbers of horned cattle and sheep' were purchased there by Louth farmers each year to be fattened in the county)[11] and for his 'manly heroism' in saving the life of Butler he 'received a well-merited reception' when he was carried shoulder high through the streets as thousands gathered to see the man who had 'so signalised himself by his honest manliness in the corrupt jury room'.[12] Mathews' sentiments were, of course, very much a by-product of a different time – the height of the Land War of the early 1880s and the growth of the Home Rule movement – but the story perhaps revealed how Coleman had dealt with his own sense of ambiguity in a changing Ireland.

At any rate, Butler was remanded to the following assizes as the jury did not have the power to acquit him and so Judge Fletcher sent him back to prison with the intention of retrying him at the next assizes. According to law, the hung jury had to be discharged 'on the verge of the county'. As that was several miles from Dundalk and it was now almost midnight, Serjeant Joy requested that they be discharged 'convenient to town'. The defence counsel did not object, so the jury were taken together on a sociable to the end of the town's boundary at Lady's Well bridge, accompanied by the high sheriff, a guard of soldiers and Fletcher who there discharged them of their duties and told them to go their separate ways.[13]

On 7 April 1818, McCullough, Sheenan, Keegan, Smith and McQuillan were brought to their place of execution at Reaghstown. McCullough looked 'remarkably clean and seemed to have a white dress under his great coat'. McQuillan stood up on the sociable, sat down, rose up again and exclaimed to the crowds: 'That my soul may perish if ever I saw Wildgoose Lodge.' The *Belfast Newsletter* reported that 'since their conviction these unhappy men continued to evince the most determined resolution of dying declaring their innocence'.[14] Pendleton reported to Gregory:

> The conduct of these men was not so ferocious as that of most of the
> others had been; but though more temperate in their manner they were

11 www.jbhll.freeservers.com/lewis_county_louth.htm (28 Sept. 2006). 12 Mathews, *The burning of Wildgoose Lodge*, p. 13. 13 *Dundalk Examiner*, 1 Oct. 1881. 14 *Belfast Newsletter*, 10 Apr. 1818; *Dundalk Examiner*, 5 Nov. 1881.

equally hardened in their guilt and died proclaiming their innocence and other ignorance of every circumstance not only of the fact for which they suffered but of everything connected with any species of unlawful association.[15]

Fr James Marron, parish priest of Tallanstown, attended the prisoners prior to execution. He later wrote to Margaret O'Reilly: 'I have constantly attended them since Sunday morning and they all have to the last moment asserted their innocence of the crime for which they suffered. The Co. Meath man [McQuillan] declared he never knew where the lodge was until he saw it from the scaffold.'[16] McCullough refused to admit his guilt but 'at the earnest request and persuasion of the Rev. Mr Marron … said he forgave the world'.[17] If all five proclaimed their innocence, this brought the total of those to have done so to twelve.

McCullough's body was taken to Louth where it was gibbeted bringing the number of gibbeted bodies on display there to four; there were four more at Corcreaghy and three in the Hackballscross area (Fr Marron wrote to Margaret O'Reilly: 'nothing but gibbets offend the eye'). The bodies of the other four men were sent to Dundalk infirmary for dissection, another departure in the trials. From the authorities' point of view dissection had the same effect as gib-beting: it was another mark of infamy; it denied the victim a Christian burial (according to Padraig Ó Macháin this was 'a deliberate attempt to prey on folk-beliefs regarding the supposed necessity for the human body to be whole and intact on the Last Day');[18] and prevented the holding of wakes that might allow for a gathering of malcontents. Why they were dissected instead of gibbeted like the others is unclear; it may be that the surgeons in Dundalk infirmary simply had requested bodies for experimentation, and were, therefore, follow-ing trends that had become popular in England since the eighteenth century.[19]

The trial of William Butler brought the Special Commission to an end. William Gregory was delighted that 'the severe example of executing 16 will have its due effect on the minds of the people'.[20] A number of men, probably six, were released on bail at this stage.[21] The authorities considered these minor players who would have been less influential in hatching disaffection in their respective localities. In closing the commission, Serjeant Joy declared that it had been the Crown's intention all along to prosecute only the ringleaders and to extend mercy to the 'minor villain'.

15 Samuel Pendleton to William Gregory, 7 Apr. 1818 (NA, SOC, series ii, box 168). 16 Letter cited in Paterson, 'The burning of Wildgoose Lodge', pp 179–80. 17 Belfast Newsletter, 10 Apr. 1818; Dundalk Examiner, 5 Nov. 1881. 18 Ó Macháin, Six years in Galmoy, p. 166. 19 For the English case, see Linebaugh, 'The Tyburn riot against the surgeons', pp 69–78. 20 William Gregory to Robert Peel, 4 Apr. 1818 (PRO, Peel papers, ADD 40205). 21 Weekly Freeman's Journal, 11 Apr. 1818.

As for the six prisoners at the bar, although there was abundant proof
of their guilt; yet as it appeared they had not [acted] in the savage
manner others had, whom it was necessary to make examples of, he
would tell them that the law which they had set at defiance would now
humanely suffer them to be discharged on entering into bail to appear
when called upon, which would entirely depend on the peaceable state
of the county.[22]

A message was being sent abroad that the countryside had to return to more
peaceful means or more men would forfeit their lives; they were effectively being
held as hostages in ransom for the return of social order.[23] On the other hand,
the authorities may have recognised that opinion was becoming increasingly
inflamed by the executions of men who were declaring their innocence.[24] It had
long been argued that multiple executions could just as likely inflame disaffection as remedy social disorder. Back in 1780, Edmund Burke had warned that
the multiple executions which followed the Gordon riots in England – a week
long orgy of looting, arson and defiance of authority – might have serious repercussions: 'The sense of justice in men is overlooked and fatigued with a long
series of executions, or with such a carnage at once, as rather resembles a massacre than a sober execution of the laws.'[25] But the executions relating to
Wildgoose Lodge had not yet finished.

The final trials

William Butler, Owen Gaynor (brother of the acquitted, Laurence), Michael
Kearnan (from Monaghan, probably around Carrickmacross), Patrick Malone
(the son of Pat Malone executed in March 1818), Thomas Tiernan (brother of
one of those hanged for the April 1816 raid) and George McQuillan (whose
brother, Patrick, had been earlier executed) were not released on bail. The case
of Patrick Waters reflected the probable confusion and probable ignorance and
terror of some of the prisoners in Dundalk jail still awaiting trial. He believed
he was awaiting trial for the burnings but on 3 April was informed that he was
to be tried for the first raid on the house. He told the court: 'he did not expect
such a trial to be brought on and was unprepared for trial'. The trials of all these
men were postponed to the summer assizes of 3 July 1818 at which time Baron

22 *Belfast Newsletter*, 7 Apr. 1818. 23 *Correspondent*, 7 Apr. 1818; *FJ*, 8 Apr. 1818; *Dundalk Examiner*,
5 Nov. 1881. 24 *Dublin Evening Post*, 11 Mar. 1818. 25 Quoted in Gattrell, *The hanging tree*, p.
20; see also Hay et al. (eds), *Albion's tree*, pp 50–1.

McClelland was back on the bench. These, the last of the Wildgoose Lodge trials, were held in the new courthouse in Dundalk, the 'neatness and comfort' of which was praised by the judge. McClelland remarked on how few prisoners there were for trial and expressed his pleasure that local disturbances had abated.[26] It seems that the multiple executions did have the required effect.

Butler, Kearnan and Gaynor were the first to be arraigned. Butler applied for another postponement of his trial until the following assizes. This was granted and he was sent back to jail. The trial of Kearnan and Gaynor seems to have generated much less coverage than those that preceded them. By now, the prosecution had established a well-defined chain of evidence so these trials were merely re-runs of what had come before them. Neither had counsel. Kearnan cross-examined James Corrigan, one of Pendleton's policemen, 'with intent to show that he had held out inducements to him to make his confession'. Pendleton produced Kearnan's statement in court in which he had sworn against Terence Marron, Hugh McCabe, Pat Craven, Edward McQuillan. The first three named had by then been executed; McQuillan was later to be released. Gaynor cross-examined several witnesses 'with a great degree of shrewdness' but to no avail. Both prisoners were found guilty. Kearnan was described as one of the 'most hardened and wicked' of those prosecuted, this being largely based on the fact that as he left the courthouse he bellowed 'forth the most horrid imprecations against his prosecutors', while Gaynor 'behaved with decency'. Both men were executed outside Dundalk gaol. Kearnan, who had originally been admitted an approver but who, as we have seen, withdrew his confession during the earlier trials, allegedly confessed his guilt saying that 'bad company brought him to his untimely grave', while Gaynor declared: 'he bore no malice to any person'. They were then, to use the cliche of the day, 'launched into eternity' and their bodies brought to Dundalk infirmary for dissection.[27]

On 4 July 1818 Thomas Tiernan, Patrick Malone, and George McQuillan (and probably Patrick Waters, James Laughran and James Morris) were admitted to bail and later released. There was something of a pattern here. Tiernan's brother, McQuillan's brother and Malone's father had already been executed for either the first or second raid on Wildgoose Lodge. Owen Gaynor was executed but his brother had earlier been acquitted. Were the authorities deliberately avoiding the execution of more than one member of a family? Eight months later, on 6 March 1819, two years after his arrest, Butler was brought back for trial before Baron McClelland who 'was happy to learn that those disturbances which had so long disgraced their country had subsided; those deluded people had

26 *Belfast Newsletter,* 7 July 1818; *Correspondent,* 8 July 1818; *Dundalk Examiner,* 5, 12 Nov. 1881.
27 *Belfast Newsletter,* 7, 10 July 1818.

found that the arm of the law was too powerful for them to contend with'.[28] Butler was finally admitted to bail on his own recognizances of £100 and eventually released after having spent two years in jail. Where he secured such a significant sum of money or what became of him afterwards is unknown.

28 Ibid., 7 July 1818; *Correspondent,* 8 July 1818; *Dundalk Examiner,* 5, 12 Nov. 1881.

Conclusion

The gibbet mast had mouldered down, the bones
And iron case were gone, but on the turf,
Hard by, soon after that fell deed was wrought
Some unknown hand had carved the murderer's name.
The monumental letters were inscribed
In times long past, but still, from year to year,
By superstition of the neighbourhood,
The grass is clear'd away, and to this hour
The characters are fresh and visible:
A casual glance had shown them, and, I fled
Faltering and faint, and ignorant of the road.

William Wordsworth, *The Prelude or, Growth of a poet's mind.*

The murder of eight people by burning to death at Wildgoose Lodge in late October 1816 makes for an intriguing examination of agrarian crime and punishment in pre-Famine Ireland. That the crime was abominable and shocking is without dispute but arguably it was the very heinous nature of it that has in the past discriminated against an objective examination of the incident and its fallout. The crime itself has been handed down in literature and lore and as this work has shown there has been an overlap between both largely as a result of the popularity of William Carleton's account. 'Wildgoose Lodge' succeeded initially because Carleton represented the crime and its motivation in terms acceptable to a literate Protestant ascendancy audience from which he sought patronage. For the likes of Sir Robert Peel, William Gregory and the Louth propertied classes – both Protestant and Catholic – Carleton's representation, without consideration of the socio-economic conditions that incubated it, relieved the establishment and the propertied classes of any form of culpability. When his version was replaced in local lore by that of John Mathew's orthodox nationalist account it reflected the seismic shift that had taken place in Irish politics and society in the intervening seventy years or so.

Until now relatively little has been written on the arrests, trials and executions all of which in their own right provide fascinating insights not only to the working of the police, forensic, and judicial systems of the time but also the complexity of the social networks that existed. Indeed, even the evidence provided at the trials by lower class witnesses furnishes an exceptional insight to the social lives and culture of that class (not all of which has been alluded to in this study).

Of course, there will always be questions remaining to be answered in relation to the committal of the atrocity itself. There may be some who will argue that this work does not reveal the full facts of what happened on the night because the evidence presented here is largely based on approvers' evidence and this work has time and again questioned the reliability of those state witnesses. But that would be to miss another important point continuously emphasised in this work, that the authorities through their investigations carried out locally over a period of months and gathered from a web of local informers (such as Rispin, Halpenny, the mysterious young woman, Thomas Woods from Corcreaghy, Owen Reilly who lived about four miles from the lodge who was forced to feed some of the raiders with a farrel of oaten bread and some milk,[1] and probably many more who remain anonymous) had already accumulated the facts before they found their approvers.

For the first time this work has placed the crime in an historical context that has illustrated the need to contemplate it within local circumstances of poverty and threatening famine resulting from the economic collapse after 1815. The burning of Wildgoose Lodge was a social crime rather than a political one. It was not carried out by Ribbonmen as historians understand the term in the present day (although Ribbon involvement in the end may have been a factor). Those involved in the crime were not members of the Ribbon Society, but certain common characteristics with more formal secret societies have clouded the distinctions: Devan and some of his followers came from a social background well represented in Ribbon circles; Devan was a hedge schoolmaster and he administered oaths; later Ribbonmen were involved in cases of murder, assault, house attacks and arms theft. But regarding the Louth society of 1816 there is no reference in the historical evidence to any type of hierarchical structure with county masters, parish masters, body masters, committeemen and ordinary members that characterised the Ribbon Society. Nor is there any mention of membership fees being paid.[2] Instead the crime was carried out at the bidding of a local agrarian society that through a system of terrorism had attempted to control the local economy, chiefly the level of conacre rents and access to land, the essence of which was probably best described by Major

---

1 *Belfast Newsletter,* 6 Mar. 1818.   **2** Jennifer Kelly has concluded that 'the amounts of money charged by the Ribbonmen, both at local lodge and higher levels within the society suggest large amounts of disposable income across the board of Ribbon membership'; Kelly, 'Ribbonism in Co. Leitrim', p. 6.

General Burnet who, when reporting on the state of Armagh and Louth in June 1816, referred to 'a lawless banditti who attempt to intimidate farmers and others from paying beyond a certain rate of rent'.[3] The rank and file were drawn predominantly from the lower classes – smallholders, farmers, unemployed weavers, cottiers and labourers – those most affected by economic depression at a time when an increasing population was putting excess strain on an already burdened land-based economy. In the pursuance of their goals their obdurate leaders showed a callous disrespect for life, even for that of a five-month-old infant.

The propertied class's culpability should not be ignored. In Louth, the landed and urban propertied classes did little to alleviate the predicament of the impoverished in 1816–18. In 1817 in a letter to the *Newry Telegraph* the afore-mentioned A. Atkinson was scathing in his criticism of the apathy of the upper classes to the plight of the poor:

> Let the opulent inhabitants of Kingscourt [Co. Cavan], Ardee and many other towns which we might name, stoop from the splendour of those seats which they have rendered of their country and take a peep into those abodes of wretchedness, which (within a pistol-shot of the finest combinations of art and nature) present the sense of the stranger with an aggregate of all which the imagination could devise, to complete a picture of horror … but which in the *ipso facto* scenes of human life, can only be excelled by the prospect of a dungeon in which the putrid carcases of the inhabitants combine with clanking chains, and the fetid effluvia of a vault, to give us, alas! a lively representation of the future condition of those sons of prosperity, who instead of manifesting their gratitude to heaven for the bounty which has distinguished them, by their charity to that nature of which they partake, sedulously avoid those objects which bring to their recollection that there is such a thing as misery in the world; and that the millions which every year are basely squandered at the card table would, in the hands of a wise and judicious charity, effectually relieve it.[4]

In December 1817, when Dundalk was ravaged by fever, £700 was raised 'by voluntary contributions from the inhabitants of the town and vicinity' and the government provided a grant of £120.[5] Just over a year before, almost £1,500

3 Abstracts of military reports by Major General Burnet, June 1816; quoted in Murray, *The burning of Wildgoose Lodge*, p. 145.   4 Quoted in 'Dundalk in 1817' in *Tempest's Annual, 1952*, pp 7–8.
5 *Dublin Evening Post*, 30 Dec. 1817.

had been pledged by the county gentry for the apprehension of those responsible for the Wildgoose murders and the government had subscribed £1,200.

This work has pointed to the fact that the post-1815 economic crisis gave rise to the social circumstances in which agrarian agitation was incubated. The numerous reports of agrarian outrages suggest that there were obviously plenty of middlemen and farmers willing to exploit market forces, unwilling to relinquish their newfound gains, and thereby willing to ignore the potential wrath of the aggrieved, while looking to the state for protection.[6] There were those like Edward Lynch who were willing to prosecute their lower class neighbours in order to protect their property. Simultaneously, the determination of local secret societies to operate within an environment free of informers contributed directly to the brutal exaction of revenge on Edward Lynch and his family for their role in the prosecution of three men who were implicated in the initial raid on Wildgoose Lodge in April 1816.

If this study tells us anything about the nature and working of underground organisations in pre-Famine Ireland it is that they were capable of callousness in the extreme. (And, given the activities of the likes of McIlroy and Gubby stretching from Dungannon and Omagh in Tyrone to south Armagh and then Monaghan, Meath and Louth, it also indicates the wide geographical area covered by individual criminals and criminal gangs.) This makes it seem all the more remarkable that within a short time Daniel O'Connell had managed to somehow divert much of the same violent energy into a constitutional mass movement in the campaign for Catholic Emancipation (even if the potential for violent disorder remained as long as the underlying social causes prevailed.)[7] Whereas Catholic freeholders of the type who sat on the Wildgoose juries had looked to the state for the protection of their property rights, in a loose alliance with Protestant landlords, gentlemen farmers and businessmen in 1816, the forty-shilling freeholders were prepared to revolt against the bidding of their landlords in Monaghan and Louth in the general election of a decade later.[8] The reasons for this so-called revolt are obviously varied and complex and not confined to local issues. Nonetheless, Catholic grievance with the legal and judicial system was an important contributory element and the Wildgoose Lodge trials may very well have compounded this grievance in the years following,[9] and influenced the likes of John Coleman to lead the Catholic Emancipation and later Repeal movements in Dundalk.

Until now the social motivation behind the crime was clouded by the store of lore that has survived. Indeed, there will always remain some uncertainty

---

6 For a contemporary view on this see Lewis, *Local disturbances*, p. 43. **7** See Garvin, 'Defenders, Ribbonmen and others', p. 219. **8** Livingstone, *The Monaghan story*, pp 184–8. **9** See, for example, letter of 'Poplicola' to editor in *Correspondent*, 21 Mar. 1818.

regarding possible ulterior motives behind the Wildgoose atrocity. As already noted, local lore, time and again, has suggested that local considerations might even have been personal – an opportunity for somebody with social clout such as Patrick Devan to settle an old score.[10] But we will probably never know if this might have been, for example, because Devan's love for Lynch's daughter was unrequited (or even disallowed by her father) nor, indeed, will we probably ever fathom how to reconcile Devan, the honest industrious worker, well conducted and peaceable as testified to by his parish priest and further suggested in the tone of his surviving letters to his father with the hardened villain that was capable of murdering an innocent five-month-old child (along with seven others), allegedly justifying it with the execrable pronouncement that the nits should not be allowed to grow into lice? Did something exceptional drive Devan to the extremes of barbarity carried out by him personally or directed by him that night? If Devan was tried in a later era, more accurate forensic evidence might have explained a great deal about his state of mind at the time. But in the early-nineteenth century, the mental element was of relative unimportance and it would be some years before insanity and criminal responsibility would figure in the Irish homicide trial.[11] Similarly, in a later era, other extenuating circumstances such as the levels of intoxication of the perpetrators, which accentuated passions in some and possibly even induced temporary insanity in others, might also be revealed and taken into consideration. The levels of intoxication of the approvers who alleged they were at Wildgoose Lodge would also have been considered in the context of their ability to provide scrupulous evidence in the later identification of men they had never met before the night of 29–30 October who could only have been scurrying shadows in the mayhem of a dark night.

Almost certainly a defence counsel in a later era would alert an unpartisan jury to so many discrepancies in the approvers' evidence that they would have had no choice but to release many of the prisoners purely on the element of doubt created in the jurors' minds. As it was, the government and its officials showed very little concern as to whether or not those tried and eventually executed were actually guilty or not. They used approvers and other witnesses unscrupulously – in most cases the wrong type of people who were motivated by the prospects of saving their own lives or at least improving their economic situation rather than truth and justice – in an attempt to address lawlessness

---

10 For the general case of Ribbon crimes see MacDonagh, *Ireland*, p. 144. 11 For treatments of this subject see, for example, Finbarr McAuley, *Insanity, psychiatry and criminal responsibility* (Dublin, 1993); The Law Reform Commission, *Consultation paper on homicide: the mental element in murder* (Dublin, 2001).

and to break a 1798-type conspiracy that was more a figment of the magistracy's imagination than a reality. In the cases which Sergeant Joy prosecuted he made sure to point out to the jurors the importance of their station: 'It was their office to maintain the laws and secure the impartial distribution of justice, to preserve social order and protect public property.'[12] As the trials unfolded, it became clear that the preservation of social order and the protection of property took precedence over 'the impartial distribution of justice' with the result that innocent men were executed along with the guilty. It was not the guilt or innocence of the convicted that mattered but rather the public example.

From Robert Peel and William Gregory at the top of the Castle administration, down to the Louth magistracy under the influence of John Foster, and with the connivance of reproachable judges who owed their position to favour, a less than reputable chief police magistrate, and the general complicity of the propertied classes who comprised the juries there was collusion to bring suspects to trial and to have them executed in order to crush the social anarchy sweeping through Louth and surrounding areas in 1816–18. This was merely symptomatic of a society in which patronage dictated how business should be carried out through social connections. In the process, the fabrication of evidence based on information provided by informers and then fed to willing approvers was never a moral issue. On 4 April 1818, at which stage most of the suspects had been tried and executed, William Gregory wrote to Robert Peel: 'One good effect must certainly follow from the conviction of so many on the testimony of approvers, that the system of union for lawless purposes must be shaken.'[13] The fact that the vast majority of the jurors were prepared to believe the suspect evidence of vacillating and highly questionable characters and to turn a blind eye to the most glaring evidential contradictions in almost every case tried proved their acquiescence in this process. In a heavily ironic twist, Judge Fletcher in his address to the grand jury at the spring assizes in Armagh in 1818, shortly after he had left Dundalk, told them:

> That admirable system of jurisprudence, under which it is our good fortune to live, requires that no man should be put even to answer on any criminal charge, until a jury of his country, on their oaths, see sufficient grounds for subjecting him to trial on the accusation. It is, therefore, that it is required that twelve of your number should agree to every indictment, ere it can be returned to this court as a true bill ... [in the past] the only evidence placed before you was the examinations taken

12 *Newry Telegraph*, 4 April 1818.   13 William Gregory to Robert Peel, 4 April 1818 (British Library, Peel papers, ADD 40205).

by the magistrates – and you must all of you gentlemen be aware how fallacious these may often be. We all know how greatly the heat of passion – the first feeling of resentment – the ignorance of some – the fraud of others, must necessarily discolour objects; the incapacity of the magistrate, often his prejudice or malice, or party feeling, mixing with or thwarting his reason and his sense of justice. If these … have had anything to do in originating the accusation, their mischievous evidence will be stopped by your conscientious examination of *civa voce* evidence.[14]

When the Louth agitation reached its apex with the murders at Wildgoose Lodge it was deemed expedient to bend the rules to address the threat to the state, irrespective of the underlying socio-economic conditions that incubated the atrocity. Thus, as already noted, Peel told the Commons in 1816: 'Formerly tumult and outrages might be traced to particular causes; but those which now prevailed seemed to be the effect of a general confederacy in crime – a systematic opposition to all laws and municipal institutions.'[15] Those in authority regarded multiple executions as the most reliable means of doing so. In 1816 Peel had learned this in the Castle's attempts to pacify an equally disturbed Tipperary. He wrote to the British prime minister, Lord Liverpool:

> In Tipperary we are … making a terrific but necessary example under the Special Commission we have sent there. There have been thirteen capital convictions for offences amounting to little short of rebellion, and fourteen sentenced to transportation for the destruction of a barrack. All these sentences will be carried into execution without mitigation … You can have no idea of the moral depravation of the lower orders in that county. In fidelity to each other they are unexampled, as they are in their sanguinary disposition and fearlessness of the consequences.[16]

Liverpool replied:

> I am happy to find you have been so successful in your convictions under the Special Commission. Though it is dreadful to think of so many executions as must take place in consequence, yet I am thoroughly persuaded there is no chance of peace for the country except by so extensive an example as cannot fail to strike terror into the minds of the disaffected.[17]

14 Quoted in Murray, *The burning of Wildgoose Lodge*, pp 249–50. **15** *Annual Register, 1816*. **16** Quoted in Gash, *Mr Secretary Peel*, p. 175. **17** Quoted in Parker, *Peel correspondence*, vol. i, p.

In 1824 similar tactics were to be used in Co. Kilkenny. Charles Kendal Bushe, solicitor-general during the Wildgoose Lodge trials, went there as lord chief justice of the King's Bench to preside over the trials of six men suspected of murdering landlord John Marum during a period of intense agrarian activity. Bushe sentenced six men to death and thereafter: 'the state of Galmoy and the border area of its neighbouring barony in the Queen's County, Upper Ossory, went from chaos to quiet. The authorities could be well pleased with the turn of events in an area that, since 1819 and earlier, had defied all efforts by them to control it.'[18] Arguably, Bushe and the authorities had learned from his/their Louth experiences.

While one must be very careful when making comparisons over time, there are some interesting parallels between the actions of Peel's Castle administration in 1816–18 and that of W.T. Cosgrave's administration in 1922 when draconian legislation was introduced by Dáil Eireann to deal with the threat posed to the embryonic Free State by Republican opponents of the treaty. The special emergency powers resulted in the execution of seventy-seven men between November 1922 and May 1923. These men were executed without the formality of a trial for, as Tom Garvin points out, 'no particular crime other than being on the wrong political side'.[19] (Peel, on the other hand, had preserved the forms of law, even if somewhat tenuously.) The Cosgrave administration's response to republicanism, along with its attempts to introduce a general amnesty for those who would repudiate the republic, helped bring an end to systematic terrorism in Ireland. Shortly after the first batch of executions during the Irish Civil War, Cosgrave pointed out: 'The executions have had a remarkable effect … The unfortunate thing about them is you have to execute the unfortunate dupes, and the responsible people were not got.'[20] Similarly, the Wildgoose Lodge executions, along with something akin to a general amnesty, had the desired effect of cowing leaders and followers and ending systematic terrorism in the borderlands. Innocent men were executed, while more who were much more culpable escaped in the amnesty. However, sporadic outbreaks of agitation were to continue in the borderlands into the decades preceding the Great Famine, particularly the early 1820s, and the legitimacy of the state was not to be recognised by all its inhabitants. In comparison, neither did the threat to the state disappear after the Irish Civil War. Splinter groups of the IRA sporadically threatened violence and within a decade the Fianna Fáil party, which had been built upon a republican ideology (though of a type that Wolfe Tone would hardly have recognised), and comprised of many of the most hardened opponents of the treaty was to assume power.

207. **18** Ó Macháin, *Six years in Garmoyle*, p. 170. **19** Tom Garvin, *1922: the birth of Irish democracy* (Dublin, 1996), pp 162–3. **20** Quoted in ibid., p. 163.

In many respects the Wildgoose Lodge trials stand out as an obvious anomaly to such generalisations as Irish petty juries tended to acquit a far greater proportion of suspects than their English counterparts; interventions by the state to pack juries were not as great as they could have been; levels of repression inherent in the law were more likely to be experienced in Surrey than Munster; and that in the Irish case 'the number of reports of irregularity and manipulation are admittedly limited'.[21] In Co. Louth in 1816–18 'the deep depravity and wickedness' of the crime was met with the 'terrible retribution' of the law.[22] This, in turn, as Baron McClelland's opening address at the summer assizes of 1818 suggested, had the desired short term effect and so on 5 April 1819, after a period of calm, the magistrates of Louth petitioned the lord lieutenant to proclaim that the baronies of Ardee, Louth, and Upper and Lower Dundalk were once again restored to peace and good order.[23] (When Joy and Gregory sought legal advice on the Luddite trials in York[24] they were also aware of the effects of the multiple executions in their aftermath about which one contemporary wrote: 'The effect was tremendous, for whereas the town had been full of excited mobs of a threatening character, hardly a person was to be seen outside his house on the following day'.)[25] On 12 April 1819 the lord lieutenant ordered the Louth constabulary to remove the gibbets within the county. Within three days, Pendleton and twenty-four of his men had removed the last of them, three months short of two years since Devan had been the first to be executed.[26] Tradition has it that during all this time, no fruit from Corcreaghy and the surrounding areas was bought in Dundalk as 'it was believed that the flies might alight on the fruit after feasting on the remains of the unfortunate men in the gibbets'.[27] This was the favoured part of the story told by this author's great-grandfather to his father, but, of course, it had come to him via William Carleton's account.

When the gibbets were removed, John Foster, on behalf of the Louth magistrates, wrote to William Gregory that it was their earnest hope that:

> They have remained sufficient time to impress on the people the ready & determined resolution of the magistrates to apply with energy the powerful arm of the law, to check and put down any attempt tending

21 Garnham, *The courts, crime and criminal law*, pp 142, 259–60. 22 *Correspondent*, 11 Mar. 1818. 23 Memorial of Co. Louth magistrates assembled at Castlebellingham, 5 Apr. 1819 (NA, SOC, 2075/31). 24 See chapter five. 25 Quoted in Gatrell, *The hanging tree*, p. 98. 26 Joseph Holmes to William Gregory, 12 Apr. 1819 (NA, SOC 2075/29); Resolution passed by Louth magistrates at Castlebellingham, 5 Apr. 1819 (NA, SOC 2075/31). 27 Carleton, *Autobiography*, p. 117; Mathews, *The burning of Wildgoose Lodge*, p. 13.

to disturb the peace and tranquillity of their county and to bring to
severe justice the promoters and perpetrators of any more attempts.[28]

What was left of the decomposed bodies was brought to Dundalk jail and
interred within its walls in graves packed with lime.[29] As Gatrell concludes
regarding the English example: 'Anatomization, decapitation, and gibbeting
struck at popular anxieties deliberately. Burial policies also struck at them deliberately – particularly the consignment of hanged bodies to unconsecrated and
quicklimed graves inside prisons.'[30] Was gibbeting successful in its primary aim
of discouraging future crime? Writing about twenty years after Devan's execution, James Anton thought not:

> How far the sentence of the law in thus exposing the carcases of crim-
> inals may have the intended effect of deterring others from attempting
> the like crimes, I shall leave for the consideration of those who are more
> deeply versed than myself in the workings of the human mind. I am
> led to think, however, that where the criminals form only the operative
> part of an extensive body it might be better to let their bones lie hid in
> the dust with their crimes than to excite public feeling in favour of sor-
> rowing relations and oath-bound associates who register the criminals
> in the calendar of martyrs and saints.[31]

The truth of Anton's conclusions was in some respects reflected in Devan's
own journey into nationalist martyrdom as described in chapter one. It was not
until the 1832 Reform Act that gibbeting and anatomising were ended and over
thirty years more before public executions were replaced by executions hidden
behind prison walls.

In retrospect, rough justice it might have been but the contemporary
reportage on the executions in the press were in the main un-emotive. The hangings, it might be said, were seen to be legitimate and just, at least by those
beyond the communities who supplied the victims. In contemporary England
there was an old axiom: 'Men are not hanged for stealing horses, but that horses
may not be stolen' and contemporary thinking, at least amongst tories, was as
late as 1868 captured by an English MP who stated that the question was not
'one of softening the heart or saving the souls of murderers, but of preventing
the Queen's subjects from being murdered'.[32] In Ireland in 1816–18, there were
few in authority who felt that multiple executions such as those in Co. Louth

28 John Foster to William Gregory, 5 Apr. 1819 (NA, SOC, 2075/31).   **29** Weekly police report,
Louth district, 19 Apr. 1819 (NA, SOC 2075/33).   **30** Gattrell, *The hanging tree*, p. 87.   **31** Anton,
Retrospect of a military life, p. 233.   **32** Gattrell, *The hanging tree*, p. 5.

were counter-productive and even the likes of Judge Fletcher who promoted the enquiry into mitigating social circumstances which determined criminal activity were loath to put an end to capital punishment. In England in the nineteenth century 'those who had political influence and a public voice were richer people who feared theft but were protected from violence (so theft was the crime most acted against then)'.[33] In Ireland the situation was similar but was further complicated by the fact that the local ruling elite, predominantly Protestant and unionist, feared a general uprising of the masses that might have sectarian as well as political repercussions. Thus the alarmism of the magistracy in Louth and neighbouring counties in 1816–18 reflected such fears and was significantly grounded in the recent memories of 1798.

All of those executed, with the exception of Thomas McCullough (and to a lesser extent Patrick Devan), were lower class, marginalised people. For those in authority, newspaper editors and correspondents or members of the upper class it mattered little whether one of the hanged was McQuillan, McCullen or Cullen; Kearnan, Kiernan or Kieran; James Smith or Thomas Smith; or for that matter where exactly they came from. Judges and prosecutors, the Castle administration, the Louth magistracy, unsympathetic newspaper editors and correspondents, and later writers such as Carleton and Anton simply saw the suspects as 'monsters', 'nefarious villains', 'deluded wretches', 'obdurate and hardened miscreants', 'inhuman miscreants', 'barbarians' and so on. That this in some way impacted upon the mindset of the lower orders is suggested by the fact that Patrick Devan (and even he was sometimes Devane, Devaun and Devine) was the only one whose name passed into local lore, largely thanks to William Carleton, and into notoriety for the best part of three quarters of a century until the regeneration of Irish nationalism from the early 1880s found a place for him in Irish martyrdom. There is no record of what happened to his family but given their socio-economic status it is possible that they, as well as the families of many of the others executed, later became victims of the national catastrophe that was the Great Famine of 1845–51. The names of most of those destroyed in the fire were also lost in local lore, except for Lynch and Rooney whose infamy as informers in nationalist circles superseded the sympathy accorded to them by the authorities and establishment-minded commentators in the immediate aftermath of the atrocity. What is more certain is that for generations the fallout from the burning of Wildgoose Lodge hung like a dark shadow over a large area of north Louth and south Monaghan, particularly the Reaghstown area.

What of the other protagonists who have featured in this work? It is widely accepted that secret societies in Ireland, be they of a social or political nature,

33 Ibid., p. 14.

were continuously susceptible to the prevalence of informers. One should consider that at a time of extreme economic depression members of the lower classes could only have been tempted by any opportunity to provide for themselves or their families. A £200 reward of the type on offer for information on the murders at Wildgoose Lodge was the equivalent of at least twenty years' wages for a labourer. Financial reward allied to promises of pardons (with some possible degree of coercion) enticed Gubby, Gollogly, McIlroy, Murphy and Clarke to provide the necessary evidence in court. The notoriety of these characters plus their unreliability as authentic witnesses has been much commented on in this work. Of them all, Gubby was the least likely to have been at Wildgoose Lodge on the night of 29–30 October 1816, yet on his evidence Terence Marron, James Smith, John Keegan, Thomas McCullough, Thomas Sheenan, Pat Craven, John Kieran, Michael Floody and Bryan Lennon were all executed and William Butler was lucky to evade the gallows. Gubby has become the most infamous of the approvers, the one who is most likely to be named in local accounts, probably because he was the only one named by Carleton in his autobiographical account of his stay in Killanny or possibly because he was an outsider born in Co. Tyrone, so it was somewhat easier to talk of him as the chief informer than blame any of the local community.

Murphy appeared as approver in the trials of fourteen of the prisoners and was the sole approver in the trials of Michael Kearnan, James Loughran, James Morris and Hugh Tiernan. Peter Gollogly witnessed against twelve of the suspects. Bernard McIlroy's unreliability as a witness was fully exposed when Michael Kearnan admitted that McIlroy 'put him up to saying he knew of the circumstances of the business'.[34] Kearnan's confession carried no weight and McIlroy's evidence became crucial to the conviction and execution of Patrick Devan, James Smith, Hugh McCabe, Pat Craven, John Kieran, Michael Floody and Bryan Lennon. Alice Rispin and Patrick Halpenny were the main corroborators as opposed to approvers, although the distinction is merely a technical one. These were neighbours of Edward Lynch and by extension neighbours of most of those they testified against. One cannot be sure that these were the only neighbours of Lynch called as Crown witnesses but it is almost certain that at least a few more provided information covertly outside the courts.

The other notable informer was Terence Cassidy of Ratheady who, it seems, made something of a living by providing the authorities with information on members of secret societies and their oath swearing activities. On 26 March 1816, a short time after most of the suspects had been arrested, he was mentioned in a letter from Edward Lucas of Castleshane in Co. Monaghan (notably

34 *Belfast Newsletter,* 6 Mar. 1818; *Kilkenny Moderator,* 12 Mar. 1818; see also chapter six.

son-in-law of William Ruxton of Red House near Ardee, a close associate of John Foster) to William Gregory in connection with information he had provided to the Monaghan magistracy.[35] He was probably the secret informer that Pendleton referred to in his communications with Gregory. Raymond Murray speculates that he may have been related to Ann Cassidy who died in the fire at Wildgoose Lodge, but there is no evidence of this. As described in chapter five Patrick Clarke met his death very soon after the Devan trial and McIlroy disappeared some time after September 1819. The date of Cassidy's brutal murder was more definite. He was battered to death at Mullacrew, near the town of Louth, on 3 July 1818, the first day of the summer assizes that saw the beginning of the end of the Wildgoose trials. He had been seen earlier that day speaking with J.J. Biggar, a local magistrate and himself a regular correspondent with the Dublin Castle administration. Cassidy's head was reduced to pulp with a stone and a note was pinned to his body: 'Here's the end of an informer there's none to inform about him.'[36] The newspaper reported: 'It was generally supposed by the lower order of people in this country that Cassidy had given private information respecting the burning of Wildgoose Lodge; he is reported to have advised Kieran, who was hung, and had got the mark of gunpowder on his face, to give information, for that his face would betray him.'[37] When in 1819 his widow, Mary, later petitioned Lord Talbot, lord lieutenant of Ireland, for a reward her petition stated that it had been 'reported and understood in the country that he [her husband] had given informations against the Threshers & that he was to give evidence at that assizes [summer 1818]' when he was murdered. At that stage Mary Cassidy and her family were still living in Dundalk, 'a great object of charity having six young children & no means of providing for them'.[38] Mary Cassidy was eventually granted an annuity of £15 per annum by the government from the date of her husband's murder.

Three approvers/informers (at least) therefore met untimely brutal deaths. What of those prosecution witnesses who survived? On 5 April 1819, a committee was appointed by the Louth magistrates gathered at Castlebellingham to consider the state of the Wildgoose Lodge funds.[39] £1,242 of the originally pledged £1,500 had been raised through the original subscribers. Regarding the shortfall, the committee concluded: 'Several of the original subscribers have not, however, paid their proportions; and your committee are of opinion, there

35 See, for example, Edward Lucas to William Gregory, 26 Mar. 1816 (NA, SOC, 1816, 1765/65). 36 *Belfast Newsletter*, 10 July 1818; Letter from Thomas Duffy to Richard Filgate, 18 Aug. 1821 (Dundalk Library, WGL papers). 37 *Belfast Newsletter*, 10 July 1818; also *Dundalk Examiner*, 5 Nov. 1881. 38 Petition of Mary Cassidy, [?] Sept. 1819 (NA, SOC 2075/27). 39 Report of meeting of Louth magistrates at Castlebellingham, 5 Apr. 1819 (PRONI, Foster papers, D562/776).

MAGISTRATES

OF THE

County of Louth.

WE *the undersigned being the Committee appointed at your Meeting, at Castlebellingham, on the 5th April, 1819, for the purpose of collecting a sufficient Sum from the Subscription, entered into, in order to Reward Persons, giving information respecting the Burning of Wildgoose Lodge, think it necessary to report their proceedings.*

Your Committee have by applications to the several Subscribers, raised the Sum of £1242 18s. 0½d. being Sixty per Cent. on the original Subscription of such Individuals as have contributed to the above Sum. Several of the original Subscribers have not, however, paid their proportions; and your Committee are of opinion, there is little or no hope of being able to raise any more Money. A list of the defaulters shall, nevertheless, be laid before you, at the next Meeting you may choose to appoint for the consideration of the state of the Wildgoose Lodge Funds.

Your Treasurer has, by order, made Payments, from this Fund, to the amount of £1064 1s. 4½d. and a Balance of £178 16s. 8d. now remains in his Hands, to be disposed of as you may think most fit. But your Committee deem it right to inform you, that besides the four Prosecutors, viz. GILROY, GOLLOGLY, GUBBY, and MURPHY, to whom a Sum of £800, has been paid, three other persons have made applications for remuneration, from this Fund, viz. the Widow of TERENCE CASSIDY, a Woman Named ALICE RISPEN, and a Man of the name of HALFPENNY.

Your Committee beg leave to suggest, that as the 7th February next is appointed for holding a Sessions, for the investigation of Presentments, it probably might prove convenient to enter into the business of the Wildgoose Lodge Fund, on that Day, when your Treasurer will be ready to lay before you a detailed account of his Receipts and Payments.

HENRY BRABAZON.
GEORGE FORSTER
JAMES FORDE. } *Committee.*
GERVAIS TINLEY.
JOHN STRATON.

PARKS, PRINTER, DUNDALK.

23 Proclamation of the magistrates of Co. Louth announcing
the payment of rewards, *c.*5 April 1819.

is little or no hope of being able to raise any more money.'[40] In late August, early September 1819, £200 each was finally transferred to Gubby, McIlroy, Murphy and Gollogly.[41] By then, Gubby, Murphy and Gollogly had fled to Dublin where they lived in fear for their lives and as noted in chapter five McIlroy was later murdered in Longford. On 14 August 1819, Murphy had claimed that his passage to America had been paid 'this week past' and he wanted

40 Murray, *The burning of Wildgoose Lodge*, p. 315. **41** H. Brabazon to William Gregory, 4 Sept. 1819 (NA, SOC 2075/33); Report of meeting of Louth magistrates at Castlebellingham, 23 Aug. 1819 (PRONI, Foster papers, D562/3786).

to get out of the country as soon as possible.[42] Whether Murphy, Gollogly and Gubby subsequently fled the country is unknown but the reward payment books show that by late 1819 only the wives of Gollogly and Murphy were receiving allowances from the government.[43]

Alice Rispin had also made application to the reward committee but had not been paid by the spring of 1820. On 15 March that year she wrote to William Filgate looking for help because of 'the state of the times and the distress of my family'. Since the trials, she had moved with her family from Dublin to Kildare and back again to Dublin. (One of her sons was at that stage imprisoned in Monaghan.)[44] The government eventually provided her with lodgings at Islandbridge in Dublin. Later in March 1820 she went to see John Taylor at Dublin Castle who gave her the £3 15s. of 'government money', which he told her she was to get quarterly in the future as well as £15 per annum from the county of Louth.[45] The latter sum came from the Louth magistrates' decision to invest £250 in the purchase of an annuity for her life from an insurance company.[46] But by 1825, she was still begging money from the Louth magistracy.[47] She continued to receive quarterly payments of £3 15s. until at least 1827.[48] After that she either died or simply reverted to becoming another anonymous member of the lower classes.

Those responsible for contributing to the arrests of the suspects had also claim to rewards and there was, it seems, no shortage of claimants.[49] Constables George Payne, William Leary and John Burke all claimed £200 for their role in the arrest of Devan. John Shore the postmaster at Navan claimed £200 for the arrest of McIlroy. George Wright, the sub-constable at Dungannon claimed 'part of reward' for the arrest of Gubby. William Smart, the gaoler at Trim, claimed £20 for 'useful information' emanating from Murphy. John Armstrong, chief constable at Drogheda, claimed £200 for the arrest of Gubby. Thomas Hunter and the other police constables at Corcreaghy looked for 'benefit of reward in such proportions etc. for apprehending 12 persons'. Pendleton did not think that 'Payne being the bearer of the warrant [for Devan's arrest], or Leary the person who made the actual capture ... should entitle either of them

42 Pat Murphy to John Foster, 14 Aug. 1819; Thomas Gubby and Peter Gollogly (jointly) to Sir John Foster, 22 Aug. 1819 (PRONI, Foster papers, D562/3787, 3789). **43** Murray, *The burning of Wildgoose Lodge*, pp 320–1. **44** Ibid., p. 318. **45** Alice Rispin to William Filgate, 15 Mar. 1820 (Dundalk Library, Wildgoose Lodge papers). **46** Samuel Pendleton to John Foster, 5 Apr. 1819 (PRONI, Foster papers, D567/780). **47** Lord Oriel [John Foster] to William Filgate, 12 Nov. 1825; ibid. **48** Payment account books, 1816–19 (PRO, CO 904-4-5); taken from Murray, *The burning of Wildgoose Lodge*, p. 321; also, Samuel Pendleton to William Gregory, 19 July 1818 (NA, SOC, series ii, box 168). **49** Samuel Pendleton to Alex Mangin, n.d. [1818] (NA, SOC, series ii, box 168).

exclusively to this reward'. Instead he recommended £100 to be given to the police at Louth and another £100 to the police at James' Street: 'to be distributed in such manner as the respective magistrates of these establishments shall think best'.

But while there were always the willing informers, there was just as likely to be a community anxious to conceal perpetrators of agrarian and political crimes or to punish those who betrayed them. (This remained such a feature of Irish society that coercive legislation was eventually passed between 1847 and 1875 that recognised the need to punish those who refused to give evidence and to punish communities in which agrarian murders were perpetrated through a system of communal fines and the levying of compensation.)[50] In spite of rewards on offer it seems that many more neighbours witnessed for the defence than the prosecution. In each trial the defence was able to call on numerous neighbours, relatives and friends (and even the brother of Edward Lynch) who were prepared to provide alibis (and in many cases perjure themselves) in an attempt to have the prisoners released. Press reports on the Smith, Gaynor and McQuillan trial stated that while the jury were considering their verdict: 'the court remained very full and some of the friends of the prisoners were permitted to speak with them'. The disdain that some had for the law (and for the Catholic clergy) was suggested in a report that James Smith's sister in open court told her brother:

> To die hard, if he was found guilty – never to forgive his prosecutors – and, dead or alive, to have revenge. She conjured him not to let anything that the clergy could say have any effect upon him, nor ever persuade him to confess his guilt – and, when going to be hanged to throw off his hat.[51]

The murders at Wildgoose Lodge and the subsequent executions had repercussions for wider political, social and religious issues. The nature of the crime hardened the attitudes of the likes of John Foster, Sir Harcourt Lees, William Gregory, William Saurin and Robert Peel (at least for another thirteen years) to Catholic Emancipation. Peel continued as chief secretary of Ireland until 1818. As noted previously, one of his biographers, Norman Gash, has contended that the murders at Wildgoose Lodge was one of the 'barbarous incidents ... which in their ugliness made a profound impression upon his [Peel's] mind'.[52] The

---

50 Vaughan, *Landlords and tenants*, p. 184. 51 *Drogheda Journal*, 4 Apr. 1818; *Belfast Newsletter*, 7 Apr. 1818; see also accounts reproduced in *Dundalk Examiner*, 22 Oct. 1881. 52 Gash, *Mr Secretary Peel*, p. 171.

murders influenced Peel to propose an amendment to the Peace Preservation Act in March 1817 allowing discretion to the lord lieutenant in council to allow for public funds to be used in part to meet the expenses incurred in preserving peace in proclaimed districts, thereby taking some of the financial burden off the local landlords.[53] Peel's extended and complex political career has been well documented. Amongst his later political appointments was home secretary (1822–7, 1828–30) where he expended considerable time and energy in: 'the formulation of the criminal law and the mechanics of policing, through indictment, trial, and sentencing, to punishment on the scaffold, in prison and in penal colonies'.[54] However, V.A.C. Gattrell argues that Peel's reputation as a reformist has been largely misplaced and contends that he 'was famously a man of paradoxes'. While others have contended that Peel advocated in parliament the removal of the death sentence in all cases where it was practicable, Gattrell argues: 'Far from dismantling the bloody code, or intending to begin to dismantle it, his statutory considerations were intended to outflank the wholesale reform advocated by the Whig radicals and to retain the legal values of the *ancien regime* in their essentials.' Gattrell maintains that when he did abolish capital punishment it was for crimes for which people were unlikely to be hanged anyway and points to the fact that more people were hanged in England in the 1820s during his terms as home secretary than under any of his predecessors. Gattrell, who makes no reference to Wildgoose Lodge in his work, concludes that 'we often find a knowing disingenuousness as he massaged evidence to support his goals' and that he was reluctant to concede that rising crime might have been attributable to general distress preferring to blame 'the unruly passions and corrupt nature of human beings',[55] evidence of which can be clearly seen in the events surrounding the Wildgoose Lodge incident.

In 1827–8, Peel conceded grudgingly that Catholic Emancipation was inevitable. He went on to serve two terms as prime minister of Great Britain in 1834–5 and 1841–6, the latter term coinciding with the beginning of the Great Famine in Ireland. He died in June 1850 as a result of injuries sustained in a fall from his horse.[56]

William Gregory remained as under-secretary until 1830, intensely Conservative in his politics and a firm believer that the success of the Second Reformation – the evangelical campaign in Ireland – would resolve many of the country's problems.[57] Like Saurin, Gregory continued to oppose any further concessions to Catholic agitation 'which he was convinced sought the destruction of the established church, the Protestant ascendancy, and eventu-

53 Ibid., p. 184.   54 Prest, 'Peel' (4 Mar. 2005).   55 Gattrell, *The hanging tree*, pp 567–85.   56 Prest, 'Peel' (4 Mar. 2005).   57 Grey, 'Gregory' (4 Mar. 2005).

ally the union itself'. When Peel supported Emancipation in 1829, Gregory 'expressed both despair and a sense of personal betrayal'.[58] He was removed from office the following year, marking the return of Lord Anglesey as lord lieutenant of Ireland. He died in 1840.[59]

Gregory would have found an easy ally in Sir Harcourt Lees, the Protestant rector of Killanny. As noted earlier in this work, in July 1820 an informer at the trial of those accused of his attempted murder in Killanny claimed that one of the suspects had said that Lees and William Filgate Jr were both 'damned bad' men who were 'not worthy to live', thereby suggesting that both suffered from a similar reputation amongst the Catholic lower classes. Lees, who died in 1852, continued to attract much controversy and censure for his rabid anti-Catholic emancipationist views long after 1816. In January 1823, for example, the editor of *The Times* of London reproached him for the over-zealous tone of his writings that he contended drove men into the ranks of the Ribbonmen. Lees could hardly have been flattered by the editor's description of him: 'The poor crazy creature is the son of a long-headed Scotchman, who migrated to Dublin some 50 years ago, and feathered the nest in which this addled egg was deposited.'[60] Lees' reputation became such a tarnished one that local lore would have one believe that the horses drawing his hearse refused to pull it up 'the minister's hill' (that led from Essexford Glebe) and that the rats followed the cortege to his burial place. The fact that he neither died in nor was buried in Killanny seems irrelevant.

William Filgate lived until 1868. He survived his two eldest brothers who both died unmarried (Alexander, 1771–1827 and Thomas, 1773–1830) and therefore inherited his father's house at Lisrenny, between Tallanstown and Ardee, and estates in Louth and Monaghan. Of all those party to the arrest and conviction of the suspects William Filgate felt the fallout most acutely. During the 1820s he survived numerous plots to assassinate him (in this respect the contribution of his estate management policies should not be discounted) and for a considerable time from at least November 1816 had military protection.[61] In 1831, he was contemplating standing for election in Louth when his campaign was damaged by accusations of his association with the fallout from the Wildgoose murders. Berkely Stafford was the one accused of having impugned Filgate's name but he denied this in a letter to Filgate: 'I did not even hint or glance at it [mention of Wildgoose Lodge] in the most remote degree – nor was

58 Ibid. **59** His grandson's widow was Augusta Lady Gregory (1852–1932), playwright, folklorist, literary patron and co-founder of the Irish Literary theatre in 1899 along with W.B. Yeats and Edward Martyn. **60** *The Times*, 11 Jan. 1823. **61** Murray, *The burning of Wildgoose Lodge*, p. 138; see also chapter one.

the idea present in my mind on that occasion.'[62] Filgate was never elected. The surviving estate papers are too fragmented to allow for a comprehensive analysis of his estate management during his tenure but there is clear evidence that the Great Famine had a detrimental economic effect: by 1854, Filgate had petitioned the Encumbered Estates Court to sell large parts of his estates in Louth and Monaghan.[63] But he survived this potential calamity and his family continued to live at Lisrenny to well into the twentieth century.[64] His uncle, Townley Patten Filgate, was awarded £90 in compensation for his material losses at Wildgoose Lodge. In January 1819, he removed the kitchen grate from its ruins to his home at Lowther Lodge.

John Foster, later created first Baron Oriel, was in the twilight of a rather illustrious political career that had seen him hold position as chancellor of the exchequer and (last) Speaker of the Irish House of Commons when the murders at Wildgoose Lodge took place. Despite being in his seventies, he determinedly and single-mindedly orchestrated the capture and conviction of as many men as was necessary to restore the four baronies of Louth to more peaceful ways. His methods raise a number of questions regarding existing work on Foster. A.P.W. Malcomson in his introduction to the Foster papers on deposit in PRONI points out that many exceedingly minor matters of local concern are copiously represented but that 'There is a suspicious dearth of material on Catholic Relief, Catholic Emancipation and the Union (to name only the most obvious political issues of the day), and possibly high politics are under-represented in what survives'.[65] Malcomson contends that what has been 'lost' was an accident of history but simultaneously points out that Foster spent much of his retirement years sorting and filing his papers. It is therefore debatable whether they were 'lost'; presumably Foster was acutely aware of how history might judge him and therefore he may just as likely have deliberately culled his papers, possibly even many important documents relating to the atrocity at Wildgoose Lodge.

Foster may not have been a bigot, as his biographer contends, and there is ample evidence of his paternalism in his estate improvements but he very much mistrusted the Catholic lower classes. Malcomson contends that Foster believed in 'the generally good disposition of the Catholic masses, if given proper leadership and shown proper example.' As evidence of this he quotes Foster's remarks following the establishment of the Irish militia in 1793: 'Our militia is in excellent state and, though the majority of men are Catholic, I believe they would all

62 Berkeley Stafford to William Filgate, 29 Sept. 1831 (PRONI, Filgate papers, T2354/2/26). 63 Encumbered Estates Court rental in the matter of the estate of William Filgate to be sold 5 May 1854 (in private possession). 64 *Burke's Irish family records* (London, 1976 ed.), pp 412–14. 65 http://www.proni.gov.uk/records/private/fossmass.htm, 23 Feb. 2006.

stand or fall with their officers'[66] Foster's use of the conjunction 'though' is somewhat ambiguous. It might just as well suggest his mistrust of the Catholic rank
and file. Moreover, Foster's actions in Louth and Meath towards the predominantly Catholic Defenders and United Irishmen of the late eighteenth century
raise further questions. For his activities, contemporaries heavily censured him,
but his political standing well protected him.[67] Ultimately Foster was a landlord
who, like his father before him, preferred, where possible, to keep Protestant
tenants around him with the result that by 1812 the Collon area of Louth was
the most Protestant in the county with a ratio of 130 Protestants to 1,000
Catholics.[68] There may have been some degree of economic sense in this – the
colony brought linen weaving experience with them[69] – but he probably regarded
the importation of Protestants into the area as a safeguard against Catholic lower
class agitation. He died in 1828, a year before Emancipation was granted. He
had lived long enough to witness the revolt of the forty-shilling freeholders in
the general election in Louth in 1826 that was to initiate the process that would
ultimately break the Foster monopoly of one of the Louth seats.[70]

Serjeant Henry Joy's career took off after the trials of the Wildgoose Lodge
suspects. In 1822 he was appointed solicitor-general, then attorney general in
1827 and chief baron of the exchequer in 1831. He died in 1838. Charles Kendal
Bushe remained solicitor-general of Ireland until 1822 when he was appointed
lord chief justice of the King's Bench. He resigned in 1841 due to ill health and
died in 1843.[71] William Saurin, who had been appointed attorney general in
1807 became: 'exceptional among Irish law officers for retaining the office for
an unsurpassed span of fifteen years'. During that time he remained central to
all opposition to further Catholic concessions.[72] In 1822, Lord Wellesley became
lord lieutenant for Ireland and Saurin was removed from his post. Although he
did not take too kindly to this, Saurin returned to the bar and continued to
play an active role in Irish affairs, most notably as an active promoter of the
Brunswick clubs that were formed ostensibly to resist Catholic Emancipation.
He died in 1839. Baron James McClelland, as noted already, was not finished
with controversial trials. He died in 1831 at his home at Annaverna in Dundalk.
Judge Fletcher died eight years before in 1823. Some time after Leonard
MacNally's death in February 1820 MacNally was exposed as a Castle spy.[73]
Patrick Geoghegan has written of his activities:

Quoted in Malcomson, 'Foster' (www.oxforddnb.com/view/article/9960). **67** See A County
Meath Freeholder, *A candid and impartial account of the disturbances in the Co. Meath in the years
1792–'3–'4* (Dublin, 1794). **68** Malcomson, *John Foster*, p. 139; Smyth, *Men of no property*, p. 51.
69 Malcomson, *John Foster*, p. 272. **70** Ibid. **71** Benson and Agnew, 'Bushe' (4 Mar. 2005).
72 Huddleston, 'Saurin' (4 Mar. 2005). **73** J.M. Rigg, revised by M.D. Evans, 'Leonard MacNally'

24 The remains of Wildgoose Lodge in the 1970s
(Dundalk County Library, WGL papers).

Some recent attempts have been made to defend MacNally from odium
by arguing that he was a spy, acting out of what he perceived as the
public good, and not therefore an informer. For a barrister to betray
the integrity of his office, and every principle of law and justice, for
whatever reason, is deserving of total condemnation ...[74]

Samuel Pendleton's success in Louth possibly changed Peel's negative attitude towards him. By January 1820, he had returned to Dublin from whence
he was sent to Galway to quell growing disorder there. Nine of the county's
thirteen baronies had been proclaimed. He and his police force met with a great
deal of hostility and violence but 'under his ferocious leadership' scores were
arrested and at the spring assizes of 1820 twenty-eight felons were convicted

in H.C.G. Matthew and Brian Harrison (ed.), *Oxford dictionary of national biography*, vol. 35
(Oxford, 2004), p. 934; Stephen Gwynn, *The history of Ireland* (New York, 1923), p. 405. **74**
Patrick Geoghegan, *1798 and the Irish Bar* (Dublin, n.d.), p. 9. **75** Palmer, *Police and protest in
England and Ireland*, pp 219–20.

(including seven capital convictions and four life transportations).[75] Shortly after he arrived in Galway, John Foster assured Lord Norbury (who later tried the Galway suspects and who in 1816 had tried Murphy and Gollogly for the Sillery robbery) that Pendleton would not let the Galway magistracy down: 'If when you write to him [Lord Clonbrock] tell him from me that the more confidence he places in Pendleton the more he will value him & his police. I never saw a man better fitted for the job he is now employed in.'[76] When order was more or less resumed in April, Pendleton resigned. S.H. Palmer claims that it was 'in part from exhaustion, but also because of his abrasive relations with military officers and local magistrates and his over zealousness in prosecution'.[77]

As already noted, of the fifty-seven jurors only John Coleman became something of a communal folk hero because of his defence of William Butler but the other fifty-six jurors by no means became targets of open hostility. Some of the jurors must have been apprehensive about the consequences of their participation in the trials and some possibly felt threatened for a long time afterwards. But there was a socio-economic cut off point where the type of people chosen for jury participation in the Wildgoose Lodge trials had little reason to fear for their future; most of these men were able to surround themselves with protection, perhaps in the form of their own retainers or the local yeomanry of which the likes of Alexander Shekleton were serving officers. They were more secure from revenge attacks on them or their property than farmers such as Lynch, while those from the town of Dundalk had the added assurance of a large military presence. Even the less overt types of intimidation that could have been practiced on the town merchants such as boycotting of their businesses seems to have been completely absent in the years following. Thus the likes of Shekleton, McAlister, Brown, Tallan, Dickie and so on remained very prominent businessmen/professionals for many years afterwards and their descendants continued to play important roles in the social and political life of Dundalk and Louth. For example, Alexander Shekleton's son, also Alexander, became secretary for many years to the Louth grand jury; he was also secretary of the Royal Agricultural Society's Cattle Show and secretary to the board of superintendence of the county gaol. His brother, James, succeeded his father as proprietor of the iron works and ran it until his death in 1870: 'He was most enterprising, and extended the works largely, devoting himself principally to the manufacture of agricultural implements of all kinds, and his work was to be found all over Ireland.'[78] Robert Dickie's son, Joseph, a solicitor 'was an exten-

76 John Foster to Lord Norbury, 3 Feb. 1820 (PRONI, Foster papers, D562/3988). 77 Palmer, *Police and protest in England and Ireland*, p. 220. 78 'Biographical notes' in *Tempest's Annual, 1959*, p. 135. 79 Ibid., p. 123.

sive and able practitioner in Dundalk for many years'.[79]

Likewise, stories concerning 'little' Fr McCann committing suicide have no basis in fact. He died in 1822. Fr Marron remained parish priest of Tallanstown until his death in 1839. In January 1818, Fr Patrick Duffy who, as prison chaplain, had accompanied the prisoners to their place of execution, received a letter and £50 from the Castle via Samuel Pendleton. He replied that he was grateful that

> the government thought proper to give me for the honest discharge of my duty as chaplain to the jail of Dundalk [the sum of £50]. As the gift was totally unexpected by me I feel the more grateful. It shall be the peculiar study of my life to merit the approbation of that humane government which sees and relieves in the humblest situations the wants of its faithful adherents.[80]

In different ways, all three priests had illustrated the ambiguous attitude of the Catholic clergy towards agrarian agitation and the complex web of social relations that existed at local level between the Catholic clergy, the Catholic gentry, the lower classes, the Protestant elite, parish vestries and the government.

A story concerning another priest from a different era is appropriate to bring this work to a close. Pádraig Ó Conchubhair, this author's former primary school teacher, related it after we met by accident in the Public Record Office of Northern Ireland for the first time in many years. When Pádraig first came to Carrickmacross from Co. Kerry in the early 1970s he was at early mass one Sunday morning at which a young curate, recently arrived in the parish from elsewhere in the diocese of Clogher, delivered a sermon condemning a recent atrocity committed in Northern Ireland. 'Thank God', the curate concluded, 'that nothing like that ever happened around here!' As Padraig left St Joseph's church he overheard one old man say to another: 'Somebody should tell him about the burning of Wildgoose Lodge'.

---

80 Fr Patrick Duffy to Robert Peel, 19 January 1818 (NA, SOC, series ii, box 168).

Stanzas from John Graham, Sir Harcourt's vision: an historical poem *(Dublin, 1823)*

In a chapel called Stonehouse, not far from Ardee,
For Wildgoose Lodge bound to proceed,
A blood-thirsty gang did the Baronet see
All Plotting a murderous deed.

Full forty assassins in dreadful array,
The number 'gainst Paul that combin'd,
From an altar erected to GOD took their way,
With the spirit of Hell in their mind.

Sir Harcourt beheld them their torches upraised,
To the roof of the lodge on the hill,
Eight victims to Popery died in the blaze!
And the blood in his body ran chill.

A judge too he heard with a tremulous breath,
No foe to the clergy of Rome,
Beseech them to punish these dealers in death,
On Diven pronouncing his doom.

But little that judge, all unspotted himself,
Of the gownsmen he call'd upon knew,
How strong was their love to their Pope and their poll,
To their oaths and religion how true.

No meeting of bishops or clergy was call'd,
At Reaghstown or Stonehouse to say,
That deeds of such horror their pastors appall'd,
Who these felons would drag into day.

Oh! No – for the leaders whom Ribbonmen swear,
At twelve hours call to obey,

Are their titular teachers, whose pastoral care,
Their follies could argue away.

Two oaths in this island – no man will dispute,
Exist in this wonderful day;
The one of Rome's bishops to persecute,
And heresy to banish away.

The other of Ribbonmen – dreadful to say,
On a very short notice to rise,
Their innocent Protestant neighbours to slay,
And the sixth great commandment to despise.

Samuel Pendleton's summary of all those tried for the murders at Wildgoose Lodge

Prisoner name	Date of arrest	Place of arrest	By whom apprehended	Name of approver	Result of trial	Observation
Pat Malone	12 Mar. 1817	Meath	Sml. Pendletone	Gollogly, Murphy and police	Gibbeted at Louth, 12 Mar. 1818	
*James Campbell	Ditto	Ditto	Ditto	Gollogly, Murphy	Gibbeted at Corcreaghy, 12 Mar. 1818	
Hudy McElearney	Ditto	Ditto	Ditto	Gollogly, Murphy	Gibbeted at Louth, 12 Mar. 1818	
Terence Marron	Ditto	Monaghan	Ditto	Gollogly, Murphy,	Gibbeted at Corcreaghy, 12 Mar. 1818	'had solicited to be admitted an approver yet died declaring himself innocent'
Michael Kearnan	Ditto	Ditto	Ditto	Murphy	Hanged, Dundalk, 4 July 1818	'had been admitted an approver, when produced as a witness denied his confession – at the gallow admitted his guilt'
Pat Meegan	Ditto	Meath	Ditto	Gollogly, Murphy	Gibbeted at Corcreaghy, 12 Mar. 1818	
James Smith	Ditto	Louth	Louth police	Gubby, McIlroy**	Hanged at Reaghstown, 7 Apr. 1818	
John Keegan	Ditto	Ditto	Ditto	Gubby	Hanged at Reaghstown, 7 Apr. 1818	'also indicted for the original burglary on Lynch'
Hugh McCabe	Ditto	Ditto	Ditto	Gilroy, Gollogly	Gibbeted at Louth, 12 Mar. 1818	'also indicted for the original burglary on Lynch'
*Thomas McCullough	Ditto	Ditto	Ditto	Gubby, Gollogly, Murphy	Gibbeted at Louth, 7 Apr. 1818	
George McQuillan	Ditto	Ditto	Ditto	Murphy	Admitted to bail, 4 July 1818	
Edward McQuillan	Ditto	Ditto	Ditto	Murphy	Admitted to bail, 4 July 1818	
Thomas Sheenan	Ditto	Ditto	Ditto	Gubby	Hanged at Reaghstown, 7 Apr. 1818	'also indicted for the original burglary on Lynch'
*Pat Craven	16 Mar. 1817	Ditto	Ditto	McIlroy, Gubby	Gibbeted at Louth, 12 Mar. 1818	'confessed his guilt and named many others'

Prisoner name	Date of arrest	Place of arrest	By whom apprehended	Name of approver	Result of trial	Observation
*John Kieran	Ditto	Ditto	Ditto	McIlroy, Gubby	Gibbeted at Hackballscross 12 Mar. 1818	'confessed his guilt and named many others'
Pat Malone	Ditto	Ditto	Ditto	McIlroy	Admitted to bail, 4 July 1818	
James Loughran	31 Mar. 1817	Ditto	Ditto	Murphy	Admitted to bail, 4 July 1818	
Pat McQuillan	Ditto	Meath	Ditto	Gollogly, Murphy	Hanged at Reaghstown, 4 July 1818	
Laurence Gaynor	11 Apr. 1817	Ditto	Ditto	Gollogly, Murphy	Acquitted 7 Apr. 1818	
Owen Gaynor	Ditto	Ditto	Ditto	Gollogly, Murphy	Hanged at Dundalk, 4 July 1818	
James Morris	Ditto	Ditto	Ditto	Murphy	Admitted to bail, 4 July 1818	
William Butler	Ditto	Louth	Ditto	Gubby, Gollogly	Put off his trial, 4 July 1818	'had been tried in March, the jury could not agree, the foreman stated that one only was for acquittal, is also indicted for the original burglary'.
Patrick Devan	21 May 1817	Dublin	Dublin and Louth police	McIlroy, Clarke	Gibbeted at Corcreaghy, 24 July 1817	
Michael Floody	1 July 1817	Monaghan	Louth police	McIlroy, Gubby	Gibbeted at Hackballscross, 12 Mar. 1818	'confessed his guilt'
*Bryan Lennon	8 Oct. 1817	Monaghan	Ditto	McIlroy, Gubby, Gollogly	Gibbeted at Hackballscross, 12 Mar. 1818	'pleaded guilty; named many others'
Hugh Tiernan	22 Dec. 1817	Louth	Ditto	Gollogly Murphy	Admitted to bail, 4 July 1818	'brother of Tiernan, hanged for the original burglary'.

* 'these marked thus leaders on this and many other occasions'.
** Referred to as Gilroy in original

Source: Return of all persons apprehended for the burning of Wildgoose Lodge, compiled by Samuel Pendleton (NA, SOC 1828/16).

Bibliography

Manuscript Sources

National Library of Ireland
Ainsworth reports of private collections [Bellew of Barmeath; Francis Tipping; W.P. Ruxton; Henry Coddington]
Bath estate papers
Blayney Balfour papers
T.P. Filgate papers
William Filgate papers
Chichester Fortescue papers
W.P. Ruxton papers
National Archives of Ireland, Dublin
State of the Country Papers [Series 1 and 2]
Chief Secretary's Office, Registered Papers, outrage reports
Official papers, series ii, 1790–1803
Rebellion papers
Public Record Office, Northern Ireland
T.P. Filgate papers
Chichester Fortescue papers
Sir John Foster papers
Roden papers
Shirley papers
Flax growers' bounty lists
British Library
Correspondence of Sir Harcourt Lees with 2nd earl of Liverpool, MSS 38291–95
Sir Robert Peel papers
British Museum
Letters of William Gregory [MS 40,203, consulted on microfilm in NLI]
Dundalk Library
Wildgoose Lodge [Filgate] papers
Dundalk Museum
Filgate papers
Cardinal Tomás Ó Fiaich Memorial Library & Archive, Armagh
Archive of the Archdiocese of Armagh (including Armagh diocesan parish collections)
Emory University, Atlanta, Georgia
William Gregory papers

Private Possession
Papers relating to Wildgoose Lodge in the possession of Eddie Filgate, Louth Village
A.H.C. Pollock papers in possession of Pollock family, Mountainstown, Navan, Co.
Meath.

Parliamentary Papers

Papers relating to disturbances on the county of Louth, HC 1817, vol. viii (263). 491
*Minutes of evidence taken before the select committee appointed to enquire into the distur-
bances in Ireland,* HC 1825, vol. vii, 20
*Minutes of evidence taken before the select committee of the House of Lords appointed to
inquire into the state of Ireland, more particularly with reference to the circumstances in
that part of the United Kingdom,* HC 1829, vol. ix (181). 1
First report of inquiry into the condition of the poorer classes in Ireland & appendix A, HC,
1835, vol. xxxii (369)
*A return of the number of murders, waylayings, assaults, threatening notices, incendiary
fires or other crimes of an agrarian character, reported by the constabulary within the
counties of Louth, Armagh and Monaghan, since the 1st of January 1849 ...* HC 1852,
xlvii
*Report from the select committee on outrages (Ireland); together with the proceedings of the
committee, minutes of evidence, appendix and index,* HC 1852 (438), xiv
Hansard parliamentary debates, House of Commons

Acts

An act to suppress insurrections and prevent disturbance of the public peace in Ireland. 47
Geo. III (2), c.13 [1 Aug. 1807]
*An act for more effectually preventing the administering and taking of unlawful oaths in
Ireland, and for the protection of magistrates and witnesses in criminal cases.* 50 Geo. III,
c. 102 [20 June 1810]
*An act to provide for the better execution of the laws in Ireland, by appointing superintend-
ing magistrates and additional constables in counties, in certain areas.* 54 Geo. III, c. 131
[25 July 1814].
*An act to provide for the preserving and restoring of peace in such parts of Ireland as may
at any time be disturbed by seditious persons, or persons entering into unlawful combinations or conspiracies.* 54 Geo. III, c. 180 [30 July 1814]
*An act to continue an act made in the fifty-fourth year of his present majesty's reign, intit-
uled an act to provide for the preserving and restorng of peace in such parts of Ireland as
may at any time be disturbed by seditious persons, or by persons entering into unlawful
combinations or conspiracies.* 57 Geo. III, c.50 [27 June 1817]

Newspapers, journals etc.

Annual Register, 1816
Belfast Newsletter
Correspondent
Drogheda Journal
Dublin Evening Mail
Dublin Evening Post
Dundalk Examiner and Louth Advertiser
Enniskillen Chronicle and Erne Packet

Faulkner's Dublin Journal
Freeman's Journal
Irish Times [Benedict Kiely's series
  'Return to Wildgoose Lodge',
  12 July–21 September 1972]
Kilkenny Moderator
Newry Telegraph

Works of reference

Bassett, G.H., *Louth county guide and directory* (Dublin, 1886)
Boylan, Henry, *Dictionary of Irish biography* (New York, 1978)
Burke's landed gentry of Ireland (various editions)
Collins, Peter, *County Monaghan sources in the Public Record Office of Northern Ireland*
  (Belfast, 1998)
Connolly, S.J., (ed.), *The Oxford companion to Irish history* (Oxford, 1998)
Jones, Mark Bence, *A guide to Irish country houses* (London, 1988 revd. ed.)
Lewis, Samuel, *A topographical dictionary of Ireland*, 2 vols (London, 1837)
Matthew, H.C.G., and Harrison, Brian, (eds), *Oxford dictionary of national biography*
  (Oxford, 2004)
Pigot's Directory of Ireland (Dublin, 1934)
Thom's Irish almanac & official directory for the year 1844 (Dublin, 1844)

Contemporary published

A County Meath Freeholder, *A candid and impartial account of the disturbances in the
  county of Meath in the years 1792, 1793 and 1794* (Dublin, 1794)
*A list of registered freeholders of the county of Louth, 1822, consisting of the baronies of Ardee,
  Louth, Upper and Lower Dundalk* (Dundalk, 1822)
A member of the Church of England, *Strictures on The Antidote, L'Abeja and Cursory
  View of Sir Harcourt Lees* (Dublin, 1820)
*An Anglo-Irish dialogue: a calendar of the correspondence between John Foster and Lord
  Sheffield 1774–1821* (Belfast, n.d.)
*An inquiry into the influence of the excessive use of spirituous liquors in producing crime,
  discord and poverty in Ireland* (Dublin, 1830)
Anton, James, *Retrospect of a military life* (Edinburgh, 1846)
*A report of the meeting of the Roman Catholics of the County of Monaghan held on Tuesday
  January 10th 1826* (Monaghan, n.d.)
Atkinson, A., *Ireland exhibited to England* (London, 1823)
Barrington, Jonah, *Historic memoirs of Ireland,* vol. ii (London, 1835)
Bassett, G.H., *Louth county guide and directory* (Dublin, 1886)

Brett, William, *Reminiscences of Louth: being an authentic and truthful narrative of polit-ical and social events which occurred in the county of Louth* (Enniskillen, 1857)

Carleton, William, *The life of William Carleton: being his autobiography and letters; and an account of his life and writings, from the point at which the autobiography breaks off,* Two volumes (London, 1896) [ed. David J. O'Donoghue]

—, *Traits and stories of the Irish peasantry,* 2 vols (1842–4)

Coote, Charles, *Statistical survey of county Cavan* (Dublin, 1802)

—, *Statistical survey of the county of Monaghan* (Dublin, 1801)

D'Alton, John, and J.R. O'Flanagan, *The history of Dundalk and its environs from the earliest historic period to the present time* (Dundalk, 1864)

[E.N.], *A full report of the important trial and execution for the burning of the Wildgoose Lodge* (Drogheda, 1824)

Fisher, John, *The history of landholding in Ireland* (London, 1877)

Hall, James, *Tour through Ireland,* vols i and ii (London, 1813)

Lampson, G. Locker, *A consideration of the state of Ireland in the nineteenth century* (London, 1907)

Lees, Sir Harcourt, *The antidote: or 'Nouvelles a la main' recommended to the serious atten-tion of the Right Hon. W.C. Plunkett* (Dublin, 1819)

—, *The mystery: being a short but decisive counter-reply to the few friendly hints of the Rev. Charles B. Stennett at present an officiating popish priest in the Religious College of Maynooth* (Dublin, 1820)]

—, *An address to the King's friends throughout the British Empire on the present awful and critical state of Great Britain* (Dublin, 1820)

—, *The crisis or patriotism explained and popery exposed in four letters addressed to the upright and eloquent barrister, Daniel O'Connell, Esq.* (Dublin, 1820)

—, *An address to the Orangemen of Ireland relative to the late riot at the Theatre Royal, Hawkins St.* (Dublin, 1823)

Lewis, G.C., *On local disturbances in Ireland and on the Irish church question* (London, 1836)

MacNevin, Thomas, (ed.), *The speeches of the Rt. Hon. Richard Lalor Sheil MP with a memoir* (Dublin, 1845)

Marmion, Anthony, *Ancient and modern history of the maritime ports of Ireland* (Holborn, 1855)

Mason, W.S., *A statistical account or parochial survey of Ireland drawn up from the com-munications of the clergy* (Dublin, 1814–19)

Mathews, John, *The burning of Wildgoose Lodge* (Dundalk, 1882)

Musgrave, Richard, *Memoirs of the different rebellions in Ireland from the arrival of the English,* 2 vols (Dublin, 1802)

O'Hagan, T., *Occasional papers and addresses* (London, 1884)

O'Neill Daunt, W.J., *A life spent for Ireland* (London, 1896)

—, *Ireland since the Union* (Dublin, n.d. [1888])

Ó Néill, Pádraig (ed.), *Journal of Henry McClintock* (Dundalk, 2001)

O.S. [John Graham], *Sir Harcourt's vision: an historical poem* (Dublin, 1823)

Pollard, H.B.C., *The secret societies of Ireland: their rise and progress* (London, n.d.)

Ross, Noel (ed.), 'The diary of Marianne Fortescue 1816–1818' in *Journal of the County Louth Archaeological and Historical Society*, 24:4 (2000), 474–503

— (ed.), 'The diary of Marianne Fortescue 1816–1818' in *Journal of the County Louth Archaeological and Historical Society*, 24:2 (2002), pp 101–28

Rushe, D.C., *Historical sketches of Monaghan from the earliest records to the Fenian movement* (Dublin, 1895)

Shirley, E.P., *Some account of the territory or dominion of Farney* (London, 1845)

Sigerson, George, *History of the land tenures and land classes of Ireland with an account of the various secret agrarian confederacies* (London, 1871)

Trotter, J.B., *Walks through Ireland in the years 1812, 1814 and 1817* (London, 1819)

Secondary published

Adams, J.R.R., *The printed word and the common man* (Belfast, 1987)

Archer, J.E., *Social unrest and popular protest in England, 1780–1840* (Cambridge, 2000)

Bailey, V. (ed.), *Policing and punishment in nineteenth century Britain* (New Brunswick, NJ, 1981)

Ballard, Linda May, 'The folklorist and local history' in Gillespie and Hill (eds), *Doing local history*, pp 47–61

Barnard, Toby, 'The eighteenth-century parish' in Raymond Gillespie and W.E. Neely (eds), *The laity and the Church of Ireland, 1000–2000* (Dublin, 2005)

Bartlett, Thomas, 'An end to moral economy: the Irish militia disturbances of 1793' in *Past & Present* 99 (May, 1983), pp 41–64

—, *The fall and rise of the Irish nation, the Catholic question, 1690–1830* (Dublin, 1992)

Beames, M.R., *Peasants and power: the Whiteboy movements and their and their control in pre-famine Ireland* (New York, 1983)

Beames, M.R., 'The Ribbon societies: lower class nationalism in pre-Famine Ireland' in *Past & Present*, 97 (Nov., 1982), pp 128–43

—, 'Rural conflict in pre-Famine Ireland: peasant assassinations in Tipperary, 1837–1847' in Philpin (ed.), *Nationalism and popular protest*, pp 264–81

Beattie, J.M., *Crime and courts in England, 1660–1800* (Oxford, 1986)

Belchem, John, 'Freedom & friendship to Ireland: Ribbonism in early-nineteenth century Liverpool' in *International Journal of Social History*, no. 39 (1994), pp 33–56

Blackstock, Allan, *An ascendancy army: the Irish yeomanry, 1796–1834* (Dublin, 1998)

Boué, André, 'William Carleton as a short-story writer' in Patrick Rafroidi and Terence Browne (eds), *The Irish short story* (Gerrards Cross, 1979), pp 81–101

Bourke, Angela, *The burning of Bridget Cleary* (London, 1999)

Broeker, Gaelen, 'Robert Peel and the Peace Preservation Force' in *Journal of Modern History*, 33 (1961), pp 363–73

Broeker, Gaelen, *Rural disorder and police reform in Ireland, 1812–36* (London and Toronto, 1970)

Burke, Helen, *The people and the poor law in 19th century Ireland* (Littlehampton, 1987)

Carroll-Burke, Patrick, *Colonial discipline: the making of the Irish convict system* (Dublin, 2000)

Casey, D.J., and R.E. Rhodes (eds), *Views of the Irish peasantry 1800–1916* (Hamden, Connecticut, 1977)

—, 'Carleton in Louth' in *Journal of the County Louth Archaeological and Historical Society*, 17:2 (1970), pp 97–106

—, 'Wildgoose Lodge: the evidence and the lore' in *Journal of the County Louth Archaeological and Historical Society*, 18:3 (1975), pp 211–31; 18:2 (1974), pp 140–61

Casey, J.P., *The office of the attorney general in Ireland* (Dublin, 1980)

Chesnutt, Margaret, *Studies in the short stories of William Carleton* (Goteborg, 1976)

Clark, Samuel, *Social origins of the Irish land war* (Princeton, 1979)

Clark Samuel and J.S. Donnelly, J.S. (eds), *Irish peasants: violence and political unrest 1780–1914* (Manchester, 1983)

Clinton, Georgina, 'Relief committee membership in the Union of Dundalk during the Great Irish Famine' in *Journal of the County Louth Archaeological & Historical Society*, 24:1 (1999 for 1997), pp 51–9

Comerford, R.V., *The Fenians in context: Irish politics and society, 1848–82* (Dublin, 1985)

—, *Ireland* (London, 2003)

—, *Charles J. Kickham: a biography* (Dublin, 1979)

Connell, K.H., *The population of Ireland, 1750–1845* (Oxford, 1950)

Connolly, S.J., *Religion and society in nineteenth century Ireland* (Dundalk, 1985)

Connolly, S.J., 'Aftermath and adjustment' in W.E. Vaughan (ed.), *A new history of Ireland*, vol. v (Oxford, 1989), pp 1–22

—, 'Union government, 1812–23' in W.E. Vaughan (ed.), *A new history of Ireland*, vol. v (Oxford, 1989), pp 48–73

—, 'Mass politics and sectarian conflict, 1823–30' in W.E. Vaughan (ed.), *A new history of Ireland*, vol. v (Oxford, 1989), pp 74–106

—, 'Albion's fatal twigs: justice and law in the eighteenth century' in Rosalind Mitchison and Peter Roebuck (eds), *Economy and society in Scotland and Ireland, 1500–1939* (Edinburgh, 1988), pp 117–25

Corish, P.J. (ed.), *Radicals, rebels and establishments: historical studies xv* (Belfast, 1985)

Crawford, E. Margaret, 'Dietary considerations in pre-Famine Ireland and its environs' in Raymond Gillespie and Harold O'Sullivan (eds), *The borderlands: essays on the history of the Ulster-Leinster border* (Belfast, 1989), pp 107–27

Crawford, W.H., 'Economy and society in south Ulster in the eighteenth century', in *Clogher Record*, 8:3 (1975), pp 241–57

—, 'Ulster as a mirror of the two societies' in T.M. Devine and David Dickson (eds), *Ireland and Scotland, 1600–1850* (Edinburgh, 1983), pp 60–9

—, 'The reshaping of the borderlands c.1700–1840' in Raymond Gillespie and O'Sullivan, Harold (eds), *The borderlands: essays on the history of the Ulster-Leinster border* (Belfast, 1989), pp 93–105

Crossman, Virginia, 'Emergency legislation and agrarian disorder in Ireland, 1821–41' in *Irish Historical Studies*, 27:108 (Nov. 1991), pp 309–23

—, *Politics, law and order in nineteenth century Ireland* (Dublin, 1996)

Cullen, L.M., *An economic history of Ireland since 1660* (London, 1972)

—, *The emergence of modern Ireland 1600–1900* (New York, 1981)

Curtin, N.J., 'The transformation of the Society of United Irishmen into a mass-based revolutionary organisation, 1794–6' in *IHS*, 24 (Nov. 1985), pp 463–92

Curtis, L.P., *Apes and angels: the Irishman in Victorian caricature* (Newton Abbot, 1971)

Daly, Mary E., *Social and economic history of Ireland since 1800* (Dublin, 1981)

Danaher, Kevin, *The year in Ireland: Irish calendar customs* (Cork, 1972)

Dickson, David, Cormac Ó Gráda and S. Daultrey, 'Hearth Tax, household size and Irish population change 1672–1821' in *Proceedings of the Royal Irish Academy*, 82 (1982), pp 125–82

Dickson, David, Dáire Keogh and Kevin Whelan (eds), *The United Irishmen: republicanism, radicalism and rebellion* (Dublin, 1993)

Donnelly, J.S., Jr, 'The Rightboy movement 1785–8' in *Studia Hibernica*, 17 & 18 (1977–8), pp 120–202

—, 'The Whiteboy movement, 1761–5' in *IHS*, 21 (Mar. 1878), pp 20–54

—, 'Hearts of Oak, Hearts of Steel' in *Studia Hibernica*, 21 (1981), pp 7–73

Donnelly, J.S., Jr, 'Irish agrarian rebellion: the Whiteboys of 1769–76' in *Proceedings of the Royal Irish Academy*, 83, no. 12 (1983), pp 293–331

—, 'Pastorini and Captain Rock: millenarianism and sectarianism in the Rockite movement of 1821–4 in Samuel Clark and J.S. Donnelly Jr (eds), *Irish peasants: violence and political unrest 1780–1914* (Manchester, 1983), pp 102–39

— and Kirby Miller (ed.), *Irish popular culture, 1650–1850* (Dublin, 1998).

Duffy, P.J., *Landscapes of south Ulster: a parish atlas of the diocese of Clogher* (Belfast, 1993)

Dunne, Tom (ed.), *The writer as witness: literature as historical evidence* (Cork, 1987)

—, *Rebellions: memoirs, memory and 1798* (Dublin, 2004)

Elliott, Marianne, *Partners in revolution: the United Irishmen and France* (New Haven, 1982)

—, 'The Defenders in Ulster' in David Dickson, Dáire Keogh And Kevin Whelan (eds), *The United Irishmen: republicanism, radicalism and rebellion* (Dublin, 1993), pp 222–33

—, *The Catholics of Ulster: a history* (London, 2001)

Evans, E. Estyn, 'Peasant beliefs in nineteenth century Ireland' in D. J. Casey and R.E. Rhodes, *Views of the Irish peasantry, 1800–1916* (Hamden, CN, 1977), pp 37–56

Gash, Norman, *Mr Secretary Peel: the life of Sir Robert Peel to 1830* (London, 1985 ed.)

Evans, E.J., *Sir Robert Peel: statesmanship, power and party* (London and New York, 1991)

Fegan, Melissa, '"Something so utterly unprecedented in the annals of human life": William Carleton and the Famine' in Peter Gray (ed.), *Victoria's Ireland? Irishness and Britishness, 1837–1901* (Dublin, 204), pp 131–40

FitzGerald, Garret, 'Estimates for baronies of minimum level of Irish-speaking amongst successive decennial cohorts: 1771–1781 to 1861–1871' in *Proceedings of the Royal Irish Academy*, 84 (1984), pp 117–55

Flanagan, Thomas, *The Irish novelists, 1800–1850* (New York, 1959)

Foley, Tadhg, and Sean Ryder (ed.), *Ideology and Ireland in the nineteenth century* (Dublin, 1998)

Foster, R.F., *The Irish story: telling tales and making it up in Ireland* (London, 2001)

Foucault, Michel, *Discipline and punish: the birth of the prison* (London, 1979)

Froggatt, Peter, 'The census in Ireland of 1813–15' in *IHS*, 14, (1964–5), pp 227–55

Garnham, Neal, *The courts, crime and the criminal law in Ireland, 1692–1760* (Dublin, 1996)

Garvin, Tom, 'Defenders, Ribbonmen and others: underground political networks in pre-Famine Ireland' in C.H.E. Philpin (ed.), *Nationalism and popular protest in Ireland* (Cambridge, 1987), pp 219–43

Gash, Norman, *Mr Secretary Peel: the life of Sir Robert Peel to 1830* (London, 1961)

—, *Mr Secretary Peel: the life of Sir Robert Peel after 1830* (London, 1972)

Gaskill, Malcolm, 'Reporting murder: fiction in the archives in early modern England' in *Social History*, 23 (1998), pp 1–30

Gattrell, V.A.C., *The hanging tree: execution and the English people 1770–1868* (Oxford, 1994)

Geary, Laurence (ed.), *Rebellion and remembrance in modern Ireland* (Dublin, 2001)

Gibbons, S.R., *Captain Rock, night errant: the threatening letters of pre-Famine Ireland, 1801–1845* (Dublin, 2004)

Gillespie, Raymond and Harold O'Sullivan (eds), *The borderlands: essays on the history of the Ulster-Leinster border* (Belfast, 1989)

Glassie, Henry, *Passing the time: folklore and history of an Ulster community* (Dublin, 1982)

Griffin, Brian, 'Prevention and detection of crime in nineteenth century Ireland', in N.M. Dawson (ed.), *Reflections on law and history: Irish legal history society discourses and other papers, 2000–2005* (Dublin, 2006), pp 99–125

Gough, Henry and David Dickson (ed.), *Ireland and the French revolution* (Dublin, 1990)

Hart, Peter, *The IRA and its enemies: violence and community in Cork, 1916–1923* (Oxford, 1998)

Hay, Douglas et al. (eds), *Albion's fatal tree: crime and society in eighteenth-century England* (London, 1975)

Hayley, Barbara, *Carleton's traits and stories and the 19th century Anglo-Irish tradition* (Gerrards Cross, 1983)

Henry, Brian, *Dublin hanged: crime, law enforcement and punishment in late eighteenth-century Dublin* (Dublin, 1994)

Hill, J.R., 'The legal profession and the defence of the ancien regime in Ireland, 1790–1840' in Daire Hogan and W.N. Osborough (eds), *Brehons, serjeants and attorneys* (Dublin, 1990), pp 181–210

Hill, Myrtle, 'Reading the past: literature and local history' in Raymond Gillespie and Myrtle Hill (eds), *Doing Irish local history: pursuit and practice* (Belfast, 1988)

Hoppen, K.T., *Elections, politics and society in Ireland 1832–1885* (Oxford, 1984)

—, *Ireland since 1800: conflict and conformity* (London, 1989)

Jeffares, A. Norman, *Anglo-Irish literature* (Dublin, 1982)

Johnson, D.S., 'The trials of Sam Gray: Monaghan politics and nineteenth century Irish criminal procedure' in *Irish Jurist*, 20 (1985), pp 109–34

Katsuta, Shunsuka, 'The Rockite movement in County Cork in the early 1820s' in *IHS* 33:131 (May 2003), pp 278–96

Kavanagh, Patrick, *Tarry Flynn* (London, 1948)

Kelly, James, *Gallows speeches from eighteenth-century Ireland* (Dublin, 2001)

Kelly, Jennifer, 'An outward looking community?: Ribbonism & popular mobilisation in Co. Leitrim 1836–1846' (unpublished PhD thesis, University of Limerick, 2005)

Kenny, Colum, 'The exclusion of Catholics from the legal professions in Ireland, 1537–1829' in *IHS*, 25:100 (Nov. 1987), pp 337–57

Kenny, Kevin, *Making sense of the Molly Maguires* (New York, 1998)

Keogh, Dáire, *A patriot priest: the life of Fr James Coigly, 1761–1798* (Cork, 1998)

Kerr, Donal, *Peel, priests and politics: Sir Robert Peel's administration and the Roman Catholic Church* (Oxford, 1982)

Kiely, Benedict, *Poor scholar: a study of William Carleton* (Dublin, 1947)

Lee, Joseph, 'The Ribbonmen' in T.D. Williams (ed.), *Secret societies in Ireland* (Dublin, 1973), pp 26–35

Leerssen, Joep, *Remembrance and imagination: patterns in the historical and literary representation of Ireland in the nineteenth century* (Cork, 1996)

Linebaugh, Peter, 'The Tyburn riot against the surgeons' in Douglas Hay et al., *Albion's fatal tree: crime and society in eighteenth-century England* (London, 1977), pp 65–117

Litvack, Leon, and Glenn Hooper (ed.), *Ireland in the nineteenth century: regional identity* (Dublin, 2000)

McAnally, Henry, *The Irish Militia, 1793–1816* (London, 1949)

McBride, Ian, 'Memory and national identity in modern Ireland' in Ian McBride (ed.), *History and memory in modern Ireland* (Cambridge, 2001), pp 1–42

McCabe, Desmond, 'Social order and the ghost of moral economy in pre-Famine Ireland' in Raymond Gillespie and Gerard Moran (eds), *'A various country': essays in Mayo history, 1500–1900* (Westport, CN, 1987), pp 91–112

—, '"That part that laws or kings can cause or cure": crown prosecution and jury trial at Longford assizes, 1830–45' in Raymond Gillespie and Gerard Moran (eds), *Longford: essays in county history* (Dublin, 1991), pp 153–72

MacDonagh, Oliver, *States of mind: a study of Anglo-Irish conflict, 1780–1980* (London, 1983)

MacDonagh, Oliver, W. F. Mandle and Pauraic Travers (eds), *Irish culture and nationalism, 1750–1950* (London, 1983)

MacDonald, Brian, 'Monaghan in the age of revolution' in *Clogher Record*, 17:3 (2002), pp 751–79

—, 'The Monaghan militia and the tragedy of Blaris Moor' in *Clogher Record*, 16:2 (1998), pp 123–43

McDowell, R.B., *Ireland in the age of imperialism and revolution, 1760–1801* (Oxford, 1979)

—, *The Irish administration 1801–1914* (London, 1964)

McEldowney, J.F., 'The case of the Queen v McKenna (1869) and jury packing in Ireland' in *Irish Jurist*, 12 (1977), pp 338–54

McGogg-McCann, Michelle, *Melancholy madness: a coroner's casebook* (Cork, 2003)

McMahon, R.J., 'Homicide, the courts and popular culture in pre-Famine and Famine Ireland' (unpublished PhD thesis, UCD, 2006)

Malcolm, Elizabeth, 'Popular recreation in nineteenth-century Ireland' in Oliver MacDonagh, W.F. Mandle and Pauraic Travers (eds), *Irish culture and nationalism, 1750–1950* (Hampshire and London, 1983), pp 40–55

Malcomson, A.P.W., *John Foster: the politics of the Anglo-Irish ascendancy* (Oxford, 1978)

Marnane, D.G., 'Land and violence in nineteenth-century Tipperary' in *Tipperary Historical Journal* (1988), pp 53–89

Miller, D.W., 'The Armagh troubles 1784–95' in Samuel Clark and J.S. Donnelly Jr (eds), *Irish peasants: violence and political unrest 1780–1914* (Manchester, 1983)

Mooney, Desmond, 'The origins of agrarian violence in Meath 1790–1828' in *Riocht na Midhe*, 8:1 (1987), pp 49–67

Murray, A.C., 'Agrarian violence and nationalism in nineteenth-century Ireland: the myth of Ribbonism' in *Economic and Social History*, 13 (1986), pp 56–73

Murray, Raymond, *The burning of Wildgoose Lodge: Ribbonism in Louth, murder and the gallows* (Monaghan, 2005)

O'Brien, George, *The economic history of Ireland from the Union to the Famine* (New York, 1921)

Ó Ceallaigh, Tadhg, 'Peel and police reform in Ireland, 1814–18' in *Studia Hibernica*, 6 (1966), pp 25–48

Ó Ciosáin, Niall, *Print and popular culture in Ireland, 1750–1850* (London, 1997)

O'Ferrall, Fergus, *Catholic Emancipation: Daniel O'Connell and the birth of Irish democracy* (Dublin, 1985)

Ó Gráda, Cormac, 'Poverty, population and agriculture, 1801–45' in W.E. Vaughan, (ed.), *A new history of Ireland*, vol. v, *Ireland under the union, 1801–70* (Oxford, 1989), pp 108–36

O'Neill, J.W., 'Popular culture and peasant rebellion in pre-Famine Ireland' (PhD thesis, University of Minnesota, 1984: University Microfilms International version)

O'Neill, Kevin, *Family and farm in pre-famine Ireland: the parish of Killeshandra* (Wisconsin, 1984)

Osborough, W.N., 'The regulations of the admission of attorneys and solicitors, 1600–1866' in Daire Hogan and W.N. Osborough (eds), *Brehons, serjeants and attorneys* (Dublin, 1990), pp 101–52

O'Sullivan, Harold, 'The background to and the events of the Insurrection of 1798 in Dundalk and north Louth' in *County Louth Archaeological and Historical Journal*, 24:2 (1998), pp 165–95

Owens, Gary, 'The Carrickshock incident, 1831: social memory and an Irish *cause célèbre*' in *Cultural and Social History* (2004), 1

Palmer, S.H., *Police and protest in England and Ireland, 1780–1850* (Cambridge, 1988)

Patterson, T.G.F., 'The burning of Wildgoose Lodge' in *County Louth Archaeological Journal*, 12:2 (1950), pp 159–80

Pomfret, J.E., *The struggle for land in Ireland 1800–1923* (Princeton, 1930)

Philpin, C.H.E. (ed.), *Nationalism and popular protest in Ireland* (Cambridge, 1987)

Rafroidi, Patrick, and Terence Browne (eds), *The Irish short story* (Gerrards Cross, 1979)

Roberts, P.E.W., 'Caravats and Shanavests: Whiteboyism and faction fighting in east Munster, 1802–11' in Clark Samuel and J.S. Donnelly Jr (eds), *Irish peasants: violence and political unrest 1780–1914* (Manchester, 1983), pp 64–101

Robins, Joseph, *The miasma: epidemic and panic in nineteenth century Ireland* (Dublin, 1995)

Rushe, D.C., *Monaghan in the eighteenth century* (Dublin, 1916)

—, *Historical sketches of Monaghan from the earliest records to the Fenian movement* (Dublin, 1895)

Shipkey, R.C., *Robert Peel's Irish policy, 1812–1846* (New York, 1987)

Sloan, Barry, *The pioneers of Anglo-Irish fiction 1800–1850* (Gerrards Cross, 1986)

Smyth, Jim, *The men of no property: Irish radicals and popular politics in the late eighteenth century* (Basingstoke, 1992)

Smyth, W.J., 'Flax cultivation in Ireland: the development and demise of a regional staple' in W.J. Smyth and Kevin Whelan (eds), *Common ground: essays on the historical geography of Ireland* (Cork, 1988), pp 234–52

Somerville, Edith and Martin Ross, *An incorruptible Irishman: being an account of Chief Justice Charles Kendal Bushe and his wife Nancy Crampton and their times, 1763–1843* (London, 1932)

Sweeney, Frank (ed.), *Hanging crimes: when Ireland used the gallows* (Dublin, 2005)

—, *The murder of Connell Boyle, 1898* (Dublin, 2002)

Ua Dubhthaig, Pádraig, *The book of Dundalk* (Dundalk, 1946)

Vaughan, W.E., *Landlords and tenants in mid-Victorian Ireland* (Oxford, 1994)

— (ed.), *A new history of Ireland*, vol. v, *Ireland under the union, 1801–70* (Oxford, 1989)

Waldron, Jarlath, *Maamtrasna: the murders and the mystery* (Dublin, 1992)

Whelan, Anthony (ed.), *Law and liberty in Ireland* (Dublin, 1993)

Whelan, Kevin, 'The United Irishmen, the Enlightenment and popular culture' in David Dickson, Dáire Keogh and Kevin Whelan (eds), *The United Irishmen: republicanism, radicalism and rebellion* (Dublin, 1992)

Williams, T.D. (ed.), *Secret societies in Ireland* (Dublin, 1973)

Zimmerman, G.D., *Songs of Irish rebellion: Irish political street ballads and rebel songs 1780–1900* (Dublin, 2000 ed.)

Websites

www.jbhall.freeservers.com

www.oxforddnb.com

www.bbc.co.uk/history/war/easterrising/songs

www.louth.goireland.com

Index

by Brad Morrow

Tipping, Thomas, 95
Tisdal, Thomas, juror, 172n
Tollymore Park, Co. Down, seat of earls
  of Roden, 76
Tone, Wolfe, 165
Townley Hall, Drogheda, 85, 86
Treanor, farmer near Ball's Mills, South
  Armagh, 125
Trench, Ann, married to William
  Gregory, 130
Trench, Power le Poer, archbishop of
  Tuam, 99
Trench, Hon. Col. Robert le Poer, 130
Trench, W.S., land agent, 49
Trench, Wm, 1st earl of Clancarty, 130
Trim, 162
Trotter, J.B., 143
Trotter, W.H., 119f
Tully, townland near Corcreaghy, Co.
  Louth, 63

Ua Dubthaigh, Pádraig, 47, 54
United Irishmen, 95, 96, 153, 154, 253

'Valley of Knockanure, The', ballad, 55,
  56n
Vaughan, W.E., 68, 90

Wainwright, Revd, inspector of Dundalk
  jail, 159, 164
Waldron, Jarlath, 17n, 187n

Walmesley, Bishop Charles, 41
Ward, Patrick, tailor, 221f
Waters, Patrick, 231, 232
Wellesley, marquis of, lord lieutenant,
  253
Whelan, Kevin, 94n
Whiteboy Acts, 58, 84, 113
Whiteboys, 90, 115, 117, 211
Whitworth, Lord, lord lieutenant, 102,
  152
Wildgoose Lodge; owned by T.P. Filgate
  in 1816 and tenanted by Edward
  Lynch, 18, 19; map of surrounding
  area, 108; *ills*, 111, 254
Wildman, John, owner of WGL (1886),
  54
Willcocks, Richard, chief magistrate, 152
Wolff, R., 28n
Wolffe, John, 78n
Woods, Thomas, neighbour of Patrick
  Devan, informer, 116, 152, 165, 235
Woolsey, John, agent to Mrs J.W. Foster
  and WGL juror, 172
Wordsworth, William, 234
Wright, Sub-constable George, 159, 163,
  248
Wynne, Robert, 176f

Yeats, W.B., 30n

Zimmerman, G.D., 62